ARITHEMATICS

ROBERT L. JOHNSON
CHARLES R. McNERNEY

University of Northern Colorado

ARITH<small>metic</small>EMATICS
<small>math</small>

A TEXT FOR ELEMENTARY SCHOOL TEACHERS

MACMILLAN PUBLISHING CO., INC.
New York
Collier Macmillan Publishers
London

Printed in the United States of America

Macmillan Publishing Co., Inc.
866 Third Avenue
New York, New York 10022

Collier-Macmillan Canada, Ltd.

Library of Congress Cataloging in Publication Data

Johnson, Robert Leo.
   Arithematics; a text for elementary school teachers.

   Includes bibliographical references.
   1. Arithmetic—Study and teaching (Elementary)
2. Arithmetic—1961 –   I. McNerney, Charles R.,
joint author.   II. Title.
QA135.5.J67   372.7'2'044   73-3891
ISBN 0-02-360880-3

Printing: 1 2 3 4 5 6 7 8   Year: 4 5 6 7 8 9 0

Dedicated to our wives,

Sallie and
Mari-lynn

Preface

In view of the abundance of texts designed for the prospective teacher of mathematics in the elementary school, it is reasonable to ask: Why present another? The answer is that the authors of this text have been teaching from many of the texts now available and have found that there is a definite need for a text organized around those concepts that form a basis for elementary school mathematics programs. At face value, most mathematics textbooks for elementary school teachers seem appropriate. It is difficult to argue that their content is not relevant and it is readily apparent that these texts lack the rigor contained in textbooks written for an in-depth study of mathematics. We believe, however, that most of these textbooks, excellent as they may be, tend to ignore the problems that elementary education students have in identifying with mathematics content and in developing a need to know it.

We have attempted to alleviate these problems by using a rhetoric throughout this book which helps the teacher to identify with mathematics, to realize that children continually re-create mathematics concepts, and to see relationships between what he should know and what he will teach. Most of the concepts in this text have been developed in a context that makes reference to mathematical, psychological, and pedagogical aspects of learning them.

This text is written with several assumptions in mind regarding the student who uses it as well as the teacher who teaches from it. First, it is assumed that the prospective elementary school teacher will have had at least one year of algebra and considerable informal experience with geometry. For this reason our exercises will quite frequently involve the use of material that is yet to be formally developed in the text. Although some people may not consider this procedure suitable, we feel that a fundamental objective of this text is to build a deeper understanding of the concepts and a greater mastery of the skills which the student has acquired in his precollege mathematical experiences. This deeper understanding and greater mastery is prerequisite to meaningful mathematics instruction. If the student does not have the mathematical background we have described, it is assumed that he will be prepared to study certain sections of the text with more care than other students or will be prepared to pursue individualized activities which will serve to develop understandings and simple skills at least in the area of elementary algebra. A further assumption is that the user of this text is concerned about the relationship between the topics discussed here and the responsibility of being an elementary school teacher of mathematics. It is on the basis of this assumption that the authors have written their materials in such a way as to illustrate, through dialogues and descriptions, the elementary school classroom and student.

The assumption is also made that the prospective teacher of elementary school mathematics and the teacher of such teachers should find delight in mathematics as something to do as well as something to teach. For this reason an effort has been made to allow the reader to discover some ideas on his own and to present some ideas that are not at all difficult but are interesting and within the reach of the elementary school teacher and the elementary school student.

Mathematics is sometimes thought by the man in the street to be a mysterious subject that has remained constant throughout all of history. We hope to be able to dispel some of the mystery that may surround some of the ideas of mathematics, and we hope to be able to place mathematics in a historical perspective through historical vignettes which may help to show that mathematics has been created by man and is a dynamic, vital, and changing subject.

Anticipating a national change to the metric system of measure, we have used both the English and the metric system for illustrations so that prospective teachers will feel comfortable with both systems of measurement. This emphasis has been made throughout the text but is a special feature of the chapter on geometry.

Two national agencies continue to have considerable influence in directing the development of the curriculum in mathematics for the prospective teacher of elementary school mathematics. The Mathematics Association of America has its Committee on the Undergraduate Program in Mathematics (CUPM) and has made recommendations regarding the training of such teachers. The Cambridge Conference names another group of people concerned with the development of the curriculum in mathematics. We believe that the goals we have in mind for the students using this text are consistent with the philosophies and goals of these two bodies.

We believe the book has three major applications. First, it is intended to be a resource book that prospective teachers can use to supplement and enrich the presentations by instructors of mathematics courses for elementary education students. We assume that the presentations of most instructors will be rather systematic and we hope that they will give considerable attention to exploratory activity.

Second, it is intended to be an "on the teacher's desk" resource book for elementary school teachers who would like to better understand what they teach through self-study during a school year. We hope that in having pupils complete some workbook activities dealing with sets, operations, or integers, the teacher will refer to these concepts to attain a better understanding of them and, perhaps, create some ways to extend and enrich the workbook activities.

Third, the book is intended to be a resource for in-service workshops in mathematics for teachers. Our hope is that an instructor and a class of teachers can identify and solve problems associated with learning mathematics and with utilizing the acquired knowledge to improve classroom instruction.

We gratefully acknowledge the help of our colleagues, our students, and our families during the development of the text. Special thanks are due to Kathy Antonopoulis for typing the manuscript. Our editor was very helpful in obtaining reviews of the early forms of the material and we appreciate help from all the departments at Macmillan.

Greeley, Colorado   R. L. J.
                                                                              C. R. M.

Contents

Contents

Contents

Chapter 1

Mathematical Language

1.1

INTRODUCTION

Look at the following collection of sentences and read each one very carefully so that every word has equal importance.

> I think that I shall never see
> a fahrquar lovely as a tree.

> I
> SEE THE
> THE BIRD SITTING ON THE
> THE TOP OF THE PRETTY BIRDHOUSE

> All mimsy were the borogoves
> and the mome raths outgrabe.

No doubt several things came to your attention as you read these sentences, including the fact that they seem to make little sense. Our purpose in using these sentences to begin a chapter on the language of mathematics is to illustrate some features of language in general and of mathematical language in particular.

The first point we wish to make is simply that words are *given* meaning by the user, and until someone tells how he uses a certain word his listeners will not know what he means by that word. The sentence using the word "fahrquar" is an example of this notion and disastrously affects this well-known thought of Joyce Kilmer.

A second point is that reading mathematical language calls for special care in noticing each symbol. In the second sentence did you notice that the word "the" is used too many times? It is not wise to skim when reading mathematical literature because each symbol carries with it a great deal of meaning.

The final point is that we must take care to agree on the meaning of words that we use, the ways in which these words are used in mathematical sentences, and the kind of thinking that underlies the use of the words. In the excerpt from Lewis Carroll it is clear that there is some kind of formal sense to the sentence, even though none of us know what most of the words mean. The sense seems to rise from the form that the sentence takes, for we recognize that the subject of the first portion is "borogoves" which are "mimsy."

The sections of this chapter are designed to introduce the details of the language of mathematics, and the second chapter should give you some idea about mathematical ways of thinking.

1.2

SENTENCES AND SIMPLE LOGIC

As is true of any language, the language of mathematics is written in sentences consisting of subject and predicate. This may surprise you at first because you may have thought that mathematics deals with numbers, points, lines, and other objects, but hardly ever deals with sentences. Yet if you reflect a bit, you will see that we use sentences to talk about numbers and the other objects of mathematics. For instance, "$2 + 2 = 4$" is a sentence with the subject being "$2 + 2$" and the predicate being "$= 4$." If we use words rather than symbols, the sentence structure might stand clear: "Two plus two is equal to four."

Considering the number of words that can be used in mathematics, an infinite number of sentences could be formed, but, as with the English language, not all of them would have any substantive meaning. For example, "A triangle is greater than 7" uses mathematical words but has no meaning. Of course, some sentences have meaning to one reader but not to another, such as "He's cool, man." You know what is meant by this, but most of your grandmothers would not. A mathematics example might be "Every principal ideal domain is a unique factorization domain." All the words are mathematical and some readers might know what the sentence means.

So there are two concerns that we have about sentences. First, we must insist that the sentences we use in mathematics have substantive meaning; that is, they must make sense. Second, we must be careful that these sentences make sense to you, the reader.

Some sentences concerning mathematics that make sense have an additional quality. They are either true or false. Such meaningful sentences are called *statements* and are said to have *truth value* T or *truth value* F depending on whether the statement is true or false.

> A *statement* is a meaningful sentence that is either true or false.
>
> The *truth value* of a statement is T if the statement is true and F if it is false.

The fact that mathematical statements do not have "shades of gray" or "credibility gaps" makes the language and logic of mathematics a great deal simpler than would otherwise be the case. In the famous debates of history there were shades of truth that led to the possibility of interesting arguments based on sound logic. Aristotle, Webster, and Lincoln were masters of debate and made use of these shades of truth. In mathematical argument there is little room for debate, for the statements of our concern are either true or false.

If we restrict the kinds of sentences we consider to those which are meaningful, then there are only three kinds of sentences that will be of interest in elementary mathematics: true sentences, false sentences, and sentences that are neither true nor false. For the first two kinds of sentences, which we have agreed to call statements, it is convenient to use capital letters as representatives or names of certain examples. For instance, "P" may stand for the statement "Five is an even number." Of course, P happens to be a false statement. "Q" might represent the statement "One meter is approximately equal to 39.4 inches." Statement Q is a true statement.

The third type of sentence is a sentence that is neither true nor false. Consider the sentence "It weighs 90 kilograms." Is this sentence true? Is it false? The sentence does indeed make good sense, but its truth value cannot be known because "It" might refer to any one of

4

a number of objects. The mathematical sentence "x is greater than 7" also makes good sense, but it has no truth value because "x" might refer to any of a variety of numbers or other objects. Such sentences are not statements; but if the word "It" were replaced by "Explorer II satellite" and if the symbol "x" were replaced by "8," then both become statements because the first is false and the second is true.

In both our cases, the truth value of the original sentence is *open*, pending a replacement of the word "It" and the symbol "x" by names of appropriate objects. These sentences are called *open sentences*, and such symbols as "It" and "x" are called *variables* or *placeholders*.

> An *open sentence* is a sentence containing a symbol which, when replaced by the name of an appropriate object, becomes a statement.
>
> A symbol that holds a place for names of objects, as in an open sentence, is called a *variable* or a *place-holder*.

For the remainder of this section let us restrict our consideration to statements and return at a later point to discuss open sentences.

Let the letter P name an arbitrary statement. (If you wish, make up your own statement.) We have agreed that P may be either true or false; that is, the only possible truth values are T and F. A table summarizes these possibilities:

Statement	P
Truth values	T
	F

If two arbitrary statements, P and Q, are to be considered, there are four possible combinations of truth values, as shown in the table:

Statements	P	Q
	T	T
Possible	T	F
truth values	F	T
	F	F

If three arbitrary statements, P, Q, and R, are to be considered, there are eight possible combinations of truth values.

5

P	Q	R
T	T	T
T	T	F
T	F	T
T	F	F
F	T	T
F	T	F
F	F	T
F	F	F

Study these three tables. Note the system that is used to ensure that all possibilities are accounted for. If three statements are involved, it has been shown that there are eight possible combinations of truth values. How many possible combinations would there be when four statements are considered? When five statements are involved? When an arbitrary number of statements, say n, are involved?

If $"P"$ represents the statement "A triangle has four sides," then a new statement, called the negation of P, may be formed using the word "not." The wording may need to be changed to maintain good grammar. The new statement using the word "not" would be "A triangle does not have four sides." If $"P"$ names the original statement, then the negation of P is named by $"-P,"$ read "not P." It seems reasonable to agree that if P is true, then $-P$ is false, and if P is false, then $-P$ is true. Thus, P and $-P$ have opposite truth values.

> If P is a statement, the *negation of P* is a statement derived from P using the word "not" and having truth values as given by the table. Write $"-P"$ for "not P."
>
> | P | $-P$ |
> |---|---|
> | T | F |
> | F | T |

The agreement concerning the truth value of the negation $-P$ constitutes a definition that is reflected in the table, called a *truth table*.

According to our agreement about statements, when P is true, $-P$ is false, and when P is false, $-P$ is true. This agreement can be used to determine when one statement is the negation of another. No confusion should arise, but it sometimes does. Therefore, let us illustrate a possible source of confusion with two statements P and Q, where P is the statement "Today is Wednesday" and Q is the statement "Today is Thursday." Is Q the negation of P? Let's test by using the definition of negation. If the statement "Today is Wednesday" is true, then the statement Q is false. So far, so good. If the statement "Today is Wednesday" is false, then is the statement "Today is Thursday" true? Not necessarily, because today might well be Sunday! If today is Sunday, P and Q are both false at the same time.

When one statement is the negation of another, the two statements are called *contradictory statements*. When two statements are such that it is impossible for them to be simultaneously true but it is possible for them to be simultaneously false, the statements are said to be *contrary statements*. Thus, "Terry is a good boy" and "Terry is not a good boy" are contradictory statements, but "Today is Wednesday" and "Today is Thursday" are contrary statements.

> If statement Q is the negation of statement P, then P and Q are called *contradictory statements*.
>
> If statements P and Q cannot be both true at the same time but are possibly false at the same time, then P and Q are called *contrary statements*.

Look at the following truth tables for statements P and Q. These tables illustrate the possible truth values for the two kinds of statement pairs just discussed.

Contradictory Statements			Contrary Statements	
P	Q		P	Q
T	F		T	F
F	T		F	F
			F	T

Possible truth values for contradictory and contrary statements.

Another way to create new statements is to connect two statements with the word "and." If P represents the statement "The night is young" and Q represents the statement "You're so beautiful," then a new statement, called the *conjunction* of P and Q and symbolized

7

by "$P \wedge Q$," is "The night is young and you're so beautiful." This compound sentence is certainly false if either or both of the two statements P and Q are false. In fact, the only way the compound statement can be true is when both components P and Q are true. This constitutes the definition of conjunction shown in the truth table.

If P and Q are statements, the *conjunction* of P and Q, symbolized by "$P \wedge Q$" and read "P and Q," is the statement derived from P and Q using the word "and" and having the following truth values:

P	Q	$P \wedge Q$
T	T	T
T	F	F
F	T	F
F	F	F

Notice again that the conjunction of P and Q is true only under the most stringent of conditions: both P and Q must be true.

A new statement may also be formed using P and Q and the word "or." If we use the examples of the preceding paragraph, the new statement is "The night is young or you're so beautiful." A statement formed in this way is called a *disjunction* and is symbolized by "$P \vee Q$." It seems reasonable that $P \vee Q$ is a true statement in every possible condition except when P is false and Q is false. This is reflected in the definition and truth table for disjunction.

If P and Q are statements, the disjunction of P and Q, symbolized by "$P \vee Q$" and read "P *or* Q," is the statement derived from P and Q using the word "or" and having the following truth values:

P	Q	$P \vee Q$
T	T	T
T	F	T
F	T	T
F	F	F

Notice that the disjunction is true under very loose fitting requirements: as long as one or both of P or Q is true.

You may be wondering about the agreement made about the word "or" as shown in the truth table making up the definition. In the English language the word "or" has an "exclusive" and an "inclusive" usage. We use the word "or" in the exclusive sense when we mean that one or the other *but not both* of two sentences is true. The occurrence of one prohibits the occurrence of the other; that is, the truth of one *excludes* the truth of the other. A truth table could be conveniently used to define this use of the word "or" as shown:

P	Q	P or Q (exclusive use)
T	T	F
T	F	T
F	T	T
F	F	F

An example of this use of the word "or" is the statement "You are 18 or you are 19." There is no way for both of the component statements to be true at the same time.

The second use of the word "or" is the *inclusive* sense, by which we mean that it is possible for the statement $P \vee Q$ to be true when both P and Q are true. You may have seen the symbol "and/or" in some documents. This use of "or" is called the inclusive use for it includes the case when both component statements are true. This is the sense in which the word "or" is used in mathematics, and we find that it is very convenient. Remember that our common use of the word "or" in this book will include the possible case when both P and Q are true; in this case, the sentence $P \vee Q$ will be true.

A final means of generating new statements will serve our purposes for the present. "The night is young *when and only when* you're so beautiful" exemplifies this method of statement formation. The words "when and only when" are often replaced by "if and only if" in mathematical literature. Such a compound statement is called the *biconditional* and is symbolized by "$P \Leftrightarrow Q$," which is read "P if and only if Q."

Agreement regarding the truth value of such a statement is not as easily reached as in the case of negation, the conjunction, and the disjunction of statements because the reasoning involved is a bit unusual. Nevertheless, it is agreed that $P \Leftrightarrow Q$ is true as long as both P and Q have the same truth value, that is, when P and Q are both true or both false. The definition is shown in the truth table.

> If P and Q are statements, the *biconditional* formed with P and Q, symbolized by "$P \Leftrightarrow Q$" and read "P if and only if Q," is the statement formed from P and Q using the words "if and only if" and having the following truth values:
>
> | P | Q | $P \Leftrightarrow Q$ |
> | --- | --- | --- |
> | T | T | T |
> | T | F | F |
> | F | T | F |
> | F | F | T |

All the preceding remarks dealing with the formation of new statements from others concerned arbitrary statements P and Q whose truth values gave rise to four possible cases. In practice, the truth or falsity of many statements is known, and interest centers on deriving the truth or falsity of newly formed statements derived from the given statements. What is desired is a means of deciding which compound statements are true, given that certain statements are true or false. The means for making such decisions lie in the domain of mathematical logic where the student of mathematics *deduces* the consequences of assumptions. More must be said later concerning some of the aspects of *deduction*, but let us clear away a few details now.

First, suppose that we are concerned with determining the truth values of the compound statement $-(P \wedge Q)$, which might be a representation of the statement "It is not the case that Jim is a wrestler and Jack is the best student." We can determine the truth values of this statement by applying the definitions given for negation and conjunction to a truth table.

P	Q	$P \wedge Q$	$-(P \wedge Q)$
T	T	T	F
T	F	F	T
F	T	F	T
F	F	F	T
		Step 1	2

Step 1 is taken by recalling that a conjunction is true only when both P and Q are true, and step 2 takes advantage of the definition of negation. It is seen that $-(P \wedge Q)$ is false only when P and Q are both true.

Again, suppose that the truth values of $(-P) \vee (-Q)$ are desired. As in the first instance, truth tables provide a way.

P	Q	$(-P)$	$(-Q)$	$(-P) \vee (-Q)$
T	T	F	F	F
T	F	F	T	T
F	T	T	F	T
F	F	T	T	T
		Step 1	2	3

Hence, two applications of the definition of negation and an application of the definition of disjunction provide the means of determining that $(-P) \vee (-Q)$ is true in every case except when both P and Q are true.

Finally, notice that the truth values for both $-(P \wedge Q)$ and $(-P) \vee (-Q)$ are exactly the same for each possible combination of truth values for P and Q. Whenever this happens, we say that statements such as $-(P \wedge Q)$ and $(-P) \vee (-Q)$ are *equivalent statements*.

> Two statements M and N are *equivalent statements* if they have exactly the same truth values for all possible combinations of truth values for their component statements.

By using truth tables, we can study a number of compound statements to determine which are equivalent. Among those which can be easily checked are

$P \wedge Q$ is equivalent to $Q \wedge P$
$P \vee Q$ is equivalent to $Q \vee P$
$(P \wedge Q) \wedge R$ is equivalent to $P \wedge (Q \wedge R)$
$(P \vee Q) \vee R$ is equivalent to $P \vee (Q \vee R)$
$P \wedge (Q \vee R)$ is equivalent to $(P \wedge Q) \vee (P \wedge R)$
$P \vee (Q \wedge R)$ is equivalent to $(P \vee Q) \wedge (P \vee R)$

Here is a typical dialogue in a fifth-grade classroom, which may serve to show that there is a definite relationship between what we

11

have been saying about equivalent statements and what is said in the classroom. Read the dialogue and imagine that you are the teacher.

> MISS QUE: Kids, remember that a multiple of five is a number like 0, 5, 10, 15, 20, . . .?
>
> LINDA: Yes, it's a number you can get by counting by fives.
>
> MISS QUE: Good! Then what are some multiples of six?
>
> JUAN: 0, 6, . . . uh, 12, 18, and so on.
>
> MISS QUE: Great! So what is a multiple of six?
>
> ROBERT: It must be a number you can get to by counting by sixes.
>
> MISS QUE: That's just right. Now, who can give us an example of a number that is a multiple of five and at the same time is a multiple of six?
>
> JANE: 35!
>
> MISS QUE: Oh? Let's think about that. What do you others think?
>
> JANE: But 35 is a number I get by counting by fives, I mean, it's a multiple of five.
>
> ROBERT: Yeah, but it's not a number you can get by counting by sixes!
>
> MISS QUE: Ah ha! That's the point isn't it, because we wanted a number that was a multiple of both five and six. Who has another choice?

Do you see that there are two statements involved here? One is "35 is a multiple of five" (call this one P), and the other is "35 is a multiple of six" (call this one Q). The teacher and children were able to see that the statement "35 is a multiple of five and 35 is a multiple of six" is a false statement. It is false because "35 is a multiple of six" is false. You know that $P \wedge Q$ must be false when Q is false, simply from the definition of conjunction (or the word "and"). But you also know more than this. You know that if $P \wedge Q$ is false, then $-(P \wedge Q)$ is true. You also know that $-(P \wedge Q)$ is equivalent to $-P \vee -Q$. So, if you are the teacher, you will know that your statement "35 is not a multiple of five and of six" is true just because the statement "35 is not a multiple of six" is true.

You probably are thinking that the example used above is a little far-fetched and you may be right. However, it is true that you will find many uses for knowledge of equivalent statements. Suppose that you want to check some of these suspected statements to see if they are truly equivalent. As suggested earlier, you only need to check truth tables built for the statements in question. You have seen the comparison of the truth tables for $-(P \wedge Q)$ and $-P \vee -Q$. Here is another such comparison. Note that columns 4 and 5 have the same truth values.

P	Q	$-P$	$-Q$	$P \vee Q$	$-(P \vee Q)$	$-P \wedge -Q$
T	T	F	F	T	F	F
T	F	F	T	T	F	F
F	T	T	F	T	F	F
F	F	T	T	F	T	T
		1	2	3	4	5

Columns 1 and 2 are developed from the definition of negation, and column 3 comes from the definition of disjunction ("or"). Column 4 is simply the negation of column 3, and column 5 is the result of using the definition of conjunction ("and"). You see, column 5 is true in just the one case in which both $-P$ and $-Q$ are true (that's the definition of conjunction).

The two sets of equivalent statements for which we have provided truth tables are very important for our use in this text as well as for your use in the classroom. These two statements of equivalence are called De Morgan's laws, after the famed English mathematician, Augustus De Morgan, who incidentally would be regarded as a true friend of students, for he hated competitive examinations!

> The following equivalent paired statements are called De Morgan's laws:
>
> $$-(P \wedge Q) \text{ is equivalent to } -P \vee -Q$$
> $$-(P \vee Q) \text{ is equivalent to } -P \wedge -Q$$

As you gain experience with statement forms and have a chance to examine truth tables, you will begin to notice an interesting class of statement forms. One such example is

P	$-P$	$P \vee -P$
T	F	T
F	T	T

You can see that the statement $P \vee -P$ is always true regardless of the truth value of P. Another example is

13

P	$-(-P)$	$P \Leftrightarrow -(-P)$
T	T	T
F	F	T

Again, regardless of the truth value of P, the statement $P \Leftrightarrow -(-P)$ is always true. Such statements as $P \vee -P$ are called *tautologies*.

Consider the statement $-(P \wedge Q) \Leftrightarrow (-P \vee -Q)$. A look at the truth table gives another clue about equivalent statements, which is connected to the idea of tautologies just mentioned.

P	Q	$P \wedge Q$	$-(P \wedge Q)$	$-P \vee -Q$	$-(P \wedge Q) \Leftrightarrow (-P \vee -Q)$
T	T	T	F	F	T
T	F	F	T	T	T
F	T	F	T	T	T
F	F	F	T	T	T

The final column in the truth table indicates that the statement $-(P \wedge Q) \Leftrightarrow (-P \vee -Q)$ is always true no matter what the truth values of P and Q. It seems apparent, then, that all the equivalent statements give us tautologies when we introduce the biconditional $\Leftrightarrow$.

EXERCISES (Section 1.2)

1. Read each of the following sentences. Which are statements and which are open sentences?
   a. $2 + 2 = 4$.
   b. George McGrumple is alive and living in Pasadena.
   c. She is older than she looks.
   d. $x + 2 = 2,341$.
   e. A meter is equivalent to approximately 39.64 inches.
   f. A line extends on and on in two directions.
   g. The galumptikyte is a multicolored orakithon.
   h. A very good girl is she.

2. For those sentences of Exercise 1 that you find to be statements, which are true?

3. A standard technique in many elementary texts is to use boxes, circles, triangles and the like as variables in open sentences. Here are some open sentences. What names would you use in place of the variables to make the sentences true statements?
   a. $\square + 5 = 76$
   b. $17 - \triangle = 9$
   c. $2 \cdot \bigcirc - 8 = 46$

14

 d. $3\square + 17 = 32 - 2\square$
 e. $12 > \square > \triangle$
 f. $(12 \div \triangle) + 5 = 8$
 g. $(18 \div \square) - 7 = \bigcirc$

4. Using the definition of negation, conjunction, disjunction, and the bi-conditional, build truth tables for the statements given.
 a. $-P \wedge Q$
 b. $P \vee -Q$
 c. $(P \wedge Q) \vee -Q$
 d. $-P \vee (Q \wedge P)$
 e. $P \vee (Q \wedge R)$
 f. $P \Leftrightarrow (Q \vee -R)$

5. Make a list of the pairs of equivalent statements that have been mentioned so far.

6. Write a dialogue between you and a typical student of the third grade in which the words "and," "or," and "not" are used in a natural way.

7. Give two examples of pairs of statements that are contradictory and two examples of pairs of statements that are contrary.

8. Suppose you know that it is true that "Elmdale elementary teachers will get a substantial raise next year or the Elmdale library will get 500 new books." Suppose you also learn that the Elmdale library is not going to get 500 new books. From what you have learned about the truth table for disjunction (or) can you make any conclusion?

9. Make use of De Morgan's laws and form grammatically correct negations of the following statements.
 a. Roses are red and violets are blue.
 b. Juanita is 7 or 8 years old.
 c. You should get out and stay out.
 d. $-P \wedge -Q$.
 e. $P \vee -Q$.
 f. $-P \vee Q$.

10. What is the truth value of each of the following?
 a. $(6 > 1) \wedge (5 + 2 = 7)$
 b. $(6 > 1) \vee (6 = 1)$
 c. $(6 > 1) \wedge (6 = 1)$
 d. $(3^2 = 9) \Leftrightarrow (3 = -3)$

11. From your local newspaper take one of the letters to the editor. Identify the statements in the letter and speculate on their truth value. Discuss why the arguments of the letter may be difficult to follow.

1.3
SETS

The concept of *set* is so simple that it is remarkable how useful the notion is in unifying and simplifying much of mathematics. A set, intuitively, is a collection of objects called elements. The word "collection" is a good synonym provided it is used with flexibility. Let us explain. We shall want to consider sets of numbers, sets of points in space, sets of many elements, sets with just one element, and even sets with no elements. If the word "collection" allows for all these possibilities, then it provides a good synonym.

Capital letters near the beginning of the alphabet are often used to name arbitrary sets and small letters are used to name elements. The set of all fifth-grade boys in Hope Elementary School, for example, might be called set A, and if Jesse James is a fifth-grade boy in that school, then Jesse is an element of that set. If the letter x names an arbitrary fifth-grade boy in that school, we write "$x \in A$" to say "x is an element of set A." Helen Highwater is a fifth-grade girl in Hope Elementary School and not an element of our set A. If the letter y names an arbitrary object that is not in set A, we write "$y \notin A$" to say that "y is not an element of set A."

> If A is a set and x is an element of set A, while y is not an element of set A, we write
>
> $$x \in A, \qquad y \notin A$$

We said that the word "collection" is a good synonym for the word "set" if used with a degree of flexibility. Does your use of the word "collection" extend to the collection of everything? The collection or set of everything is commonly called the *universe*. Often we shall want to talk about a large set, but not as large as the universe. For example, we may want to talk about the huge set of numbers. For purposes of that particular discussion the set of numbers *is* the universe. Such a set is called the *universe of discourse*.

> A set of elements to which discussion is limited is called a *universe of discourse* (or universal set).

A set is said to be *well defined* when it is possible to demonstrate whether or not a given object of the universe belongs to that set. The set of all whole numbers (zero, one, two, three, etc.) is a well-defined set because given any object in the universe, it is easy to determine whether or not that object is a whole number. The set of all members of the Z club, whose membership is a strictly held secret, is not a well-defined set, for there is no apparent method available to determine who is a member and who is not.

If A is a well-defined set, it is often convenient to portray the set as a circular region like that shown in Figure 1-1. A small dot portrays an object x, which is an element of set A, and another dot portrays an object y, which is not an element of set A.

Figure 1-1

It is possible to find that the elements of a set are also sets. For example, the set of all service organizations in one community contains the following elements: Rotary, Kiwanis, Soroptimist, and Lions. Each element of this set of organizations is actually a set of people. Although Jim Townsend is an element of the set of Kiwanians, Jim is not an element of the set of service organizations, for he is not an organization.

There are two basic ways of describing the elements of a set. The *roster* notation simply lists the names of the elements within braces. For instance,

$$\{\text{Jim, Frank, John, Betsy}\}$$

names a set consisting of the four people whose names appear within the braces. It is important to notice that it is the *names* of the objects and *not* the objects themselves which appear between the braces. Another example,

$$\{1, 2, 3, 4, 5, 6, 7, 8, 9, 10\}$$

names the set of counting numbers from one through ten. The names of these numbers (called numerals) appear within the braces. A variation on this notation is the following, in which the three dots imply that

17

the pattern established in the first three names is to continue until the last name is reached:

$$\{1, 2, 3, \ldots, 10\}$$

This is a convenient notation, for consider the alternative for the set

$$\{1, 2, 3, \ldots, 10,000\}$$

This set names the set of counting numbers from one through ten thousand.

Incidentally, once an element of a set has been named within braces, it is unnecessary, in fact redundant, to name that element again. Thus, the set $\{1, 3, 3, 3, 4, 4\}$ is just the set $\{1, 3, 4\}$, because having named 3 and 4 as elements of the set leaves nothing to be gained by saying so again.

The other basic method of naming the elements of a set is called the *set-builder notation* and makes use of the notion of open sentences discussed earlier. To illustrate, consider the set of all even whole numbers. This set may be described as

$$\{x : x \text{ is an even whole number}\}$$

(read "The set of all x such that x is an even whole number"). Using the roster method, the set is named by

$$\{0, 2, 4, 6, 8, \ldots\}$$

with the three dots implying that the pattern established is to continue *ad infinitum*. The open sentence "x is an even whole number" is called the *defining property* of the set. The variable x is to be replaced by names of objects, and if the resulting statement is true for any such object, then that object qualifies for membership in the set. Testing 12, for example, we can easily see that the statement "12 is an even whole number" is a true statement, so 12 is an element of this set. Testing 7 results in the false statement "7 is an even whole number," so it follows that 7 does not belong to the set.

In what has been said so far, there is no reason not to test numbers like $\frac{1}{2}$, $3\frac{1}{4}$, 5, and others. Some clue was present in the set-builder description of the set, however, and that clue was the term "whole number." We were only to consider whole numbers that might be even. Hence, our variable x was replaced only by names of whole numbers as we tested objects for membership. The set of objects that is in some

18

way identified as appropriate for replacement in the open sentence defining the set is called the *replacement set*. How logical! Those elements of the replacement set for which the defining property is a true
statement form the set. The set is often called the *truth set* or *solution
set* for the open sentence. [Read "$p(x)$" as "p of x."]

> If $p(x)$ is an arbitrary open sentence containing the
> variable x, then a set of objects whose names are
> suitable replacements for the variable x is called a
> *replacement set* for the open sentence $p(x)$. The set of
> objects from the replacement set for which the open
> sentence $p(x)$ becomes a true statement is called
> a *solution set* or *truth set*. The solution set is named
> by the symbols
>
> $$\{x : p(x)\}$$
>
> which is read "The set of all x such that $p(x)$."

To illustrate, consider as our open sentence "three times x is less than
seven," or, in good algebraic form, "$3x < 7$." If the replacement set
is the set of whole numbers, then the solution set is the set $\{0, 1, 2\}$,
because the following three statements are all true:

$$3 \text{ times } 0 \text{ is less than } 7$$
$$3 \text{ times } 1 \text{ is less than } 7$$
$$3 \text{ times } 2 \text{ is less than } 7$$

Therefore, $\{x : 3x < 7\}$ is the set $\{0, 1, 2\}$. Observe that if the replacement set includes the fractional numbers there are many other elements in the set named by $\{x : 3x < 7\}$, because $\frac{1}{2}$ belongs to the set
since

$$3 \text{ times } \tfrac{1}{2} \text{ is less than } 7$$

is a true statement. In fact, any fractional number less than $\frac{7}{3}$ belongs
to the set. Do you see why?

Knowledge of the appropriate replacement set is obviously very
important, for it determines the specific elements of a set named with
the set-builder notation. When the replacement set is the set of whole
numbers we have seen that

$$\{x : 3x < 7\}$$

19

contains the elements 0, 1, and 2. Using the same set of whole numbers as the replacement set,

$$\{x : x \text{ is an even whole number less than } 10\}$$

must be the set $\{0, 2, 4, 6, 8\}$. The set

$$\{x : 2x + 1 = 13\}$$

must be the set $\{6\}$, containing just one element; and

$$\{x : 2x = 5\}$$

contains no elements at all. There is no whole number replacement for the symbol x used to make the sentence "$2x = 5$" a true statement. This set is called the *empty set* or the *null set*. The symbol used to name the empty set is "∅."

> The set containing no elements is called the *empty set* and is named by the symbol "∅."

Don't get confused about the empty set. It contains no elements at all. What's wrong with the sentence "$0 = ∅$?" The symbol "0" stands for the number zero and the symbol "∅" stands for a set of no elements. The number 0 does not equal the empty set (at least in this context), for 0 is a thing, a number, just as 1, 2, and 3 are things. What's wrong with saying "$∅ = \{0\}$?" This can't be true, because there is at least one element in $\{0\}$, the element 0.

Be prepared also to meet sets whose elements are also sets. Consider the set of all fraternities on campus. Sigma Nu, Theta Xi, Sigma Chi, and so on, are all fraternities, but each is itself a set of men. $\{\{1, 2\}, \{1, 2, 3\}\}$ is a set with two elements, the set $\{1, 2\}$ and the set $\{1, 2, 3\}$. In fact, you can imagine sets of sets of sets.

EXERCISES (Section 1.3)

1. The following sets are named by using the set-builder notation. Rename the elements of each set using the roster method.
   a. $A = \{x : x \text{ is a whole number and } x^2 = 16\}$
   b. $B = \{x : x \text{ is an odd whole number and is less than } 10\}$
   c. $C = \{y : y \text{ is a rational number and } y^2 = \frac{9}{25}\}$
   d. $D = \{z : z \text{ is a rational number and } 2z - 6 = 11\}$
   e. $E = \{x : x \text{ is an integer and } -7 < x < 0\}$
   f. $F = \{y : y \text{ is an integer and } y^2 = 16\}$
   g. $G = \{m : m \text{ is a natural number and } m + 8 = 3\}$

2. The following sets are named by the roster method. Rename these sets using the set-builder notation.
   a. $H = \{1, -1\}$
   b. $I = \{15, 17, 19, 21\}$
   c. $J = \{\frac{1}{10}, \frac{1}{5}, \frac{3}{10}, \frac{2}{5}, \frac{1}{2}, \frac{3}{5}, \frac{7}{10}, \frac{4}{5}, \frac{9}{10}\}$
   d. $K = \{1, 4, 9, 16, 25, 36, \ldots\}$
   e. $L = \{2, 3, 5, 7, 11, 13, 17, 19, \ldots\}$

3. For the sets shown, answer the true–false questions that follow. If the statement is false, say why.

   $A = \{1, 2, 3, 4, 5, 6, 4\},$ $B = \{1\},$ $C = \{1, 2, \{3, 4\}, \{5, 6\}\},$
        $D = \emptyset,$ $E = \{\emptyset\},$ $F = \{\emptyset, \{1, 2\}, \{1, 2, 3\}, \{1\}\}$

   a. Set A contains exactly six elements.
   b. Set A is the same set as set C.
   c. $3 \in A$.
   d. $3 \in C$.
   e. $\{1, 2\} \in C$.
   f. $B \in A$.
   g. $B \in F$.
   h. $D \in F$.
   i. F contains exactly four elements.
   j. Some of the elements of C are themselves sets.
   k. Set E contains no elements.

4. What is wrong with the following dialogue?
   JOANNE: The teacher said that this set contained Jimmy and Freddie and Trudy. How do I name this set?
   JACKIE: You put Jimmy, Freddie, and Trudy between braces!

5. Let set $A = \{x : 2x^2 + x - 1 = 0\}$.
   a. What is the defining property of set A?
   b. If the replacement set for the defining property of set A is the set of natural numbers $\{1, 2, 3, \ldots\}$, what is the solution set for this defining property? In other words, what are the elements of set A if the replacement set is the set of natural numbers? Try a few and see what happens!
   c. What are the elements of set A if the replacement set is the set of integers $\{\ldots, -2, -1, 0, 1, 2, \ldots\}$?
   d. What are the elements of set A if the replacement set is the set of rational numbers?

6. Make up a dialogue between you and a primary student in which the empty set comes up in a natural way.

7. Explain the difference between 17 and $\{17\}$.

8. Explain the difference between $\{17\}$ and $\{\{17\}\}$.

9. You have seen that some sets have just a few elements while others have a great many.
   a. How many elements are there in the empty set?
   b. How many elements are there in the set $A = \{0\}$?

c. How many elements are there in the set $B = \{156.241\}$?

d. How many elements are there in set $C = \{0, 156.241\}$?

e. How many elements are in the set $D = \{0, 1, 2, 3, \ldots, 100\}$?

f. How many elements are in the set $E = \{0, 1, 2, 3, \ldots\}$?

g. How many elements are in the set $F = \{0, 2, 4, 6, \ldots\}$?

10. Sets E and F of Exercise 9 are different types of sets than sets A, B, C, and D. What is this difference? Can you say something about this difference *without* talking about number? In the next section look for a way to distinguish such sets without using the word number.

1.4

SET RELATIONSHIPS

Just as there are relationships between numbers, such as equality, less than, greater than, and the like, there are also some interesting relationships between sets. First, let us explain the way in which equality will be used in this text. Whenever a sentence of the form

$$a = b$$

is presented, it will mean that the symbols *"a"* and *"b"* name the same object, that is, whatever object is named by *"a"* is also named by *"b."* For instance, we might have

$$\frac{6}{2} = \frac{24}{8}$$

and our meaning is that "$\frac{6}{2}$" and "$\frac{24}{8}$" are names of the same object, the number 3. As another example, suppose that line segment $\overline{AB}$ and line segment $\overline{CD}$ are pictured as shown in Figure 1-2, and suppose

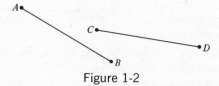

Figure 1-2

that both segments have the same measure, 3 centimeters. According to our agreement we cannot say that $\overline{AB}$ equals $\overline{CD}$, because "$\overline{AB}$" does not name the same object that "$\overline{CD}$" names, for they are different line segments. We can say, however, that the measure of $\overline{AB}$ equals the measure of $\overline{CD}$, because both measures are the same number.

In view of these comments concerning the meaning of equality, sets A and B are equal if and only if "A" and "B" name the same set. But this means that any element of set A is an element of set B and any element of set B is an element of set A, because "A" and "B" name the same set. This gives us a usable criterion for deciding when two sets, no matter how complicated their description, are equal.

> If A and B are sets, $A = B$ if and only if every element of A is an element of B and every element of B is an element of A.

To illustrate the use of this criterion, let us show that if $A = \{x : 2x + 1 = 5$ or $2x + 1 = 7\}$ and $B = \{x : 4x - 1 = 7$ or $4x - 1 = 11\}$, then $A = B$. First, note that the elements of A are 2 and 3. Now 2 is an element of B because 4 times 2 minus 1 is 7. Also, 3 is an element of B because 4 times 3 minus 1 is 11. So every element of set A is an element of set B. Finally, we see that the only elements of set B are 2 and 3, which we have seen to be elements of set A. Therefore, the two sets A and B are equal. Of course, it would have been simpler in this case to determine the solution set of the defining properties of sets A and B, that is, $\{2, 3\}$, and conclude that the two sets are equal since they both name the same set.

Before leaving the discussion of equality, it would be wise of us to point out some properties of equality for future use. First, it should be clear that it is always the case that $a = a$, for any a, because "a" and "a" certainly name the same object whatever it may be. This is called the *reflexive* property of equality. Second, if $a = b$, then it must be that $b = a$, because if "a" and "b" name the same object, then "b" and "a" also name the same object. This is called the *symmetric* property of equality. Third, if $a = b$, and $b = c$, then it must follow that $a = c$. This is reasonable, because "a" and "b" name the same object and "b" and "c" name the same object, so "a," "b," and "c" all name the same object and, in particular, "a" and "c" name the same object, so $a = c$. This last property is called the *transitive* property of equality.

> *Properties of Equality*
> For any a, $a = a$ (reflexive property).

If $a = b$, then $b = a$ (symmetric property).
If $a = b$, and $b = c$, then $a = c$ (transitive property).

Consider the sets C, D, E, and F:

$$C = \{a, b, c, d\}, \qquad D = \{a, c, d\}, \qquad E = \{b, d, e\}, \qquad F = \{b, d, c, a\}$$

Look at C and D. Are they equal sets? No, they are not equal, but there is some relationship between them: every element of set D is an element of set C. We can say that D is a *subset* of set C and write "$D \subseteq C$." Set E is *not* a subset of set C because $e \in E$, but $e \notin C$. We can write "$E \nsubseteq C$" to state this fact.

Set A is a *subset* of set B if and only if every element of set A is an element of set B. We write "$A \subseteq B$" to say "A is a subset of B."

Set A is *not a subset* of set B if set A contains at least one element, say x, such that x is *not* an element of set B. We write "$A \nsubseteq B$" to say "A is not a subset of B."

Using the definition of subset it is easy to check that F is also a subset of set C in the preceding examples. However, C is also a subset of F. Therefore, every element of F is an element of C and every element of C is an element of F, and it follows that $C = F$. This gives us another workable criterion for determining when two sets are equal.

If A and B are sets, $A = B$ if and only if $A \subseteq B$ and $B \subseteq A$.

Look again at C, D, and F. It has been seen that $D \subseteq C$ and $F \subseteq C$, but F is a "stronger kind of subset of C than D. We distinguish between these two kinds of subsets by saying that D is a *proper* subset of C because C has at least one element, in this case b, that is not found in D. We say that F is an *improper* subset of C since $F = C$. We can distinguish the proper subset by use of a slight change in the subset symbol and indicate, for example, that D is a proper subset of C by writing "$D \subset C$."

If A and B are sets, then A is a *proper subset* of B if A is a subset of B and B contains at least one element,

say x, such that x is not an element of A. We write
"$A \subset B$."

A is an *improper* subset of B if $A = B$.

There is another relationship between sets that was discovered centuries ago by ancient man. Today, in primitive societies, use of this principle continues when a tribesman tells how many cattle he has by emptying a pouch of small pebbles or by holding out a collection of notched sticks. His meaning is clear: to each pebble there corresponds a cow and to each cow there corresponds a pebble (or notch on a stick). This is the essence of the notion of a one-to-one correspondence. Children establish one-to-one correspondences as their earliest mathematical experiences. For example, they match their two hands with two mittens, a set of fingers with their age, the kitchen chairs with the members of the family, and eventually they match sounds with words on a page. Look at the following sets. Can you find a one-to-one correspondence between them?

$$A = \{a, b, c\}, \qquad B = \{x, y, z\}$$

One such correspondence pairs a with x, b with y, and c with z. But there are several one-to-one correspondences between these two sets. We picture all of them next in a convenient form:

$$
\begin{array}{cccccc}
a-x, & a-x, & a-y, & a-y, & a-z, & a-z \\
b-y & b-z & b-x & b-z & b-x & b-y \\
c-z & c-y & c-z & c-x & c-y & c-x
\end{array}
$$

Do you see the method used to ensure that all possible pairings of elements are listed? Suppose that we consider sets with just two elements.

$$C = \{m, n\}, \qquad D = \{p, q\}$$

What are the one-to-one correspondences here? Do you see that there are exactly two?

$$
\begin{array}{cc}
m-p, & m-q \\
n-q & n-p
\end{array}
$$

If the two sets contained exactly one element each, how many one-to-one correspondences would there be? Here is a table summarizing what we have found so far. Can you extend it?

Number of Elements in Each Set	Number of One-to-One Correspondences
1	1
2	2
3	6
4	?
5	?
.	.
.	.
.	.
n	?

Two sets for which a one-to-one correspondence exists are called *equivalent sets*. Thus, A and B in the preceding paragraph are equivalent sets and C and D are equivalent sets. Are the two sets E and F equivalent sets?

$$E = \{1, 2, 3, 4, 5\}, \qquad F = \{m, n, p, q, r, s, t\}$$

No, they are not equivalent, because no one-to-one correspondence can be found between the elements of the sets. Any attempt to pair the elements of set E with the elements of set F so that each element of E is paired with one element of F and each element of F is paired with one element of E is doomed to failure! Some elements of F will be left over. Hence, E and F are not equivalent sets.

> If A and B are sets, a *one-to-one correspondence* between A and B is a pairing of the elements of A and B so that each element of A is paired with one unique element of B and each element of B is paired with one unique element of A.
>
> If there exists a one-to-one correspondence between A and B, then A and B are said to be *equivalent sets*. We write "$A \sim B$."

Notice that word "unique" in the definition of one-to-one correspondence. If $A = \{1, 2\}$ and $B = \{x, y, z\}$, then a pairing like 1 with x, 2 with y, and 1 with z is *not* a one-to-one correspondence, because 1 is paired with x *and* with z, which violates the requirement that each element of A be paired with a *unique* element of B.

In some sense you may feel that set equivalence has something to do with "number" for, in the examples wherein two sets were equivalent, it seems that equivalent sets have the same number of elements. (Of course, the word "number" is being used in an intuitive sense here, because we have not yet defined what number is.) However, if we agreed that two equivalent sets do indeed have the same number of elements, we are led to some interesting conclusions. For instance, if W names the set of whole numbers and E names the set of *even* whole numbers, we can show that the two sets are equivalent in the following way:

$$
\begin{array}{rl}
0- & 0 \\
1- & 2 \\
2- & 4 \\
3- & 6 \\
4- & 8 \\
5- & 10 \\
6- & 12 \\
\vdots & \vdots \\
n- & 2n \\
\vdots & \vdots
\end{array}
$$

Whole numbers   Even whole numbers

If equivalent sets have the same number of elements, then there are the same number of *whole numbers* as there are *even whole numbers*. Of course, what this number is has not been made clear, but it is certainly not a small number.

Although it is not convenient to develop a definition of the concept of number at this time, we can clear up a little matter that was mentioned in Exercise 10 of Section 1.3. That matter was concerned with making a distinction between finite and infinite without using the word "number." In the preceding paragraph you saw that we could find a one-to-one correspondence between the set of whole numbers (W) and the set of even whole numbers (E). That correspondence is illustrated by pairing each whole number with its double. Since each even whole number is the double of some whole number, we are sure that this correspondence is a one-to-one correspondence. You can see that the set E is a proper subset of the set W, because every even whole number is a whole number; but there are lots of whole numbers that aren't even. So we have exhibited a one-to-one correspondence between the set of whole numbers (W) and a *proper subset* of the whole numbers (E). This is a very important characteristic of set W. Let's see if we can find a proper subset of set $A = \{1, 2, 3, 4, 5\}$ that can be placed in a one-to-one correspondence with set A. One proper subset

27

of set A is the set $B = \{1, 2, 3, 4\}$. Can set A be placed in a one-to-one correspondence with set B? No! Any such attempt always leaves one element of set A without a partner in set B. In fact, set A cannot be matched with any of its proper subsets to form a one-to-one correspondence, and this is what really distinguishes set A from set W. It is the distinction between finite and infinite sets.

> A set K is an *infinite set* if K contains a proper subset that can be placed in a one-to-one correspondence with set K.
>
> A set is *finite* if it is not infinite.

If someone names a set and asks you to show that it is an infinite set, you have two steps to take. First, you must find a proper subset of the set given to you and, second, you must show that this proper subset can be placed in a one-to-one correspondence with the given set. There may be several proper subsets of the given set that you could use, but the definition simply asks for one such proper subset. But you must show that this proper subset can be placed in a one-to-one correspondence with the set itself.

EXERCISES (Section 1.4)

1. Read each of the following statements. Decide whether the statements are true or false. If they are false, revise them with substantive changes so that the statements are true.
   a. If $7 = 9$, then $9 = 7$ by virtue of the reflexive property of equality.
   b. If $12 = 76$ and $76 = 39$, then $12 = 39$ by the symmetric property of equality.
   c. $4x = 4x$ by the reflexive property.
   d. If $12x = 17y$ and $17y = 32z$, then $12x = 32z$ by the transitive property.
   e. $13 = 52 \div 4$ by the reflexive property of equality.

2. If set $M = \{1, 2\}$,
   a. Is $\{1\} \subseteq M$? Is $\{1\} \in M$?
   b. Is $1 \subseteq M$? Is $1 \in M$?
   c. Is $\emptyset \in M$? Is $\emptyset \subseteq M$?
   d. Is $\{1, 2\} \subseteq M$? Is $\{1, 2\} \in M$?
   e. Make a list of all the subsets of set M. You should find that there are four such subsets.

3. If set $N = \{a, b, c\}$,
   a. What are the proper subsets of set N? You should find that there are seven proper subsets.

b. What are the improper subsets of set N?

c. Altogether, how many subsets does set N have?

4. What are the subsets of set $L = \{4\}$?

5. What are the subsets of the empty set $\emptyset$?

6.

If a Set Contains This Many Elements,	It Must Have This Many Subsets,	and This Many Proper Subsets.
0		
1		
2		
3		
4		
.		
.		
.		
n		

7. Complete the table on page 26.

8. Name a set that is equivalent to the set $R = \{a, b, c, d, e\}$. Show why the two sets are equivalent.

9. Name a set that is equivalent to the set

$$O = \{1, 3, 5, 7, 9, \ldots\}$$

Show why the two sets are equivalent.

10. We have seen that the set of whole numbers is infinite because it contains a proper subset, the even whole numbers, which can be placed in a one-to-one correspondence with the set of whole numbers. Is there any other proper subset of the whole numbers that you can place in a one-to-one correspondence with the whole numbers? Name that set and show how the one-to-one correspondence goes.

11. The set of even whole numbers also ought to be an infinite set. Can you find a proper subset of the even whole numbers and show how to place the elements of this proper subset in a one-to-one correspondence with the even numbers?

12. Exhibit a one-to-one correspondence between
    a. The hours on the clock and the months of the year.
    b. The inch marks on a ruler and the hours on a clock.
    c. The fingers on both hands and the dimes in a dollar.

13. We have seen that equality has the three properties called reflexive, symmetric, and transitive. Verify that set equality has these three properties by checking the definition of set equality. Specifically, check that for every set A, $A = A$; that if $A = B$, then $B = A$; and that if $A = B$ and $B = C$, then $A = C$.

14. Explain why it is that set equivalence also has the properties of reflexivity, symmetry, and transitivity. That is, show why every set A is equivalent to itself ($A \sim A$); why if $A \sim B$, then $B \sim A$; and why if $A \sim B$ and $B \sim C$, then $A \sim C$.

1.5

OPERATIONS ON SETS

In our discussion earlier of mathematical statements it was discovered that new statements may be formed from old statements. From the statements P and Q were formed new statements $P \wedge Q$, $P \vee Q$, $P \Longleftrightarrow Q$, and $-P$. In elementary arithmetic, with the numbers 4 and 5, we can form new numbers $4 + 5$, 4×5, $4 \div 5$, $^-4$, and $^+5$. Likewise, if we begin with two sets A and B, we may form new sets in many different ways.

If A and B are sets, the *intersection* of the two sets is the set of all elements that are simultaneously elements of A and of B. If $A = \{a, b, c, d\}$ and $B = \{c, d, e, f\}$, then the intersection set is $\{c, d\}$, because c and d are elements of both A and B. We write this symbolically as

$$A \cap B = \{c, d\}$$

which we read "The intersection of A and B is the set containing c and d." Pictorially, if the region inside a circle is considered to represent set A and the region inside another circle represents set B, the intersection of the two sets is the region of overlap of the two circles (see Figure 1-3). Diagrams of this sort, which illustrate sets and their relationships, are called *Venn diagrams* after a mathematician who used them years ago. They are a convenient means of illustrating ideas. We shall use them again. Of course, it may happen that the two sets have no elements in common, in which case the intersection set is the empty set, and we would write "$A \cap B = \emptyset$." Pictorially, we might show sets A and B as circles that do not overlap, as in Figure 1-4. When

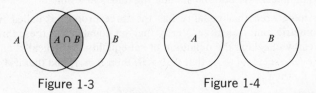

Figure 1-3   Figure 1-4

the intersection of two sets is the empty set, we say that the two sets are *disjoint*.

If A and B are sets, the *intersection* of A and B is the set of elements that are simultaneously elements of both A and B. To name this set, we write "$A \cap B$." If $A \cap B = \emptyset$, we say that A and B are *disjoint* sets.

Let us name the intersection of sets A and B by use of the set-builder notation introduced earlier.

$$A \cap B = \{x : x \in A \text{ and } x \in B\}$$

The use of the word "and" is consistent with the way it was defined in the section on statements, because if x is replaced by the name of some element, the statement is true only if the statements "$x \in A$" and "$x \in B$" are true for the same replacement.

Recall that statements $P \wedge Q$ and $Q \wedge P$ are equivalent statements. It follows that whenever a replacement for x makes the statement "$x \in A$ and $x \in B$" a true statement, the statement "$x \in B$ and $x \in A$" is also true for that replacement. From this remark it can be seen that $A \cap B = B \cap A$. This property is called the *commutative property* of intersection. For three sets A, B, and C it is possible to give meaning to the expression "$A \cap (B \cap C)$" in the following way:

$$A \cap (B \cap C) = \{x : x \in A \text{ and } x \in (B \cap C)\}$$

But to say that $x \in (B \cap C)$ is to say that $x \in B$ and $x \in C$, so

$$A \cap (B \cap C) = \{x : x \in A \text{ and } (x \in B \text{ and } x \in C)\}$$

Finally, if we recall some equivalent statements from an earlier section, we may have a sequence of equalities:

$$
\begin{aligned}
A \cap (B \cap C) &= \{x : x \in A \text{ and } (x \in B \text{ and } x \in C)\} \\
&= \{x : (x \in A \text{ and } x \in B) \text{ and } x \in C\} \\
&= (A \cap B) \cap C
\end{aligned}
$$

This property is called the *associative property* of intersection.

Here are some illustrations of these properties. Let $A = \{1, 2, 3, 4, 5\}$, $B = \{3, 4, 5, 6\}$, and $C = \{4, 5, 6, 7, 8\}$. From the definitions it follows that

$$
\begin{array}{ll}
A \cap B = \{3, 4, 5\}, & (A \cap B) \cap C = \{4, 5\} \\
B \cap C = \{4, 5, 6\}, & A \cap (B \cap C) = \{4, 5\}
\end{array}
$$

Likewise,

$$A \cap B = \{3, 4, 5\}, \qquad B \cap A = \{3, 4, 5\}$$
$$B \cap C = \{4, 5, 6\}, \qquad C \cap B = \{4, 5, 6\}$$

> If A, B, and C are sets, then it is true that
>
> i. $A \cap B = B \cap A$ (the *commutative* property of set intersection).
>
> ii. $A \cap (B \cap C) = (A \cap B) \cap C$ (the *associative* property of set intersection).

If A and B are sets, the *union* of A and B is the set of elements that are in set A *or* in set B. For instance, if set $A = \{1, 2, 3, 4\}$ and set $B = \{3, 4, 5, 6\}$, then the union of A and B, named by "$A \cup B$," is the set of elements $\{1, 2, 3, 4, 5, 6\}$. If we portray sets A and B as circular regions, then the union of sets A and B is the set of all the region inside the two circles, including the overlapping section (see Figure 1-5).

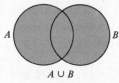

$A \cup B$

Figure 1-5

> If A and B are sets, the union of A and B is the set of elements in A or in B. Symbolically,
>
> $$A \cup B = \{x : x \in A \ or \ x \in B\}$$

Do you see that our use of the word "or" is consistent with the way it was used in the section on sentences and statements? An element has an easy way to be a member of the union of sets A and B, for all it must do is be in set A *or* in set B. To be a member of the intersection of A and B, it must be in *both A and B*.

Again if we make use of equivalent statements discussed in an earlier section, we can derive some properties of set union.

$$
\begin{aligned}
A \cup B &= \{x : x \in A \ or \ x \in B\} \\
&= \{x : x \in B \ or \ x \in A\} \qquad (P \vee Q \text{ is equivalent to } Q \vee P) \\
&= B \cup A
\end{aligned}
$$

Therefore, $A \cup B = B \cup A$, and set union also has a commutative property.

$$(A \cup B) \cup C = \{x : x \in (A \cup B) \text{ or } x \in C\}$$
$$= \{x : (x \in A \text{ or } x \in B) \text{ or } x \in C\}$$
$$= \{x : x \in A \text{ or } (x \in B \text{ or } x \in C)\}$$
$$= A \cup (B \cup C)$$

Therefore, $(A \cup B) \cup C = A \cup (B \cup C)$, and set union has an associative property.

> If A, B, and C are sets, then
>
>   i. $A \cup B = B \cup A$ (*commutative* property).
>   ii. $(A \cup B) \cup C = A \cup (B \cup C)$ (*associative* property).

From the discussion of set operations so far it is obvious that intersection of sets is related to conjunction of statements in the sense that both concepts are dependent on the word "and." Also, set union is related to disjunction in the sense that both are related by the word "or." From the collection of equivalent statements derived earlier, note that $P \wedge (Q \vee R)$ is equivalent to $(P \wedge Q) \vee (P \wedge R)$. This may suggest an analogous relation between set intersection and set union. To be specific,

$$A \cap (B \cup C) = \{x : x \in A \text{ and } x \in (B \cup C)\}$$
$$= \{x : x \in A \text{ and } (x \in B \text{ or } x \in C)\}$$
$$= \{x : (x \in A \text{ and } x \in B) \text{ or } (x \in A \text{ and } x \in C)\}$$
$$= \{x : x \in A \cap B \text{ or } x \in A \cap C\}$$
$$= (A \cap B) \cup (A \cap C)$$

This property is called a *distributive* property of set intersection over set union. It is also true that set union is distributive over set intersection, but we shall let you show in the exercises why this is so. Here is an example which may be used to verify that set intersection is distributive over set union. Let $A = \{1, 2, 3, 4\}$, $B = \{3, 4, 5, 6\}$, and $C = \{5, 6, 7, 8, 9\}$.

$(B \cup C) = \{3, 4, 5, 6, 7, 8, 9\}$ and $A \cap (B \cup C) = \{3, 4\}$
$(A \cap B) = \{3, 4\}$ while $A \cap C = \emptyset$

33

So

$$(A \cap B) \cup (A \cap C) = \{3, 4\}$$

Verify that set union distributes over set intersection in the same way.

Suppose that $A = \{a, b, c, d\}$ and $B = \{c, d, e\}$. Then there are some elements of A that are not elements of B, that is, a and b. This set of elements is in some sense a difference between A and B. Let us be specific and make a definition.

> If A and B are sets, then the *complement* of B *with respect to A* (sometimes called the difference of B from A) is the set of elements in A that are not in B. Symbolically,
>
> $$A - B = \{x : x \in A \text{ and } x \notin B\}$$
>
> Similarly, the complement of A with respect to B is
>
> $$B - A = \{x : x \in B \text{ and } x \notin A\}$$

In our example it can be seen that $A - B = \{a, b\}$ and that $B - A = \{e\}$. If we introduce a third set, $C = \{b, d, e, f, g\}$, then $A - C = \{a, c\}$; so it is clear that the complement of A depends on the set with respect to which that complement is found.

Very often some major set is identified as a domain for discussion. For example, there have been several occasions so far in which we have limited our discussion to the set of whole numbers. Such a set to which consideration is limited is called a *universe of discourse*, or simply a *universe*, as mentioned in Section 1.3. Under the presence of such a universe the complement of a set A may be defined with respect to that universe. In such a case this derived set is simply called the *complement* of set A. Pictorially, if the rectangular region of Figure 1-6 represents the universe and the circular region represents set A, then the region outside of set A yet within the rectangle is called

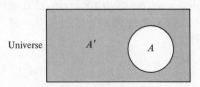

Figure 1-6

the complement of set A and is named by the symbol "A'," read "A complement" or "A prime."

> If A and U are sets, where U is a universe, then the complement of set A, denoted A', is the set of elements in the universe that are not in A. Thus,
>
> $$A' = \{x : x \notin A\} = \{x : x \in U \text{ and } x \notin A\}$$

Notice again how convenient the Venn diagram is in presenting these ideas. Most ideas are easier to understand if there is a simple illustration that can be used to clarify the relationships.

This section has dealt with operations on sets as distinct from relationships between sets. The relationships between sets included equality, proper subset, subset, and equivalence. All these relationships express facts about the way in which one set is related to another. The operations on sets have included set intersection, union, and complementation. These operations have been used to name new sets rather than to express a relation between sets. Given a pair of sets, their intersection is another set. In arithmetic, given a pair of numbers, their sum is another number. So, sum and product of numbers name new numbers, and we say that addition and multiplication of numbers are operations rather than relationships. In a later section we shall introduce the concept of function and show that these operations are functions. In the meantime, remember that set operations name new sets, whereas set relationships express some relation between sets.

EXERCISES (Section 1.5)

1. A Venn diagram portraying three sets A, B, and C within a universe of discourse U is shown. Various regions have been assigned numbers for reference. For each set named in the exercises, list the numbers of the regions in the Venn diagram that make up the set. *Example:* $(A \cap B) \cup C$ is made up of regions numbered 2, 7, 4, 5, and 6.

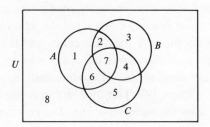

a. $A \cap B$	h. $(A \cup B) \cap C$	o. $A \cap (B \cap C)$
b. $A \cup C$	i. $(A - B) \cap C$	p. $(A \cup B) \cap C$
c. $B - A$	j. $(A \cap B) \cup (A \cap C)$	q. $A \cup (B - A)$
d. $U - A$	k. $(A - B) \cup (B - A)$	r. $A \cap (B - A)$
e. A'	l. $A' \cap C$	s. $A \cup B$
f. $B - C$	m. $A' \cap B'$	t. $(A - B) \cap (B - A)$
g. $C - B$	n. $A \cap (B \cup C)$	u. $(A \cup B) - (A \cap B)$

2. As a result of Exercise 1, you should be able to make some conjectures about operations on sets. For instance, you should be able to conjecture that $B - C$ is not generally the same set as $C - B$. Find at least four other conjectures that seem to be true (in addition to the commutative, associative, and distributive properties for set union and intersection).

3. Remember that we have examined some relations between sets in Section 1.4 and have examined some operations on sets in this section. Make a list of the relationships that have been defined, and make a list of the operations that have been defined. Are new sets created from relationships? Are new sets created from operations on sets?

4. For each of the following sets, sketch a Venn diagram and shade in the region named.

a. $A - B$	d. $(A \cap B) \cup (A \cap C)$	g. $A' \cap (B' \cap C')$
b. $(A - B) \cap A$	e. $(A \cup B)'$	h. $(A - C) \cup (B - C)$
c. $A \cap (B \cup C)$	f. $A' \cap B'$	i. $(A \cup B) - C$

1.6

PRODUCT SETS

You have now seen three operations on sets: set intersection, set union, and set complementation or set difference. In each case, given two sets A and B, a new set was created, $A \cap B, A \cup B, A - B$, or A'. There is another important operation on sets that we shall use repeatedly in the developments which follow, but we need a few words of introduction to make the new operation clear.

Think of a pair of dice. Are you thinking of two little cubes with dots on their faces? Now imagine that one die (the singular) is a brilliant blue and the other is a sensational red. In all other respects these dice are like ordinary dice for they are cubes and the faces have dots (from one through six). Now roll the dice onto an imaginary table (make it green!). Let us describe what you might see on the top of the dice, as shown in Figure 1-7. The blue die may have a three on top while the red die may be showing a five. Do you agree that this is a

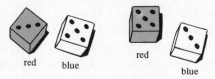

Figure 1-7

different roll than when the blue die shows a five and the red die shows a three? There is a convenient way to name these pairs. It makes use of parentheses and the agreement that the numeral showing on the blue die is listed first while the numeral on the red die is listed second. Thus, "(3, 5)" names the outcome of the experiment described first. The pair (5, 3) can be used to indicate that the blue die showed a five and the red die showed a three. We agreed that these were two different rolls of the dice, so the pair (3, 5) is not the same as the pair (5, 3), for the *order* in which the numerals are listed is different. For this reason these pairs are called *ordered pairs*. Here is the formal agreement.

> An *ordered pair* of elements is a pair of elements having the following property:
>
> $(a, b) = (c, d)$ if and only if $a = c$ and $b = d$
>
> If (a, b) is an ordered pair, the element a is called the *first component* (or first entry) and the element b is called the *second component* (or second entry).

The agreement that we made about the pair (3, 5), that the first component indicated the roll of the blue die while the second component indicated the roll of the red die, is consistent with the property of ordered pairs given. That is, $(3, 5) \neq (5, 3)$ because $3 \neq 5$.

What is the total set of pairs that come from rolling these two dice? Since the first component is one of the numbers 1, 2, 3, 4, 5, 6 and the second component is also one of these numbers, it seems reasonable that if the blue die comes up with a "1" on top, there are six ways for the red die to roll. These rolls are indicated by the pairs

$$(1, 1), \quad (1, 2), \quad (1, 3), \quad (1, 4), \quad (1, 5), \quad (1, 6)$$

But the blue die could just as easily come up with a "2," "3," "4," "5," or "6." So the total set of pairs representing all the possible rolls of these two dice must be

$$\begin{bmatrix} (1, 1), (1, 2), (1, 3), (1, 4), (1, 5), (1, 6) \\ (2, 1), (2, 2), (2, 3), (2, 4), (2, 5), (2, 6) \\ (3, 1), (3, 2), (3, 3), (3, 4), (3, 5), (3, 6) \\ (4, 1), (4, 2), (4, 3), (4, 4), (4, 5), (4, 6) \\ (5, 1), (5, 2), (5, 3), (5, 4), (5, 5), (5, 6) \\ (6, 1), (6, 2), (6, 3), (6, 4), (6, 5), (6, 6) \end{bmatrix}$$

Here is another example that results in a set of ordered pairs. Billy has three shirts, a blue one, a red one, and a striped one. He also has a pair of blue jeans and a pair of brown slacks. What is the set of outfits he can wear today? If we agree to list these outfits as pairs with shirts as first component and slacks as second component, the set of pairs must be

$$\left\{ \begin{array}{l} \text{(blue, blue), (blue, brown)} \\ \text{(red, blue), (red, brown)} \\ \text{(striped, blue), (striped, brown)} \end{array} \right\}$$

Notice that each of his shirts is paired with each of his slacks to give us six pairs or outfits.

In the two examples involving pairs of objects you can see that we paired the objects of one set with the objects of another (or possibly the same) set. Such a set of pairs is called a product set.

> If A and B are sets, the *product set*, written "$A \times B$," read "A cross B," is the set of all pairs with the first components being elements of set A and the second components being elements of set B. In set-builder notation it is given as follows:
>
> $$A \times B = \{(a, b); \, a \in A \text{ and } b \in B\}$$

Remember that $A \times B$ is the set of *all* pairs (a, b) with a an element of A and b an element of B. If $A = \{b, r, s\}$ and $B = \{b, n\}$, then $A \times B = \{(b, b), (b, n), (r, b), (r, n), (s, b), (s, n)\}$, which could be an abbreviation for the set of outfits that Billy can wear.

Later we shall explain how useful the notion of product set is when we talk about multiplication. For now it will be enough to ask you some leading questions. When set A contains three elements and set B contains two elements, how many pairs are there in $A \times B$? Do you agree that there will be six pairs? If set A contains five elements and set B contains four elements, how many pairs are there in $A \times B$? Suppose that set A contains m elements (where m is just some arbitrary number) and set B contains n elements. How many pairs will there be in $A \times B$?

You have been using the notation $x \in A$ to say that x is an element of set A. Suppose that (b, c) is one of the pairs in the product set $A \times B$. Then it must be that (b, c) is an element of $A \times B$, for $A \times B$ is the set of all such pairs. Therefore, it makes sense to write "$(b, c) \in A \times B$" to express this fact.

If set $M = \{p, q, r, s\}$ and set $N = \{r, s, t\}$, the product set

$$M \times N = \begin{cases} (p, r), (p, s), (p, t) \\ (q, r), (q, s), (q, t) \\ (r, r), (r, s), (r, t) \\ (s, r), (s, s), (s, t) \end{cases}$$

What are the pairs in the product set $N \times M$? The definition of product sets makes it clear that the first components must come from set N and the second components from set M. Therefore,

$$N \times M = \begin{cases} (r, p), (r, q), (r, r), (r, s) \\ (s, p), (s, q), (s, r), (s, s) \\ (t, p), (t, q), (t, r), (t, s) \end{cases}$$

Would you say that $M \times N$ and $N \times M$ are equal sets? No! Although some of the elements of $M \times N$ are found in $N \times M$, not every element of $M \times N$ is an element of $N \times M$. For instance, (p, r) and (p, s) are elements of $M \times N$, but they are not elements of $N \times M$. Notice that (r, p) is an element of $N \times M$, but $(r, p) \neq (p, r)$ because these are *ordered* pairs. Hence, $M \times N \neq N \times M$. These two sets do have a certain common property, however. Do you see what it is?

Suppose that set $A = \{1, 2, 3\}$ and set $B = \emptyset$. What is the set $A \times B$? The definition of product set should tell us the answer. If (a, b) is one of the pairs in $A \times B$, then a is an element of A and b is an element of B. But what elements are in B in this example? There are none! Therefore, since there are no possible second components for any pairs of $A \times B$, there must not be any pairs in $A \times B$. In other words, $A \times B$ is the empty set. In fact, whenever either $A = \emptyset$ or $B = \emptyset$ (or both), then $A \times B = \emptyset$.

EXERCISES (Section 1.6)

1. What is the total set of pairs that are the result of tossing a penny and a dime? Of course, let's assume that each coin can come up only heads (H) or tails (T).

2. Suppose that Jimmy has a blue tie and a green tie as well as an orange shirt, a yellow shirt, and a pink shirt. How many tie–shirt pairs can he wear? (Disregard good taste!)

3. Jeff has a drawer full of socks. He has pairs of black socks and pairs of brown socks and no other colors. In the dark early one morning he begins to pull socks from the drawer. How many must he remove from the drawer to be sure that when he gets to the kitchen where the light is he will have a matching pair?

4. If $A = \{1, 2, 3\}$ and $B = \{\#, \$\}$, exhibit the pairs in $A \times B$ and then exhibit the pairs in $B \times A$. Show why $A \times B \neq B \times A$.

5. As you have seen, it is generally not true that $A \times B$ is the same as $B \times A$. What restrictions would need to be made so that $A \times B = B \times A$?

6. One of the difficulties in learning about $A \times B$ is that the elements of $A \times B$ are *pairs*. How many elements (pairs) are there in the set $A \times B$ of Exercise 4? How many pairs are there in the set $B \times A$? Can you make a generalization?

7. Give a simple example of three sets A, B, and C, and for this example show that $A \times (B \cup C) = (A \times B) \cup (A \times C)$.

8. Provided $A \subseteq B$, would it be true that $(A \times C) \subseteq (B \times C)$? Find an example which shows that this is true or false.

9. Does the following expression make sense?

$$A \cup (B \times C) = (A \times B) \cup (A \times C)$$

If it does, is it true? If it doesn't make sense, show why not. If it does make sense but is false, show why.

10. Suppose that $A \subseteq C$ and $B \subseteq D$. Is it true that $A \times B \subseteq C \times D$? If it is true, could you give an argument that would convince a fellow student? If it is false, can you give an example which shows that it isn't always true? Do so.

11. Suppose that $A \times B = \{(9, 7), (6, 4), (0, 1), (3, 2), (3, 4), (9, 4), (9, 1)\}$. Can you name the elements of set A? What must be the elements of set B? Is the set named as $A \times B$ really correct? What's wrong here? What should have been the list of elements in $A \times B$?

12. If $A \subseteq B$ and $C \subseteq D$, is it true that $(A \times B) \subseteq (C \times D)$? Give an example that shows what you believe to be true or false.

1.7

RELATIONS AND LATTICE POINTS

Remember the pair of dice we used in Section 1.6 to introduce the concept of product set? We used a blue die to name the first component in an ordered pair and a red die to name the second component. So the pair (4, 2) named the outcome that occurred when the blue die showed a symbol for four and the red die showed a symbol for two. Suppose that you are a first-grade teacher and you want to help your children learn to recognize the number associated with the dots on the faces of the die and also to begin to learn about the concept of "less than" and "greater than." Here is a simple game that two children can play which will help them learn these ideas. One child is given the blue die and another child the red die. They are to roll their die in order, first the blue die, then the red die. If the number represented on the blue die is greater than the number represented on the red die, the youngster rolling the blue die wins. If the red die has a greater value than the blue die, the youngster rolling the red die wins. If both dice show the same number of dots, no one wins, and the dice must be rolled again. The first child to win five times is the winner of the game.

What is the set of pairs of numbers representing the rolls of the dice that are winning outcomes for the boy with the blue die (the first die rolled)? Do you see that the pair (2, 1) is one such roll? So is (6, 2). Here is the entire set of pairs representing winning outcomes for the blue die.

$$D = \left\{ \begin{array}{l} (2,\ 1),\ (3,\ 1),\ (4,\ 1),\ (5,\ 1),\ (6,\ 1) \\ \qquad (3,\ 2),\ (4,\ 2),\ (5,\ 2),\ (6,\ 2) \\ \qquad\qquad (4,\ 3),\ (5,\ 3),\ (6,\ 3) \\ \qquad\qquad\qquad (5,\ 4),\ (6,\ 4) \\ \qquad\qquad\qquad\qquad (6,\ 5) \end{array} \right\}$$

Set E is the set of pairs representing the outcomes in the game in which the boy with the second die, the red die, is the winner.

$$E = \left\{ \begin{array}{l} (1,\ 2) \\ (1,\ 3),\ (2,\ 3), \\ (1,\ 4),\ (2,\ 4),\ (3,\ 4) \\ (1,\ 5),\ (2,\ 5),\ (3,\ 5),\ (4,\ 5), \\ (1,\ 6),\ (2,\ 6),\ (3,\ 6),\ (4,\ 6),\ (5,\ 6) \end{array} \right\}$$

41

Set F is the set of pairs representing the cases in which neither boy wins.

$$F = \{(1, 1), (2, 2), (3, 3), (4, 4), (5, 5), (6, 6)\}$$

Remember that if $A = \{1, 2, 3, 4, 5, 6\} = B$, then $A \times B$ is the set of all pairs (a, b), where the a is an element of A and b is an element of B. So $A \times B$ in this example is the set of partially listed pairs:

$$A \times B = \begin{Bmatrix} (1, 1), (2, 1), (3, 1), \ldots, (6, 1) \\ (1, 2), (2, 2), (3, 2), \ldots, (6, 2) \\ \vdots \quad \vdots \quad \vdots \quad \quad \vdots \\ (1, 6), (2, 6), (3, 6), \ldots, (6, 6) \end{Bmatrix}$$

The sets D, E, and F, which represented winning combinations for the child with the blue die; the child with the red die; and dies are simply *subsets* of $A \times B$.

There are many other games that may be played with a pair of dice, and a great many of them can be described by means of subsets of the product set $A \times B$. For example, suppose that the rule for the game is that a child rolls both dice and if the sum of the numbers represented on each die is 7 (or whatever number you wish) the child wins; if not, he loses. What are winning combinations for this game?

$$G = \{(1, 6), (2, 5), (3, 4), (4, 3), (5, 2), (6, 1)\}$$

Again, G is a subset of $A \times B$.

Such subsets of a product set like $A \times B$ are called *relations between sets* or simply *relations*. One important relation is the relation known as the "less than" relation in the set of whole numbers. If W names the set of whole numbers, $\{0, 1, 2, \ldots\}$, the product set $W \times W$ is mighty large. Here is the way you might visualize a part of the product set $W \times W$.

$$W \times W = \begin{Bmatrix} (0, 0), (0, 1), (0, 2), \ldots \\ (1, 0), (1, 1), (1, 2), \ldots \\ (2, 0), (2, 1), (2, 2), \ldots \\ \vdots \quad \vdots \quad \vdots \end{Bmatrix}$$

In many ways it looks like the product set for the pair of dice, but of course it does not stop at 6 for either component! The "less than" relation in the whole numbers is the subset of $W \times W$ containing those

42

ordered pairs like (12, 17), (6, 11), and so on. In general, the "less than" relation contains all the pairs (x, y) wherein x is *less than* y. If we call this set L, then some of the pairs belonging to L are given next in such a way as to suggest the pattern of pairs belonging to this relation.

$$L = \begin{cases} (0,\ 1),\ (0,\ 2),\ (0,\ 3),\ (0,\ 4),\ \ldots \\ (1,\ 2),\ (1,\ 3),\ (1,\ 4),\ \ldots \\ (2,\ 3),\ (2,\ 4),\ \ldots \\ (3,\ 4),\ \ldots \end{cases}$$

This relation is a very large set, but you can probably see the nature of the pairs and can see that L is indeed a subset of $W \times W$.

If P names the set of all living people, there are some common relations used in everyday language. For example, "is a brother of" is a familiar relation and includes such pairs as (Jack, Leo), (Jeff, Nancy), (Sean, Seamus), (Bob, Kay), and thousands more. If the relation "is a brother of" is named by the letter K, we can make sentences like "(Jack, Leo) is an element of K." Your roommate will think you're a little strange if you make such remarks rather than the normal "Jack is the brother of Leo." Similarly, in mathematics we hardly ever say "(4, 9) is an element of the relation less than" but say "4 is less than 9," which we shall later write as "$4 < 9$." Generally, if R is the set name of a relation and (x, y) is one of the pairs in the relation, we say either "$(x, y) \in R$" or we say "x is R-related to y," which is usually written simply "$x\ R\ y$."

> If A and B are sets, a *relation from A to B* is a subset of $A \times B$.
>
> A subset of $A \times A$ is called a *relation on set A*.
>
> If (x, y) is an element of relation R, then write either "$(x, y) \in R$" or "$x\ R\ y$" to express this fact.

Later in this section we shall present a convenient way to portray relations, but for now let us use a simple kind of pictorial representation. On the left of Figure 1-8 is a picture of a set A and on the right is a picture of a set B. The arrows suggest the pairs of a relation. Can you name the pairs of this relation? They are (A, G), (A, N), (B, G), (B, S), and (D, N), where the letters indicate the names of the people as an abbreviation. Notice that Carlos is not paired with any element of the set B, while Alice and Betty are paired with two elements each. This relation might represent "is a cousin of."

43

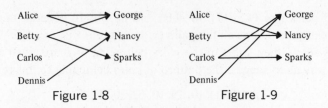

Figure 1-8   Figure 1-9

Another relation from the set *A* to the set *B* is pictured in Figure 1-9. This example might be an example of the relation known as "is a very good friend of."

Of course, there are many relations that might be found between the elements of one set and the elements of another set. If the sets were large, there would probably be too many to count.

Just for the sake of convenience, let's use a small set *A* and a small set *B* and see how many relations we can find from set *A* to set *B*. Let $A = \{1, 2, 3\}$ and let $B = \{\#, \$\}$. Any relation from *A* to *B* is a subset of $A \times B$, so let's have a look at $A \times B$.

$$A \times B = \{(1, \#), (2, \#), (3, \#), (1, \$), (2, \$), (3, \$)\}$$

How many elements are there in $A \times B$? You should agree that there are six elements in $A \times B$, for the product set consists of six pairs. Since $A \times B$ contains six elements, how many subsets does $A \times B$ have? (*Hint:* Look back at Exercise 6 in Section 1.4.) We know that any subset of $A \times B$ (even the empty set) is a relation from *A* to *B*, so there are just as many relations as there are subsets of $A \times B$. Of course, some relations are more interesting than others, as we shall see later.

Suppose that set $C = \{0, 1, 2, 3, 4\}$; then $C \times C$ contains 25 pairs of numbers. Next we describe a convenient method to use to picture this product set. Along a horizontal base line place pencil dots to represent the elements 0, 1, 2, 3, and 4, as in Figure 1-10. Next, along a

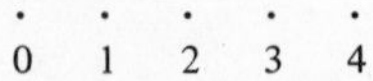

. . . . .
0   1   2   3   4

Figure 1-10

vertical line place pencil dots starting with the dot that represented the element 0 and going on to 1, 2, 3, and 4, as in Figure 1-11. Finally, place pencil dots vertically (or horizontally) from those labeled 1, 2, 3, and 4 in Figure 1-12. What you see diagrammed may be regarded as a picture of the product set $C \times C$ if we make an agreement that the pair (2, 3), for example, is portrayed by that point directly *above* the

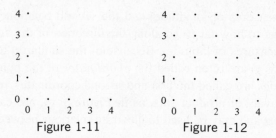

Figure 1-11   Figure 1-12

numeral 2 and directly *across* from the numeral 3, as shown in Figure 1-13. Using this agreement, every pair in the product set $C \times C$ is represented by a dot and every dot represents some pair in the product set.

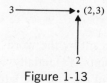

Figure 1-13

In Figure 1-14 certain points have been labeled by capital letters $S, T, U, \ldots$. What are the number pairs that correspond to these points? The point S represents the pair $(1, 3)$ because, according to our agreement, the point S is directly over the 1 on the horizontal set

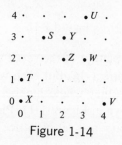

Figure 1-14

and is directly across from the 3 on the vertical set. Likewise, T corresponds to the pair $(0, 1)$, U to the pair $(3, 4)$, V to the pair $(4, 0)$, W to the pair $(3, 2)$, X to the pair $(0, 0)$, Y to the pair $(2, 3)$, and Z to the pair $(2, 2)$. Notice that the pair $(2, 3)$ and the pair $(3, 2)$ are different pairs and are represented by two different points, W and Y.

You can see that the pairs can be used to locate points as you locate points on a map of the earth. The first component in each pair gives instructions concerning how far to go along the horizontal scale (just like measures of longitude) and the second component gives instructions as to how far to go along the direction of the vertical scale (just like measures of latitude). Because of the similarity to map reading, pairs (x, y) are often called the *coordinates* of the points, and the x and y values are called the first and second coordinates, respectively.

Portrayals of product sets, as in Figure 1-14, are called sets of *lattice points* and may be used to illustrate relations between sets also.

> Representations of product sets by means of dots as models of the pairs in the product set are called *lattice points*. Each lattice point is separated or isolated from the others. The ordered pair (x, y) is called the *pair of coordinates* of the lattice point that represents the pair.

You should ask what is meant by the words separated and isolated in the definition of lattice points. Essentially what is meant is that there is some open space around each of the lattice points with no lattice points within that open space. Figure 1-15 is a picture of a lattice point showing the open space around it that contains no other lattice point.

Figure 1-15

When you draw a picture of the set of whole numbers you might draw it as shown in Figure 1-16. But each whole number is separated or isolated from every other whole number, so that a better picture might look like that shown in Figure 1-17. Pictured in this way, the set of whole numbers appears as a set of lattice points.

Figure 1-16   Figure 1-17

One of the relations on the set $C = \{0, 1, 2, 3, 4\}$ is the set $R = \{(0, 0), (1, 1), (2, 2), (3, 3), (4, 4)\}$, a subset of $C \times C$. Set R may be portrayed as a set of lattice points by marking the points that represent the pairs in R in a distinctive way, as in Figure 1-18. The points of relation R are darkened to show the nature of the relation. Such a set of points is called a *graph of the relation*.

46

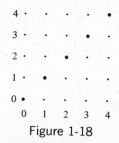

Figure 1-18

> If *R* is a relation from set *A* to set *B*, then the set of
> points that represents *R* is called the *graph* of the
> relation *R*.

Figure 1-19

Figure 1-19 portrays a graph of a relation *P*. Can you name the pairs
that belong to this relation? You should be able to see that $P =$
$\{(0, 4), (1, 3), (2, 2), (3, 1), (4, 0)\}$ or that $P = \{(x, y)$ such that x and y
are in C and $x + y = 4\}$. Do you see any learning activities that you
could devise from the ideas of lattice points and relations that would
be useful (and different) in helping children learn? Watch the exercises
at the end of the section for some suggestions.

You have seen that relations on a set A are subsets of $A \times A$.
Some of these relations on a set are especially interesting because they
have certain properties. For example, if $A = \{0, 2, 4, 6, 8\}$, an interesting relation is

$$R_1 = \{(0, 0), (2, 2), (4, 4), (6, 6), (8, 8)\}$$

The relation R_1 (which is read "R sub one") has the property that for
any element x of set A the pair (x, x) is in the relation. Another relation
with the same property is

$$R_2 = \{(0, 0), (2, 2), (4, 4), (6, 6), (8, 8), (2, 4), (6, 4)\}$$

Of course, R_2 has two more pairs than R_1, but it still has the property that, for every x in A, (x, x) is an element of R_2. Such relations on a set A are called *reflexive* relations. If the set W is the set of whole numbers $\{0, 1, 2, \ldots\}$, you may regard equality as a relation and you will see that as a relation it is a reflexive relation; because if x is any whole number, certainly $x = x$ [or the pair (x, x) belong to "equality"], so equality is a reflexive relation.

If set $A = \{0, 2, 4, 6, 8\}$ and relation $R_3 = \{(2, 4), (4, 2), (8, 6),$ $(6, 8)\}$, you can see that R_3 is not a reflexive relation. However, R_3 does have an interesting property, because whenever the pair (x, y) appears in the relation, so does the pair (y, x). Any relation on a set A is said to be *symmetric* if it has this property. The relation $R_4 = \{(8, 8), (0, 6), (6, 0), (2, 4)\}$ is not a symmetric relation because the pair $(2, 4)$ is an element of R_4, but the pair $(4, 2)$ is not. It must be the case that whenever (x, y) is contained in the relation so is the pair (y, x). Notice that the pair $(8, 8)$ is in the relation R_4 and so is the pair $(8, 8)$. (Was that too fast for you? Did you see us exchange the 8's?) If you think about equality as a relation on the set of whole numbers, you will see that equality is a symmetric relation also, for if $x = y$, then $y = x$. That is, whenever the pair (x, y) is found in the relation "equals," then the pair (y, x) is found there also.

The "less than" relation mentioned earlier has another interesting property called the transitive property. Whenever x is less than y and when y is less than z, it is always the case that x is less than z. Thus, 6 is less than 9 and 9 is less than 15, and it is true that 6 is less than 15. The reason this property is called the transitive property stems, no doubt, from the fact that the word transition involves moving across an intermediate object or idea. Here we move across the intermediate term, such as 9 in the example, to reach from 6 to 15. Why do you think the words reflexive and symmetric are used to describe the other two properties?

Sometimes it happens that a relation on set A will have all three of the properties reflexivity, symmetry, and transitivity. Whenever this is so, the relation is said to be an *equivalence relation*. Do you think that equality of whole numbers is an equivalence relation? Check transitivity, for we have already seen that equality is reflexive and symmetric.

If R is a subset of $A \times A$, then R is said to be a *relation on set A*.

If R is a relation on set A, then R is said to be a *reflex-*

ive relation if it is true that whenever x is an element of A, then (x, x) is an element of R.

If R is a relation on set A, then R is said to be a *symmetric relation on A* if it is the case that whenever (x, y) is a pair in R, then (y, x) is a pair in R.

If R is a relation on set A, then R is said to be a *transitive relation* if it is true that whenever (x, y) and (y, z) are pairs in the relation, then (x, z) is a pair in the relation.

If R is a relation on set A and R is reflexive, symmetric, and transitive, then R is said to be an *equivalence relation*.

Let us give an example of a set, an equivalence relation on that set, and portray the relation by means of a lattice-point graph. Suppose that set $B = \{a, b, c, d\}$. Then an example of an equivalence relation on this set is $E = \{(a, a), (b, b), (c, c), (d, d), (a, c), (c, a), (c, b), (b, c), (a, b), (b, a)\}$. The graph of this relation is shown in Figure 1-20. Another equivalence relation on the same set B is the relation $F = \{(a, a), (b, b), (c, c), (d, d), (a, d), (d, a)\}$. The graph is shown in Figure 1-21. As you study these two examples of equivalence relations, you

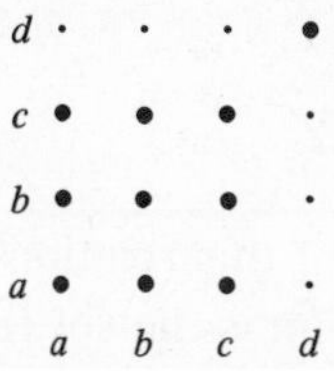

Figure 1-20 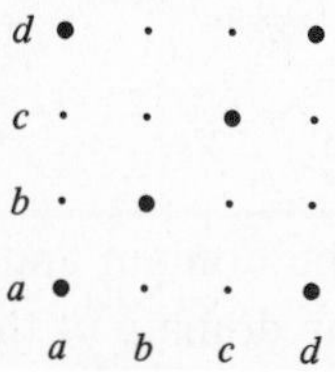   Figure 1-21

should notice that each meets the requirements of reflexivity, symmetry, and transitivity and that the graph of each relation has identifiable geometric characteristics. For example, you should be able to notice a certain symmetry of shape.

Let us summarize what has been said in this section concerning relations. We have seen that if A and B are sets then $A \times B$ names the set of all pairs such as (a, b) with a an element of set A and b an element of set B. The set $A \times B$ is called the product set. A relation from A to B is a subset of $A \times B$, and so a relation is also a set of pairs. We have seen that a special kind of relation is a relation from A to A or

49

simply a relation on set A. Some of these latter relations are reflexive relations, symmetric relations, or transitive relations. A relation on set A is an equivalence relation if it is reflexive, symmetric, and transitive. We have also seen that it is possible to portray relations by means of lattice-point graphs.

To close this section on relations, there are two terms that are commonly used to mention the first components and the second components of a relation. The set of first components of a given relation is called the *domain* of the relation and the set of second components is called the *range* of the relation. Do you see that the domain and range are sets of single elements while the relation is a set of pairs? Here is an example: set $A = \{1, 2, 3, 4, 5, 6\}$, set $B = \{3, 4, 5, 6, 7, 8\}$, and the relation $R = \{(1, 7), (2, 6), (3, 5), (4, 4), (5, 3)\}$. The domain of R is the set $\{1, 2, 3, 4, 5\}$ and the range of R is the set $\{7, 6, 5, 4, 3\}$. You can see that the domain of the relation is a subset of set A. Of course; that's because the relation is a subset of $A \times B$ so that first components come from set A. Likewise, the range is a subset of B.

Figure 1-22 is a lattice-point graph of a relation. Can you name

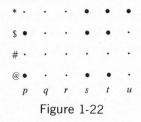

Figure 1-22

the elements in the domain and range of this relation? You should be able to see that the domain of this relation is the set $\{p, s, t, u\}$ and that the range of this relation is the set $\{@, \$, *\}$. All of this may be more easily seen perhaps if we simply list the set of pairs in the relation: $\{(p, @), (p, \$), (s, @), (s, \$), (s, *), (t, @), (t, \$), (t, *), (u, *)\}$. Just look at the list of first coordinates and you can tell what elements belong to the domain. A look at the list of second elements determines the range of the relation.

> If R is a relation from set A to set B, then the *domain of the relation R* is the set of first components of R. The *range of the relation R* is the set of second components of R.

If set $M = \{1, 2, 3, 4\}$ and set $P = \{a, b, c, d\}$, then one of the relations from M to P is the relation $R = \{(1, a), (2, a), (4, b), (4, c)\}$. Another relation derived from R is the relation known as the *inverse of R*. The inverse of R contains the following elements:

$$\{(a, 1), (a, 2), (b, 4), (c, 4)\}$$

Do you see why it is called the inverse of R? (It might better be called the reverse of R.) Of course, the inverse of R is a relation from B to A, while R is a relation from A to B.

> If R is a relation from A to B, the *inverse of R*, named by the symbol R^{-1}, is defined by
>
> $$R^{-1} = \{(y, x) : (x, y) \text{ is an element of } R\}$$

One of the common relations on the set of whole numbers is the relation discussed earlier called "less than." The symbol "$<$" is often used to name this relation. Here are a few of the pairs in this relation:

$$< = \{(0, 1), (0, 2), (0, 3), (1, 2), (1, 3), \ldots\}$$

What is the inverse of the "less than" relation?

$$<^{-1} = \{(1, 0), (2, 0), (3, 0), (2, 1), (3, 1), \ldots\}$$

Do you know another name for $<^{-1}$? Of course; it's known as the "greater than" relation.

A number of new ideas have been presented in this section, and you may be feeling some discomfort because there seem to be too many ideas. We hope that the exercises that follow will serve to make you feel more comfortable and that they will also serve to show you that each of these ideas is directly applicable to your situation as a classroom teacher. Of course, each of these ideas is also important in what we have to say in subsequent sections.

EXERCISES (Section 1.7)

1. A common dice game called craps involves throwing two dice. A player is a winner, among other more complicated possibilities, if he rolls either a seven or an eleven, that is, if the sum of the numerals on the two dice is 7 or 11. What are the winning pairs?

2. In the same game a player loses and must pass the dice on to the next player if he rolls a sum of 2, 3, or 12. How many such combinations are there? What are they?

51

3. A game can be played with two dice by multiplying the numbers represented instead of adding. Winning a roll means that the product is a perfect square (such as 1, 4, 9, 16, etc.). What are the winning combinations?

4. A game is fair if there is an equal chance of winning and of losing. Suppose that a game is to be played in which the numbers represented on the two dice are to be added, and a player wins on a roll of the dice if the sum of the numbers is greater than 7. How many winning combinations are there? Is the game fair?

5. Give three examples of relations which are in common usage that deal with the elementary school. For example, "is a student of" names a relation between students and teachers.

6. Let $A = \{1\}$ and $B = \{a\}$. How many nonempty relations are there from A to B? What are they? How many pairs are in $A \times B$?

7. Let $A = \{1, 2\}$ and $B = \{a\}$. What are the nonempty relations from A to B? How many are there? How many pairs are in $A \times B$?

8. Let $A = \{1, 2\}$ and $B = \{a, b\}$. What are the nonempty relations from A to B and how many are there? How many pairs are in $A \times B$?

9. Complete the following chart:

Number of Elements in Set A	Number of Elements in Set B	Number of Elements in $A \times B$	Number of Nonempty Relations from A to B
1	1	1	1
2	1	2	3
2	2	4	15
2	n	$2n$	?
m	n	?	?

10. Make a lattice-point representation of the following product set and then represent the indicated relations.

$$A = \{1, 2, 3, 4, 5\}, \qquad B = \{1, 2, 3, 4\}$$

a. On the lattice-point portrayal of $A \times B$, illustrate the relation $R = \{(1, 1), (1, 2), (1, 4), (4, 1)\}$.
b. Represent the relation $S = \{(1, 1), (2, 2), (3, 3), (4, 4)\}$.
c. Represent the relation $T = \{(1, 2), (2, 3), (1, 3)\}$.
d. Represent the relation $U = \{(1, 3), (3, 1), (3, 4), (4, 3)\}$.

11. What are the domains and ranges of the four relations R, S, T and U of Exercise 10?

12. Consider the relation $M = \{(a, 1), (a, 2), (b, 1), (b, 3)\}$ from set $X = \{a, b, c\}$ to the set $Y = \{1, 2, 3\}$. What is the inverse of this relation? What is the domain and what is the range of M? What generalization concerning the relationship do you see?

13. Suppose that set $A = \{a, b, c, d, e\}$. Give examples of relations on set A as called for.
a. Symmetric relation on set A.

b. Reflexive relation on set A.
c. Transitive relation on set A.
d. Equivalence relation on set A.
e. Symmetric but not reflexive relation on set A.
f. Reflexive but not symmetric relation on set A.
g. Symmetric and transitive but not reflexive relation on set A.

1.8

FUNCTIONS

Children are often aware of their height as compared with others in their class. The tallest youngster in the class is known to all and so is the shortest. Sometimes the teacher will keep records of the height of each child in the room and may have the children make graphs from the recorded data. Suppose that you have a small class of students, have measured each child, and have recorded these measures. What mathematical concepts are associated with making a graph of these data?

Name	Height (nearest centimeter)
Abby	125
Betsy	115
Charles	135
David	130
Esther	105
Frank	121
Guiseppe	130
Helen	130
Iola	128
Jimmy	138
Kathy	117
Lupe	117
Manuel	131
Nat	125

One mathematical concept associated with these data is that of *relation*, because we see here a set of ordered pairs: $\{(A, 125), (B, 115), (C, 135), \ldots, (N, 125)\}$. The domain of this relation is the set of children in the class, and the range of the relation is the set of centimeter measures given. There is something special, however, about this mathematical relation: each element of the domain is paired with *just one element* of the range. Several relations that we have examined have not had this property. The relation "is a brother of," for example, does not have this property because David is the brother of Steve and David is the brother of Peggy, so that David is paired with at least two elements of the range of this relation.

When a relation has the property that each element of the domain is paired with exactly one element of the range, the relation is called a function. The "height in centimeters" relation is a function, because each child is paired with just one number.

> A *function* is a relation which has the property that each element of the domain is paired with a single element of the range.
>
> In other words, a relation is a *function* if whenever (a, b) and (a, c) are pairs in the relation then $b = c$.

Still another statement may help explain the meaning of the word function: a relation is a function if no two ordered pairs of the relation have the same first component.

The pictures in Figures 1-23 and 1-24 are similar to those which were used in the preceding section to illustrate relations. Can you tell

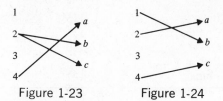

Figure 1-23   Figure 1-24

which of the pictures is an illustration of a function and which is a relation that is not a function? Figure 1-23 suggests a relation that is not a function because two ordered pairs contain the same first component. These two pairs are $(2, b)$ and $(2, c)$. Figure 1-24 suggests a function because each element of the domain is paired with exactly one element of the range.

Remember that we have found the lattice-point graphs of some relations. In Figure 1-25 are two such graphs. Which is the graph of a function? The relation on the left is not a function because the pairs

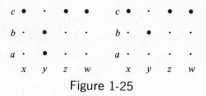
Figure 1-25

(y, a) and (y, b) are both elements of that relation and $a \neq b$. The relation on the right is a function because no two pairs have the same first component.

You have seen that the domain of some relations between two sets A and B is a proper subset of A and the domain of others is equal to set A. The relations whose graphs are shown in Figure 1-25 both had as their domain the set $\{x, y, z, w\}$. Some writers (and teachers) are very particular in their use of the word "function" and require that a function from a set A to a set B be a relation from A to B having no two ordered pairs with the same first component (as we have done), *and also having the property* that the domain of the relation is set A. They reason that if we are to speak of a function *from A to B*, then it should be *from A;* that is, every element of set A is paired with something in B. There are good reasons for this rather stringent requirement beyond a matter of precision in language, as we shall soon see. In any case, the requirement can be easily adopted at this point in our development, and we do so in our next definition.

> A *function from set A to set B* is a relation from set A to set B that meets the following requirements:
>   i. The domain of the relation is set A.
>   ii. If (a, b) and (a, c) are pairs in the relation, then $b = c$.

The second property is the one we have been requiring all along and says that if x is any element of set A, then x can be paired with *no more than one* element of set B. The first requirement is this new one mentioned and says that every element of set A must be paired with something in set $B;$ that is, each element of set A must be paired with *at least one* element of set B. Taken together, these requirements state that each element of set A must be paired with exactly one element of set B. Given any element of set A, the element of set B with which it is paired in a function is called the *image* of that element of set A.

> If the pair (x, y) is a pair in a function called f, then y is called the *image of x under the function f.*
>
> We may write either "$(x, y) \in f$" or "$y = f(x)$" to state this fact.

Look back at the set of data given at the beginning of this section and you will see that it exemplifies a function from the set of children in the classroom to the set of whole numbers. Each of the children of the class is paired with exactly one number, called the height of that child. The image of Abby is 125, and we can say that (Abby, 125) is an element of this function, or that the image of Abby is 125 under the height function (h), or that $h(\text{Abby}) = 125$.

What are some other functions that the elementary teacher is likely to find important in the teaching of elementary mathematics? Here is one that will suggest many others. Remember that a function is a relation from one set to another, so we must first start with two sets A and B. Suppose that the first set, A, is already a set of pairs, while set B is just a set of elements. The function we have in mind is pictured (in part) in Figure 1-26 and is a function from A to B. Can

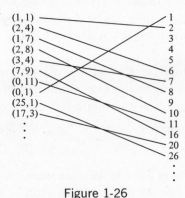

Figure 1-26

you find the common name for this function? No doubt you are able to see that the function suggested here is commonly known as addition of whole numbers. If we called this function s (for *s*um), we would have such statements as $((1, 1), 2) \in s$, $((2, 8), 10) \in s$, $((25, 1), 26) \in s$, and so on. In everyday use we would say, however, that the sum of 1 and 1 is 2, the sum of 2 and 8 is 10, the sum of 25 and 1 is 26, and so on. It is surprising to discover that when we consider the operation of addition of whole numbers as a function we derive the benefit of a fresh understanding of the meaning of that operation. For example, the fact that this is a function from the set of all pairs of whole numbers to the set of all whole numbers reminds us that every pair of whole numbers (the set A) must have an image in the set of whole numbers (the set B). Hence, if (x, y) is one of the pairs in set A, there must be some element of B that is the sum of x and y. This is more often referred to as the *closure* property for the operation of addition, but you have seen that it is simply the requirement that the domain of the function be set A. The other property requires that any object of set A must be paired with no more than one element of set B. In the case of the function called addition of whole numbers this simply means that the sum of x and y is unique, or that the sum of x and y is just one whole number. Thus, 2 plus 3 is 5, and 2 plus 3 is never anything else in whole number addition. More will be said about such operations in later chapters.

The word "function" is a common word in the English language and is used in much the same way as in mathematical language. For instance, we read that "the average annual income is a function of the national rate of employment." What is meant is that there is some way of determining the average annual income from data about the rate of employment. This determination may not be very precise or accurate, but there is some relationship in the sense that when the rate of employment is low, the average annual income is also low.

Another example is "Athletic ability is a function of age." What is implied is that given a certain person's age it is possible to determine his athletic ability. The relationship may be illustrated by a graph such as the one shown in Figure 1-27.

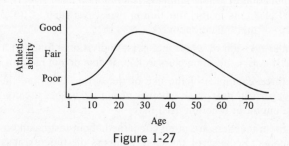

Figure 1-27

The point is that in all these examples given an element in a first set (national rate of employment, age, etc.) there corresponds to it some element in a second set (average annual income, athletic ability, etc.). The distinction is that in the English-language usage of the word "function," the relationship is apt to be quite general and loosely established. On the other hand, the use of the word "function" is quite specific and strictly established in the context of mathematics.

EXERCISES (Section 1.8)

1. Find three examples of relations that are not functions from set $A = \{7, 8, 9\}$ to set $B = \{s, t, p\}$.

2. Find three examples of functions similar to the height function for the children in the classroom.

3. If set $A = \{1, 2, 3, 4\}$ and set $B = \{a, b, d, c\}$,
   a. Give an example of a function from A to B.
   b. What is the inverse of your function in part a?
   c. Is the inverse of your function in part a also a function? Is it just a relation from B to A and not a function?
   d. Give another example of a function from A to B, find its inverse, and determine whether the inverse is again a function from B to A.

4. Give a lattice-point illustration of a relation that is not a function and tell why it is not a function.

5. The sum function (s) from the set $W \times W$ (where W names the set of whole numbers) to the set W was partially illustrated earlier. Give an example of pairs that belong to the sum function as well as some pairs that do not belong to this function.

6. Subtraction of whole numbers includes such pairs as $((6, 2), 4)$, because $6 - 2 = 4$. Name three other pairs that belong to the operation of subtraction. Name some pairs that do not belong to this operation. Is subtraction of whole numbers a closed operation?

7. Multiplication of whole numbers is a function from $W \times W$ to W. Name several elements in this function in two ways, such as $((3, 5), 15)$ is an element of multiplication and $3 \times 5 = 15$.

8. Consider division of whole numbers. Is division a function from $W \times W$ to W? If not, name some pairs in $W \times W$ that do not have an image in W.

9. Find three examples of the use of the word "function" in your daily newspaper and determine whether or not the usages are consistent with the definition of function used here.

10. Classroom teachers are often concerned about testing and evaluation of test scores. Because of the large numbers of students, it is often convenient to group the data from such testing and to display the results in a graph. A sample of such data is

Score Interval	Number of Students Scoring in This Interval
95–100	2
90–94	3
85–89	6
80–84	12
75–79	12
70–74	15
65–69	10
60–64	8
55–59	3
50–54	0
45–49	1
40–44	2
35–39	1

Make at least two graphs that represent these data, such as a bar graph, line graph, pictorial graph, or other form. Is there a function here?

Georg Cantor

(1845–1918)

Born in St. Petersburg, Russia, Georg Cantor emigrated to Germany with his parents when he was 11. He was a very capable student and went on for study at the University of Berlin. There, as often has happened in the history of mathematics, he was recognized for his potential by an older and famous mathematician, Karl Weierstrass. Cantor was one of that unique breed of men who have the courage to reexamine the fundamental notions that are commonly accepted as truth. For hundreds of years mathematicians had ignored the concept of an actual infinity, often excusing their action by contending that such matters were more theological and philosophical than mathematical. But Cantor saw that the concept of number could logically be extended beyond the finite numbers of everyday use to transfinite numbers or infinite numbers. In fact, he discovered that there are different kinds of infinite numbers. The core of his study

involved classifying sets of objects, and from his studies evolved the subject matter that is now called set theory.

Cantor's writings were severely criticized by his contemporaries and he was alternately bitterly angered and hopelessly depressed by these attacks. He was a sincerely religious man and felt that the reactions were unwarranted, for he had arrived at his conclusions through diligent study and faithful adherence to religious principles. Over a period of thirty years or more, Cantor defended his results in spite of these distasteful confrontations, but he became less and less able to bear the strain of the conflict. As 1900 came and passed, Cantor became ill both physically and mentally and died in a mental hospital in 1918. Although he was unable to fully appreciate the turn of events, prior to his death he had come to be recognized for the great mathematician that he was. Today the subject matter of set theory extends from the elementary school curriculum through almost all branches of the tree of mathematics.

Chapter 2

Mathematical Thinking

2.1
INTRODUCTION

Mathematics is a creation of man's mind, consisting of patterns of related ideas and patterns of thought. One of the more beautiful qualities of mathematics is the relatedness of the ideas, processes, and ways of thinking that form the essence of mathematics. Unfortunately, it is impossible in a single chapter to present mathematics as a whole, together with its myriad interrelationships. Quite frequently many ideas will flood one's mind in an instant, but these ideas must line up and await their turn for expression. The same is true regarding any book on mathematics. Thus, we began in Chapter 1 by considering a single facet of mathematics, that is, mathematics as a language. We now consider mathematics as a way of thinking. To do so, we shall expand upon the ideas presented earlier. Throughout the study of this book, you should constantly attempt to see how the various ideas of mathematics, necessarily presented chapter by chapter, are related.

2.2

THE ROLE OF LOGICAL THINKING IN MATHEMATICS

We might begin this section by asking the question "What is mathematics?" Mathematics has been described at various times as a language, a study of patterns, an art, an organized structure of knowledge, and as a way of thinking. One very short definition is that mathematics is what a mathematician does. At first, this definition may appear trite, but upon further consideration you will see that one of the more important activities of a mathematician is the creation of new mathematics. This creation of new mathematics, in turn, involves the study of patterns to discover new relationships, the use of mathematical language to express these relationships, and the use of deductive reasoning to prove the relationships. The mathematician must rely upon his imagination and ingenuity in the quest for knowledge. This quest and the resulting creative process is indeed an art.

More than anything else, mathematics is concerned with methods of correct reasoning and the development of mathematical systems. The study of the methods of correct reasoning is called *logic*. In one way or another, relating ideas in mathematics, making conjectures regarding possible relationships of ideas, showing that a generalization is true, making definitive statements, or developing a mathematical system has its basis in logic.

It is not surprising that the invention and study of logic is not new. The processes used by man to think or to reason were first investigated by the ancient Greeks. The great Greek philosopher Aristotle (384–322 B.C.) systematized these principles and is generally recognized as the founder of logic. Logic became one of the trivium of grammar, logic, and rhetoric that was looked upon during the Middle Ages as three of the seven liberal arts required of the educated man. Thus, the study of logic has been part of the curriculum for at least 20 centuries.

The logic of Aristotle was concerned with only four kinds of statements, having the following classification:

1. *All S* is *P*.
2. *No S* is *P*.

3. *Some S* is *P*.
4. *Some S* is *not P*.

In each of these statements the letters *S* and *P* are used to designate subject and predicate. The following are examples of these statements:

1. All birds are animals.
2. No fish are birds.
3. Some birds are parrots.
4. Some birds are not parrots.

Aristotle and others were concerned with arguments about objects of the universe and so were interested in how one can decide whether or not a certain line of arguing or line of reasoning is correct. To make such decisions, early logicians tried various combinations of statements, such as shown previously, with the result that some were seen to be particularly useful. These combinations of statement types were called syllogisms.

Reasoning became the application of 14 syllogisms involving the use of the preceding four statement forms. An additional five syllogisms were added during the Middle Ages. We formally define a syllogism as

A *syllogism* is an argument consisting of two propositions called premises and a third proposition called the conclusion.

To illustrate how the syllogism was used in reasoning, consider the *hypothetical syllogism*, which is as follows:

All teachers are people.
All people are kind.
Therefore, all teachers are kind.

The form of this argument is independent of the words "teacher," "people," and "kind." We might just as well have argued that

All multiples of 8 are multiples of 4.
All multiples of 4 are multiples of 2.
Therefore, all multiples of 8 are multiples of 2.

Do you see how the set concept of subset can be used to illustrate the validity of the hypothetical syllogism? Figure 2-1 depicts the

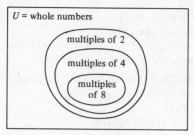

Figure 2-1

various set relationships described by the syllogism regarding multiples.

Probably the most famous syllogism is the *Socratic argument*, which is as follows:

> All men are mortal.
> Socrates is a man.
> Therefore, Socrates is mortal.

More will be said concerning this syllogism in Section 2-4.

The logic of Aristotelean logic is found to be lacking in several respects. Each of the four statements in Aristotelean logic is a simple statement. There are no compound statements involving the connectives "or" and "and." The manner of deducing conclusions is tedious, since syllogistic reasoning is dependent upon both subject and predicate relations and the use of the four basic forms.

It was not until 1848 that a logic which differed significantly from the logic of Aristotle was produced by an English schoolteacher and mathematician named George Boole (1815–1864). Boole applied symbols and the language of sets to logic. The verbiage of Aristotle and his followers was reduced to a relatively easy and simple type of algebra. Systematic reasoning became, in this algebra, a matter of manipulating formulas. Simple variables such as P came to represent a single statement, such as "All students work hard." Thus, George Boole became the founder of symbolic logic, that branch of formal logic used most frequently in mathematics today.

EXERCISES (Section 2.2)

1. Draw a Venn diagram to illustrate each of the following.
   a. All birds have feathers.
   b. Some girls like mathematics.

    c. No odd numbers are even.

    d. Some boys do not like girls.

    e. For every even number n, n is a whole number.

    f. For no odd number m, m is divisible by 2.

2. Translate each of the following into the language of sets.

    a. Some men are nice.

    b. No girls are boys.

    c. All triangles are closed figures.

    d. Some whole numbers are not even.

    e. Bill is a man.

    f. The number 3 is not even.

3. Which of the following conclusions can be validly deduced from the given premises? If necessary use Venn diagrams to help you.

    a. All girls are pretty.
       Brenda is a girl.
       Therefore, Brenda is pretty.

    b. All art is valuable.
       The Mona Lisa is valuable.
       Therefore, the Mona Lisa is a work of art.

    c. All even numbers are whole numbers.
       3 is not an even number.
       Therefore, 3 is not a whole number.

    d. No even numbers are odd numbers.
       4 is an even number.
       Therefore, 4 is not an odd number.

    e. All dogs have four legs.
       No cats are dogs.
       Therefore, no cat has four legs.

    f. Only men are allowed inside.
       Robbie is not inside.
       Therefore, Robbie is not a man.

    g. No birds like cats.
       No cats like dogs.
       Therefore, no birds like dogs.

    h. All squares are rhombuses.
       Some rectangles are squares.
       Therefore, some rectangles are rhombuses.

    i. All sweet fruit contains sugar.
       All bananas are sweet.
       Therefore, all bananas contain sugar.

    j. All x is y.
       All z is y.
       Therefore, all x is z.

4. Change each of the following open sentences into true logical statements by using the words "for all," "for some," and "for no." Assume the replacement set to be the set of whole numbers unless otherwise stated.

a. $x = x$

b. $x + 1 > 0$

c. $x^2 + 1 = 0$

d. $u + u = u$

e. $a + b = b + a$

f. $(A \cap B) \cap C = A \cap (B \cap C)$,
   where A, B, and C are sets

5. Quite frequently, children will make generalizations that are incorrect, such as "Teachers are mean!" or "Nobody in here likes me!" How would you convince a child that these generalizations are not true? List five more statements that an elementary school child might make regarding mathematics which are not true, and give your response to the generalization.

2.3

INDUCTIVE AND DEDUCTIVE LOGIC

Basically, logic is divided into two parts: inductive logic and deductive logic. Inductive logic is a reasoning process that leads from particular cases to acceptable general conclusions. For example, a child's experience with toy boats sailing on a small stream, with rainwater in the drain, with irrigation water in a ditch, and with dad's flooded patio after a rain leads the child to inductively conclude that water runs downhill! Such conclusions may or may not be correct, owing to the necessary uncertainty of basing the conclusions upon inductive logic. Many laws of science are necessarily modified when the universality of the law is found lacking.

Deductive logic, the older of the two parts of logic, is the reasoning process that leads from accepted general principles to valid conclusions. For example, a generally accepted principle of learning is that if a student is ready to read, he will read. If we know that Tom is ready to read, then it follows deductively that Tom will read. Both Aristotelean and symbolic logic are parts of deductive logic.

Each type of logic plays an important role in mathematical reasoning and, for that matter, in the learning of mathematics. Too frequently, the deductive nature of mathematics is overemphasized, resulting in a deemphasis of inductive reasoning. To do so is unfortunate, since inductive logic is the logic of discovery. Before a generalization can be proved, it must first be formulated as a conjecture based upon discovery. As Morris Kline so aptly states:

Before mathematicians can obtain a body of knowledge that warrants the deductive organization which Euclid gave to geometry they must spend decades and even centuries in creating the material. And unlike the logical organization, the creative work does not proceed step by step from one argument to another, each supported by some axiom or previously established conclusion. What the creative process does involve is groping, blundering, conjecturing and hypothesizing. Imagination, intuition, divination, insight, experimentation, chance association, luck, hard work, and immense patience are applied to grasp a key concept to formulate a conjecture, and to find a proof.*

The role of inductive logic in the learning of elementary mathematics can be illustrated in the following manner. Everyone knows that children generally learn from experience. It is desirable for initial mathematical learning experiences to involve manipulation of objects, such as small wooden or plastic cubes. Suppose that, after a period of trial and error, a child recognizes that odd whole numbers can be represented by the block arrangements of Figure 2-2, and that the even whole numbers can be represented by the block arrangements of Figure 2-3. While manipulating the cubes, a child may discover further

Figure 2-2   Figure 2-3

that the representations of two odd numbers can be combined to give the representation of an even number. His example might appear as in Figure 2-4. At first, this *observation* may seem strange, so the child

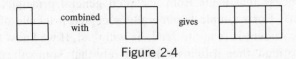

Figure 2-4

may repeat the process of manipulating the cubes, this time using two different representations of odd numbers. Once again the child *observes* that the combination of the representations of the two odd numbers gives the representation of an even number. Observing this common quality about numbers is a first step in the abstraction proc-

* Morris Kline, "The Nature of Mathematics," *Mathematics in the Modern World*, San Francisco: W. H. Freeman and Co., 1968, p. 2.

ess. The child may then make the *generalization* that two odd numbers may be combined to give an even number. To further convince himself of the "truth" of this generalization, the child may try more examples, further *testing* his generalization. Since these examples consistently give the same results, his belief that his generalization is "true" is reinforced.

What has been described is an instance of inductive reasoning, the type of thinking that is extremely important in the creation of new mathematics and particularly important in the teaching of both elementary and secondary mathematics. Children initially learn mathematics through inductive reasoning, the logic of discovery.

You will need to provide many activities that allow children to observe, abstract, generalize, and test generalizations. Therefore, study this book in earnest. It is our sincere hope that you will apply in the classroom what you learn from this text.

In the preceding reasoning process, the child has not proved his generalization that any two odd whole numbers may be combined to give an even whole number. He has accumulated a great deal of empirical evidence that his generalization is "true," but a mathematical proof is a consequence of deductive reasoning, that is, the reasoning process which proceeds from general principles to valid conclusions.

The process by which the truth of a conclusion is established is called a *proof*. Mathematical proofs proceed from hypotheses, or given statements, that are generally accepted. These hypotheses and other previously accepted statements are then deductively linked, usually by short steps, from which a conclusion follows. The child, in his experimental process, has not proceeded from the general to the specific by the deductive process. Rather, he has gone from the specific cases that he has constructed to the general case. Once proved, a generalization is called a *theorem*. The ability to reason deductively is what you hope children acquire. Such an ability is a desired objective of mathematics education.

The elementary child is not expected to be able to construct a proof. To quote the *California Strands Report:*

> Logical thinking at the elementary school level does not imply formal proofs or a study of logic per se. Logical thinking and deductive reasoning at the elementary level is a matter of well-organized common sense. Common sense can be sharpened by the use of standard logical techniques such as Venn diagrams and truth tables. (p. 53)

Later in the child's mathematical education, a primary objective will be to learn logic and the nature of proof. The pupil will then construct deductive arguments for many of the generalizations that he discovered inductively in earlier stages of his mathematical development. With regard to any given mathematical idea, the emphasis in school gradually shifts from inductive to deductive reasoning.

One final point should be made. The inductive process through which the child discovered the odd-number generalization can be used to give hints as to the possible causes or reasons for the "truth" of the generalization. By using the model of representing even whole numbers as $2 \times n$ rectangles formed from squares and of representing odd whole numbers as $2 \times n$ rectangles with one "extra" square attached, the child is very close to the abstractions that all even whole numbers can be expressed as $2 \cdot n$ (the area of a rectangle) and all odd whole numbers can be expressed as $(2 \cdot m) + 1$ (the area of a rectangle plus one more unit), where n and m are whole numbers. The key to the mathematical proof that the sum of two odd numbers is an even number is based upon the recognition of these forms for odd and even whole numbers. If *all* even whole numbers have the form $2 \cdot n$ and *all* odd whole numbers have the form $(2 \cdot m) + 1$, then if a and b are whole odd numbers that can be represented as

$$a = (2 \cdot \bigcirc) + 1$$
$$b = (2 \cdot \triangle) + 1$$

where $\bigcirc$ and $\triangle$ are elements of the set of whole numbers, then

$$a + b = [(2 \cdot \bigcirc) + 1] + [(2 \cdot \triangle) + 1]$$
$$= 2 \cdot \bigcirc + 2 \cdot \triangle + 1 + 1$$
$$= 2 \cdot (\bigcirc + \triangle) + 2 \cdot 1$$
$$= 2 \cdot (\bigcirc + \triangle + 1)$$

But, since $\bigcirc + \triangle + 1$ is just some whole number, which we may call $\square$, then $a + b = 2 \cdot \square$, where $\square$ is an element of the set of whole numbers. What this implies is that $a + b$ is an even whole number. With the addition of a few additional steps, this reasoning process would become a proof of the theorem

The sum of any two odd whole numbers is an even number.

An objective of this text is that you will, upon completion of the text, be able to supply correct reasons for many of the steps in a given proof.

70

EXERCISES (Section 2.3)

1. Observe the pattern; then name the next five members in each sequence.
   a. 1, 3, 5, 7, 9, . . .   e. 2, 1, 4, 3, 6, 5, . . .
   b. 1, 4, 9, 16, 25, . . .   f. 0, 1, 8, 3, 4, 8, . . .
   c. 1, 1, 1, 2, 1, 4, 1, 8, . . . g. 1, a, b. 4. c. 6. . . .
   d. 1, 1, 2, 3, 5, 8, . . .   h. O, T, T, F, F, S, S, E. . . .

2. Study the patterns of the numbers in the squares shown, then describe the arrangement of the numbers in each. Complete the chart.

   a.

1	2	6	7
3	?	?	?
4	?	12	?
?	11	15	16

   b.

2	3	6	?
1	?	5	8
?	?	14	?
9	?	?	?

3. Complete the following patterns. Make a conjecture from each pattern.

   a. $1 \cdot 2 \cdot ? = 6 \cdot 1$
      $2 \cdot ? \cdot 4 = 6 \cdot 4$
      $3 \cdot 4 \cdot 5 = ?$
      $4 \cdot 5 \cdot 6 = ?$
   b. $4 = 2 + ?$
      $6 = ? + 3$
      $8 = ? + 5$
      $? = 7 + 3$
   c. $1 \cdot 2 \cdot 3 \cdot 4 = ? - 1$
      $2 \cdot 3 \cdot 4 \cdot 5 = ? - 1$
      $3 \cdot 4 \cdot 5 \cdot 6 = ? - 1$
      $4 \cdot 5 \cdot 6 \cdot 7 = ? - 1$
   d. $1 = 1^2$
      $1 + 3 = ?$
      $1 + 3 + 5 = ?$
      $1 + 3 + 5 + 7 = ?$
   e. $3^2 - 1 = ?$
      $5^2 - 1 = ?$
      $7^2 - 1 = ?$
      $9^2 - 1 = ?$
   f. $5 = ? + 4$
      $13 = 4 + ?$
      $? = 1 + 16$

4. Complete the Pascal triangle shown, and determine at least three patterns from the triangle (try to find more).

$$
\begin{array}{ccccccccccc}
 & & & & & 1 & & & & & \\
 & & & & 1 & & 1 & & & & \\
 & & & 1 & & 2 & & 1 & & & \\
 & & 1 & & 3 & & 3 & & 1 & & \\
 & 1 & & ? & & ? & & ? & & 1 & \\
1 & & ? & & ? & & ? & & ? & & 1 \\
\end{array}
$$
$$
\begin{array}{ccccccccccccc}
1 & & ? & & ? & & ? & & ? & & ? & & 1
\end{array}
$$

5. The following are whifbams:

$$
\begin{array}{cccc}
\begin{array}{c} \cdot\cdot \\ \cdot\cdot \\ \cdot\cdot \end{array} &
\begin{array}{c} \cdot\cdot\cdot \\ \cdot\cdot\cdot \\ \cdot\cdot\cdot \end{array} &
\begin{array}{c} \cdot\cdot\cdot\cdot \\ \cdot\cdot\cdot\cdot \\ \cdot\cdot\cdot\cdot \end{array} &
\begin{array}{c} \cdot\cdot\cdot \\ \cdot\cdot\cdot \\ \cdot\cdot\cdot \end{array} \\
4 & 6 & 8 & 9
\end{array}
$$

The following are *not* whifbams:

```
 ..    ...    .....    .......
 2      3       5         7
```

Which of the following are whifbams?   10, 11, 14, 13, 15, 51.

6. The following are akalahs:

```
                    .
             .     ..    ..
       .    ..    ...    ...
 .    ..    ...    ...    ....
 1     3     6      10
```

The following are *not* akalahs:

```
             ..     ..    ...
 ..    ..    ...    ....
 2      4      5      7
```

Which of the following are akalahs?   15, 20, 21, 26, 28.

7. There are several conjectures that you might make from the following patterns. Make an incorrect conjecture based on the evidence; then find a counterexample to disprove this conjecture. Try to make up a correct conjecture that appears to stand the trial of testing.

$$2 \times 2 = 4 \qquad 2 + 2 = 4$$
$$\left(\tfrac{3}{2}\right) \times 3 = 4\tfrac{1}{2} \qquad \tfrac{3}{2} + 3 = 4\tfrac{1}{2}$$
$$\left(\tfrac{4}{3}\right) \times 4 = 5\tfrac{1}{3} \qquad \tfrac{4}{3} + 4 = 5\tfrac{1}{3}$$
$$\left(\tfrac{5}{4}\right) \times 5 = 6\tfrac{1}{4} \qquad \tfrac{5}{4} + 5 = 6\tfrac{1}{4}$$
$$\vdots \qquad\qquad\qquad \vdots$$

8. Determine the numerical value of each letter in each of the following.

a.
```
  S E N D
+ M O R E
M O N E Y
```

b.
```
  F O R T Y
    T E N
+   T E N
S I X T Y
```

2.4

CONDITIONAL STATEMENTS

There are statements in the English language that when used in a conversation, give the idea of cause and effect. For example, the statement "What goes up must come down" gives the impression that if I were to throw something up in the air that something must come down. The statement "My appendix scar turns blue whenever it is going to rain" means that "if it is going to rain, then my appendix scar will turn blue."

Statements of the form "if—then" are compound statements and are defined as follows:

> If P and Q are statements, the statement "if P, then Q" is called a *conditional statement*. The statement P is called the *antecedent* or the *premise*, and the statement Q is called the *consequent* or *conclusion*. We say that P implies Q and write $P \Rightarrow Q$.

Examples of conditional statements are

1. *If* 10 centimeters is equivalent to 1 decimeter, *then* 10 decimeters is equivalent to 1 meter.
2. *If* $4 + 3 = 7$, *then* $3 + 4 = 7$.
3. *If* the sky does not fall, *then* 14 is divisible by 2.
4. *If* all multiples of 2 are even and 10 is a multiple of 2, *then* 10 is even.
5. *If* you are President of the United States, *then* you must be a citizen of the United States.

It is possible to restate example 5 in two different statements, each of which occurs in daily conversation. If we let

$A:$ You are President of the United States and
$B:$ You are an American citizen,

then we can restate $A \Rightarrow B$ by each of the following equivalent statements:

1. A *necessary* condition for being President of the United States is that you are an American citizen, or
2. A *sufficient* condition for you being an American citizen is that you be the President of the United States.

The use of the words "necessary" and "sufficient" are used in logic in exactly the same way that we use them in everyday life. For example, suppose that I were an immigration officer and you were the President of the United States. If I stop you at a port of entry and demand that you prove that you are an American citizen, it is sufficient that you show me that you are the President of the United States, since I know that one of the conditions for being the President is that you are an American citizen. In other words, a sufficient condition for citizenship is the presidency of the United States. Also, it is necessary that you be an American citizen in order to be the President of the United States.

It was mentioned earlier that the teaching of logical thinking should be a commonsense approach. Situations continually arise in the classroom that can be used to develop logical thinking. For example, a simple statement such as "Air is necessary for life" may arise in the teaching of a unit on science. If air is necessary for life, does this mean that air is the only necessity for life? The children can see that heat, food, and water are also necessary for life. We see that air is a necessary condition for life but not a sufficient condition for life. The teacher may then ask the question "Does the presence of life imply that there must be air?" Obviously, the answer is yes, since life cannot exist without air. We then say that life is sufficient for air. We may summarize all the preceding by the statements

"If we have life, then we must have air," or
"Air is necessary for life," or
"Life is sufficient for air."

As with the compound statements encountered earlier, the truth values assigned to the conditional depend upon the truth values assigned to the statements P and Q. The definition to be given probably is not what you would expect. However, the definition will seem more reasonable if the following is kept in mind:

1. Very rarely are we ever concerned with conditional statements in which the antecedents (premises) are false.
2. Very rarely are we ever concerned with conditional statements in which the antecedent and the consequent (conclusion) are unrelated.
3. This definition stems from formal logic, which is *not* concerned with the *meaning* of statements but rather with the *form* of the statements. We shall say more about this later.

These considerations prompt us to make the following definition:

If P and Q are statements, the statement "if P, then Q," designated by $P \Rightarrow Q$, is false when P is true and Q is false. Otherwise, $P \Rightarrow Q$ is true. The truth table is

P	Q	$P \Rightarrow Q$
T	T	T
T	F	F
F	T	T
F	F	T

There are several mnemonic devices that can be used to remember the method for assigning a truth value to a conditional statement. Suppose that we have the statements

$P:$ Bill wins the bet
$Q:$ George will pay $2 to Bill

In conditional form $P \Rightarrow Q$, we have if Bill wins the bet, then George will pay $2 to Bill. Notice that if both P and Q are true there is no source for argument since Bill won the bet and George paid $2. Also, if Bill does not win the bet (P is false) and George still pays Bill $2 ($Q$ is true), there still is no cause for argument. If Bill does not win the bet (P is false), and George does not pay Bill $2 ($Q$ is false), there still is not cause for contention. Finally, if Bill does win the bet (P is true) and George does not pay Bill $2 ($Q$ is false), there is real cause for debate (and sometimes fisticuffs). This case may be interpreted as the one case in which $P \Rightarrow Q$ is false.

It should be pointed out that the importance of the conditional statement is prompting its early introduction to the elementary classroom today. Both the Socratic argument syllogism and the language of sets are being used as a vehicle for introducing this important concept. Consider the following example:

Syllogism	Set Translation	Conditional Translation
All squares are rectangles.	{squares} $\subseteq$ {rectangles}	*If* a figure is a square, *then* the figure is a rectangle.
$ABCD$ is a square.	$ABCD \in$ {squares}	$ABCD$ is a square.
$\therefore ABCD$ is a rectangle.	$\therefore ABCD \in$ {rectangles}	$\therefore ABCD$ is a rectangle.

This example can be illustrated as in Figure 2-5.

A word of caution and explanation is in order at this point. You should realize that it is *not* necessary to have a subset relation between the antecedent P and the consequent Q in order to have a conditional

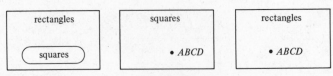

Figure 2-5

statement $P \Rightarrow Q$. This may startle you, since you are so accustomed to using conditional statements to show cause-and-effect relationships that are meaningful in everyday life. What you must realize is that the logic you are learning is designed to be useful in your teaching; however, this logic is also a part of formal logic. The word "formal" is used to accentuate the interpretation, "pertaining to form." The *meanings* of the statements we are considering are of no concern in formal logic. In fact, we turn to variables to represent statements so that we need not concern ourselves with the meaning of the statement. The *form* that the variable or variables assume, together with the symbols $\vee$ (or), $\wedge$ (and), $-$ (not), and $\Rightarrow$ (imply), is what is important.

For example, the variable P may stand for the statement "Teachers are overpaid." Regardless of the meaning and the truth value assigned to P (we all know that this statement is false), the rules of formal logic require that the statement

$$-(-P) \Longleftrightarrow P$$

must always be true (in case you have forgotten why this is true, see page 14). It is interesting to note that the assignment of the truth value to P is subject to debate and is arbitrarily assigned. Those of us in the teaching profession insist that P is false; those who pay our salaries insist that P is true. The logician is not concerned as to who is right. He is concerned that either T or F can be assigned to P. He then works with P, not the meaning of P.

All this is a long-winded way of saying that the statement "If Athens is in Germany, then Rome is in France" is a perfectly legitimate implication where no causal relationship is apparent. In formal logic no significance is attached to the meaning of the statements "Athens is in Germany" and "Rome is in France." The form, "if _____, then _____," is of major importance.

A rather amusing example of unrelated antecedents and consequents in an implication is a statement made recently by an American militant; it read "If meat is so good, why do cows eat grass?" The examples we have stated may seem ridiculous in the context of everyday living. In the context of formal logic, each statement is quite "logical."

EXERCISES (Section 2.4)

1. In each of the following implications, list the premise or premises and then list the conclusion. For example, if a is an even number and a is prime, then a is 2.
   Premise P: a is an even number.
   Premise Q: a is a prime number.
   Conclusion R: a is 2.
   a. If a student evades the draft, he is breaking the law.
   b. If it snows, the game will be canceled.
   c. If x is a whole number greater than 1, then $x^2 > x$.
   d. If 1 meter is 100 centimeters, then 10 meters is 1,000 centimeters.
   e. If 1 kilometer is 1,000 meters, then 5 kilometers is 5,000 meters.
   f. If a, b, and c are whole numbers greater than 0 and $b > c$, then $a \cdot b > a \cdot c$.

2. Change each of the following quantified statements into conditional statements.
   a. All fish swim.   c. All even numbers are whole numbers.
   b. All birds have feathers.   d. All x are y.

3. Change each of the following statements into conditional statements.
   a. Any student who studied hard will pass the course.
   b. To know him is to love him.
   c. The meek shall inherit the land.
   d. The game will be won if Heiny doesn't foul out.
   e. To err is human.
   f. Peace is necessary for world preservation.
   g. Smile if you are happy.
   h. Faith is sufficient for salvation.
   i. A responsible citizen will vote.
   j. In order to fly to Hawaii, you must go to California.
   k. Being an even number implies divisibility by 2.
   l. $4 \times b = 8$ because $b = 2$.
   m. Two lines that intersect are not parallel.
   n. She cries whenever I date someone else.

4. Restate each of the following in the following forms:
   "a necessary condition for _____ is," and
   "a sufficient condition for _____ is."
   a. If you earn money, you must pay taxes.
   b. If you become very sick, you should go to the doctor.
   c. If n is an odd number, n^2 is an odd number.
   d. If you are to continue living, you must breathe unpolluted air.
   e. If you use the metric system, you are using multiples of 10.
   f. $a + b = a + c$ implies $b = c$.

5. List five statements involving the use of the word "necessary" that children might make in the classroom setting. Tell how you might translate these statements into conditional statements by means of a meaningful discussion.

6. Construct a truth table to show that $P \Rightarrow Q$ is equivalent to $-(P \wedge -Q)$.

7. Ben Franklin once said: "A little neglect may breed mischief; for want of a nail, the shoe was lost; for want of a shoe, the horse was lost; for want of a horse, the rider was lost." What principle of implication is illustrated by this saying?

2.5

NEGATION OF QUANTIFIERS AND THE CONDITIONAL STATEMENT

As we learned earlier, the negation of a simple statement is found by the use of the word "not." It is common usage to associate the negative "not" with the verb in a sentence. For example, if P: Terry is a good boy, then the negative of P, designated by $-P$, is Terry is not a good boy. We insist that the statement P and its negation $-P$ cannot be simultaneously true. This is a fundamental assumption. This means that if P is true then $-P$ is false; and if P is false, $-P$ is true. Statements that obey this fundamental assumption are called *contradictory statements*.

There are instances that arise in the classroom when the use of the word "not" in forming the negation of a statement is not easily translated into everyday language. Special care must be taken when the quantifiers all, some, and no are used in statements. For example, consider the statement

P: All zops are skoos.

For the negation of P, we have

$-P$: Not, all zops are skoos.

The question quickly arises as to what in heavens name do we mean by "Not, all zops are skoos." Do we mean that "All zops are not skoos?" The source of confusion lies in the use of the words "all" and "not."

There are at least two translations of $-P$ that are less ambiguous than "not, all zops are skoos." Consider the following statements

R: Some zops are not skoos.
S: No zops are skoos

(this is the same statement as all zops are not skoos). Are either of these statements a negation (contradiction) to

P: All zops are skoos

The answer to this question lies in the distinction between contradictory and contrary statements. Although *P* and *S* cannot be simultaneously true, *P* and *S* can be simultaneously false. This would be the case if there were exactly one zop that was a skoo.

Each of us has at one time or other made a statement similar to "You are always late," or "Those dumb Broncos always seem to lose the big games." The obvious way to refute such statements is to state "I am *not* always late—yesterday, I was on time," or "The Oakland game was a big game and the Broncos won that game." Few, if any of us, would state "I am never late," or "The Broncos never lose the big games" (particularly if you are a Bronco fan).

This then leads us to the following definition:

> The negation of a statement of the form *"all x are y,"* where *x* and *y* are defined, is another statement of the form *"some x are not y."* An equivalent statement is *"there is at least one x that is not y."*

Pictorially, we represent this as in Figure 2-6.

Figure 2-6

When we consider the negation of the quantifiers "some" and "no," we are led to the following definitions:

> The negation of a statement of the form *"some x are y,"* where *x* and *y* are defined, is another statement of the form *"no x are y."*

An example of the use of this definition is found in the assertion

A: For *some* whole number x, $x + 3 = 1$

To negate this statement, we would say

$-A:$ For *no* whole number x, $x + 3 = 1$

> The negation of the statement of the form "no x are y," where x and y are defined, is another statement of the form "*some x are y.*" An equivalent statement is "*there is at least one x that is y.*"

An example of the use of this definition is found in the statement *B:* No even numbers are prime numbers. To negate *B* we would state

$-B:$ Some even numbers are prime numbers

Equivalently,

$-B:$ There is at least one even number that is a prime number

The power of these definitions becomes apparent when the notion of a *counterexample* is introduced to the student. For example, suppose that the elementary school child conjectures that every whole number is divisible by itself. To disprove this conjecture, a child must demonstrate a single instance when the conjecture is not true. This involves the negation of the conjecture. To negate this statement that "all whole numbers are divisible by themselves," the child must show that "there is at least one whole number that is not divisible by itself." This number is, of course, the whole number zero. Also, to find a counterexample to statement *B*, the child must show "at least one" even number that is prime. This number is the whole number 2.

It was stated earlier in this chapter that the construction of formal proofs is not a primary objective of the elementary school mathematics curriculum. However, the ability to disprove a conjecture by means of demonstrating a counterexample to the conjecture is an extremely powerful tool for the child to have at his disposal. The construction or demonstration of a counterexample lies in the realm of inductive reasoning and is generally found during the testing phase of a generalization. Logically, the formulation of a counterexample to a statement is equivalent to negating the statement.

Teachers must be particularly careful in negating the statement that uses the quantifier "some." The first inclination is to form the negation of "some" with "some are not." This is incorrect, because we may find that the initial statement involving "some" may, in fact, include the possibility that "some are not." For example, the statement "Some whole numbers are even" cannot be negated by the statement

"Some whole numbers are not even," since both statements are simultaneously true. This contradicts our basic premise that a statement and its negation cannot be simultaneously true. The correct negation is "No whole number is even."

> N: *Some* whole numbers are even.
> $-N$: *No* whole numbers are even.

This is illustrated in Figure 2-7.

Figure 2-7

We have only considered to this point the negation of statements involving quantifiers. We now turn our attention to the conditional statement and its negation. Again, we rely upon the truth table of the conditional to determine a reasonable way of negating the conditional $P \Rightarrow Q$.

Consider the following statement:

> P: If Sean is a student, then Sean studies.

The only way this statement can be false is if

> $-P$: Sean is a student *and* Sean does *not* study.

This observation leads us to the following definition:

> If $P \Rightarrow Q$ is a statement, then the negation of $P \Rightarrow Q$, designated by $-(P \Rightarrow Q)$, is the statement "P and not Q," designated $(P \wedge -Q)$. Symbolically, $-(P \Rightarrow Q)$ is equivalent to $(P \wedge -Q)$.

The following are examples of conditional statements and their negations:

> A: If it rains, then I will go home.
> $-A$: It is raining and I will not go home.
> B: If $x + 3 = 7$, then $x = 5$.
> $-B$: $x + 3 = 7$ and $x \neq 5$.
> C: If the number n is even, then n is divisible by 2.
> $-C$: The number n is even and n is not divisible by 2.

EXERCISES (Section 2.5)

1. State the negations of each of the following statements. Do not merely preface each statement with the word "not."
   a. All men are married.
   b. Some girls are pretty.
   c. Some days are not beautiful.
   d. No work is fun.
   e. There is at least one equation that has a solution.
   f. There is at least one number that is not prime.
   g. If you go to school, you must study.
   h. If you measure water in liters, you are using the metric system.
   i. Not all whole numbers are perfect squares.
   j. A number is a negative number and it is not less than zero.
   k. For all x, $x \geq 0$.
   l. For some x, $x^2 = 9$.
   m. For some x, $x/x \neq 1$.
   n. If x is not greater than zero, then $x/x \neq 1$.

2. State the negations of the following propositions:
   a. If some people go swimming, some people will drown.
   b. If all counting numbers are whole numbers, then there exists at least one whole number that is not a counting number.
   c. If N is a whole number, then N can be written in the form $2 \cdot B$ or $2 \cdot B + 1$, where B is a whole number.
   d. If some isosceles triangles are equilateral, then some isosceles triangles are not equilateral.

3. Construct the truth table to show that $P \Rightarrow Q$ is equivalent to $-(P \wedge -Q)$.

4. Construct a truth table to show that $-(P \wedge -Q)$ is equivalent to $-P \vee Q$.

5. What conclusion can be drawn from Exercises 3 and 4?

6. Construct a truth table to show that $P \Rightarrow Q$ is equivalent to $-Q \Rightarrow -P$.

2.6

INFERENCE

For almost twenty centuries the syllogism provided the primary means for deriving a conclusion from certain stated premises. With the advent of symbolic logic came a new inference scheme, which is defined as follows:

If statement P is true and if the statement $P \Rightarrow Q$ is true, then the statement Q must be true. This inference rule is called the *rule of detachment*, or modus ponens.

The rule of detachment states that we can conclude or deduce statement Q to be true whenever both statements P and $P \Rightarrow Q$ are true. Notice that we must show that *both* statements P and $P \Rightarrow Q$ are true in order to "detach" the truth of Q. If we know only that $P \Rightarrow Q$ is true, it is possible that Q is false. You should be able to determine why this is true.

Children as well as adults frequently use the rule of detachment in their everyday thinking. For example, most children realize that if the weather outside is terrible, the schools will be closed. Upon arising on a cold, blizzardy morning, a child is apt to say, "There will be no school today." This conclusion is based upon the truth of the conditional "if the weather outside is terrible, the schools will be closed," and upon the truth of the statement "the weather outside is terrible." Unfortunately for the schoolchildren, the criteria used for determining "terrible weather" are generally set by the district school superintendent, not the child. Many children have been disappointed to find the school open on a snowy day. The only flaw in the child's thinking was in the determination of the truth value for the statement "the weather outside is terrible."

Many children use an indirect mode of thinking in drawing conclusions. Consider the child who, while watching a football game on television with his father, makes the statement "The wind isn't blowing at the football game." More frequently than not, a statement such as this will warrant further investigation by the parent, especially if the child is quite young and the game is being played in another part of the country where the weather is not apparent. When asked how he knew that the wind was not blowing, the child may respond "because the flag is not waving." Some parents will immediately know the reasoning process used by the child. Most parents will not.

The reasoning process used by the child is an example of indirect reasoning. The child reasoned as follows: "If the wind is blowing, the flag will wave." "Since the flag is not waving, the wind is not blowing." This inference scheme is defined as follows:

> If $-Q$ is true and if $P \Rightarrow Q$ is true, then the statement $-P$ must be true. This inference rule is called the *rule of contrapositive inference.*

It can be shown in formal logic that $P \Rightarrow Q$ is equivalent to its *contrapositive* $-Q \Rightarrow -P$.

Contrapositive reasoning many times is much easier than direct reasoning, particularly in the construction of mathematical proofs. For example, the statement "if x^2 is an odd number, then x is an odd number" is more easily proved by proving the equivalent statement "if x is not odd, then x^2 is not odd." What we must now demonstrate is "if x is even, then x^2 is even."

Quite frequently, we see children and adults alike drawing improper or incorrect conclusions from a given implication. A common mistake is a result of confusing the conditional $P \Rightarrow Q$ with its *converse*, $Q \Rightarrow P$. For example, many children upon leaving the school building and seeing the street wet will exclaim "It must have rained!" Undoubtedly, what they are thinking is as follows:

1. If it rains outside, the street is wet.
2. The street is wet.
3. Therefore, it rained.

Somehow or other, the childrens' reasoning has become reversed. The child has applied the rule of detachment to the converse of the statement $P \Rightarrow Q$. Many of us have been guilty of this spurious reasoning at some time in our lives. How many of us would conclude upon seeing a uniformed policeman enter our neighbor's apartment that our neighbor was in trouble with the law. Our reasoning might be as follows:

1. If our neighbor is in trouble with the law, the police will come to visit him.
2. The police came to visit our neighbor.
3. Therefore, our neighbor is in trouble with the law.

One other form of incorrect reasoning warrants attention. Many times parents will try to impress upon their children that a college education is important because, among other things, the college education will provide an opportunity for a good job. What the parents are saying to the youngster is "If you get a college education, then you will have the opportunity for a good job." Some children will translate their parents statement into the following: "If I do *not* get a college education, then I will *not* have the opportunity for a good job." The parents, with good intention, made the assertion $P \Rightarrow Q$. The child assumed that $P \Rightarrow Q$ and its *inverse* statement $-P \Rightarrow -Q$ have the same meaning. This is not always true.

In concluding this section, one final point should be made. We stated earlier that an implication and its contrapositive are equivalent statements. It can also be shown in formal logic that the converse of an implication is equivalent to the inverse of the implication. That is, if $P \Rightarrow Q$ is an implication, then $Q \Rightarrow P$ and $-P \Rightarrow -Q$ are equivalent statements.

EXERCISES (Section 2.6)

1. Build a truth table to show each of the following:
   a. $(P \lor Q) \Rightarrow R$ is equivalent to $-R \Rightarrow (-P \land -Q)$.
   b. $P \Rightarrow (Q \land R)$ is equivalent to $(-Q \lor -R) \Rightarrow -P$.
   c. $P \Rightarrow (Q \lor R)$ is equivalent to $(-Q \land -R) \Rightarrow -P$.
   d. $(P \land Q) \Rightarrow R$ is equivalent to $-R \Rightarrow (-P \lor -Q)$.

2. Write the converse, inverse, and contrapositive of each of the following. Use De Morgan's laws when applicable.
   a. If I eat, I will get fat.
   b. If I use a fluoride toothpaste, I will have fewer cavities.
   c. If I do not pass this course, I will be sad.
   d. If I do not get an A or a B, I will lose my scholarship.
   e. If I get an A in math and a B in science, I will make the Dean's list.
   f. If she smiles, she is either scheming against me or she likes me.
   g. If I have a drink, it must have ice and mix in it.
   h. If $x^2 = 4$, then $x = 2$ or $x = -2$.
   i. If x is a whole number, $x + 1 > x$.
   j. If $a > b$, then $a^2 > b^2$.

3. From the given statement, determine whether each of the following inferences is valid or invalid. If the inference is valid, name the inference scheme being used. If invalid, identify the error.

   A: If you study mathematics, you study inference schemes.

   a. You study inference schemes. Therefore, you study mathematics.
   b. You do not study inference schemes. Therefore, you do not study mathematics.
   c. You do not study mathematics. Therefore, you do not study inference schemes.
   d. You study mathematics. Therefore, you study inference schemes.

   B: If a girl is blonde, she has more fun.

   e. Joan is a blonde. Therefore, she has more fun.
   f. Cathy has more fun. Therefore, she is a blonde.

g. Lisa does not have more fun. Therefore, she is not a blonde.
h. Rita is a redhead. Therefore, Rita does not have more fun.

C: If a man is healthy, he is happy.

i. Bill is unhealthy. Therefore, he is unhappy.
j. Pete is happy. Therefore, he is healthy.
k. Oscar is unhappy. Therefore, he is unhealthy.
l. Don is healthy. Therefore, he is happy.

D: Work keeps me from going to the football games.

m. I worked last night. Therefore, I didn't go to the football game.
n. There was no football game last night. Therefore, I didn't work.
o. I didn't work last night. Therefore, I went to the football game.
p. I didn't go to the football game last night. Therefore, I didn't work.

4. The following riddle*may be solved by combining deduction, analysis, and sheer persistence. Each man has a different name, a different-colored house, a different car, and each likes a different drink. Find each man's living habits, using the following statements:
   1. There are five houses in a row.
   2. Ralph lives in the red house.
   3. Ruben owns a dog.
   4. Coffee is drunk in the green house.
   5. George drinks tea.
   6. The green house is just to the right of the ivory house.
   7. The man who drives a Thunderbird owns snails.
   8. A Mustang is driven by the man who lives in the yellow house.
   9. The man in the middle house drinks milk.
   10. Fred lives in the first house.
   11. The man with the Pinto lives next to the man with a fox.
   12. The man who drives a Mustang lives next to the man who owns a horse.
   13. The driver of the Model A drinks orange juice.
   14. Glen drives a Model T.
   15. Fred lives next to the blue house.
   16. The man in the green house owns a zebra.
   17. The man who lives next door to the horse enjoys drinking water.
   18. The man who drinks milk lives in the red house.

* Presented in a math workshop by Barbara Paul.

2.7
FLOW CHARTING

One of the primary concerns of the elementary school teacher is the teaching of the various procedures for the addition, subtraction, multiplication, and division of whole numbers. For example, the first-grade teacher teaches the procedure for performing the operation $32 + 13$. The most frequently used process is a column-addition procedure whereby ones are added to ones and tens are added to tens. The procedure used is called an algorithm.

> An *algorithm* is a complete, unambiguous procedure for solving a problem in a finite number of steps.

An algorithm for computing the sum $32 + 13$ may be described as follows:

1. Write the two addends, one below the other with the ones' digits and the tens' digits aligned.
2. Draw a line beneath the two aligned addends.
3. Use the basic addition facts to add the ones' digits.
4. Write the sum of the ones' digits directly below the ones' digits of the two addends.
5. Use the basic addition facts to add the tens' digits.
6. Write the sum of the tens' digits directly below the tens' digits of the two addends.
7. The sum is represented by the numeral formed by steps 4 and 6.

What has been described is a logical, step-by-step analysis of the column-addition algorithm. A graphical representation of each of these steps is called *flow charting*. Generally, each step of the flow chart is represented by a geometric shape, each shape depicting a different operation or function of the over-all flow-chart diagram. For example, if we were to generalize the column-addition algorithm for the addition of any two two-digit numbers, we might construct a flow chart as shown in Figure 2-8.

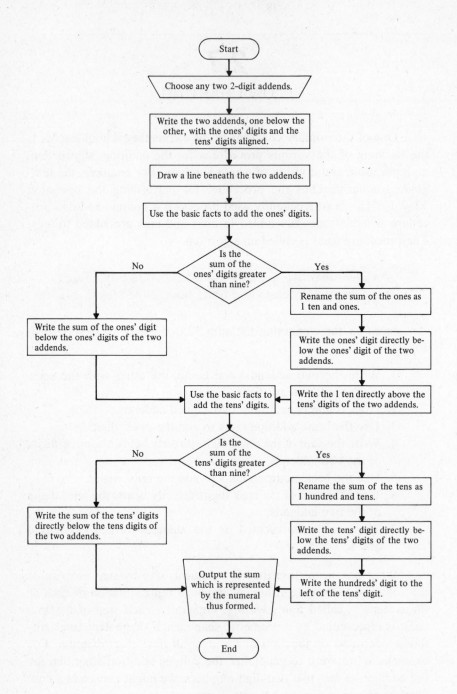

Start

Choose any two 2-digit addends.

Write the two addends, one below the other, with the ones' digits and the tens' digits aligned.

Draw a line beneath the two addends.

Use the basic facts to add the ones' digits.

Is the sum of the ones' digits greater than nine?

No

Yes

Write the sum of the ones' digit below the ones' digits of the two addends.

Rename the sum of the ones as 1 ten and ones.

Write the ones' digit directly below the ones' digit of the two addends.

Use the basic facts to add the tens' digits.

Write the 1 ten directly above the tens' digits of the two addends.

Is the sum of the tens' digits greater than nine?

No

Yes

Write the sum of the tens' digits directly below the tens digits of the two addends.

Rename the sum of the tens as 1 hundred and tens.

Write the tens' digit directly below the tens' digits of the two addends.

Output the sum which is represented by the numeral thus formed.

Write the hundreds' digit to the left of the tens' digit.

End

Figure 2-8

In the construction of the flow chart, several geometric shapes were connected by arrows, which indicate the flow or sequence of the steps to be performed. Each shape contained one step of the algorithm. Several shapes are relatively standard in meaning.

1. The *beginning* and the *end* of a flow chart are designated by an oval (Figure 2-9).

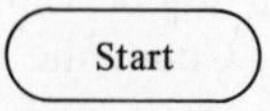

Figure 2-9

2. *Simple declarative statements* are indicated by a rectangle (Figure 2-10).

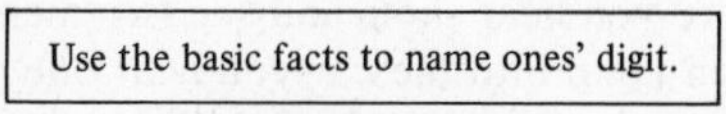

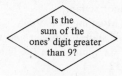

Figure 2-10

3. *Decision statements* are indicated by a diamond (Figure 2-11).

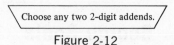

Figure 2-11

4. *Input–output statements* are represented by a trapezoid (Figure 2-12).

Figure 2-12

One final remark is in order. When the problem to be solved requires the repetition of certain steps in an algorithm, a *loop* is used. Basically, a loop is a sequence of steps that is executed repeatedly a finite number of times in the execution of the algorithm. The standard division algorithm is an example of an algorithm which requires looping in that the same steps are executed repeatedly each time a partial quotient is found.

The process of flow charting will be used throughout this text as an instructional device.

EXERCISES (Section 2.7)

1. Construct flow charts for each of the following:
   a. To start a car.
   b. To compare and print the greater of two numbers.
   c. To find the telephone area code of Boston, Massachusetts.
   d. To find and print the average of a list of numbers.
   e. To sort a list of 25 whole numbers into two lists, E for even numbers and O for odd numbers. Count the number of each list as you sort the numbers.

2. Construct a flow chart to show the standard algorithm for the multiplication of a one-digit number times a two-digit number.

3. Construct a flow chart to solve the following problem: Suppose that you are a policeman driving your car on patrol. The night is dark. As you pass a liquor store you hear shots and see two men run out of the liquor store. As the men jump into the car you hear one man yell to the driver "Get going Smitty—here comes the fuzz!" You pursue the car but cannot apprehend it because one of the robbers shoots out your front tire. You notice the following things about the suspects' car:

   1. The car is either blue or green.
   2. The car is a four-door sedan.
   3. The car is either a Mustang or a Vega.
   4. The license is out of state but green and white.
   5. You can't read all six symbols on the license plate, but the first five symbols are HY 352.

   How would you use this information to find the suspects?

George Boole

(1815–1864)

In a day and age when social and educational advancement is difficult for large segments of our society, we look for, and take encouragement from, men and women who overcome the restriction imposed by a malevolent society and grow to greatness. George Boole was one such individual.

Born in 1815 at Lincoln, England, George Boole was the son of a poor shopkeeper. The lower class into which Boole was born was not even

recognized in the eyes of the English upper classes. Children born into Boole's social class existed to serve those classes above them. They were ignorant servants of the rich. The school, if it could be called that, which Boole attended was established for the purpose of keeping the poor in their hopeless place in society.

George Boole taught himself Latin (looked upon as the mark of an educated man), Greek, French, German, and Italian. He mastered enough Latin that, at the age of 12, he translated an ode of Horace into English verse. His father, proud of his son's accomplishment, precipitated a minor controversy when he had the verse published in the local newspaper. A local master of the classics charged that a boy of 12 could not possibly have produced such a translation.

After four years as a teacher's aide and four years in preparation for the clergy, George Boole opened his own school. He felt that mathematics should be taught to his students and so, because he was largely unschooled in mathematics, he began a program of mathematical self-education. In this process he mastered two of the most difficult mathematical masterpieces ever written.

In 1848 George Boole published a slim pamphlet entitled *The Mathematical Analysis of Logic*. One year later he was rewarded with an appointment as Professor of Mathematics at Queen's College in the city of Cork, Ireland. It was at Queen's College in 1854 that Boole produced his masterpiece, *Laws of Thought*. In this book logic was developed as an abstract mathematical system wherein the elements of the system were propositions and the operations were conjunction, disjunction, and negation. Logic was then reduced to a special kind of algebra. Statements were represented by symbols, hence avoiding the ambiguity of everyday language. Reasoning upon material became a matter of manipulating simple algebraic formulas. In this way errors in reasoning were reduced once the logical problem was translated into the appropriate algebraic symbolism.

George Boole died in 1864 of pneumonia, which he contracted after faithfully keeping a lecture engagement when he was soaked from a rainfall. His life and achievements should serve as an encouragement to all who strive to high achievement.

Chapter 3

Numbers and Numeration

3.1
INTRODUCTION

From the earliest beginnings of civilized mankind through the eventful history of the development of Eastern and Western civilizations and even to the present, the concept of number has been as essential as language. Indeed, there is justification in calling mathematics and number the universal language for all peoples, for there is more agreement as to the meaning of the numerical symbols of mathematics than there is for any basic language of communication.

This chapter should give you the chance to learn about the concept of number as we use the notion today and also give you some ˙˙˙ into the history of numbers. You should be able to distinguish ˙˙e symbols used for naming numbers and the concept of ˙˙ou should find that you can understand the system of ˙˙uter uses, and you may be able to invent your

opportunity to learn about ways children ˙s that the kindergarten teacher does to help ˙ting as an important phase of the develop- ˙natics.

3.2
WHAT IS A NUMBER?

Surely everyone knows what a *number* is, but let's try to give a good definition of the word. "Number is a quality of a set denoting quantity." This first try leaves something to be desired because we need a definition of "quantity," and it seems likely that "quantity" will be defined in terms of "number" — so we had better try again. It doesn't seem to be as easy as we thought. Let's look back in time to ancient man.

Imagine the following scene: a lonely valley with a small clan of cliff dwellers living comfortably in the shelter of a cave. They have captured and domesticated a large group of sheep, which is brought into a pen each night and released again the next morning. The chief of the clan, being of a suspicious nature, fears that not all the sheep return each night to the pen and that the reason is that certain clansmen are enjoying extra rations at the chief's expense. How can he know that all the sheep which leave the pen in the morning are returned to the pen at night? Suddenly, with the insight of true genius, the chief realizes that as each animal leaves the pen in the morning he can place a small pebble in a pouch. One sheep — one pebble, one sheep — one pebble, ... When all the sheep have left the pen, he will hold the pouch of pebbles until they return in the evening. As the sheep return, he can remove one pebble for each sheep until all the sheep have apparently returned. If there are any pebbles remaining in the pouch, his suspicions will be confirmed.

There truly is an element of genius involved in this chief's invention, and it represents the first step in developing the concept of number. The notion he invented is the concept of a one-to-one correspondence, which we discussed earlier in the context of equivalent sets. The point is that whatever number of sheep there were and whatever number of pebbles he held in the pouch, because there was a one-to-one correspondence between the set of sheep and the set of pebbles, he could be sure that both sets had the same number.

Notice that the chief did not yet have the complete concept of number. He only understood that the two sets were related in a very specific way: that is, there was a one-to-one correspondence between them. The definition of number must provide for this property; that is, whatever number means, two sets have the same number if there is a one-to-one correspondence between them.

What would be the next step in the historical development of the concept of number? Surely it is clear that early man must have come to notice that there is a one-to-one correspondence between the set of arms and the set of legs, between the set of eyes and the set of ears, between the set of hands and the set of feet on his body. Extending this correspondence beyond his body, he must have noticed the one-to-one correspondence between his set of hands and other objects in his surroundings. Out of many such correspondences eventually came the conception of *twoness*. Our language provides an illustration of the ways in which twoness is found in common usage: couple, pair, brace, twin, duet, span, mates, and so forth.

So it came to be that a sense of twoness became a concept all by itself. It was an idea separate from the notion of a pair of hands, a brace of pheasants, or a span of horses. In fact, the word "two" was used to name the property held in common by all sets that could be placed in a one-to-one correspondence with a man's hands.

Today it is helpful to think of the number two as naming the set of all sets that can be placed in a one-to-one correspondence with the pair of hands. This may be a bit more than you wish to accept at this time, but let's follow this a little further. The number two, named also by the symbol "2," is the set of all sets that can be placed in a one-to one correspondence with your set of hands. Therefore,

$$two = \{\{a, b\}, \quad \{Jeff, Nancy\}, \quad \{Sean, Seamus\}, \ldots\}$$

So, the number two is a set. It's a huge set. It consists of all sets that can be placed in a one-to-one correspondence with a pair of hands. Remember that we used the word "equivalent" to say that two sets could be placed in a one-to-one correspondence. So the number two is the set of all sets that are equivalent to the set of your hands. Once again,

$$two = \{\{left\ hand, right\ hand\}, \quad \{x, y\}, \quad \{\#, @\}, \ldots\}$$

This large set of sets is called a *class* of sets. Notice that any pair of sets are equivalent sets. For this reason, the large set is called an *equivalence class*.

What has just been said provides an answer to the question posed earlier: "What is a number?" It now appears that a number is a set of equivalent sets. The number two is the set of sets equivalent to the set of a man's hands. The number four is the set of sets equivalent to the set of a man's arms and legs. This idea (that a number is a set) may not seem too reasonable at this point, but we promise to improve the idea in what follows.

> A *natural number* is a set of sets each of which is equivalent to each other. That is, if A and B are two such sets, there is a one-to-one correspondence between them.

All this may be interesting reading, but you may be wondering when we can begin to think of numbers — eight, nineteen, fifty-six, and so on. Can we avoid reference to parts of the body, or must we always refer to a pair of hands, or an arm and two legs? Let's review and extend some ideas from Chapter 1 and see if it is possible to make this fit together more simply.

Remember that an equivalence relation on a set A is a relation that is reflexive, symmetric, and transitive. That is, for every element of set A, say x, it must be that x is related to x (reflexivity). If x is related to y, then y must be related to x (symmetry). If x is related to y and y is related to z, then x must be related to z (transitivity). Here is an example of a set A and an equivalence relation on that set:

$A = \{p, q, r, s, t\}$
$R = \{(p, p), (q, q), (r, r), (s, s), (t, t), (p, q), (q, p), (q, t), (t, q), (p, t),$
$\quad (t, p), (r, s), (s, r)\}$

Check to be sure that all three requirements for an equivalence relation are met. What elements of set A are related to p? That is, what elements of A are paired with p in this relation? Do you see that p, q, and t are all paired with p? This set of elements is called the *equivalence class* of elements related to p. What is the equivalence class of elements related to s? You should find that s and r are both related to s; that is, s and r are both paired with s in this relation. This set of elements is called the equivalence class of elements related to s. We have now found two equivalence classes:

$$\{p, q, t\} \quad \text{and} \quad \{s, r\}$$

What would be a good symbol to use to name the equivalence class of elements paired with p? Why not use "$[p]$"? The brackets haven't been used for any other purpose in this text so far, and the symbol suggests something special about the element p. Therefore,

$$[p] = \{p, q, t\} \qquad \text{and} \qquad [s] = \{s, r\}$$

What elements belong to $[q]$? It has been agreed that this names the set of all elements paired with q in the relation; in other words, it names the equivalence class of elements related to q. Therefore,

$$[q] = \{q, p, t\}$$

Do you notice that $[p] = [q]$? What of $[t]$? $[r]$? It seems clear, from this example at least, that any element of an equivalence class can be used to name that equivalence class. In this example,

$$\{p, q, t\} = [p] = [q] = [t]$$
$$\{s, r\} = [s] = [r]$$

> If R is an equivalence relation on set A, the set of all elements of A that are paired with the element x is called the *equivalence class* of elements related to x. This equivalence class is named by $[x]$. Symbolically,
>
> $$[x] = \{a : a \in A \text{ and } (a, x) \in R\}$$
>
> If $b \in [x]$, then $[b] = [x]$. That is, any element of an equivalence class may be used to name that class.

Consider the set of all sets. Call this huge set U. Is it true that set equivalence is an equivalence relation on U? It is certainly a reflexive relation, because every set can be placed in a one-to-one correspondence with itself (reflexivity). If set X is equivalent to set Y, then there is a one-to-one correspondence between them. But then there must be a one-to-one correspondence between Y and X, so Y is equivalent to X (symmetry). Finally, if there is a one-to-one correspondence between set X and set Y and another one-to-one correspondence between set Y and set Z, then there is a one-to-one correspondence between set X and set Z.

Figure 3-1 may help you to see why the transitive property holds true. Since X is equivalent to Y, there is a one-to-one correspondence between them such as the one shown. Since Y is equivalent to Z, there is a one-to-one correspondence between them such as the one shown. From these two correspondences can you see that there is assured to

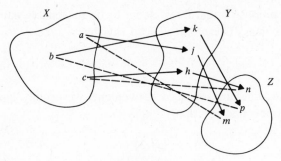

Figure 3-1

be a one-to-one correspondence between X and Z? Just follow the lines from the elements of X through to the elements of Z so that a is paired with m, b is paired with p, and c is paired with n.

So you can see that equivalence of sets is an equivalence relation. The set of all sets equivalent to your pair of hands is an equivalence class much like the equivalence classes described in the preceding example. What would be a good name for this equivalence class? We have used "two" and "2" to name this equivalence class, but we could use any element from the equivalence class if we place brackets around the name, as we have done for $[p]$ and $[s]$ in our example. However, this seems awkward, doesn't it?

$$[\{x, y\}] = \{\{\text{left hand, right hand}\}, \{a, b\}, \{x, y\}, \ldots\}$$

If there were a standard set included in this equivalence class, that standard set might serve as a good representative of the equivalence class. Isn't it true that $\{1, 2\}$ is one of the sets in this huge equivalence class of all sets equivalent to the set of your hands? Of course, the symbols "1" and "2" in this little set mean nothing in particular at this point. This little set is indeed one of the sets in this huge equivalence class and could serve us well as a representative of the total class. We shall call this set the *standard set* for the number two. What would be the standard set for the number three? We agree that the standard set for the number three is $\{1, 2, 3\}$, where the symbols "1," "2," and "3" mean nothing in particular in this context. They serve only to indicate that each set in the equivalence class called "three" is equivalent to a set containing these distinct objects. In general, the standard set of an equivalence class of sets equivalent to the set containing n objects, n a natural number, is the set $\{1, 2, 3, \ldots, n\}$. Since any element of an equivalence class can be used to name the total equivalence class, then these simple standard sets seem to be reasonable names for the equivalence class. Therefore, we can say that

two = [{1, 2}] = {{left hand, right hand}, {x, y}, {1, 2} . . .}

Because the standard set is so convenient, we usually just drop the bracket symbols and say that

$$
\begin{aligned}
\text{two} &= \{1, 2\} \\
\text{three} &= \{1, 2, 3\} \\
\text{four} &= \{1, 2, 3, 4\} \\
&\ \vdots \\
n &= \{1, 2, 3, \ldots, n\}
\end{aligned}
$$

> The *standard set* for the natural number k is the set $\{1, 2, 3, \ldots, k\}$. The standard set may be used as a *representative* for the equivalence class of sets equivalent to the standard set.
>
> We may write "$k = \{1, 2, 3, \ldots, k\}$."

How is the idea of number used? Of course, you know that the idea is used in many ways, but one of the most useful ways is in counting. The question is asked, "How many?" The answer is found by finding some standard set that can be placed in a one-to-one correspondence with the objects in question, counting the objects (that is, exhibiting a one-to-one correspondence), and assigning the number of which the standard set is a representative to the set of objects being counted.

Here is an example. Suppose that a kindergarten boy asks how many marbles he has. He places the marbles in front of him and exhibits a one-to-one correspondence between the set of marbles and the appropriate standard set (see Figure 3-2). This standard set is a

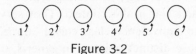

Figure 3-2

representative of the number six and he then assigns the number six to the set of marbles. This is called the count of the set.

If the elements of a set can be placed in a one-to-one correspondence with the elements of a standard set $\{1, 2, 3, \ldots, k\}$, then the number k is called the *count of the set.*

If A is a set that can be placed in a one-to-one correspondence with the standard set $\{1, 2, 3, \ldots, k\}$, then we write

$$n(A) = k$$

to say that the *count of set A is k* or that the *cardinal number of set A is k.*

Notice that to determine the count of a set (or the cardinal number of a set) one must find a standard set that can be placed in a one-to-one correspondence with the elements of the set, exhibit such a one-to-one correspondence, and finally assign the number represented by the standard set as the count of the set (or its cardinal number).

It is also worth noticing that there is a *functional* aspect to the concept of the cardinal number or count of a set. To be specific, if you can conceive of the set of all those sets that can be represented by a standard set, then the assignment of a cardinal number to a given set is a function. Figure 3-3 is an illustration that resembles some of the

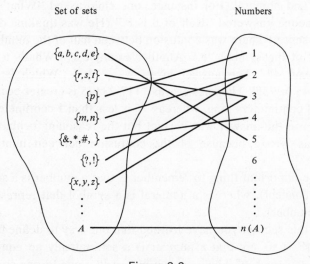

Figure 3-3

sketches used in Chapter 1 to describe functions. Notice that the cardinal number function assigns the same number to several sets. As shown, both sets $\{r, s, t\}$ and $\{x, y, z\}$ are assigned to the number three.

The cardinal numbers one, two, three, and so on, are called the *natural numbers*. The set of all these natural numbers is usually named by the letter N. The symbols used to name natural numbers are called numerals. Some distinction is made occasionally between symbols like "1," "2," and "3" and symbols like "one," "two," and "three." Strictly speaking, both types of symbols are numerals because they name numbers, but the latter are sometimes called *number names* to distinguish them as words rather than numerical symbols. As children learn more and more about numbers, they come to know that there are many numerals that name the same number. For instance, "7 + 2," "27 ÷ 3," "3 × 3," and "11 − 2" are all numerals that name the number nine.

> The set of *natural numbers*, N, is the set of cardinal numbers one, two, three, ...
>
> Numerals are names of numbers and include the symbols such as "1," "2," "3," "one," "two," "three," as well as others.

It is important that the teacher be sure of the distinction between number and numeral. For instance, one child asked "What's half of 8?" Someone answered "Half of 8 is ε." (He was thinking of half in a visual sense.) There was confusion between half of the number eight and half of the symbol "8." Another example is "What's a number bigger than 4?" The answer given was "4." "Which is greater, 117.23145 or 75?" The answer was "117.23145 is greater because it's almost 3 centimeters long, whereas 75 is less than 1 centimeter long." In this case the answer was correct but the reasoning behind the answer was wrong because of the confusion between number and numeral.

The important thing to remember is that a number is a set (or an idea or concept), whereas a numeral is a symbol that represents the set (or number).

In this section you have learned that one way to define the word "number" is to say that a number is a set, actually an equivalence class of sets each of which can be placed in a one-to-one correspondence with every other set in the class. You have learned that a good representative set for a number is the standard set. You have learned also that counting involves use of a standard set, exhibiting a one-to-one correspondence, and assigning a number as the count of the set. The set of numbers developed in this way has been called the set of natural numbers, N. Along the way you have reviewed some of the concepts of equivalence relations from Chapter 1. Finally, you have learned to be careful of the distinction between a number and a numeral.

The following exercises may help you to understand many of these ideas.

EXERCISES (Section 3.2)

1. What are some devices used commonly today that designate answers to the question "How many?" For instance, the baseball umpire raises fingers for each strike and ball.

2. Name five sets that belong to the equivalence class known as four, and show why it can be seen that they all belong to the same class.

3. If set $A = \{a, b, c, d\}$, give examples of relations as called for:
   a. Reflexive but not symmetric relation.
   b. Transitive but not reflexive relation.
   c. Reflexive and symmetric but not transitive relation.
   d. Reflexive and transitive but not symmetric relation.
   e. Symmetric and transitive but not reflexive relation.

4. Consider the relation on the set of whole numbers defined as

   a is related to b if and only if the remainder, upon division by 4, is the same for a and b

   a. Name five pairs of whole numbers that are related in this way. (For example, 13 and 5 are so related because the remainder is the same when 13 is divided by 4 and when 5 is divided by 4.)
   b. Show that this relation is reflexive by use of a number of examples.
   c. Show that this relation is symmetric.
   d. Give some examples illustrating that the relation is also transitive.
   e. You can see from what has been said that this is an equivalence relation. What are some of the elements in the equivalence class that contains 3? What are some in the equivalence class that contains 16?
   f. How many different equivalence classes are there?

5. How do you think children begin to learn how to count? Do you believe that they learn the concept of number before learning to count or after? Can you give some examples from your experience that support your point of view?

6. The standard set for the number seven is $\{1, 2, 3, 4, 5, 6, 7\}$. Is this the

same set as $\{1, 7, 6, 4, 3, 2, 5\}$? Why? What concept of counting is missing when a child finds a one-to-one correspondence between the standard set named in this way and a set of objects?

7. Put quotation marks in appropriate places in the following sentences so that the distinction is clear between an object and its name.
   a. Walla Walla feels good when you say it out loud.
   b. Denver has a population of approximately 750,000.
   c. Denver has two syllables.
   d. We use 13 to name thirteen.
   e. Can you use Abraham Lincoln in a sentence?
   f. 17.145690314 is larger than 36.
   g. The numerator of $\frac{17}{18}$ is odd.
   h. The symbol $\frac{34}{36}$ is another name for $\frac{17}{18}$.
   i. The numerator of $\frac{34}{36}$ is odd.

3.3

NUMERATION

Following the invention of the one-to-one correspondence and the recognition of the concept of numbers, it was quite natural that early man sought ways to name numbers and ways to organize these names systematically. Every civilization developed a system of counting and a process for assigning names to numbers according to a set of rules. Such a system is called a *system of numeration*.

> A *system of numeration* is a system of counting together with a process of assigning names to numbers according to a set of rules.

The Egyptian civilization, which flourished from about 5,000 B.C. to the time of Alexander, developed a simple system of numeration that was capable of dealing with a great many problems of mathematics.

The basic counting unit of the Egyptian system was ten. Such a number is called the *base* of the numeration system. The symbol used to name the number one was a vertical slash mark: /; for the number two they used two slash marks: //; for each number through nine, the Egyptians simply used one more slash mark. The symbol used for the number ten resembles an arch or the mark of a heel in the sand: ∩.

Of course, one could use ten slash marks, but the rule was that ten slash marks names the same number that one heel mark names. For twenty through ninety, the Egyptians used additional heel marks, so that the symbol for forty-seven was $\begin{array}{l} \cap\cap//// \\ \cap\cap/// \end{array}$.

Figure 3-4 is a display of the symbols used by the Egyptians.

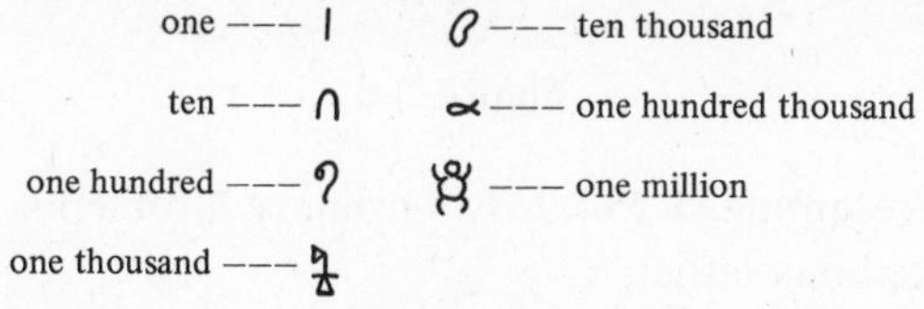

one ---		ϱ --- ten thousand
ten --- $\cap$		$\propto$ --- one hundred thousand
one hundred --- φ		--- one million
one thousand ---		

Egyptian numeration

Figure 3-4

You can see that the system of numeration is simple, because the only skill needed is a counting skill and knowledge that ten marks of one type names the same number that one mark of the next higher type names. Notice too that there is no significance to the order in which these symbols are used. That is, each of the symbols of Figure 3-5

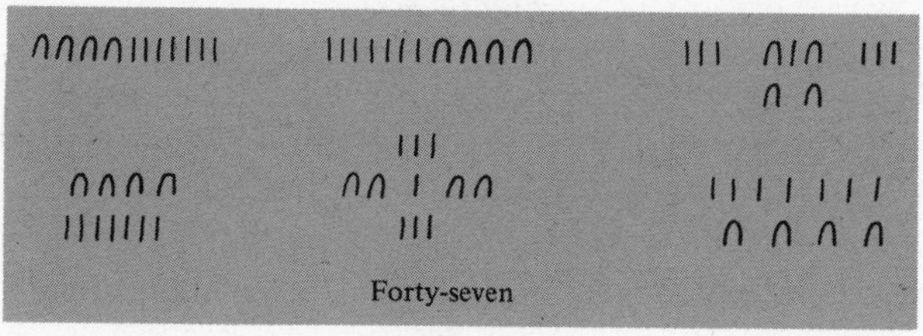

Figure 3-5

names forty-seven. Sometimes the symbols were arranged in an artistic fashion but generally symbols naming equal numbers were grouped together for convenience. This is an example of an *additive system*. Why?

The power of the system of numeration of the Egyptians is evident from the multitude of problems they solved using these symbols. In fact, the arithmetic of the Egyptians was adequate to allow them to resurvey the boundaries of the farms that were covered each year by the flooding Nile River. The Greeks were able to capitalize upon the advances of the Egyptians in later years, with the result being a great thrust forward for the development of mathematics, science, and all mankind.

The symbols were indeed adequate for many tasks. For instance, the representation of large numbers was relatively easy. Figure 3-6 is

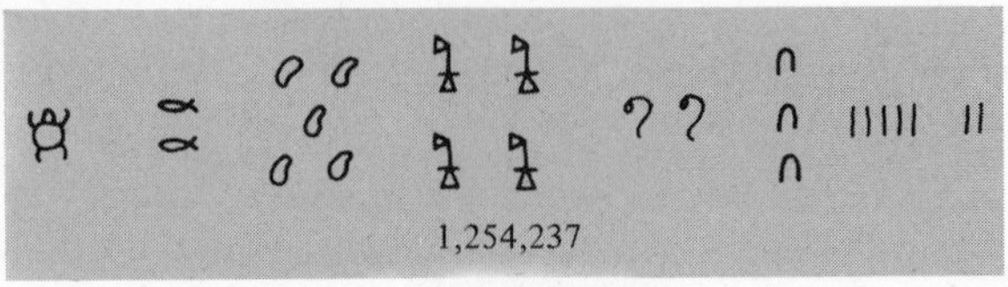

1,254,237

Figure 3-6

a symbol representing 1,254,237. Ordinary problems of arithmetic were not too tedious either.

Try this system of numeration with some simple problems of arithmetic. For instance, $145 + 278 + 684$ (Figure 3-7). The sum is

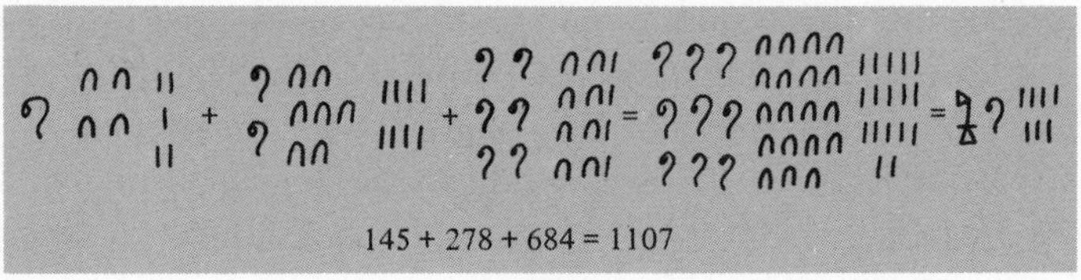

$145 + 278 + 684 = 1107$

Figure 3-7

1,107. You can see that there are basically two things one needs to know to be able to add in the Egyptian motif. One needs to know how to count how many ones, tens, hundreds, and so on, there are all together, and one needs to know how many ones make a ten, how many tens make a hundred, and so on. Essentially, adding becomes counting and converting.

Another simple problem of arithmetic, which is easily done using the Egyptian numeration system, is $1,845 - 672$ (Figure 3-8). In this process there is a preliminary step of conversion of the 8 hundreds to

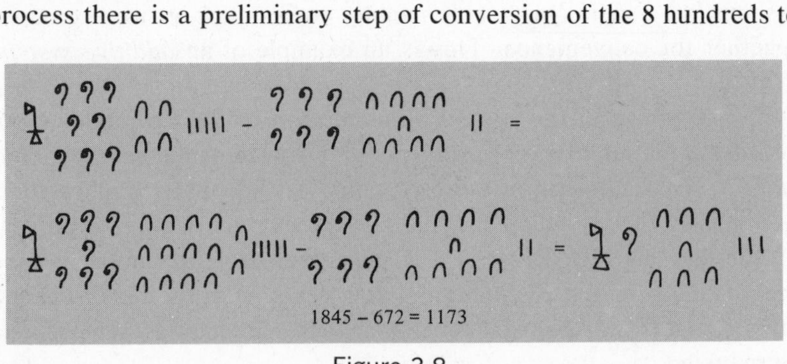

$1845 - 672 = 1173$

Figure 3-8

7 hundreds and 10 tens. From then on, it is simply a matter of counting to determine how many ones, tens, and so on, are to be removed or subtracted. Notice that subtraction and addition almost become physical activities of putting together and taking away.

The Romans also used a system based on a basic unit of ten, but with a variation using fives. The symbols used by the Romans were

one	I	one hundred	C
five	V	five hundred	D
ten	X	one thousand	M
fifty	L		

For numbers greater than 1,000, the Romans used various devices at one time or another in history. At one time they drew a long line over the numerals representing 10,000 and more to indicate that these values are to be multiplied by 1,000. 3,653,788 would be represented as

$$\overline{\text{MMMDCL}}\text{MMMDCCLXXXVIII}$$

3 6 5 3 7 8 8

This feature introduces a multiplication principle to the Roman numeration system. The basic system of the Romans greatly resembles that of the Egyptians, except for the use of half-units such as five and fifty. Both systems of numeration make use of counting and conversion facts.

The Roman numeration system evolved gradually, of course, and later manuscripts show that they used a *subtractive principle*. You know of this principle, no doubt, for you recognize "IX" to be a name for nine. Similarly, "XL" is a name for forty and "XC" is a name for ninety. This use of a symbol designating a small unit to precede a symbol for a larger unit implies the *subtraction* of the number represented by the first symbol from the number represented by the second symbol.

Operations of addition and subtraction using the Roman system of numeration are not too difficult, but multiplication and division are very tedious. In fact, the Romans had no routines for performing these operations on paper and pencil. Such routines (called algorithms) were slow to develop and actually came in common use only after the introduction of the Hindu–Arabic system of numeration. The Romans used a counting board to work out their calculations. The counting board is a simple device consisting of a set of parallel lines or grooves on a smooth board or stone. The bottom line contains pebbles showing the number of ones or units, the next row shows the number of tens, the next shows the number of hundreds, and so on. Figure 3-9 shows a counting board representation of 4,683. Later counting boards made use of the "five" position between the ones row and the tens row, the tens and the hundreds, and so on. Thus, the later version of the counting board would represent 4,683 as in Figure 3-10. With the under-

——— 0000 ———————	4,000
——— 000000 ————	600
——— 00000000 ———	80
——— 000 ————	3

Figure 3-9

——— 0000 ———————	4,000
0	500
——— 0 —————	100
0	50
——— 000 ————	30
——— 000 ————	3

Figure 3-10

standing that five pebbles on a row is the equivalent of one pebble in the space above and that two pebbles in a space is equivalent to one pebble on the line above, the operations of addition and subtraction are very easy to perform on the counting board. Multiplication and division are not very difficult to perform either.

If you are familiar with the abacus as a device for representing numbers and performing arithmetic operations, you will notice its similarity to this early form of counting board. The abacus continues in use today and is a handy device for the elementary school classroom. More about this in Chapter 4.

The Egyptian system of numeration was adequate for the four fundamental arithmetic operations of addition, subtraction, multiplication, and division, but was exceedingly tedious. The Roman system of numeration was really no better in this regard except for the invention of the counting board and the abacus. The world awaited a better system of numeration at this point in history, and it was soon to come. About the year 570 A.D. the prophet Mohammed was born in Mecca and soon after began the unification of the state of Islam. Within a few years there came to be a large Arabic sphere of influence, extending from Spain on the west to India on the east. Through the exchange of ideas between the peoples contacted in this era, there gradually developed a new and convenient system of numeration. The Hindu people of India had a contribution to make and the Arabic peoples themselves provided the force that eventually yielded the Hindu–

Arabic system of numeration. (The system probably should be called either the Hindu–Muslim or the Indian–Arabic system, for the religions of the two peoples are Hindu and Muslim, while their political divisions are Indian and Arabic.)

The essential features of the Hindu–Arabic numeration system consist of a standard base of ten, like the Egyptian and Roman systems, and a *positional* notation. Unlike the Egyptians and Romans, the Hindu–Arabic system does not need a different symbol for ten, hundred, thousand, ten thousand, and so on. Instead, the Hindu–Arabic system makes use of a positional agreement. In order to achieve this positional agreement, the system was developed to include a different symbol for each of the numbers zero, one, two, three, . . . , nine. These basic symbols are called the *digits* of the positional system. The early forms of these symbols looked something like those shown in Figure 3-11. The positional agreement made was that a digit,

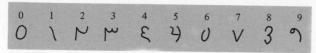

Figure 3-11

for example 5, may mean five ones, five tens, five hundreds, and so on, depending upon its position with respect to the other digits in the numeral. Therefore, the symbol "2" in the numeral "6,245" means two hundreds, while the symbol "6" means six thousands. In the numeral "45,651" the symbol "5" is used twice with two different meanings.

Of course, the first significant advantage of the Hindu–Arabic system is that the numerals become much shorter. The second advantage, perhaps more important, is that computation in this system is more easily performed. The four fundamental operations are easily performed by learning a few routines or algorithms and a set of basic facts regarding addition and multiplication of the first ten numbers. More will be said about these basic facts and the algorithms in Chapter 4.

Before we proceed with our discussion of the meaning of numerals in our current version of the Hindu–Arabic numeration system, it is appropriate to review some elementary concepts from algebra. Do you remember what the symbol "5^4" means? It means that 5 is to be used as a factor 4 times; that is,

$$5^4 = 5 \times 5 \times 5 \times 5 = 625$$

In general, $a^m = a \times a \times a \times \cdots \times a$, with a being used as a factor m times.

What would be a simple way to name the product $4^3 \times 4^5$?

$$4^3 \times 4^5 = (4 \times 4 \times 4) \times (4 \times 4 \times 4 \times 4 \times 4) = 4^8$$

because 4 is used as a factor 8 times. If a is some number and m and n are numbers, then it appears that $a^m \times a^n = a^{m+n}$. Here is another example of this type:

$$7^4 \times 7^2 = (7 \times 7 \times 7 \times 7) \times (7 \times 7) = 7^6 \qquad (6 = 4 + 2)$$

What would be an appropriately simple way to name the quotient $4^5 \div 4^3$? Often we write such quotients like this:

$$\frac{4^5}{4^3} = \frac{4 \times 4 \times 4 \times 4 \times 4}{4 \times 4 \times 4} = 4 \times 4 = 4^2$$

You can see that $5 - 3 = 2$, so it seems likely that in general

$$\frac{a^m}{a^n} = a^{m-n} \qquad (a \neq 0)$$

What about the symbol a^1? It must mean that a is to be used *once* as a factor; that is, $a^1 = a$. What about 5^0? How can one use five as a factor zero times? This reasoning doesn't seem to make sense, so let's try thinking another way. We have seen that $5^3/5^3 = 5^{3-3}$. But $3 - 3 = 0$, so $5^3/5^3 = 5^{3-3} = 5^0$. But $5^3/5^3 = 125/125 = 1$. So it seems reasonable to conclude that $5^0 = 1$.

What meaning could be given to 5^{-2}? Here is one way of thinking about it:

$$5^{-2} = \frac{5^1}{5^3} = \frac{5}{5 \times 5 \times 5} = \frac{1}{5 \times 5} = \frac{1}{5^2}$$

So it seems reasonable to conclude that $5^{-2} = 1/5^2$.

Now let's see what we have said about the expression "3^4." In the first place, this expression is referred to as the fourth power of three. The four is called the *exponent*, the three is called the *base*, and 3^4 is called the fourth power of three (or you may say that 81 is the fourth power of three because $81 = 3 \times 3 \times 3 \times 3$). Likewise, 5^3 is called the third power of five (or five cubed), 7^5 is called the fifth power of seven, 9^2 is called the second power of nine (or nine squared), and so on.

Second, we have seen that there are properties which seem to hold true concerning these powers and exponents and bases. $2^4 \times 2^5 = 2^9$, $3^5/3^2 = 3^3$, $6^0 = 1$, and $7^{-2} = 1/7^2$ are examples of these properties. There is one more property, which you may remember from your study of algebra in high school. It's not often used in elementary arithmetic but should be included for the sake of completeness. An example of this final property is

$$(3^2)^4 = 3^2 \times 3^2 \times 3^2 \times 3^2 = (3 \times 3) \times (3 \times 3) \times (3 \times 3) \times (3 \times 3) = 3^8$$

Similarly, $(6^3)^2 = 6^3 \times 6^3 = (6 \times 6 \times 6) \times (6 \times 6 \times 6) = 6^6$. The general property may be stated as follows: if a is a number and m and n are numbers, then $(a^m)^n = a^{m \times n}$.

Here is a summary of the remarks that have been made about powers, exponents, and bases. On the left is the general statement and on the right is an example that may illustrate the statement.

The symbol "a^m" is called the mth power of the base a. The number m is called the *exponent*, a is called the *base* and the number a^m is called the *power* of the base.	power $\cdots \left\{ 7^5 \right.$ exponent, base
If m is a natural number then a^m means $\underbrace{a \times a \times a \times \ldots \times a}_{m \text{ times}}$	$4^3 = 4 \times 4 \times 4 = 64$
The symbol "a^0" names 1 provided a is not zero.	$6^0 = 1$
$a^{-m} = \dfrac{1}{a^m}$	$3^{-4} = \dfrac{1}{3^4} = \dfrac{1}{81}$
$a^m \times a^n = a^{m+n}$	$12^8 \times 12^9 = 12^{17}$
$a^m \div a^n = a^{m-n}$	$\dfrac{8^7}{8^4} = 8^3$
$(a^m)^n = a^{m \times n}$	$(2^3)^4 = 2^{12}$

We must apologize for the brevity of this discussion of exponents, as well as for the fact that we shall now assume that you are prepared to make use of some of the simpler properties. Perhaps the exercises may help to reinforce your understanding of these concepts.

Now we must show you the relevance of this discussion of exponents with respect to the Hindu–Arabic system of numeration. What does the symbol "6,245" represent in the Hindu–Arabic system? Does it mean $6 + 2 + 4 + 5$? Certainly not. As indicated earlier, it means six thousands, two hundreds, four tens, and five ones because of the position of the digits in the numeral. Let us say this another way and show how we may use our knowledge of exponents.

$$6{,}245 = (6 \times 1{,}000) + (2 \times 100) + (4 \times 10) + (5)$$
$$= (6 \times 10^3) + (2 \times 10^2) + (4 \times 10^1) + (5 \times 10^0)$$

This last form of a name for 6,245 is called *expanded notation* for the number. This notation is helpful because it shows the meaning of the individual digits without regard to the position of the digits.

Here is another example of the use of expanded notation and exponents in helping to name a number.

$$624.513 = (6 \times 100) + (2 \times 10) + (4) + (5 \times \tfrac{1}{10}) + (1 \times \tfrac{1}{100}) +$$
$$(3 \times \tfrac{1}{1000})$$
$$= (6 \times 10^2) + (2 \times 10^1) + (4 \times 10^0) + (5 \times 10^{-1}) + (1 \times 10^{-2})$$
$$+ (3 \times 10^{-3})$$

Notice the step-by-step reduction in the exponents from left to right and the use of 10^0 for 1, 10^{-1} for $\tfrac{1}{10}$, and so on.

The following set of exercises should give you a chance to review the Egyptian, Roman, Hindu–Arabic, and some other numeration systems. You should also review the properties and meanings of exponents briefly discussed here.

EXERCISES (Section 3.3)

1. You might like to invent your own system of numeration, including special symbols for the digits needed in your system. Devise a numeration system that is *not* a positional system using a base of six. Next, devise a positional system in a base of nine.

2. Write a name for 635,271 in the Egyptian and then in the Roman system of numeration.

3. Write a name for 600,000 in the Egyptian and then in the Roman system of numeration. Are there advantages that you can see in the Egyptian system when compared with the Hindu–Arabic? Compare the Roman system with the Hindu–Arabic system.

4. Write names for the following numbers using the expanded notation form.
   a. 34,171   c. 17.143   e. 1,000,002.001
   b. 301,005   d. 106.002   f. 302,000

5. Here are some numerals that name numbers, but the number named is not obvious when named in this form. Using the properties of exponents discussed in this section, find the simplest name for each number.

a. $2^3 \times 2^5 \times 2^{-4}$ e. $5^2 \times \dfrac{5^4 \times 5^{-2}}{5^0}$

b. $\dfrac{6^4}{6^2} \times 6^{-1}$ f. $\dfrac{3^{84}}{3^{88}} \times 3^4$

c. $(5^2 \times 5^3)^2$ g. $\dfrac{10^1 \times 10^{-1}}{10^0}$

d. $(17^4 \times 17^{19})^0$ h. $\dfrac{(7^2) \times (7^3)}{(7^2)^3}$

6. What numbers are named?
   a. The fifth power of two.   d. The cube of 4.
   b. The third power of five.   e. The fourth power of 3.
   c. The square of 17.   f. The "zeroth" power of 6.

7. You have seen simple representations of numbers by means of a counting board in this section. Represent the following numbers as they would be shown on a counting board. (Draw a sketch as we did, or make a counting board and get some small pebbles, buttons, pennies, or other objects to use as markers.)
   a. 12,341   b. 774   c. 1,478   d. 76,579
   e. Does the modified version of the counting board (using the fives position) help simplify this notation?

8. On a simple counting board show how one can perform the following operations. Explain what you are doing to someone and see if they understand your process.
   a. $774 + 297$ b. $1,271 - 843$ c. 16×35 (Try it!)

9. One other system of numeration that was used long ago was invented by the Chinese. "Rod numerals" were used so that the first nine digits appeared as

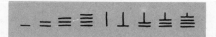

and the first nine multiples of ten appeared as horizontal rods:

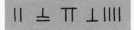

The number 27,764 was named by using these symbols *alternately* from right to left, and looks like

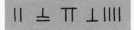

Write names for each of the following numbers in this system.
   a. 637   b. 12,451   c. 136,843   d. 15,043

10. As Exercise 9d may have suggested, one of the needs in many numera-

tion systems was for a symbol to represent the absence of a power of the base. Today we use "0," but many ancient systems were troubled by lack of a zero symbol. The Mayan civilization of the Yucatan peninsula invented a symbol for zero which looked like this: ⬢ . The system of numeration of the Mayans is also unusual because they used a base of twenty more or less combined with five. The system was a place-value or positional system with units being represented by dots and fives by horizontal bars. Therefore, eighteen would be represented as ☰ $(3 \times 5) + 3$. Rather than naming the numbers from left to right, they were named from top to bottom with the largest power of the base on top. Thus, ⁝☰ denoted 233 because it shows $(11 \times 20) + 13$.

a. Represent 45 in the Mayan numeration system.
b. Represent 326 in the system.
c. Represent 421 in the system. This isn't going to be what you might expect! You recognize that $421 = (1 \times 20^2) + (1 \times 20) + 1$, so you would believe that the Mayans would use ⁝ to name this number. However, instead of using $1 = 20^0, 20 = 20^1, 400 = 20^2, 8,000 = 20^3$, and so on, for the basic counting units in this system, they used 1, 20, 360 (which is 18×20 not 20×20), 7,200 (which is $18 \times 20 \times 20$ not 20^3), and so on. There is reason to believe that they used 18×20 because of the length of the calendar year! Therefore, $421 = (1 \times 360) + (6 \times 20) + 1$, so the Mayan would have written ⁚ as the numeral.
d. Write the numeral for 735 in the Mayan system, showing the use of the zero symbol when necessary.

3.4

POSITIONAL NUMERATION WITH BASES OTHER THAN TEN

Sooner or later you will be asked by an excited child, "Why do we use ten as the basic counting unit?" You will need to admit that it was merely the accident of biological development that gave man ten fingers and put them close enough to his head to use them as convenient representations of number concepts. What would the Hindu–Arabic numeration system be like had man developed only eight fingers?

First, there would be a need for only the following symbols as digits:

0 1 2 3 4 5 6 7

This follows because the next number concept would be represented by "10," meaning *one* bunch of eight and *no* ones. Counting would continue:

$$10 \quad 11 \quad 12 \quad 13 \quad 14 \quad 15 \quad 16 \quad 17$$

and then "20" meaning *two* bunches of eight and *no* ones. Going on,

$$20 \quad 21 \quad 22 \quad 23 \quad 24 \quad 25 \quad 26 \quad 27$$
$$30 \quad 31 \quad 32 \quad 33 \quad 34 \quad 35 \quad 36 \quad 37$$
$$40 \quad \ldots$$
$$\ldots 76 \quad 77$$

What comes after 77? We know that "77" means *seven* bunches of eight and *seven* ones. One more would give us seven bunches of eight and *eight* ones. But eight ones is just one bunch of eight, so that we now have *eight* bunches of eight. Just as ten bunches of ten is called one hundred, eight bunches of eight might be called an "eightred." So, what comes after 77? One eightred. So the counting continues: 77, 100, 101, ...

Recall that in a base ten system 697 means $(6 \times 10^2) + (9 \times 10) + 7$. Likewise, in the base eight system, the numeral "457" means $(4 \times 8^2) + (5 \times 8) + 7$. The positions of the digits "4," "5," and "7" indicate the number of eightreds, eights, and ones, respectively. So the symbol "457" in a base eight system names the same number that "$(4 \times 64) + (5 \times 8) + 7$" or "$256 + 40 + 7$" or "303" names in a base ten system.

Here are a few more examples of numbers named in the base eight system and in the base ten system:

Base Eight Numeral	Base Ten Numeral
6	6
11	9
$63 = (6 \times 8) + 3$	51
$72 = (7 \times 8) + 2$	58
$237 = (2 \times 64) + (3 \times 8) + 7$	159
$421 = (4 \times 64) + (2 \times 8) + 1$	273
513 $\quad$ . . .	?
? $\quad$ . . .	369

You should be able to determine the base ten numeral that corresponds to the base eight numeral 513 using the same technique illustrated for the earlier entries in this table.

115

How can the base ten numeral "369" be converted to a base eight numeral representing the same number? What is it that we need to know? We need to know how many ones, how many eights, and how many eightreds (sixty-fours) there are in the number named by "369" in base ten notation. How many eightreds (sixty-fours) are there in 369?

$$\begin{array}{r} 5 \\ 64\overline{)369} \\ 320 \\ \hline 49 \end{array}$$

So there are five eightreds in 369. How many eights are there in 49?

$$\begin{array}{r} 6 \\ 8\overline{)49} \\ 48 \\ \hline 1 \end{array}$$

Now you can see that there are *five* eightreds (sixty-fours), *six* eights, and *one* unit in the number represented by "369" in base ten. How should this number be named in base eight? It must be "561" because this symbol represents five eightreds, six eights, and one unit.

Here is another example. The number named by "477" in base ten is named by "735" in base eight, as the following calculations show.

$$\begin{array}{r} 7 \\ 64\overline{)477}, \\ 488 \\ \hline 29 \end{array} \qquad \begin{array}{r} 3 \\ 8\overline{)29} \\ 24 \\ \hline 5 \end{array}$$

Similarly, what would be a base eight numeral for 1,248 in base ten? Try dividing by 64 as before.

$$\begin{array}{r} 19 \\ 64\overline{)1,248} \\ 64 \\ \hline 608 \\ 576 \\ \hline 32 \end{array}$$

You can see that there are more than eight sixty-fours! We need to ask a better question than how many sixty-fours there are in 1,248. What would be the next largest counting unit in base eight? The first basic unit is one, the next is eight, the next is sixty-four (eight eights), and it must be that the next is eight sixty-fours or five hundred twelve. Divide again to find how many five hundred twelves are in 1,248.

$$
\begin{array}{ccc}
2 & 3 & 4 \\
512\overline{)1,248,} & 64\overline{)224,} & 8\overline{)32} \\
\underline{1,024} & \underline{192} & \underline{32} \\
224 & 32 & 0
\end{array}
$$

Therefore, 1,248 (base ten) is the same number as 2,340 (base eight).

We have said that 1,248 is the same number as 2,340 (base eight). Here is another way to show that these numerals name the same number.

$$
\begin{aligned}
2,340_{\text{eight}} &= (2 \times 8^3) + (3 \times 8^2) + (4 \times 8^1) + (0 \times 8^1) \\
&= (2 \times 512) + (3 \times 64) + (4 \times 8) + 0 \\
&= 1,024 + 192 + 32 + 0 \\
&= 1,248_{\text{ten}}
\end{aligned}
$$

What would be a numeral for 1,248 (base ten) in a different base, say a base of seven? What do we need to know? First, we need to know the basic counting units in a base of seven. The first unit is the ones, the next is the sevens, the next is seven sevens or forty-nine, then seven forty-nines or three hundred forty-three. In other words, the basic counting units are 1, 7, 49, 343, 2,401, and so on; using the exponential notation, these units are 1, 7^1, 7^2, 7^3, 7^4, and so on. Now to name 1,248 (base ten) by means of base seven numerals we must know how many of each of these units there are in 1,248 (base ten). We can find these as before by dividing.

$$
\begin{array}{cccc}
& 3 & 4 & 3 \\
7^3 = 343, & 343\overline{)1,248,} & 7^2 = 491, \quad 49\overline{)219,} & 7\overline{)23} \\
& \underline{1,029} & \underline{196} & \underline{21} \\
& 219 & 23 & 2
\end{array}
$$

From this information we can now say that 1,248 (base ten) is the same number as 3,432 (base seven).

From these examples you should be able to name any number by a numeral in base ten, eight, seven, six, or almost any base. You always need to know the size of each power of the base and how many of each of these there are in the number. Of course, you also need to know how to use positional notation to name numbers. For example, you need to know that in base six the only digits needed are 0, 1, 2, 3, 4, and 5, and you need to know that 45,103 (base six) means $(4 \times 6^4) + (5 \times 6^3) + (1 \times 6^2) + (0 \times 6^1) + (3 \times 6^0)$.

117

> In a notation system using a base b the only digits are 0, 1, 2, 3, . . . , $b - 1$. Furthermore, if a_0, a_1, a_2, a_3, . . . , a_n are digits in this notation system, then the number named by the numeral "$a_n \cdots a_2 a_1 a_0$" is
> $$(a_n \times b^n) + \cdots + (a_3 \times b^3) + (a_2 \times b^2) + (a_1 \times b^1) + (a_0 \times b^0)$$

It would be convenient for the purpose of expressing numerals in other bases if there were a simple routine or algorithm that could be used. There is such an algorithm, which we shall illustrate for the next example. It shows how to convert the numeral "1,746" in base ten to the corresponding numeral in base five.

$$\begin{array}{r} 349 \\ 5\overline{)1,746} \end{array}$$ with remainder 1. This means that $1,746 = (349 \times 5) + 1$.

$$\begin{array}{r} 69 \\ 5\overline{)349} \end{array}$$ with remainder 4. This means that $349 = (69 \times 5) + 4$.

$$\begin{array}{r} 13 \\ 5\overline{)69} \end{array}$$ with remainder 4. This means that $349 = (69 \times 5) + 4$.

$$\begin{array}{r} 2 \\ 5\overline{)13} \end{array}$$ with remainder 3. This means that $13 = (2 \times 5) + 3$.

Notice that in the sequence of numbers 349, 69, 13, and 2, the last number, 2, is the only one less than five.

Now

$$\begin{aligned}
1,746 &= (\underline{349} \times 5) + 1 \\
&= [(69 \times 5) + 4] \times 5 + 1, \quad\text{because } 349 = (69 \times 5) + 4 \\
&= (\underline{69} \times 5^2) + (4 \times 5) + 1 \\
&= [(13 \times 5) + 4] \times 5^2 + (4 \times 5) + 1, \\
&\quad\text{because } 69 = (13 \times 5) + 4 \\
&= (\underline{13} \times 5^3) + (4 \times 5^2) + (4 \times 5) + 1 \\
&= [(2 \times 5) + 3] \times 5^3 + 4 \times 5^2 + 4 \times 5 + 1, \\
&\quad\text{because } 13 = (2 \times 5) + 3 \\
&= (\underline{2} \times 5^4) + (\underline{3} \times 5^3) + (\underline{4} \times 5^2) + (\underline{4} \times 5) + \underline{1} \\
&= 23,441 \quad\text{(base five)}
\end{aligned}$$

All these comments serve to show you why the little routine shown next works as it does.

$$\begin{array}{r} 2, \text{ remainder } 3 \\ 5\overline{)13}, \text{ remainder } 4 \\ 5\overline{)69}, \text{ remainder } 4 \\ 5\overline{)349}, \text{ remainder } 1 \\ 5\overline{)1,746} \end{array}$$

$23,441_{\text{five}} = 1,746_{\text{ten}}$

Having followed the details of this illustration, you can see that the routine provides a very simple means for naming numbers by notations using bases other than ten.

Example $4,178 = \underline{\hspace{2cm}}$ (six)

$$\begin{array}{r} 3, \text{ remainder } 1 \\ 6\overline{)19}, \text{ remainder } 2 \\ 6\overline{)116}, \text{ remainder } 0 \\ 6\overline{)696}, \text{ remainder } 2 \\ 6\overline{)4,178} \end{array}$$

$31,202_{\text{six}} = 4,178$

To learn to compute using a base other than ten in our notation, there are two methods open to us. One method is to learn a new set of basic facts. For a system using a base of eight, the addition facts are shown in the first table and the multiplication facts in the second.

+	0	1	2	3	4	5	6	7
0	0	1	2	3	4	5	6	7
1	1	2	3	4	5	6	7	10
2	2	3	4	5	6	7	10	11
3	3	4	5	6	7	10	11	12
4	4	5	6	7	10	11	12	13
5	5	6	7	10	11	12	13	14
6	6	7	10	11	12	13	14	15
7	7	10	11	12	13	14	15	16

×	0	1	2	3	4	5	6	7
0	0	0	0	0	0	0	0	0
1	0	1	2	3	4	5	6	7
2	0	2	4	6	10	12	14	16
3	0	3	6	11	14	17	22	25
4	0	4	10	14	20	24	30	34
5	0	5	12	17	24	31	36	43
6	0	6	14	22	30	36	44	52
7	0	7	16	25	34	43	52	61

In addition to the basic facts in this system, one must also learn algorithms for adding two-digit numbers, multiplying large numbers, and all the other algorithms that you now take for granted as a part of your early training. Do you begin to appreciate the learning task that faces the child in elementary school?

There is another way you can learn to compute in this system. This method resembles what you would do if you tried to communicate in French instead of English, because the task becomes one of translation. For example, in base eight the product of 5 times 6 is 36, but you think

five times six is thirty . . . but thirty is three eights plus six . . . so five times six is thirty-six in the base eight system. . . .

In this manner of translation you should be able to use the usual algorithms and do computation in base eight (or any other base) without too much difficulty. Here is an example and the lines of thought you might use to solve the problem.

246	$6 + 7 + 4 + 1$ is 18, which is two eights plus two, that is,
157	22 in base eight . . .
614	$4 + 5 + 1 + 5 + 2$ is 17, which is two eights plus one, that
+ 351	is, 21 in base eight . . .
$1,612_{\text{eight}}$	$2 + 1 + 6 + 3 + 2$ is 14, which is one eight plus six, that is, 16 in base eight.

Even multiplication is possible using this method of translation, as the following example shows.

354	6×4 is 24, which is three eights plus zero, that is, 30 in
× 6	base eight . . .
2,610	6×5 is 30 plus the 3 that was carried makes 33, which is four eights plus one, that is, 41 in base eight . . .
	6×3 is 18 plus the 4 that was to be carried makes 22, which is two eights plus six, that is, 26 in base eight.

You must realize by now the fact that you know a great deal about the base ten system of numeration. You should also realize that you can use your knowledge of the base ten system to help explain to others concepts of positional systems with bases other than ten. Finally, you may have begun to realize how much the elementary school child must learn about some system of numeration in order to reach the level of understanding you already possess.

Lest you feel that we have exhausted the subject of bases other than ten, let us briefly consider numerals for fractions and use a "decimal" notation in the process. To refresh your memory you will remember that "24.165" means 2 tens plus 4 ones plus 1 tenth plus 6 hundredths plus 5 thousandths. If we use exponents as we have done earlier in this section, we should agree to use $10^1 = 10$, $10^0 = 1$, $10^{-1} = \frac{1}{10}$, $10^{-2} = \frac{1}{10}^2 = \frac{1}{100}$, $10^{-3} = \frac{1}{10}^3 = \frac{1}{1,000}$, and so on. These uses of exponents are consistent with their use earlier.

With these agreements, $24.165 = (2 \times 10^1) + (4 \times 10^0) + (1 \times 10^{-1}) + (6 \times 10^{-2}) + (5 \times 10^{-3})$, or you may say $24.165 = 20 + 4 + \frac{1}{10} + \frac{6}{100} + \frac{5}{1,000}$. Continuing in the same vein but with a base of eight, what is the meaning of the numeral "146.23"? Using the same form used for the base ten numerals, it must be that

$$146.23_{\text{eight}} = (1 \times 8^2) + (4 \times 8^1) + (6 \times 8^0) + (2 \times 8^{-1}) + (3 \times 8^{-2})$$
$$= (1 \times 64) + (4 \times 8) + 6 + \frac{2}{8} + \frac{3}{64}$$

The number 146.23_{eight} can now be seen to be the number $64 + 32 + 6 + \frac{1}{4} + \frac{3}{64}$, or $102\frac{19}{64}$ in base ten. It can be seen that the "decimal" point is no barrier to the consideration of fractional numbers in bases other than ten.

Here is another example, which we shall rename in base ten.

$$205.452_{\text{six}} = (2 \times 6^2) + (0 \times 6^1) + (5 \times 6^0) + (4 \times 6^{-1}) + (5 \times 6^{-2})$$
$$+ (2 \times 6^{-3})$$
$$= 72 + 0 + 5 + \frac{4}{6} + \frac{5}{36} + \frac{2}{216}$$
$$= 77\frac{176}{216} = 77\frac{22}{27}$$

In each of the examples in this section the number base chosen as an alternative to base ten has been some number less than ten. You should know that for many years there has been an organization of people who felt that the number base should be changed to twelve because of the frequency of multiples of twelve in everyday use. There are twelve months, twelve hours, twelve in a dozen, twelve dozen in one gross, twelve inches in one foot, and many more. Such a number system is called a *duodecimal* system. We might have naturally developed this number system had we all been born with twelve fingers. To count in this system we need two new digits, which we shall call Jack and Queen (not the common choice as you may imagine) and for which the numeral will be "J" and "Q." Thus, a counting chart looks like this:

0	1	2	3	4	5	6	7	8	9	J	Q
10	11	12	13	14	15	16	17	18	19	1J	1Q
20	...										
.											
.											
.											
90	91	92	93	94	95	96	97	98	99	9J	9Q
J0	J1	J2	J3	J4	J5	J6	J7	J8	J9	JJ	JQ
Q0	Q1	Q2	Q3	Q4	Q5	Q6	Q7	Q8	Q9	QJ	QQ
100	101	...									

The symbol "100" in this system means $(1 \times 12^2) + (0 \times 12^1) + (0 \times 12^0)$. Computational skill using base twelve numerals is not an objective of this text, but you may find it interesting to note that Queen times Queen is Jackety Queen!

This section has presented bases other than ten and has shown the significance of the invention of a positional system such as the Hindu–Arabic. The section may have also shown the reasons why youngsters have difficulty in elementary arithmetic.

EXERCISES (Section 3.4)

1. Here is a set of problems dealing with a base three positional system of numeration.
   a. In base three, count from one to fifty.
   b. The following numerals name base ten numbers. Convert these numerals to base three numerals that name the same numbers.

   71   98   155   579

   c. Convert the following base three numerals to base ten.

   122   2,101   20,212   100,001

   d. Here are some addition and subtraction problems in base three notation. Solve each of these problems in two ways: by operating in base three and by converting to base ten numerals, operating in base ten, and then renaming in base three.

122	121,101	2,212	21,021
101	+ 220,102	− 1,201	− 12,112
+ 211	?	?	?
?			

   e. Here are some multiplication problems in base three notation. Solve these two problems in both of the ways described in part d.

212	12,201	21,012
× 2	× 21	× 2,012
?	?	?

f. Finally, here are two problems of division in base three notation. Solve these in two ways also.

$$2\overline{)2,101}^{\,?} \qquad 212\overline{)12,201}^{\,?}$$

2. In this section you found a division algorithm that permits one to convert base ten numerals to numerals in other bases. Use this algorithm to change $3,564_{ten}$ to the corresponding numeral in base
   a. nine   b. seven   c. six   d. five   e. two

3. The algorithm used in Exercise 2 also serves well for converting from any base to any other base. The only difference is that the division must be performed by use of the original base numeration system. Here is an example that shows how 417_{eight} may be renamed in base five. As in the earlier examples, notice that the divisor in each case is five but the operations are performed in base eight.

$$\begin{array}{l} 2 \text{ with remainder } 0 \\ 5\overline{)12} \text{ with remainder } 4, \qquad 417_{eight} = 2,041_{five} \\ 5\overline{)\,66} \text{ with remainder } 1 \\ 5\overline{)\,417}_{eight} \end{array}$$

As a check, notice that

$$417_{eight} = (4 \times 8^2) + (1 \times 8) + 7 = 271_{ten}$$
$$2,041_{five} = (2 \times 5^3) + (0 \times 5^2) + (4 \times 5) + 1 = 271_{ten}$$

   a. Using base eight operations, convert 537_{eight} to the corresponding numeral in base five.
   b. Convert 537_{eight} to the corresponding numeral in base six.
   c. Convert 537_{nine} to the corresponding numeral in base six.

4. Convert the following base ten numerals to base twelve numerals:
   a. 97   b. 161   c. 880   d. 2,341

5. Convert the following base twelve numerals to base ten numerals.
   a. J9   b. 89   c. JQ1   d. 156J   e. JQ019

6. Solve each of the following problems written in base twelve notation.

   a. $\begin{array}{r} 90J \\ 177 \\ +2Q1 \\ \hline ? \end{array}$ b. $\begin{array}{r} 189 \\ -\ QJ \\ \hline ? \end{array}$ c. $\begin{array}{r} 628 \\ \times\ 45 \\ \hline ? \end{array}$ d. $17\overline{)2J8}^{\,?}$

7. Elementary school children are often asked to count the number of ice cream sticks in a box found on a work table. If a child can only count from one to seven, and there are forty-six sticks on the table, what is he likely to do and what will be his most likely response to the question "How many?"

8. The positional character of the Hindu–Arabic system is often described by saying that the system is a place-value system. Explain what is meant by the expression "place value."

9. To reinforce as well as to further explain the positional or place-value nature of the decimal (base ten) system, some teachers use a "pocket board" made of tag board or other material like this:

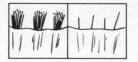

(three bundles of ten sticks
and four single sticks)

In the left-hand pocket children place bundles of ten and in the right-hand pocket they place any objects left over after bundling as many bunches of ten as they can. Usually tongue depressors, ice cream sticks, or other long, flat objects are used. Devise some activities like this one that would help to explain the place-value concept in decimal numeration.

3.5

HOW CHILDREN LEARN TO COUNT

You have already seen the importance of the concept of one-to-one correspondence in the development of the concept of number. You have also come to recognize the set $\{1, 2, 3, 4, 5, 6\}$ as a standard set for the number six. It may be the case that you have been led to believe that these two notions are the only ideas needed to learn to count. In fact, we have stated that the count of a set, or the cardinal number of a set, is the number k such that the standard set $\{1, 2, 3, \ldots, k\}$ can be shown to be in a one-to-one correspondence with the given set. However, there is one more concept needed by young children who are learning to count the number of objects in a given set. That concept is the concept of *order*.

Children must learn that one is the first number to use in counting, that two is the second, that three is the third, and that k is the last number if the given set contains that many elements. Because of your maturity, you can see that the question of order of numbers is really a question of subset relationship. That is, the next number after one is two because the standard set for one is $\{1\}$, which is a subset of the standard set for two, $\{1, 2\}$. Three comes before five because the standard set for three is a subset of the standard set for five. Therefore, to order the natural numbers means to name the natural numbers in such a way that the standard set for each natural number is a subset of the next. Hence, one is the first natural number in this order because $\{1\}$ is a subset of the standard set of every other natural number.

This approach, however satisfying to you as a mature student, is not quite as simple for the child, although the essence of the idea is the same for him as it is for you. First experiences for children involve matching sets in one-to-one correspondences. In this way the child comes to recognize the property that such sets have in common; that is, they have the *same* number. Experiences which call for making a set that is "more" or making a set that is "less" than some beginning set lead the child to discover early concepts of order. Beginning with a set of a certain size, the child is then asked to make a set that is one more. Such experiences lead children to discover the concept of the next number in a sequence of numbers. Now, given a set of one object, the child can answer "How many?" with the response "One." The child and teacher might then have a dialogue something like the following.

> MISS DEAL: Form a set that is one more. How many now?
> JENNIFER: Two.
> MISS DEAL: Good! Form a set that is one more. How many?
> JENNIFER: Three.
> MISS DEAL: Just right! So what number comes just after one?
> JENNIFER: Two.
> MISS DEAL: And just after two?
> JENNIFER: Three.
> MISS DEAL: What number comes just after three?
> JENNIFER: Four. Because when I put one more in the set I get four.

Of course, many children begin school with the ability to say the number names from one to ten in the correct order. They have a *rote* level ability to count, but they often do not know why four comes after three in the sense of making a set with one more. The skill of counting, which is the immediate objective, is called *rational counting*. This level of ability implies that the child can do at least three things:

1. The child can place the objects in a set in a one-to-one correspondence with a set of number names.
2. The child can name these numbers in the proper order.
3. The child can assign the last number named to the set and identify that number as the count of the set.

When he reaches this level, he should be ready for the next steps in the development of arithmetic concepts.

In view of the importance of the concept of order in the development of counting skills, it may be appropriate to revise the concept of standard set for natural numbers. To do this, we could return to the

125

concept of ordered pairs from Chapter 1. Recall that (1, 2) is not the same ordered pair as (2, 1), whereas the set {1, 2} and the set {2, 1} are identical. In this spirit, the representative set for the natural number five should be the *ordered set* (1, 2, 3, 4, 5). This definition of standard set has the distinct advantage of being more nearly like the way in which children learn to count. This is the order in which children would place the set {1, 2, 3, 4, 5} in a one-to-one correspondence with a set of five objects. However, this definition has the disadvantage that it requires a further step in the explanation of the concept of number, which was our target in Section 3.2 when the issue first came into the discussion. Therefore, we shall choose to continue to use the unordered set {1, 2, 3, . . . , k} as the standard set for the natural number k.

Such number concepts as three, seven, and the like have been termed *cardinal* numbers because they name the cardinality of sets. Numbers may also be used to designate the order of objects in a set. Such use of numbers is called the *ordinal* use of number. We use numbers in the ordinal sense in many ways. For instance, the runner finished third, the seventeenth green, the fourth in bridge, the second base, the sixth sense, and the like.

There is another use of numerals that is often confused with the cardinal and ordinal usages. "The basketball player is number 12." The sentence does not mean that the boy is the twelfth man on the team, nor does it mean that he is the number twelve in the cardinal sense of counting. What is meant is that the numeral on his shirt corresponds to his name in the program. In this sense numerals name people, animals in a rodeo, or cars in a race. We call this use the *nominal* use of number, because it is essentially the use of the number name and not the number itself.

You can begin to see the challenges involved in teaching concepts of mathematics to young children. We hope that you will find the task as exciting and rewarding as did those who have taught you these notions.

EXERCISES (Section 3.5)

1. Distinguish between the cardinal, ordinal, and nominal uses of number in the following.
   a. Page 345.
   b. Volume 6.
   c. 1824 Buena Vista Drive.

    d. He was third in line.

    e. 1974 A.D.

    f. This is the seventeenth try.

    g. The ball is downed on the 40-yard line.

    h. He plays second base.

    i. She was number one in my book!

2. What *endings* characterize ordinal number names?

3. Look up the history of the words *first* and *second* and compare with the words *one* and *two*.

4. See if you can find some very young children and ask one or more of them to count a set of candy pieces for you. Do you spot the kind of errors they make? Are they making the one-to-one correspondence? Are they naming the numbers in order? Are they assigning the correct number as the count of the set?

5. Explain why the set $\{1, 2, 3, 4, 5, 6\}$ is the same as the set $\{6, 3, 2, 5, 4, 1\}$. Now explain why the ordered set $(1, 2, 3, 4, 5, 6)$ is not the same as the ordered set $(6, 3, 2, 5, 4, 1)$.

Niels Henrik Abel

(1802–1829)

What must one do to achieve greatness? How can it be accomplished by the time one reaches 26 years of age? The first prerequisite is genius, and Abel had all that is required for genius, and more. However, there were three strikes against him from the outset. He came from a family that was desperately poor, and lived his entire life in abject poverty, dependent upon his own resources plus those of his friends for support. His homeland was Norway, which had been at war with Sweden and England and which now found itself destitute and undergoing a famine as well. Furthermore, he did not learn French and German until he was in his early twenties and so he had difficulty communicating with the world's great mathematicians.

In spite of these handicaps, as well as the fact that he had to care for his six brothers and sisters and his mother following the death of his father when Abel was 18, by the time Abel died he was seen by many as the greatest mathematician of the nineteenth century. Perhaps you can appreciate the significance of one of his great accomplishments. You

know how to solve equations like $2x + 3 = 0$ and you may vaguely recall how to solve equations like $x^2 + 3x + 2 = 0$. These are first- and second-degree equations, respectively, and there are relatively simple methods to use to solve third- and fourth-degree equations as well. Such methods were known to mathematicians as early as the sixteenth century; but in the 300 years since, no one had been able to devise a method, simple or complex, to solve a fifth-degree equation. Abel worked on this problem and by the time he was 19 he had done what no other mathematician had been able to do; he proved that there *is no* general method that can be devised to solve the fifth-degree equation or one of any higher degree. A boy of 19 had solved a problem that had not been resolved by the greatest mathematicians, including Karl Friedrich Gauss.

The pathetic story of Abel's life continues, for he could get no one to recognize the value of what he had proved on this matter or on other truly outstanding issues. There are substantiated accounts of his manuscripts being put aside by celebrated authorities who were too vain to consider his writings, there are substantiated accounts of his manuscripts being lost in the process of publication, and some cases in which he was simply snubbed by people who could have profited most from the contact. He had been trying to gain a professorship in order to support his family and to continue his study, but tuberculosis struck him down. True to form in this pathetic tale, two days after his death from the disease he received a letter that announced his appointment as a full professor at the University of Berlin. He was 26 years old.

128

Chapter 4

The System of
Whole Numbers

4.1
INTRODUCTION

In the previous chapters you gained insight into the role of mathematics in Western culture. History is replete with instances of man refining the concepts of number to solve problems and to satisfy a basic curiosity regarding the nature of numbers. You learned that man gradually refined his methods of numeration from that of a simple tally system to the sophisticated place-value system that we use today. It is interesting to ponder where man's quest for greater efficiency in numeration will lead us.

In this and subsequent chapters we shall continue to be concerned with numeration and with numerals, the symbols we use to express our number concepts, but to a lesser degree. However, we shall now place our major emphasis on number concepts and the manner in which we teach and use numbers and their related operations. Our investigation will be systematic and will remain basically the same in each chapter.

We shall start with a set of numbers with which you are familiar and develop from this set a new set of numbers. In general, this new set of numbers will enable us to solve problems that we could not have otherwise solved. The binary operations of addition and multiplication will then be defined on the new set. These operations will be defined in terms of operations that you already know. Finally, the properties of the new set under the binary operations and under other relations, such as the ordering relation, will be examined.

One basic objective of this text is to enable you to name and basically understand each number that may be represented on the number line. This is not a trivial task. In the earliest grades the curiosity of children is aroused by the number line, which many classrooms have exhibited across the top of the front chalkboard (Figure 4-1). It is not at all uncommon to have children ask their teacher:

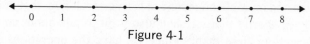

Figure 4-1

"What lies to the left of 0?" "Are there numbers that are not found on the number line?" Upon completion of this book you should be able to answer questions like these in a mathematically honest and pedagogically sound manner.

4.2

THE SET OF WHOLE NUMBERS

We are already familiar with the set N of natural or counting numbers, which is a collection of equivalence classes. Each set in a particular equivalence class is related to every other set in that class by a common property called a cardinal number. The set $\{a, b, c, d\}$ is in the same equivalence class as the set {Peter, John, Mary, Joe}, since these two sets can be matched one to one. Their common property is the cardinal number 4.

If we now define the number 0 to be the cardinal number of the empty set, we have a number that is not contained in the set of natural numbers. By considering the cardinal numbers of all the various equivalence classes, we now have the set of whole numbers, which will be designated by W.

$$W = \{0, 1, 2, 3, 4, 5, \ldots\}$$

Notice that $N \subset W$.

To talk about the system of whole numbers, we make the following definition.

> A *number system* is a set of numbers S, with one or more operations and relations defined on this set and with certain rules or properties governing these operations and relations.

Each aspect of this definition merits further attention.

We begin with a set of numbers, such as the set of whole numbers W. Upon that set we define one or more binary operations, such as addition and multiplication, and at least one relation, that of equality. You will see shortly that we shall also want to talk about an ordering relation, such as "less than." Once we have the operations and relations, we then consider properties or rules that the elements, operations, and relations satisfy, such as the grouping property of addition. Each of these considerations is important in our study of mathematics. If we change the set, the operations, and/or relations and properties, we change the system. We shall see in subsequent chapters how changes in any of these produce new mathematical systems.

For the time being we turn our attention to the idea of a binary operation. A few introductory remarks are in order regarding any binary operation.

1. We always talk about a binary operation with respect to some set S. To talk about addition is meaningless unless we know the set upon which this operation is defined.

2. A binary operation involves assigning a member of set S to each ordered pair of elements from set S. We shall not consider a process to be an operation on a set S unless each pair of elements of S is matched with an element of S. For example, division of whole numbers is *not* an operation, since the pair $(2, 4)$ is not matched with any whole number. In this case we say the operation is not *performable* or that the operation is not *closed*.

3. The number assigned to the ordered pair of numbers must be the only number which can be assigned to that pair of numbers. In other words, the assignment must be *unique*. If this is so, we say that our operation is well defined.

Figure 4-2 shows an example of a binary operation on the set

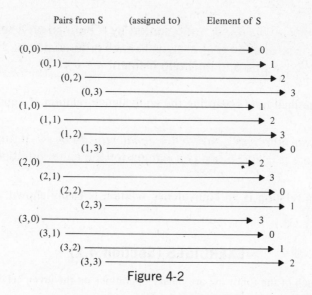

Figure 4-2

$S = \{0, 1, 2, 3\}$. Remember that each pair of elements from S is assigned to some element of S. There are 16 possible pairs that can be formed from the elements of set S, and you can see that some of these pairs have the same element in both the first and second component. Very often you will see such a binary operation portrayed by means of a table (Figure 4-3). The pairs are not explicitly identified, but

	0	1	2	3
0	0	1	2	3
1	1	2	3	0
2	2	3	0	1
3	3	0	1	2

Figure 4-3

from the table in the figure you can see that the pair $(2, 1)$, for example, is assigned to the element 3 because if you look in the *row* labeled "2" and go across to the *column* labeled "1" you will find the element 3.

An example of a relation that is not well defined is the following: Match each pair of friends with a common friend. If the two friends have more than one common friend, with which friend do you pair the two friends? The matching is not unique, since there may be more than one matching possible.

As you may have guessed:

133

A *binary operation*, represented by *, defined on a set S, is a function that assigns to each ordered pair (a, b) of $S \times S$ one and only one element $a * b$ of S.

One final note regarding the equivalence relation of equality.

Two numbers a and b are *equal*, written $a = b$, if and only if a and b are two names for the same number.

That this relation is an equivalence relation is easily shown. Do you see how?

EXERCISES (Section 4.2)

1. Which of the following are binary operations on the given set?
   a. $T = \{$people in your class$\}$.
      $a * b = a$'s sister $(a, b \in T.)$
   b. $E = \{$even whole numbers$\}$.
      $a * b = (a + b)/2$, where $+$ and division are defined on W and $a, b \in E$.
   c. $B = \{$brothers and sister you know$\}$.
      $a * b = $ a parent of a and b, provided a and b are a brother and sister.
   d. $E = \{$even whole numbers$\}$.
      $a * b = a^b$, provided $a \neq 0$ and $a, b \in E$.
   e. $O = \{$odd whole numbers$\}$.
      $a * b = a^b$, where $a, b \in 0$.
   f. $W = \{$whole numbers$\}$.
      $a * b = (2 \cdot a) + b$, where $+$ and $\cdot$ are defined on W and $a, b \in W$.
   g. $O = \{$odd whole numbers$\}$.
      $a * b = (a + b)/2$, where $+$ and division are defined on W and $a, b \in O$.
   h. $W = \{$whole numbers$\}$.
      $a * b = a$, where $a, b \in W$.

2. Suppose that you ask a third-grade child what the product 3×4 is. He replies 13. You ask the same student what the product 5×3 is and he replies 16. What rule is the child using to name his products? Is this a binary operation?

3. Suppose that you ask a second-grade child what the sum $7 + 8$ is? He replies 30. You ask the same student what the sum $4 + 2$ is and he replies 12. What rule is the child using to name his sums? Is this a binary operation?

4.3
ADDITION OF WHOLE NUMBERS

As we examine elementary textbooks we see activities designed to lead the child from the concrete to the abstract. Children manipulate objects to count the number of elements in a set, hence determining the cardinal number of the set of objects. Eventually, the children will manipulate two sets of objects, possibly a set of 3 buttons and a set of 2 beads. By their very nature these sets are disjoint, since they are composed of distinct objects. The teacher will ask questions such as

"How many buttons do you have?"
"How many beads do you have?"
"Push the buttons together with the beads. How many buttons and beads do you have altogether?"
"If you are not sure, count the members of this new set."

The procedure will be repeated time and time again, quite frequently with different sets of manipulative objects. This activity is a prelude to the teaching of the basic addition fact that $3 + 2 = 5$. Our definition of addition of whole numbers underlies the activity that the children were performing.

> Suppose that A and B are finite disjoint sets ($A \cap B = \emptyset$). If $n(A) = a$ and $n(B) = b$, where a and b are whole numbers, then $a + b = n(A \cup B)$.

The restriction that $A \cap B = \emptyset$ is rather important. If you were teaching a level three mathematics class of 23 children, and a fellow teacher was teaching a level four science class of 17 children, the total number of different children in your two classes could be less than 40. This might not seem important unless you decided to combine the two groups for a field trip and had to know how many children to provide lunches and transportation for.

As an example of the definition of addition, suppose that $A = \{1, 2, 3, 4\}$ and $B = \{a, b\}$. Then $n(A) = 4$, $n(B) = 2$, and $A \cap B = \emptyset$. Then $4 + 2 = n(A \cup B) = 6$.

We turn our attention to the properties that govern the operation of addition on W. We begin by noting that if a and b are *any* whole numbers then $a + b$ is necessarily a whole number by definition. We say that the set of whole numbers is *closed* under the operation of addition. Although this may appear to be trivial, there are many sets that are not closed under the operation of addition as defined on W. The set of odd numbers is not closed under addition since the sum of two odd numbers is not another odd number. Rather, the sum of two odd numbers is an even number, which is not an odd number. The closure property depends upon both the operation and the set of numbers.

Closure is used in higher mathematics to examine relationships between subsystems and systems, but it can also be used as a simple partial check in arithmetic computation. Every whole number is either even (E) or odd (O). The set E is closed under addition as defined on W, but the set O is not. If a child adds two even numbers, such as 356 and 786, a necessary condition that his sum be correct is that his sum be even. If his sum is not even, his answer is not correct. Also, if the child adds two odd numbers, such as 6,835 and 9,671, a necessary condition that his sum be correct is that the sum *not* be odd. That is, his sum must be even. Simple partial checks such as those just mentioned can be taught to the children at the earliest levels. These checks are also quite useful for teachers and teachers aides who have to rapidly check children's worksheets with several examples on each sheet.

If we examine a table of basic facts, such as that of Figure 4-4,

+	0	1	2	3	4	5	6	7	8	9
0	0	1	2	3	4	5	6	7	8	9
1	1	2	3	4	5	6	7	8	9	10
2	2	3	4	5	6	7	8	9	10	11
3	3	4	5	6	7	8	9	10	11	12
4	4	5	6	7	8	9	10	11	12	13
5	5	6	7	8	9	10	11	12	13	14
6	6	7	8	9	10	11	12	13	14	15
7	7	8	9	10	11	12	13	14	15	16
8	8	9	10	11	12	13	14	15	16	17
9	9	10	11	12	13	14	15	16	17	18

Figure 4-4

we see, upon first glance, 100 facts that the child must know. Upon closer examination, we recognize that $0 + n = n + 0 = n$ for any whole number n. If we teach the children that 0 plus any whole number is just that whole number, we have eliminated 19 basic facts that the child must memorize. Because there is an element of 0 of W such that $0 + n = n + 0 = n$, where $n \in W$, we say that there is an *additive identity element for W*.

Also, as we look along the main diagonal in.the figure we see that our figure is symmetric about this diagonal. If we were to cut out the figure and carefully fold it about the diagonal, identical numerals would coincide. A "5" would coincide with a "5," and so forth. If we were to look along the row whose addend is 4 and down the column whose addend is 2, we would see the sum 6. The sum "6" would fold onto a "6" from the row whose addend is 2 and from the column whose addend is 4. What this implies is that $4 + 2 = 6$ and $2 + 4 = 6$. The order in which we add two whole numbers does not make a difference in the sum. We say that *W is commutative under the operation of addition.* That is,

$$a + b = b + a, \quad \text{for each } a, b \in W$$

Knowledge of this property further reduces the number of facts to be memorized by 36 facts. We now have reduced our table of basic facts to be memorized to 45 facts. This is a considerable reduction in time and energy.

We could get very formal about the previously stated properties and prove that W, under $+$, has an additive identity and a commutative property. To show commutativity, we remember from Chapter 1 that the union of sets is commutative. Hence,

$$\begin{aligned} a + b &= n(A) + n(B) \\ &= n(A \cup B) \\ &= n(B \cup A) \\ &= n(B) + n(A) = b + a \end{aligned}$$

Also

$$\begin{aligned} a + 0 &= n(A) + n(\emptyset) \\ &= n(A \cup \emptyset) \\ &= n(A) = a \end{aligned}$$

We also notice that $(a + b) + c = a + (b + c)$ for all whole numbers a, b, and c. In children's books this property is quite frequently called the grouping property for addition. In mathematics we say that *W is associative under the operation of addition.* You are asked in the exercises to show this property is true by using set properties.

> Given the set of whole numbers with a binary operation of addition defined as
>
> $$a + b = n(A \cup B), \quad \text{where } A \cap B = \emptyset$$
> $$\text{and} \quad n(A) = a, \; n(B) = b$$
>
> then
> 1. *W* is *closed* under the operation of addition.
> 2. *W* is *commutative* under the operation of addition.
> 3. *W* is *associative* under the operation of addition.
> 4. There exists an *additive identity* 0 such that $a + 0 = 0 + a = a$ for each $a \in W$.

EXERCISES (Section 4.3)

1. In each of the following examples, state whether the associative, commutative, closure, or identity property was applied.
   a. $3 + 8 = 8 + 3$
   b. $2 + 4 = 6$
   c. $(1 + 2) + 3 = 1 + (2 + 3)$
   d. $8 + 0 = 8$
   e. $(2 + 3) + 3 = (3 + 2) + 3$
   f. $10 + 0 = 0 + 10$

2. Show that $(a + b) + c = a + (b + c)$ by using the properties of sets and the definition of addition.

3. Use the associative property to show that $9 + 6 = 15$. (*Hint:* Rename 6 and use a numeration property.)

4. Describe how you would use the *definition of addition* of whole numbers and the properties of sets to illustrate to a child that the set of whole numbers is commutative under addition.

5. Suppose that we redefine the addition of whole numbers in the following manner: if $n(A) = a$ and $n(B) = b$, then $a + b = n(A \cup B) + n(A \cap B)$. Use this definition to show that $8 + 6 = 14$ if $A = \{z, b, c, d, e, f, g, h\}$ and $B = \{g, h, i, j, k, l\}$.

6. Suppose that you are to find the sum

$$\begin{array}{r} 1 \\ 9 \\ +\,9 \\ \hline \end{array}$$

Would you add from the top down or from the bottom up? Why? How do you know the results will be the same?

7. Suppose that we have a finite number system where addition is defined by the table given. $D = \{2, 4, 6, 8\}$. Study the table, and then answer the following questions.
   a. Is D closed with respect to $*$?
   b. Is there an additive identity for D?
   c. Is D commutative under $*$?

*	2	4	6	8
2	2	2	2	2
4	2	4	2	4
6	2	2	6	2
8	2	4	2	8

8. Suppose that we have a finite number system where addition is defined on the set $A = \{1, 2, 3, 4\}$ in the following way: $a * b = a$. Complete the table, and then answer the following question.
   a. Is A closed with respect to $*$?
   b. Is there an additive identity in A?
   c. Is A commutative under $*$?
   d. Is A associative under $*$?

*	1	2	3	4
1	1	1	1	1
2	2	?	2	?
3	3	3	?	?
4	4	?	?	?

9. A child writes the following four examples:
$$2 + 7 = 16, \quad 0 + 7 = 14, \quad 3 + 2 = 12, \quad 1 + 9 = 17$$
What definition for addition might he be using?

4.4

MULTIPLICATION OF WHOLE NUMBERS

There are several ways to teach children the meaning of multiplication. One method uses a repeated addend approach. For example,

$2 + 2 + 2 = 6$, or
2 three times $= 6$, or
3 times $2 = 6$. That is, $3 \times 2 = 6$.

This is a meaningful way of defining what we mean by the multiplication of two whole numbers. What we are saying is that $a \times b$ means that a sets of b each can be explained for $a > 1$.

> If a and b are whole numbers, $a > 1$, then the operation of multiplication assigns $a \times b$ to (a, b), where
>
> $$a \times b = \underbrace{b + b + b + \cdots + b}_{a \text{ times}}.$$

This definition, while time honored, sheds little light on why $0 \cdot n = 0$ or $1 \cdot n = n$. Considering n as an addend zero times, or one time, to many children is meaningless.

Another approach to multiplication, quite popular today, circumvents the above-mentioned inadequacies of the repeated addend approach. The popularity of this approach may be due to the fact that it deals with the cross product of sets, a concept that permeates mathematics. Let us consider an example.

Suppose that we have the sets $A = \{p, m, b, f\}$ and $B = \{at, an, it\}$. The cross product of A and B is found in the following manner: Each member of A can be paired with an element of B in three ways (see Figure 4-5). Hence,

$A \times B = \{(p,$ at$), (p,$ an$), (p,$ it$), (m,$ at$), (m,$ an$), (m,$ it$), (b,$ at$), (b,$ an$), (b,$ it$), (f,$ at$), (f,$ an$), (f,$ it$)\}$

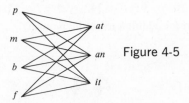

Figure 4-5

Since $n(A) = 4$ and $n(B) = 3$, then $n(A \times B) = 12$. We formally define this concept.

> If $a = n(A)$ and $b = n(B)$, then $a \times b = n(A \times B)$. Remember: if either A or B is the empty set, $A \times B = \emptyset$.

Our definition implies that W is closed under multiplication, since two members of W are matched with the cardinal number of $A \times B$, which is a whole number.

The property of closure of W under multiplication can be used in the teaching of children in exactly the same manner that was discussed in the previous section. The set E is closed under multiplication. Hence, the product of two even numbers must be even. The set O of odd numbers is closed under multiplication. Hence, the product of two odd numbers must be odd. If a child multiplies two even or two odd numbers, a necessary condition that his answer be correct is that he maintain closure under the operation of multiplication.

There are numerous concrete applications of this definition that can be used to motivate both the definition and properties of W under this operation. Consider the desk arrangement in a mythical classroom shown in Figure 4-6. If a teacher were standing in the front of the

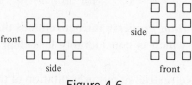

Figure 4-6

classroom, she would see a 3 × 4 array of pupil desks. If she then moved to the side of the classroom, she would see a 4 × 3 arrangement of desks. Has the number of desks changed as the teacher moved from the front to the side of the classroom? What is being demonstrated is the *commutative property of multiplication*. Of course, we could again become rigorous and use the properties of sets to show that $a \times b = b \times a$.

To demonstrate that W is associative under multiplication, a simple shoe box can be used (see Figure 4-7). We know that the vol-

Figure 4-7

ume of the shoe box is given by $V = w \times l \times h$. This formula can be interpreted to mean V = (area of base) × height, or V = width × (area of a side); $(w \times l) \times h = w \times (l \times h)$. This demonstration lends itself very well to a laboratory exercise wherein plastic containers and water can be used to illustrate a mathematical principle while integrating mathematics and science.

We found that there was a whole number 0 such that $a + 0 =$

$0 + a = a$. Is there a whole number n such that $a \cdot n = n \cdot a = a$? Upon reflection you see that the number 1 is n. The number 1 is called the *multiplicative identity element for the set W*. We state, without proof, that there can only be one multiplicative identity element for a given set of numbers. The same is true for an additive identity element.

Once again, everything that has been said about W under the properties mentioned can be put to use in the teaching of children. The 100 multiplication facts can be reduced to 45 facts if the commutative, associative, and identity properties are employed. There is an added advantage if we realize that

$$a \cdot 0 = 0, \qquad \text{for all } a \in W$$

This zero multiplication property further reduces the facts to be memorized to 40 facts, which is considerably less than the 100 we began with.

So far, we have restricted our presentation of the system of whole numbers to properties that hold for either addition or multiplication. A reasonable question to ask is "Are there any properties that hold when both binary operations are used together?" The answer is yes, and the property is best illustrated by an example.

To find the product 3×12, we generally multiply 3 times 2, multiply 3 times 10, and then add the results. Notice that we started with a multiplication problem and found our answer by multiplying *and* adding. Are we sure our procedure is correct? In other words, are we sure that

$$3 \times 12 = (3 \times 10) + (3 \times 2)$$

Once again, a physical model may help us decide (Figure 4-8). We

```
x  x  x  x  x  x  x  x  x  x │ x  x
x  x  x  x  x  x  x  x  x  x │ x  x     Figure 4-8
x  x  x  x  x  x  x  x  x  x │ x  x
```

have initially a 3×12 array, which we may count, if necessary, to see that there are 36 elements in the array. Suppose that we were now to partition the array of 36 elements into two arrays, one a 3×10 array and the second a 3×2 array. Do we still have the same number of elements as in our original array? The answer is yes, and the property we are demonstrating is called the *distributive property of multiplication over addition*.

If a, b, and c are whole numbers, then $a \times (b + c) = (a \times b) + (a \times c)$.

In our example, $10 + 2$ was represented by the numeral 12. In summary, then,

Given the set of whole numbers with a binary operation of multiplication defined as follows: $a \times b = n(A \times B)$, where $n(A) = a$ and $n(B) = b$, then
1. W is *closed* under the operation of multiplication.
2. W is *commutative* under the operation of multiplication.
3. W is *associative* under the operation of multiplication.
4. There exists *a multiplicative identity* 1 such that $a \cdot 1 = 1 \cdot a = a$ for each $a \in W$.
5. *Multiplication is distributive over addition*; that is, $a \times (b + c) = (a \times b) + (a \times c)$, where $a, b, c \in W$.

EXERCISES (Section 4.4)

1. In the following examples, state the property that was applied.
   a. $4 \times 8 = (4 \times 4) + (4 \times 4)$
   b. $3 \times 2 = 2 \times 3$
   c. $17 \cdot 1 = 1 \cdot 17$
   d. $1 \cdot 5 = 5$
   e. $3 \times (4 \times 5) = (3 \times 4) \times 5$
   f. $5 \times 7 \in W$
2. Use the distributive property to show that $5 \times 12 = 60$.
3. Construct a coordinate system to show the lattice points of $D \times D$, where $D = \{1, 2, 3, 4, 5, 6\}$. How many lattice points are there?
4. For the following tell whether the given statement is true or false. If false, tell why.
   a. $A \times B = B \times A$ for all A and B.
   b. If $n(A) = a$ and $n(B) = b$, then $a \times b = A \times B$.
   c. $A \times (B \cup C) = (A \times B) \cup (A \times C)$.
   d. $A \times (B \times C) = (A \times B) \times C$.
   e. If $a, b, c \in W$, then $a + (b \times c) = (a + b) \times (a + c)$
5. Use the distributive property to rename the following:
   a. $(2 \cdot 10) + (3 \cdot 10)$
   b. $(2^2 \cdot 5) + (2^2 \cdot 3)$
   c. $(3^3 \cdot 1) + (3 \cdot 2)$
   d. $(a + b) \cdot 3$
   e. $x^2 + x$
   f. $(1 + c) \cdot (a + b) + (c + 1) \cdot 3$
6. The formula for the volume of a cube is $V = s \cdot s \cdot s$, where s is the length

143

of a side. Explain how you can use this formula to teach the associative property of multiplication.

7. Construct a laboratory exercise for Exercise 6.

8. The repeated addend approach to multiplication can be illustrated by "jumping" on the number line. Draw a number line and show the "jumping" approach for the following:
   a. 3×2 c. 4×3
   b. 2×1 d. 5×0

9. Suppose that we have a finite number system where multiplication is defined by the table given. $S = \{0, 1, 2, 3, 4\}$.
   a. Is S closed with respect to $*$?
   b. Is there a multiplicative identity in A?
   c. Is A commutative under $*$?
   d. Is A associative under $*$?

$*$	0	1	2	3	4
0	0	0	0	0	0
1	0	1	2	3	4
2	0	2	4	1	3
3	0	3	1	4	2
4	0	4	3	2	1

10. A child writes the following four examples:
$$2 \times 7 = 16, \qquad 0 \times 7 = 2, \qquad 3 \times 2 = 8, \qquad 1 \times 9 = 11$$
What definition for multiplication might he be using?

4.5

THE ORDER RELATION

In many elementary school mathematics textbooks we encounter (in the first sections of the book) work pages designed to build the concept that the matching of the elements of any two finite sets A and B produces one of three results:

1. The elements of A match the elements of B one to one; hence, the sets have the same cardinal number; or
2. One or more elements in B remain unmatched; hence, A contains fewer members than B; or
3. One or more elements in A remain unmatched; hence, B contains fewer members than A.

If $n(A) = a$ and $n(B) = b$, then the first result states that $a = b$. The following definition states the relationship in results 2 and 3.

> If $n(A) = a$ and $n(B) = b$, where A and B are finite sets, then a *is less than* b, written $a < b$, if A matches one to one a proper subset of B. If a is less than b, we can also say that b *is greater than* a and write $b > a$. The sentences $a < b$ and $b > a$ are called *inequalities*.

A very important relation on any two elements of W is the following:

> *Law of Trichotomy.* If a and b are any two whole numbers, then one and only one of the following relations is true: $a = b$, $a < b$, or $b < a$.

Of the three relations, only the equality relation is an equivalence relation since

1. For any whole number $a = a$ (reflexive property).
2. If a and b are whole numbers such that $a = b$, then $b = a$ (symmetric property).
3. If a, b, and c are whole numbers such that $a = b$ and $b = c$, then $a = c$ (transitive property).

It can be shown rather easily that the less than and greater than relations are transitive relations only. Figure 4-9 indicates why these relations are transitive.

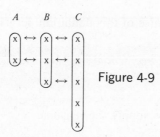

Figure 4-9

The definition given for the order relations of less than and greater than are sound pedagogically because the definitions allow for the child to manipulate objects to compare two sets. If a child is not sure that 5 is greater than 3, he can manipulate a set of 5 objects and a set of 3 objects and compare the sets to see which cardinal number is greater. However, the set definition is somewhat cumbersome when

145

a mathematician utilizes inequalities in the proof of a mathematical theorem. For that reason we have a somewhat more abstract definition of the less than (greater than) relation, which is indeed easier to use.

If a and b are whole numbers, *a is less than b*, written $a < b$ if there exists a nonzero whole number n so that $a + n = b$. To say that $a = b$ or $a < b$ write "$a \leq b$."

To illustrate this definition, we know that $3 < 8$ since there exists a nonzero whole number 5 so that $3 + 5 = 8$. A physical interpretation can be given to this definition by observing a scale where a 3-pound weight is put on one side of the scale and an 8-pound weight is placed on the other (Figure 4-10). By placing a 5-pound weight with the 3-pound weight, a balance is attained (Figure 4-11). This is one more activity that lends itself to a laboratory approach. Metric weights may be used to emphasize the metric system.

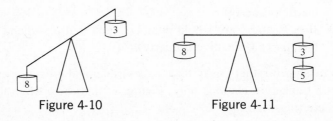

Figure 4-10   Figure 4-11

To illustrate the use of this definition, let us show that

If a, b, and c are whole numbers and $a < b$, then $a + c < b + c$.

You are asked to supply the reasons:

Steps	Reasons
1. $a < b$	1. Given.
2. $a + n = b$	2. Why?
3. $(a + n) + c = b + c$	3. Why?
4. $a + (n + c) = b + c$	4. Why?
5. $a + (c + n) = b + c$	5. Why?
6. $(a + c) + n = b + c$	6. Why?
7. $\therefore a + c < b + c$	7. Why?

For the children, we may illustrate the property by using a number-line approach. We begin by stating that if $a < b$ then a lies *to the left* of b on the number line. For example, on the number line of Figure 4-12, $2 < 5$. Hence, 2 is to the left of 5 on the number line. If we

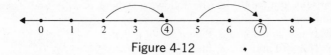

Figure 4-12

were to add 2 to 2 and then add 2 to 5, would $2 + 2$ still be to the left of $2 + 5$ on the number line? In other words, would we have preserved the order of the inequality by adding the same number? Figure 4-12 shows this to be true. The same theorem can be demonstrated very nicely by using weights and a scale as we did earlier.

If we can add the same whole number to both sides of our inequality and still preserve the order of the inequality, can we then multiply both sides of an inequality by the same whole number and still preserve order? At first glance, you might be tempted to say yes; however, we should always consider the whole number 0 when making conjectures. If there is to be an exception, 0 will probably be the exception. To show that this is an exception, we need only to show that $3 < 5$, yet $3 \cdot 0 \not< 5 \cdot 0$; that is, $3 \cdot 0$ *is not less* than $5 \cdot 0$. If we modify our hypotheses slightly, we can prove the following:

> If a, b, and c are whole numbers, $c \neq 0$ and $a < b$, then $a \cdot c < b \cdot c$.

EXERCISES (Section 4.5)

1. Suppose that A and B are finite sets and $A \subset B$. How would you convince a child that $n(A) < n(B)$?
2. What is wrong with the assertion that $A < B$, where A and B are sets?
3. List the members of each of the following sets:
   a. $\{x : x \in W \text{ and } x < 6\}$
   b. $\{x : x \in W \text{ and } x < 3\}$
   c. $\{x : x \in W \text{ and } x < 4\}$
   d. $\{x : x \in W \text{ and } x < 5\}$
   e. $\{x : x \in W \text{ where } x < 6 \text{ and } x > 3\}$
   f. $\{x : x \in W \text{ where } x < 7 \text{ and } x > 5\}$
   g. $\{x : x \in W \text{ where } x < 0\}$
   h. $\{x : x \in W \text{ where } x < 8 \text{ and } x > 7\}$

4. Suppose that you earn more money than Bill, and Pete earns more money than you. What conclusion can you make regarding Bill and Pete's earnings?

5. If you go to Las Vegas to gamble, which property guarantees that you will win, lose, or break even?

6. Present arguments for the following, where a, b, c, and d are whole numbers.
   a. If $a < b$ and $c < d$, then $a + c < b + d$.
   b. If $a < b$ and $c < d$, then $a \cdot c < b \cdot d$.

4.6

SUBTRACTION AND DIVISION OF WHOLE NUMBERS

The processes of subtraction and division have a very definite limitation when defined upon the set of whole numbers. In subtraction the problem arises when we try to match some whole number n with the ordered pair of whole numbers (a, b), where $b > a$. This is equivalent to the problem of trying to solve the equation $3 - 5 = n$, where n must be a whole number. It is impossible to find such a whole number; hence, the operation is not performable on W. We have then basically two choices:

1. We may expand the set of whole numbers to a more inclusive set within which subtraction is performable; or
2. We may define subtraction in such a way that the operation is performable on select ordered pairs of $W \times W$.

In this chapter the second choice is preferred. In Chapter 5 the first choice will be employed. As with the operations of addition and multiplication, we shall use a set approach to define the operation of subtraction. We begin by defining the following set operation:

> If A and B are sets, then the *separation* of A and B, denoted by $A - B$, is the set of all elements that belong to A but do *not* belong to B.

If $A = \{$first 10 whole numbers$\}$ and $B = \{$first 5 even numbers$\}$, then $A - B = \{$first 5 odd numbers$\}$. Also, if $C = \{$professors in the

United States} and D = {women in the United States}, then $C - D$ = {male professors in the United States}. The Venn diagrams of Figures 4-13 and 4-14 illustrate these examples. You should convince yourself that, in general, $A - B \neq B - A$. That is, the set separation is not commutative.

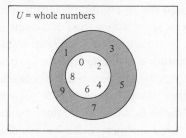
Figure 4-13

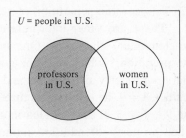
Figure 4-14

We now define subtraction.

If $n(A) = a$ and $n(B) = b$ with $B \subseteq A$, then $a - b = n(A - B)$. Again we assume that A and B are finite sets.

A number of observations are in order:

1. By using a cardinal number approach to subtraction we have restricted the set upon which we have defined the operation of subtraction to a subset of the whole numbers.
2. The definition given is a restricted definition, since we are considering only finite sets such that one set B is a subset of the other set A. A little reflection reveals that this ensures that $b \leq a$. This eliminates our $3 - 5 = n$ concern.

Let us see how children use set separation to learn the basic concepts of subtraction. The classroom exercise may begin by having the teacher choose three boys and two girls to represent set A. Notice that the set of three boys is a subset of A and the set of two girls is a subset of A. The five children are asked to stand with the teacher in front of the class.

"How many children do we have in our set?"   (five)
"How many children are boys?"   (three)
"Will the set of boys please return to their seats?"

149

"How many children are left standing in front?"   (two)
"Can anyone write a sentence showing that five minus three
   equals two?"

The activity may then continue with the children working with concrete objects at their seats or in small groups to illustrate the relationship between the separation of sets and the operation of subtraction.
There are other interpretations of subtraction that are used in
the elementary classroom. One such approach is the Family of Facts
interpretation,* which uses the commutative property and the inverse
relation property of addition and subtraction. Once the child learns
that $6 + 3 = 9$, he also knows three other "facts": $3 + 6 = 9$, $9 - 3 = 6$,
and $9 - 6 = 3$. If the child learns the initial fact $3 + 6 = 9$, then, by the
order property of addition (commutative property), he knows that
$6 + 3 = 9$. Also, since subtraction "undoes" what addition "does,"
that is, addition and subtraction are *inverse operations*, the child knows
that $9 - 3 = 6$ and $9 - 6 = 3$. When this approach is used in the classroom, basic subtraction facts are not taught as something to be learned
independent of the addition facts.
Addition and subtraction are called *inverse operations*, because
$a + b = c$ implies that $c - a = b$. Also, if $c \geq a$, then $c - a = b$ implies
that $a + b = c$. To solve the problem $15 - 9 = n$, we may solve the related problem $n + 9 = 15$. We are given the sum 15 and the addend 9,
and are asked to find the missing addend n.
Since we restricted the operation of subtraction to a particular
subset of $W \times W$, W is *not closed* under subtraction. For example,
$3 - 5$ cannot be performed within W. Since $6 - 4 \neq 4 - 6$, W is *not
commutative* under subtraction. Also, $6 - (4 - 2) \neq (6 - 4) - 2$; therefore, we do *not* have associativity for W under subtraction.
We began this section by stating that the processes of subtraction
and division have definite limitations. We have seen the difficulties
involved with the use of subtraction. The same difficulties arise with
the use of division. The operation of division is not always performable
on W. Again we have the same choices as we had with subtraction:

1. We may expand the set of whole numbers to a more inclusive
   set within which division is performable; or
2. We may define division in such a way that the operation is
   performable on select ordered pairs of $W \times W$.

* See E. R. Duncan et al., *Modern School Mathematics: Structure and Use* (Boston:
Houghton Mifflin Company, 1972).

As with subtraction, we shall restrict our definition of division in such a way that division is performable on a proper subset of $W \times W$. In Chapter 7 we shall extend our set of numbers to a more inclusive set so that *nonzero division* will always be possible.

We shall deviate slightly from our previous methods of defining addition, multiplication, and subtraction. In each of these definitions we used a set operation approach. For the operation of division we shall use an inverse operation approach.

> If a and b are whole numbers, $b \neq 0$, then $a \div b = n$, where n is a whole number such that $b \times n = a$. If no such whole number n exists, the operation of division is not performable on W.

We see that this is a Family of Facts interpretation for division, with the exception that division by a zero factor is not permissible. For example, if we know that $3 \times 5 = 15$, we also know that $15 \div 3$ and $15 \div 5$ have meaning and are, respectively, 5 and 3. If one of the factors in our Family of Facts is 0, we must be careful. For example, we know that $0 \times 6 = 0$. Hence, $6 \times 0 = 0$ and $0 \div 6 = 0$. However, $6 \div 0$ is meaningless. We illustrate this in the following manner. For $6 \div 0$ to have meaning, by definition there must be some whole number n such that $0 \times n = 6$. But this is impossible, because we know by the zero multiplication property that any whole number times 0 is 0. Hence, $6 \div 0$ is meaningless. In other words, there is no whole number c that can be assigned to the ordered pair $(6, 0)$ under the operation called division. This is a violation of our second requirement for a binary operation as given on page 132. The operation is not performable.

A word of caution is in order here. Many teachers get caught in the trap of defining $0 \div 0$ to be equal to 0 since $0 \times 0 = 0$. We point out that we can just as well define $0 \div 0$ to be 1, 2, 3, and so forth, since $0 \times n = 0$ for any whole number n. Because of this ambiguity, and the remark above, we simply agree that division by 0 is not permissible in W. In this case we are violating the third requirement for a binary operation. That is, the result is not unique; hence, the operation is not well defined.

As you might expect, W is neither closed, commutative, nor associative under the operation of division. You should be able to construct the appropriate counterexamples.

The operation of multiplication distributes over subtraction, provided the operation of subtraction is performable in W. For example

$$5 \times (12 - 2) = (5 \times 12) - (5 \times 2)$$
$$= 60 - 10$$
$$= 50$$

In summary, then:

Given the set of whole numbers with the binary operations of subtraction and division defined as follows:

$a - b = n(A - B)$ where $n(A) = a$ and $n(B) = b$

with $B \subseteq A$

$a \div b = c$, where $b \neq 0$ and $c \in W$ such that

$b \times c = a$, then

1. W is *not closed* under the operations of subtraction and division.
2. W is *not commutative* under the operations of subtraction and division.
3. W is *not associative* under the operations of subtraction and division.
4. *Multiplication is distributive over subtraction*; that is,

    $a \times (b - c) = (a \times b) - (a \times c)$,

    where $a, b, c \in W$

5. Subtraction is the *inverse operation* of addition.
6. Division is the *inverse operation* of multiplication.

EXERCISES (Section 4.6)

1. List the members of $A - B$ and $B - A$.
   a. $A = \{a, b, c, d, e\}$, $B = \{d, e, f\}$
   b. $A = \{1, 2\}$, $B = \{2, 3, 4, 5\}$
   c. $A = \{1, 2\}$, $B = \{1, 2\}$
   d. $A = \{1, 2, 3, 4\}$, $B = \{2, 3\}$
2. Draw Venn diagrams to represent $A - B$ and $B - A$ in Exercise 1.
3. Show that $7 - 3 = 4$ by using
   a. A number line approach.

b. A set definition.

c. An inverse operation definition.

4. Is it true that if $a < b$ and $c < d$, then $a - c < b - d$? Explain.

5. Is it true that if $a < b$ and $c < d$, then $a \div c < b \div d$? Explain.

6. Does division distribute over addition? Over subtraction? Explain.

7. Show that $a > b$ is equivalent to $a - b > 0$.

8. Suppose that a and b are whole numbers and $a - b = b - a$. What do you know about a and b?

9. Suppose that a and b are whole numbers and $a \div b = b \div a$. What do you know about a and b?

10. Suppose that a, b, and c are whole numbers and $a - (b - c) = (a - b) - c$. What do you know about a, b, and c?

11. Suppose that a, b, and c are whole numbers. Is it possible that $a \div (b \div c) = (a \div b) \div c$? Explain.

4.7

THE FUNDAMENTAL ALGORITHMS OF ARITHMETIC

An algorithm is a systematic procedure for performing a mathematical operation such as addition, subtraction, multiplication, or division. You recall that we defined an operation on W to be a function that related a single number from W to each pair of numbers from $W \times W$. In working with the operation of addition, the number $3 + 6$ was assigned to the number pair (3, 6). If the number pair consisted only of numbers written as single digits, we used the table of basic facts to assign the number name 9 to the sum $3 + 6$. A similar situation was true for each of the other operations. The question arises: What do we do when we have pairs of numbers written as multiple-digit numerals, such as (37, 16)? Once again, the number $37 + 16$ is assigned to this pair under the operation of addition. If necessary, we can count from 37 until we reach the desired answer of 53, or we can build a more extensive table of facts so that $37 + 16$ will be memorized to be 53. As you might expect, man has developed computational shortcuts that allow us to circumvent, whenever possible, these tedious methods for computing. These shortcuts generally take the form of an algorithm. The rationale behind most algorithms is based upon a knowledge of place-value numeration, of the properties of the system of whole numbers, and of the basic facts. The choice of the algorithms that we teach today is dependent upon the desired outcome of instruction. Generally, in the initial stages of concept development, longer algorithms are used to bridge the intermediate stages in the concept development. Later, shorter methods are used to improve speed in computation.* The following examples illustrate three algorithms used at different stages in the development of the standard addition algorithm.

Expanded notation method	Step method	Short method
$25 = 20 + 5$ $+\ 32 = 30 + 2$ $50 + 7 = 57$	25 $+\ 32$ 7 $+\ 50$ 57	25 $+\ 32$ 57

In this section we shall develop various algorithms for each of the fundamental operations. Our objective is to provide you with a basic understanding of the standard algorithms for each of the fundamental operations and to provide you with a source of algorithms that may be used for different educational outcomes. Two important points should be noted regarding the algorithms we develop for each operation:

1. The derivation of an algorithm and the algorithm itself should not be confused. The derivation of the algorithm tells us *why* the algorithm works. If the children had to go through the derivation of the algorithm each time they needed to use the algorithm, we would have a sorry state of affairs.
2. These derivations depend only upon place-value numeration and the system of whole numbers. Hence, each derivation holds regardless of the place-value numerals used in the algorithm. For example, if we are using base five numerals in our algorithm, the derivation of the algorithm is exactly the same as the derivation used with decimal numerals.

---

* For an excellent discussion of algorithms, see W. G. Quast, "Method or Justification," *Arithmetic Teacher*, **19** (Dec. 1972), 617–622.

ADDITION

We begin by deriving the standard addition algorithm for addends written with two digits with no renaming of ones as tens. We then derive the same standard algorithm with renaming of ones as tens.

Example 1 $a = 32 + 55$

Steps	Reasons
1. $a = (3 \times 10 + 2 \times 1)$ $+ (5 \times 10 + 5 \times 1)$	1. Place-value numeration
2. $= (3 \times 10) + [(2 \times 1)$ $+ (5 \times 10 + 5 \times 1)]$	2. Associative property of $+$
3. $= (3 \times 10) + [(5 \times 10 + 5 \times 1)$ $+ (2 \times 1)]$	3. Commutative property of $+$
4. $= (3 \times 10 + 5 \times 10)$ $+ (5 \times 1 + 2 \times 1)$	4. Associative property of $+$
5. $= (3 + 5) \times 10 + (5 + 2) \times 1$	5. Distributive property of $\times$
6. $= (8 \times 10) + (7 \times 1)$	6. Basic facts
7. $= 87$	7. Place-value numeration
8. $\therefore a = 87$	8. Transitive property of $=$

Example 2 $b = 19 + 43$

Steps	Reasons
1. $b = (1 \times 10 + 9 \times 1)$ $+ (4 \times 10 + 3 \times 1)$	1. Place-value numeration
2. $= (1 \times 10) + [(9 \times 1)$ $+ (4 \times 10 + 3 \times 1)]$	2. Associative property of $+$
3. $= (1 \times 10) + [(4 \times 10 + 3 \times 1)$ $+ (9 \times 1)]$	3. Commutative property of $+$
4. $= (1 \times 10 + 4 \times 10)$ $+ (3 \times 1 + 9 \times 1)$	4. Associative property of $+$
5. $= (1 + 4) \times 10 + (3 + 9) \times 1$	5. Distributive property of $\times$
6. $= (5 \times 10) + (12 \times 1)$	6. Basic facts
7. $= (5 \times 10) + (1 \times 10 + 2 \times 1) \times 1$	7. Place-value numeration
8. $= (5 \times 10) + (1 \times 10 + 2 \times 1)$	8. Identity property for $\times$
9. $= [(5 \times 10) + (1 \times 10)] + (2 \times 1)$	9. Associative property for $+$
10. $= (5 + 1) \times 10 + (2 \times 1)$	10. Distributive property
11. $= (6 \times 10) + (2 \times 1)$	11. Basic facts
12. $= 62$	12. Place-value numeration
13. $\therefore b = 62$	13. Transitive property of $=$

155

These examples are derivations of the standard addition algorithms

$$\begin{array}{r} 32 \\ +\ 55 \\ \hline 87 \end{array} \quad \text{and} \quad \begin{array}{r} 19 \\ +\ 43 \\ \hline 62 \end{array}$$

We mentioned earlier that there are several algorithms that can be used for addition and that the choice of a particular algorithm depends upon the desired outcome of instruction. Manipulative devices are quite frequently used in the initial stages of instruction to aid in concept development. One such device is the *open-ended abacus*.

Example 3 $a = 32 + 55$

1. Place 2 beads on the ones' rod and place 3 beads on the tens' rod (Figure 4-15).

1.

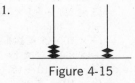

Figure 4-15

2. Place 5 beads on the ones' rod and 5 beads on the tens' rod (Figure 4-16).

2.

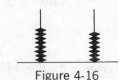

Figure 4-16

3. Count the number of beads on each rod.

3. 7 ones beads and 8 tens beads.

4. Use place-value numeration properties to name the number.

4. $a = 8$ tens $+ 7$ ones
$= 87$

Example 4 $b = 19 + 43$

1. Place 9 beads on the ones' rod and 1 bead on the tens' rod (Figure 4-17).

1.

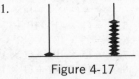

Figure 4-17

2. Place 1 bead on the ones' rod; this makes 10 ones' beads, which are "traded" for 1 tens' bead (Figure 4-18).

2.

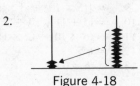

Figure 4-18

3. Place the remaining 2 ones' beads on the ones' rod, and the 4 tens' beads on the tens' rod (Figure 4-19).

3.

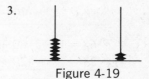

Figure 4-19

4. Count the number of beads on each rod.

4. 2 ones beads and 6 tens beads.

5. Use place-value numeration to name the number.

5. $b = 6$ tens $+ 2$ ones
$= 62$

A last manipulative device that can be used in the teaching of nondecimal and decimal computation is a *slide rule*. This device can easily be made by the student. The slide rule illustrated in Figure 4-20 is a base five slide rule, constructed by numbering two strips of paper. A decimal slide rule may be constructed in a similar manner. We use the slide rule shown in Figure 4-20 to find the *sum* $2_{five} + 14_{five}$.

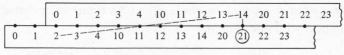

Figure 4-20

Example 5 $c = 2_{five} + 14_{five}$

1. Position the top strip of paper in such a way that the zero is aligned above the addend 2.
2. Find the addend 14_{five} on the top number line.
3. Read the sum 21_{five}, which is on the lower number line directly below 14_{five}.

SUBTRACTION

Once again, we begin with the derivation of the standard subtraction algorithm, but this time we derive only the standard algorithm for the difference of two-digit numerals with no renaming of tens as ones. Before we begin, let us use an example to point out a possible area of difficulty in the teaching of the algorithm.

Many elementary series use the *expanded notation algorithm* in teaching of subtraction:

Step 1	*Step 2*		*Step 3*	*Step 4*
$68 =$	$60 + 8$	$=$	$60 + 8$	
$-23 =$	$-(20 + 3)$	$=$	$-20 - 3$	
			$40 + 5$	$= 45$

Little or no explanation is given for the transition from step 2 to step 3. Generally the teacher justifies this transition by saying that subtracting $20 + 3$ is the same as subtracting 3 and then subtracting 20; hence, we write $-20 - 3$. We then subtract ones and tens. This seems reasonable to most children; consequently, there is little cause for concern on the teacher's part for this explanation. There are students, however, who realize that the reason given is pedagogical not mathematical. Whether we like it or not, mathematical proofs involve mathematical, not pedagogical, justification. For this reason we take time to prove to you that

$$(60 + 8) - (20 + 3) = (60 - 20) + (8 - 3)$$

It is not our intention to confuse you but rather to be mathematically honest with you. The proof is as follows:

Steps	Reasons
1. Let $r = 60 - 20$ and $p = 8 - 3$	1. By definition
2. Then $60 = r + 20$ and $8 = p + 3$	2. $+$ and $-$ are inverse operations
3. $60 + 8 = r + 20 + p + 3$	3. Definition of $+$
4. $\qquad = (20 + 3) + (r + p)$	4. Associative and commutative properties of $+$
5. $(60 + 8) - (20 + 3) = r + p$	5. $+$ and $-$ are inverse operations
6. But $r + p = (60 - 20) + (8 - 3)$	6. Definition of $+$ and step 1
7. $\therefore (60 + 8) - (20 + 3) = (60 - 20) + (8 - 3)$	7. Transitive property of $=$

As you can see, the crux of the proof depends upon the property that addition and subtraction are inverse operations. We now use the preceding theorem in deriving the standard algorithm.

Example 1 $n = 68 - 23$

Steps	Reasons
1. $n = (60 + 8) - (20 + 3)$	1. Place-value numeration
2. $\quad = (60 - 20) + (8 - 3)$	2. Theorem just proved

3. $= (6 \times 10 - 2 \times 10)$
    $+ (8 \times 1 - 3 \times 1)$ 3. Place-value numeration
4. $= (6 - 2) \times 10 + (8 - 3) \times 1$ 4. Distributive property of $\times$
5. $= (4 \times 10) + (5 \times 1)$ 5. Basic facts
6. $= 45$ 6. Place-value numeration
7. $\therefore n = 45$ 7. Transitive property of $=$

There is a method of subtraction that first appeared about 1300 A.D. *The Columbia algorithm* begins the subtraction process at the left. The following steps illustrate the use of this algorithm.

Example 2 $n = 7,689 - 4,792$

1. 3
    7̸689
    4̸792   1. 4 from 7 leaves 3.

2. 2
    3̸9
    7̸6̸89
    4̸792   2. 7 from 36 leaves 29.

3. 28
    3̸9̸9
    7̸6̸8̸9
    4̸7̸92   3. 9 from 98 leaves 89.

4. 28
    3̸9̸97
    7̸6̸8̸9
    4̸7̸9̸2̸   4. 2 from 9 leaves 7.

The answer is 2,897.

The open-ended abacus and the slide rule are again applicable for algorithmic use. Each is demonstrated in the following examples.

Example 3 $p = 43 - 16$

1. Place 3 beads on the ones' rod and 4 beads on the tens' rod (Figure 4-21).

1.

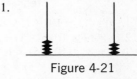

Figure 4-21

2. "Trade" 1 tens' bead for 10 ones' beads and place the 10 ones' beads on the extended ones' rod (Figure 4-22).

2.

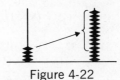

Figure 4-22

3. Remove 6 ones' beads and 1 tens' bead from the abacus (Figure 4-23).

3.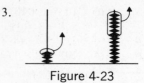

Figure 4-23

4. Count the number of ones' beads and the number of tens' beads.
5. Use place-value numeration to name the number.

4. 2 tens' beads and 7 ones' beads
5. $p = 2$ tens $+ 7$ ones
   $= 27$

Example 4 $r = 14_{seven} - 6_{seven}$

1. Position the top strip of paper in such a way that the given addend is aligned above the sum 14_{seven} (see Figure 4-24).

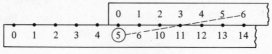

Figure 4-24

2. Find the zero on the top number line.
3. Read the missing addend, 5_{seven}, which is on the lower number line directly below 0.

MULTIPLICATION

It was explained earlier that the standard multiplication algorithm for factors written with two digits involves extensive use of the distributive property of multiplication over addition. Let us see how this principle is used in the derivation of the standard algorithm.

Example 1 $n = 35 \times 5$

Steps	Reasons
1. $n = [(3 \times 10) + (5 \times 1)] \times (5 \times 1)$	1. Place-value numeration
2. $= (3 \times 10)(5 \times 1) + (5 \times 1)(5 \times 1)$	2. Distributive property
3. $= 3 \times (10 \times 5) \times 1$ $ + 5 \times (1 \times 5) \times 1$	3. Associative property of $\times$
4. $= 3 \times (5 \times 10) \times 1$ $ + 5 \times (5 \times 1) \times 1$	4. Commutative property of $\times$
5. $= (3 \times 5) \times (10 \times 1)$ $ + (5 \times 5) \times (1 \times 1)$	5. Associative property of $\times$
6. $= 15 \times 10 + 25 \times 1$	6. Basic facts and identity property

160

7.	$= 15 \times 10 + [(2 \times 10)$ $+ (5 \times 1)] \times 1$	7. Place-value numeration
8.	$= 15 \times 10 + [(2 \times 10 \times 1)$ $+ (5 \times 1 \times 1)]$	8. Distributive property
9.	$= 15 \times 10 + [(2 \times 10)$ $+ (5 \times 1)]$	9. Identity property
10.	$= [(15 \times 10) + (2 \times 10)]$ $+ (5 \times 1)$	10. Associative property of $\times$
11.	$= (15 + 2) \times 10 + (5 \times 1)$	11. Distributive property
12.	$= (17 \times 10) + (5 \times 1)$	12. Basic facts of $+$
13.	$= 175$	13. Place-value numeration
14.	$\therefore n = 175$	14. Transitive property of $=$

Example 1 is a derivation of the standard algorithms.

Step method		*Short method*
35		^{2}35
$\times\ \ 5$		$\times\ \ 5$
25	and	175
$+\ 150$		
175		

Gelosia multiplication (so named because of its resemblance to a window grating of that name) first appeared in 1478 and is still being used in some elementary series today.*

Example 2 $r = 72 \times 23$

1.

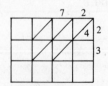

Figure 4-25

1. $2 \times 2 = 4$; write the 4 in the frame as shown in Figure 4-25.

2.

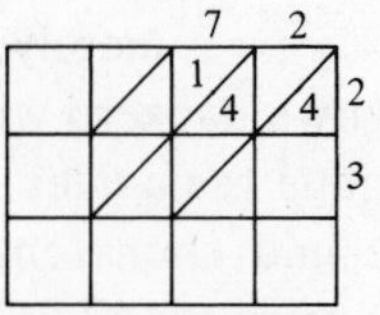

Figure 4-26

2. $2 \times 7 = 14$; write the 14 in the frame as shown in Figure 4-26.

* See Duncan et al., *op. cit.*, Book 6.

3.

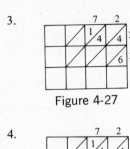

Figure 4-27

3. $3 \times 2 = 6$; write the 6 in the frame as shown in Figure 4-27.

4.

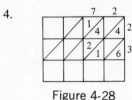

Figure 4-28

4. $3 \times 7 = 21$; write the 21 in the frame as shown in Figure 4-28.

5.

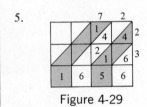

Figure 4-29

5. Add along the diagonals to obtain the answer 1,656, as in Figure 4-29.

DIVISION

There is a theorem in mathematics that states a rather basic relationship between two whole numbers a and b.

> *Division Algorithm.* If a and b are two whole numbers with $b \neq 0$, then there is one and only one pair of whole numbers q and r such that $0 \leq r < b$ and $a = b \times q + r$.

You will notice that the relationship $a = b \times q + r$ is merely the statement that when we divide a whole number a by a nonzero whole number b we get a unique quotient q and a unique remainder r. The algorithms that we are about to describe depend upon renaming the number a so that we can use the distributive property of division over addition to find the quotient q and the remainder r.

Example 1 $5,631 \div 13$ **Example 2** $5,631 \div 13$

```
              3
             30
            400
        13)5,631
          5,200
            431
            390
             41
             39
              2
```

```
        13)5,631
           2,600 | 200
           3,031
           2,600 | 200
             431
             390 |  30
              41
              39 |   3
               2 | 433
```

Notice that in each case we reduced the dividend to a sum of multiples of 13 plus a remainder. In Example 1 we wrote $5,631 = 5,200 + 390 + 39 + 2$, and in Example 2 we wrote $5,631 = 2,600 + 2,600 + 390 + 39 + 2$. In Example 2 we worry less about the estimates for partial quotients than we do in Example 1. The algorithm for Example 2 is generally longer than the algorithm for Example 1; however, the problem of estimating partial quotients is greatly reduced. The method given in Example 1 is what we shall call the *standard algorithm*. The method in Example 2 is called the *scaffold method*.

Flow charts describing each algorithm are given in Figure 4-30 and 4-31 on page 164.

EXERCISES (Section 4.7)

1. Use the expanded method of addition to find each sum.

    a.   33   b.   41   c.   63   d.   115
       + 16   + 32   + 87   + 496

2. Use the step method of addition to find each sum.

    a.   16   b.   29   c.   114   d.   233
       + 12   + 36   + 297   + 521

3. Illustrate the following by means of pictures of an open-ended abacus.

    a.   23   b.   47   c.   96   d.   43
       + 31   + 36   - 32   - 28

4. Use the Columbia algorithm to find each difference.

    a.   343   b.   417   c.   5,680   d.   6,377
       - 167   - 298   - 2,749   - 2,689

163

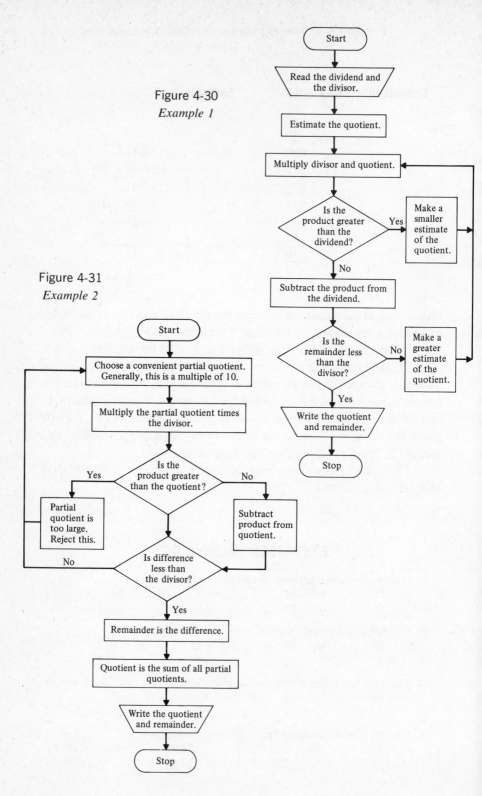

Figure 4-30
Example 1

Start

Read the dividend and the divisor.

Estimate the quotient.

Multiply divisor and quotient.

Is the product greater than the dividend?

Yes → Make a smaller estimate of the quotient.

No

Subtract the product from the dividend.

Is the remainder less than the divisor?

No → Make a greater estimate of the quotient.

Yes

Write the quotient and remainder.

Stop

Figure 4-31
Example 2

Start

Choose a convenient partial quotient. Generally, this is a multiple of 10.

Multiply the partial quotient times the divisor.

Is the product greater than the quotient?

Yes → Partial quotient is too large. Reject this.

No → Subtract product from quotient.

Is difference less than the divisor?

No

Yes

Remainder is the difference.

Quotient is the sum of all partial quotients.

Write the quotient and remainder.

Stop

5. Use the step method of multiplication to find each product.

    a. 16×8 b. 25×12 c. 153×6 d. 113×27

6. Use the Gelosia method to find each product.

    a. 27×9 b. 85×5 c. 83×13 d. 125×62

7. Use the division algorithm and the standard division algorithm to find the missing variable in the following:

    a. $58 = 7 \times q + r$ d. $639 = 15 \times q + r$
    b. $84 = 12 \times b + r$ e. $4{,}903 = 16 \times b + r$
    c. $a = 9 \times 18 + 6$ f. $8{,}611 = 306 \times q + r$

8. Express the results of the following in the form $a = b \times q + r$.

    a. $18 \div 4$ c. $108 \div 19$ e. $67 \div 108$
    b. $27 \div 11$ d. $225 \div 173$ f. $0 \div 9$

9. Name the possibilities for the remainder r for the given divisors.

    a. 3   c. 11   e. 25
    b. 5   d. 20   f. 40

10. Rename the dividend in the following in the most convenient way for using the standard algorithm to perform the division.

    a. $33 \div 6$ c. $78 \div 12$ e. $456 \div 13$
    b. $96 \div 8$ d. $88 \div 14$ f. $696 \div 387$

11. Use the scaffold method to perform each division.

    a. $86 \div 7$ c. $236 \div 17$ e. $6{,}834 \div 426$
    b. $93 \div 8$ d. $493 \div 21$ f. $9{,}301 \div 637$

12. Find the sum or difference as indicated.

    a. $12_{seven} - 6_{seven}$ e. $TE_{twelve} + 35_{twelve}$
    b. $23_{five} + 11_{five}$ f. $73_{eight} - 57_{eight}$
    c. $11{,}101_{two} + 10{,}101_{two}$ g. $35_{six} + 14_{five}$
    d. $462_{eight} - 273_{eight}$ h. $47_{eight} - 2T_{twelve}$

Norbert Wiener

(1894–1964)

Algebra was never hard for me, although my father's way of teaching it was scarcely conducive to peace of mind. Every mistake had to be corrected as it was made. He would begin the discussion in an easy, conversational tone. This lasted exactly until I made the first mathematical mistake. Then the gentle and loving father was replaced by the avenger of the blood. The first warning

he gave me was a sharp and aspirated "What!" and if I did not follow this by coming to heel at once, he would admonish me "Now do this again!" By this time, I was weeping and terrified. My lessons often ended in a family scene. Father was raging, I was weeping and my mother did her best to defend me, although hers was a losing battle. There were times for many years when I was afraid that the unity of the family might not be able to stand these stresses . . . .

These words were written by Norbert Wiener, child prodigy, outstanding American mathematician and father of cybernetics—"the theory of communication and control, wherever it may be found, whether in the machine or in the living being."

Norbert Wiener was born in Columbia, Missouri, on November 26, 1894. His father was a Russian immigrant, a student and teacher of modern languages, and the tutor of his son in mathematics and the classics. His mother was the daughter of a Kansas City department store owner. Wiener's principal deficiency in elementary school was arithmetic. The following words, taken from Wiener's autobiography *Ex-Prodigy*, can be taken as a source of encouragement for many elementary school children and teachers alike:

As to arithmetic, I counted on my fingers and continued that long after it was regarded as unpermissible by the standards of my school classes. I was puzzled by such things as the axiom that *a* times *b* equals *b* times *a* . . . I was not particularly fast in learning my multiplication tables or, in fact, anything else that had to be learned by rote (pp. 45–46).

Wiener's father pulled him from school because manipulation drill bored the child of 7. Norbert was taught algebra instead of arithmetic to provide a greater challenge and stimulus to his imagination. He went to high school at 10, graduated from college at 14, earned his Ph.D. from Harvard at 18, and studied mathematics under Bertrand Russell and G. H. Hardy at Cambridge, England. Norbert Wiener returned to the Department of Mathematics at The Massachusetts Institute of Technology at 25 and served in this department until his death in March 1964. He was one of the earliest to recognize the potential of the digital computer and to develop the theory of communication science.

Chapter 5

The Integers

5.1

INTRODUCTION

In Chapter 4 you learned about the set of whole numbers and the operations of addition and multiplication on that set. Although the set of whole numbers is adequate for solving many of man's problems, the set has some deficiencies. If the whole numbers were the only numbers we had invented, there would be no easy way to discuss midwinter temperatures in Colorado, no simple way to handle indebtedness or loss of yardage on the gridiron, and no convenient way to discuss other phenomena that require a concept of positive and negative numbers. The set of integers will provide such a concept.

There are other deficiencies of the set of whole numbers. For example, there is no whole number that makes the sentence "$7 + x = 3$" a true statement. Furthermore, the set of whole numbers is not closed with respect to subtraction, as the example "$6 - 9 = \bigcirc$" shows. Finally, only the zero has an additive inverse in the whole numbers, whereas every integer has an additive inverse; that is, there is an integer such that $5 + y = 0$ has a solution.

The set of integers is to be developed in this chapter, and you should find that all the deficiencies mentioned for the set of whole numbers are adequately met in the new system. As we near the end of the chapter you will see that the set of integers also has some deficiencies so that the invention of another number system will be needed.

You may already have considerable knowledge of the set of integers as the set of numbers in the set $\{\ldots, ^-3, ^-2, ^-1, 0, 1, 2, 3, \ldots\}$. If so, you may wonder what the purpose of the first sections of this chapter may be, for in these sections we shall develop the integers as if you knew only the set of whole numbers. Our point is that you should know at least one or two ways to construct the integers so that you may be able to diagnose the difficulties your own students have as they learn these concepts for the first time. You may also learn that there are sequential concepts in this development that dictate the order in which they must be taught. So, for the time being, pretend that you know the system of whole numbers but know nothing of the set of integers.

5.2

THE INTEGERS

You have seen that the set of whole numbers can be simply represented by means of a number line such as that of Figure 5-1. You

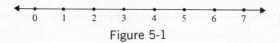

Figure 5-1

have also seen that there is no whole number that makes the following sentence true: $5 + w = 0$. Let us *invent* a new number that we shall call the *opposite of 5*, using the symbol "$^-5$," which has the property that $5 + {}^-5 = 0$. Where would you find a good representation for the opposite of 5, $^-5$, on the number line? Why not extend our representation of the number line to include points to the *left* of zero so that all these opposites are represented there? It would look as shown in Figure 5-2.

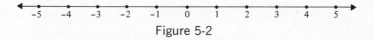

Figure 5-2

Note that the opposite of five is represented by a point that is five units left of the zero point. This extension of the number line to include opposites is not completely unreasonable to young children since many children are taught in grade one that a line "goes on and on." Several children have been known to ask teachers, "What lies to the left of zero on the number line?" Such a question is highly desirable, for it shows that the child is thinking about the nature of a line as well as the ideas behind association of numbers with points.

This seems to be a reasonable invention of a new kind of number, so let us make a formal definition.

> If a is a whole number, the *opposite of a* is the number symbolized by ^-a and having the property that $a + ^-a = 0$.
>
> The set of numbers formed by the union of the set of whole numbers and the set of opposites of whole numbers is called the *set of integers*.
>
> The set of nonzero whole numbers is called the set of *positive integers*, and the set of opposites of the nonzero whole numbers is called the set of *negative integers*. Zero is neither positive nor negative.

We shall require the operation of addition of integers to be commutative, so it will follow that $5 + ^-5 = 0 = ^-5 + 5$. From this can you determine what the opposite of $^-5$ might be? With the idea that the *opposite of a* is that number which when added to a gives 0, then it must be that the opposite of $^-5$ is 5, because $^-5 + 5 = 0$. This means that not only do the positive integers (whole numbers) have opposites, but also the negative integers have opposites. In fact, you have just noticed that the opposite of a negative integer is a positive integer, whereas the opposite of a positive integer is a negative integer. Of course, the opposite of zero is zero, because $0 + 0 = 0$. A number line may help you to visualize these ideas (see Figure 5-3).

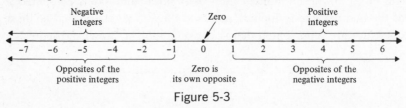

Figure 5-3

You should also notice that the opposite of the opposite of an integer is that integer. Since $^-5 + 5 = 0$, then the integer 5 must be the opposite of the opposite of 5 (Figure 5-4). This concept can be stated in symbols like this:

$$^-(^-5) = 5$$

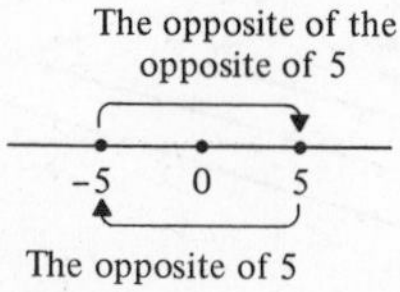

The opposite of the
opposite of 5

Figure 5-4

The opposite of 5

In general, for any integer a, $^-(^-a) = a$.

> The opposite of a positive integer is a negative integer, and the opposite of a negative integer is a positive integer. The opposite of zero is zero.
>
> For any integer a, $^-(^-a) = a$.

There is an element of confusion that we should pause to clarify at this point. First, there is no confusion that the negative integers are those numbers which we invented as the opposites of the nonzero whole numbers. Furthermore, there is no confusion about the fact that 17 is a positive integer and that $^-21$ is a negative integer. The confusion arises when someone asks "If x is an integer, is ^-x a negative integer or is ^-x a positive integer?" The answer you might be tempted to give is "^-x is negative"; but, if so, it indicates that the little symbol before the "x" is confusing you. If you read the expression, "^-x" as "the opposite of x," then perhaps you can see what the answer should be. "If x is an integer, then ^-x is a negative provided that x is positive, but ^-x is positive if x is negative." So, if x is 17, then x is positive and ^-x or $^-17$ is negative. But if x is $^-21$, then ^-x is $^-(^-21)$ or 21, which is positive. Therefore, to avoid this early source of confusion, try to remember to read "^-x" as "the opposite of x."

Figure 5-5 illustrates an interesting function that is related to the topic of opposites. The domain of the function is the set of integers as shown on the left, and the range of the function is the set of nonnegative integers (or whole numbers) as shown on the right. Notice that the image of any given positive integer is itself, and the image of any negative integer is its opposite. The image of zero is zero.

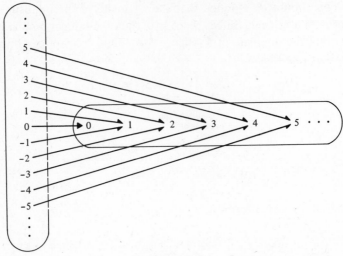

Figure 5-5

If the function shown in Figure 5-5 is described as a set of pairs, then it is the set

$$\{(0, 0), (1, 1), (^-1, 1), (2, 2), (^-2, 2), (3, 3), (^-3, 3), \ldots\}$$

The common name for this function is the *absolute value function*, or the function that yields the absolute values of the integers. The symbol "$|x|$" is used to name the absolute value of the integer x. You can see that $|4| = 4$, $|17| = 17$, $|^-21| = 21$, $|0| = 0$, $|^-42| = 42$, and so on. A formal definition of absolute value is given next, but you must be careful to recognize the use of the opposite of an integer.

> If x is an integer, the absolute value of x depends on whether x is positive or negative. If x is positive, the absolute value of x is x itself. If x is negative, the absolute value of x is the opposite of x. The absolute value of zero is zero.

Thus

$$|x| = \begin{cases} x, & \text{if } x \text{ is positive} \\ 0, & \text{if } x \text{ is zero} \\ ^-x, & \text{if } x \text{ is negative} \end{cases}$$

Notice that the absolute value of an integer is never a negative integer.

Another way of thinking about the absolute value of an integer is to consider the number of units from zero on a number line to the point that corresponds to the given integer. This helps to illustrate that $|17| = |{}^-17|$, $|{}^-8| = |8|$, and for any integer x you can see that $|x| = |{}^-x|$ (Figure 5-6).

> For any integer x, $|x| = |{}^-x|$.

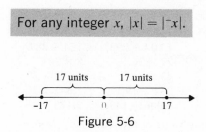

Figure 5-6

It is this concept of size or magnitude of an integer that creates a need for the concept of absolute value. Often we are concerned not so much with the direction of a number (that is, whether it is positive or negative) as we are with the size or absolute value of the number.

We close this section with one final remark concerning properties of the set of integers. The reasonableness of this property is also seen by thinking about a number line. Suppose that you are playing a game like pin-the-tail-on-the-donkey, except that the pin must land on some integer on the number line. Before you take off your blindfold, can you tell us something about the integer you have picked? See if you agree with the following statement.

> For every integer x, one and only one of the following is true:
>   i. x is positive.
>   ii. x is zero.
> iii. ^-x is positive.

This property, which is one feature of the integers that you can visualize from the number line, is called the *trichotomy property*, because it notes that there are three disjoint sets whose union is the set of integers. These three sets are the set of positive integers, the set of negative integers, and the set containing zero. On the number line, the property simply states that an integer is represented by exactly one point,

175

which is to the right of zero, the zero point, or to the left of the zero. There are no other possibilities.

EXERCISES (Section 5.2)

1. As a check on your skills with whole numbers use the following problems as a timed test. Can you do all these problems with no errors in 4 minutes?

   a. $16 + 24$, $65 - 32$, $17 + 96$

   b. $108 - 49$, $112 + 143$, $159 - 136$

   c. $1,009 + 243$, $1,104 - 293$, $124 + 887$

   d. 17×41, 27×36, 8×241

   e. 76×32, 43×84, $1,642 \times 37$

   f. $617 \div 17$, $874 \div 19$, $1,642 \div 37$

   g. $2,437 \div 9$, $2,006 \div 143$, $2,173 \div 26$

2. Find the absolute value of the following:

   a. 147   b. $^-32$ c. $^-16$ d. 4

3. Explain why 0 is not positive and why 0 is not negative.

4. What is the opposite of 0? Does this mean $0 = {}^-0$?

5. Give another name for the following integers.

   a. $^-(^-6)$ b. The opposite of 6

   c. The opposite of $^-3$ d. $^-|5|$ e. $^-|^-7|$

   f. Negative 4   g. $|^-(^-2)|$ h. $^-|^-(^-0)|$

6. If x is an integer, is x positive? Is ^-x positive? Is $^-(^-x)$ positive?

7. Why is the following not a reasonable sentence? The absolute value of the integer was $^-2$.

8. What is wrong with the following false statement?

   Every whole number is paired with two different integers in the absolute value function.

9. When we write "$^-4$," we do *not* mean "subtract 4." Why not?

5.3

ADDITION AND SUBTRACTION OF INTEGERS

Given any pair of integers, the sum of these integers can be quickly determined from your knowledge of the addition of whole numbers and from the definition of the opposite of an integer.

Since you are familiar with such sums as $6 + 9$, $12 + 4$, and $7 + 7$, we need consider only those cases in which negative integers are involved. What would be a reasonable conclusion for $^-6 + {}^-9$, $^-12 + {}^-4$, and $^-7 + {}^-7$? Several rational arguments could be given. One might be that since the sum of two debts is a greater debt, then $^-6 + {}^-9 = {}^-15$. Another argument might be that adding two negative integers ought to be nearly the same as adding two positive integers in the sense that the sum of objects of one kind is another object of that same kind. Thus, $^-12 + {}^-4 = {}^-16$, another negative integer. By considering a number line, another rational argument might be given, as illustrated in Figure 5-7. Thus, in each of these cases it seems reasonable to conclude that the sum of two negative integers is a negative integer.

Figure 5-7

Relying on the strength of some assumptions regarding the sum of integers, a more powerful argument can be given. Here is a list of properties that we shall assume hold true in the set of integers for the operation of addition. You should find them similar to properties of whole number addition.

> If Z names the set of integers and $+$ names the binary operation of addition of integers, then
> i. If a and b are in Z, then $a + b$ is in Z (closure property).
> ii. If a and b are in Z, then $a + b = b + a$ (commutative property).
> iii. If a, b, and c are in Z, then $a + (b + c) = (a + b) + c$ (associative property).
> iv. If a is in Z, then $a + 0 = 0 + a = a$. (Zero is the additive identity.)
> v. If a is in Z, then there exists ^-a in Z such that $a + {}^-a = {}^-a + a = 0$. (Every integer has an additive inverse, namely, its opposite.)

Given this set of properties, it can be shown that if x and y are integers then $^-x + {}^-y = {}^-(x + y)$. Notice that if we can show this to be true, then all three of the previous examples are easily determined. $^-6 + {}^-9 = {}^-(6 + 9) = {}^-15$. $^-12 + {}^-4 = {}^-(12 + 4) = {}^-16$. $^-7 + {}^-7 = {}^-14$. Study carefully each of the following related sentences. Each sentence illustrates one of the properties given above. Remember that we don't expect you to construct a proof, but we do want you to be able to recognize the reasons for each step of a proof. As you progress through the text, you will find that you will make progress in the ability to give reasons for the steps in a proof.

$$
\begin{aligned}
(x + y) + (^-x + {}^-y) &= (x + y) + (^-y + {}^-x) && \text{(why?)} \\
&= x + [y + (^-y + {}^-x)] && \text{(why?)} \\
&= x + [(y + {}^-y) + {}^-x] && \text{(why?)} \\
&= x + [0 + {}^-x] && \text{(why?)} \\
&= x + {}^-x && \text{(why?)} \\
&= 0 && \text{(why?)}
\end{aligned}
$$

It is shown by these sentences that $(x + y) + (^-x + {}^-y) = 0$. However, our definition of opposites stated that whenever $a + b = 0$ then a is the opposite of b (and b is the opposite of a). That is, if $a + b = 0$, then $^-a = b$. Therefore, since $(x + y) + (^-x + {}^-y) = 0$, then $^-(x + y) = {}^-x + {}^-y$.

> If a and b are integers, then $^-(a + b) = {}^-a + {}^-b$. In words, *the opposite of a sum of two integers is the sum of their opposites.*

The last type of addition problem for pairs of integers is the kind illustrated by $7 + {}^-4$, $^-8 + 6$, $5 + {}^-11$, and $^-7 + 9$. However, with what we know already about addition of integers, each of these sums can be found simply.

$$
\begin{aligned}
7 + {}^-4 &= (3 + 4) + {}^-4 = 3 + (4 + {}^-4) = 3 + 0 = 3 \\
{}^-8 + 6 &= (^-2 + {}^-6) + 6 = {}^-2 + (^-6 + 6) = {}^-2 + 0 = {}^-2 \\
5 + {}^-11 &= 5 + (^-5 + {}^-6) = (5 + {}^-5) + {}^-6 = 0 + {}^-6 = {}^-6 \\
{}^-7 + 9 &= {}^-7 + (7 + 2) = (^-7 + 7) + 2 = 0 + 2 = 2
\end{aligned}
$$

A classroom activity that can be used to illustrate the concept involves stacks of poker chips of two different colors, say red for negative and white for positive. For the sum of $^-7$ and 4 select 7 red chips and 4 white chips and place the stack of red chips next to the stack of white chips. Agree that 4 of the red chips equalize or balance the 4 white chips and show that there are 3 red chips left over. Thus, $^-7 + 4 = (^-3 + {}^-4) + 4 = {}^-3 + (^-4 + 4) = {}^-3 + 0 = {}^-3$. To find the sum $3 + {}^-2 + 4 + {}^-5 + 2 + {}^-6$, represent each number by a stack of red or white chips, combine the stacks of white and red chips, and then use the equalizing notion to determine the sum. Thus, $3 + {}^-2 + 4 + {}^-5 +$

$2 + {}^-6 = (3 + 4 + 2) + ({}^-2 + {}^-5 + {}^-6) = 9 + {}^-13 = 9 + ({}^-9 + {}^-4) =$
$(9 + {}^-9) + {}^-4 = 0 + {}^-4 = {}^-4.$

Another activity involves the use of a red rod that is 7 units long
(${}^-7$) and a black rod that is 4 units long (4). Place the two rods so that
the shorter one is on top of the longer. Agree that whatever length
protrudes represents the sum. Here 3 units of red will protrude so that
7 red plus 4 black equals 3 red. Hence, ${}^-7 + 4 = {}^-3$.

Finally, using the number line concept and the notion that positive integers are represented by segments pointing to the right and
negative integers are represented by segments pointing to the left,
the sum of integers may be determined by joining segments, as illustrated in Figure 5-8.

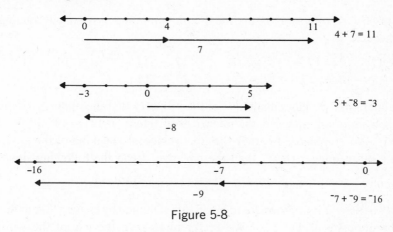

Figure 5-8

There are many other methods that may be used to generate an
understanding of the meaning of addition of integers. The essential
concept, however, is that of the opposite of an integer and the fact that
an integer plus its opposite is zero.

Subtraction of whole numbers was defined in such a way that
$a - b = c$ provided that $a = b + c$. This definition is perfectly adequate
for integers as well.

> If a, b, and c are integers, then $a - b = c$ if and only if
> $a = b + c$.

It is fairly easy to apply this definition provided one has a clear understanding of the addition of integers. For example, $17 - 11 = 6$ because
$11 + 6 = 17$. Also, ${}^-12 - 6 = {}^-18$, because ${}^-12 = 6 + {}^-18$. Furthermore,

179

$^-8 - ^-3 = ^-5$ because $^-8 = ^-3 + ^-5$. Finally, $4 - ^-9 = 13$ because $4 = ^-9 + 13$.

On the basis of this definition of subtraction, a second approach to subtraction may be established. We have said that $a - b = c$ because $a = b + c$. We contend that $a - b = a + ^-b$. To prove that this is so, we must simply prove that $a = b + (a + ^-b)$, because the term $a + ^-b$ is playing the role of the term c in the original definition. But $b + (a + ^-b) = b + (^-b + a) = (b + ^-b) + a = 0 + a = a$. So we have shown that subtraction of integers can be accomplished through addition of integers.

If a and b are integers, then $a - b = a + ^-b$.

This use of opposites is the most common practice when subtracting integers.

$$17 - 14 = 17 + ^-14 = 3, \qquad 17 - ^-14 = 17 + ^-(^-14) = 31$$
$$^-17 - 14 = ^-17 + ^-14 = ^-31, \qquad ^-17 - ^-14 = ^-17 + ^-(^-14) = ^-3$$

Notice that we have made use of the property that the opposite of the opposite of an integer is the integer itself. Here $^-(^-14) = 14$.

We emphasized earlier the importance of speaking of the opposite of an integer rather than the negative. Read the following aloud.

$$6 - ^-11 = 6 + ^-(^-11) = 6 + 11 = 17$$

We believe it is appropriate to begin this sentence by saying "Six minus the opposite of 11 . . . ." We prefer to reserve the use of the word "minus" for the operation of subtraction and to never use "minus" when speaking of the opposite of an integer or of a negative integer.

If a, b, and c are integers, it is easy to see that if $a = b$ then $a + c = b + c$. This is so because we know that $a + c = a + c$ from the reflexive property of equality. So, $a + c = b + c$, for "a" and "b" are names of the same object. In the set of integers, then,

If $a = b$, then $a + c = b + c$. (Addition Transformation Principle, or ATP).

What is the converse of this statement? Remember that the converse of $P \Rightarrow Q$ is $Q \Rightarrow P$. So the converse is

$$\text{If } a + c = b + c, \text{ then } a = b.$$

Is the converse also a true statement? The answer is yes, and it can

180

be shown to be true using the fact that the integer c has an opposite. Here is a formal argument.

$a + c = b + c$	(given)
$(a + c) + {}^-c = (b + c) + {}^-c$	(ATP)
$a + (c + {}^-c) = b + (c + {}^-c)$	(associativity)
$a + 0 = b + 0$	(definition of ^-c)
$a = b$	(definition of 0)

> If a, b, and c are integers and $a + c = b + c$, then $a = b$ (Cancellation Principle for Addition).

If you were asked to find an integer to replace the variable x to make a true statement from the sentence $x + 73 = 18$, you could make use of the cancellation principle and the knowledge that $18 = {}^-55 + 73$. Hence, $x + 73 = {}^-55 + 73$, so that $x = {}^-55$. Of course, one may also use the addition transformation principle $x + 73 = 18$, so $(x + 73) + {}^-73 = 18 + {}^-73$, from which we have that $x + (73 + {}^-73) = {}^-55$, or that $x = {}^-55$.

The process of finding integers that make such sentences true is called *solving* the equation. The integer found is called a *solution* of the equation. Most examples that are appropriate at this point in our text are almost trivial, since you have so much skill with the set of integers already. If we ask you to solve the equation $14 + x = 5$, you can tell us quickly that $x = {}^-9$ is a solution because you know that $14 + {}^-9 = 5$. However, it is important to be able to use the principles you have learned and to realize that you have all the power that any mathematician has to prove that $^-9$ is the only solution. The formal sequence of steps might be those which follow. Again we ask you to supply the reasons.

$14 + x = 5$	
$^-14 + (14 + x) = {}^-14 + 5$	(ATP)
$(^-14 + 14) + x = {}^-14 + 5$	Why?
$0 + x = {}^-14 + 5$	Why?
$x = {}^-14 + 5$	Why?
$x = {}^-(9 + 5) + 5$	$14 = 9 + 5$
$x = (^-9 + {}^-5) + 5$	Why?
$x = {}^-9 + (^-5 + 5)$	Why?
$x = {}^-9 + 0$	Why?
$x = {}^-9$	Why?

Certainly, more of the details have been provided than would be necessary for you to see that ⁻9 is the solution, but it is worth noting that only the whole number fact that $14 = 9 + 5$ is needed in this sequence in addition to the principles established for the set of integers.

EXERCISES (Section 5.3)

1. Here is a short list of problems involving addition and subtraction of integers. Test your skill to see if you can find all the sums and differences in 3 minutes without error.
   a. $17 + ⁻8$, $⁻28 + 16$, $32 + 69$, $⁻13 + 95$
   b. $⁻28 + 164$, $⁻74 − 29$, $⁻14 − ⁻16$, $73 − ⁻41$
   c. $⁻29 − 43$, $⁻36 + 59$, $142 + ⁻37 − 16 + ⁻55$
   d. $⁻1{,}421 + 643 − ⁻725$, $713 − 427 + ⁻326 − 643$
   e. $⁻473 + ⁻1{,}541 − 796 − ⁻2{,}791 + 1{,}692$

2. Give three examples which confirm that $⁻(a + b) = ⁻a + ⁻b$.

3. For the set of whole numbers, there are four sentences called the "number facts" for any set of three different numbers. For instance, given the numbers 6, 3, and 9, the number facts are

$$6 + 3 = 9, \qquad 3 + 6 = 9, \qquad 9 − 3 = 6, \qquad 9 − 6 = 3$$

   With the set of integers there are also four number facts that are associated with any three integers. For instance, given the numbers 8, ⁻5, and 3, we have

$$8 + ⁻5 = 3, \qquad ⁻5 + 8 = 3, \qquad 3 − 8 = ⁻5, \qquad 3 − ⁻5 = 8$$

   The basic form in both sets is exactly the same. Given numbers a, b, and c, the number facts are

$$a + b = c, \qquad b + a = c, \qquad c − a = b, \qquad c − b = a$$

   What are the number facts for the following sets of integers?
   a. $17, 9, 26$ b. $25, ⁻11, 14$ c. $16, 29, ⁻13$
   d. $⁻14, 11, ⁻3$ e. $⁻12, ⁻10, ⁻22$ f. $15, ⁻19, ⁻4$

4. Here are some simple equations. Find solutions for each by solving in detail and by justifying each step that you take.
   a. $x + 11 = 17$ b. $x − 8 = 14$
   c. $x + 15 = 6$ d. $x − 12 = ⁻16$
   e. $⁻14 + x = 7$ f. $15 − x = 9$
   g. $27 − x = 14 − 2x$ h. $12 − 3x = ⁻2x + 29$

5. Give appropriate names for the following.
   a. If Jimmy has 16¢ and I have x¢, how much do we have together?
   b. When I gave Helen three pieces of candy, I had m pieces left. How many pieces did I have to begin?
   c. It is t miles from here to Omaha and then it is 247 miles farther on to Ipswitch. How far is it from here to Ipswitch by way of Omaha?
   d. The principal allowed Miss Que a budget of $500 for the purchase

of mathematics laboratory supplies and equipment. She spent x dollars for equipment. How much does she have left?

6. Solve the following by giving appropriate names as in Exercise 5 and then solving as equations.
    a. Jimmy has 16¢ and together we have 85¢. How much do I have?
    b. I had twelve pieces of candy and gave Helen three. How much do I now have?
    c. From here to Ipswitch it is 723 miles by way of Omaha. How far is it from here to Omaha if it is 247 miles from Omaha to Ipswitch?
    d. I am thinking of a number. When I subtract the number from 27 I get the same as when I subtract twice the number from 14. What is the number?

7. Give examples that show whether or not subtraction is commutative and whether or not it is associative.

8. Why is it true that $0 - a = {}^-a$?

5.4

MULTIPLICATION AND DIVISION OF INTEGERS

For the four types of multiplication problems in the set of integers, let us see just what might be a reasonable conclusion on the basis of what we observe from everyday life. We shall then turn to what we know of multiplication of whole numbers and the principles established for the set of integers thus far to establish rules mathematically for the multiplication of integers.

Suppose that it is a typical cold, wintry day in Colorado and the temperature is falling at a constant rate of 2 degrees per hour. In 4 hours the temperature will have fallen 8 degrees. If the temperature at midnight is 0 degrees, at 4 A.M. (that is, 4 hours after midnight) the temperature will be 8 degrees below zero. If we agree to designate a decrease of 2 degrees as $^-2$, then we may compute the total decrease in temperature as $(4) \times (^-2) = {}^-8$. It appears reasonable that the multiplication of a negative number times a positive number yields a negative number.

On the other hand, if we ask what the temperature was at 9 P.M. (that is, 3 hours before midnight), we must agree that the temperature was 6 degrees above zero because $6 + (^-2 + {}^-2 + {}^-2) = 0$. If we agree to designate the 3 hours before midnight as $^-3$, we have $(^-3) \times (^-2) = 6$.

It appears reasonable that the multiplication of two negative integers gives a positive integer.

Now let us see what seems reasonable on the basis of what we know of multiplication of whole numbers and of the principles established for the set of integers. The four types are exemplified by the following four examples:

$$5 \times 4, \quad 5 \times {}^-4, \quad {}^-5 \times 4, \quad {}^-5 \times {}^-4$$

You will recall that 5×4 means $4 + 4 + 4 + 4 + 4$ or 20. It seems reasonable that $5 \times {}^-4$ means ${}^-4 + {}^-4 + {}^-4 + {}^-4 + {}^-4$ or ${}^-20$. What about ${}^-5 \times 4$? If we anticipate that integer multiplication should be commutative, then ${}^-5 \times 4 = 4 \times {}^-5$ and if we resort to the same meaning as above, $4 \times {}^-5$ means ${}^-5 + {}^-5 + {}^-5 + {}^-5$ or ${}^-20$. This also suggests that if a and b are integers, then $a \times {}^-b = {}^-a \times b$.

So the first three types seem to be reasonable and follow closely the model established for the whole numbers. Now consider the problem ${}^-5 \times {}^-4$. Consider the pattern

$$
\begin{aligned}
{}^-5 \times 4 &= {}^-20 \\
{}^-5 \times 3 &= {}^-15 \\
{}^-5 \times 2 &= {}^-10 \\
{}^-5 \times 1 &= {}^-5 \\
{}^-5 \times 0 &= 0 \\
\\
{}^-5 \times {}^-1 &= \quad ? \\
{}^-5 \times {}^-2 &= \quad ? \\
{}^-5 \times {}^-3 &= \quad ? \\
{}^-5 \times {}^-4 &= \quad ?
\end{aligned}
$$

Do you see that the column of numbers on the right is increasing by five at each step? If the pattern continues, then ${}^-5 \times {}^-1$ must be 5 and ${}^-5 \times {}^-2 = 10$, ${}^-5 \times {}^-3 = 15$, and ${}^-5 \times {}^-4 = 20$.

Here is another argument for the case ${}^-5 \times {}^-4$. We can anticipate that the multiplication of integers ought to be distributive over addition of integers and that the product of any integer with zero should be zero. Therefore, consider the following sequence of statements: $0 = {}^-5 \times 0 = {}^-5(4 + {}^-4) = ({}^-5 \times 4) + ({}^-5 \times {}^-4) = {}^-20 + ({}^-5 \times {}^-4)$. Thus, $0 = {}^-20 + ({}^-5 \times {}^-4)$. But $0 = {}^-20 + 20$, so we know that

$$^-20 + (^-5 \times ^-4) = ^-20 + 20$$

or

$$^-5 \times ^-4 = 20$$

from the cancellation principle of addition.

Let's use the number line as a basis for explanation of the four types. For the problem 5×4 we can recall the model used for the whole numbers (see Figure 5-9). For the problem $5 \times ^-4$ a similar

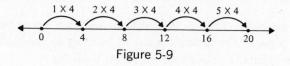

Figure 5-9

model serves (see Figure 5-10). For the problem $^-5 \times 4$ an agreement that $^-5$ means five groups of 4 in the *opposite direction* (or in the direc-

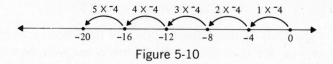

Figure 5-10

tion opposite to 4) seems to give us a good model (see Figure 5-11). Finally, the agreement that $^-5 \times ^-4$ means five groups of $^-4$ in the

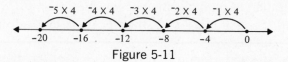

Figure 5-11

opposite direction (or in the direction opposite to that of $^-4$) provides the model (see Figure 5-12).

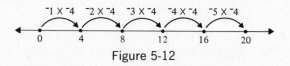

Figure 5-12

Whatever rationale is used, the definition of the operation of multiplication for the set of integers is neatly stated using the concept of absolute value.

185

If a and b are integers
  i. and a and b are both positive or both negative, then
$$a \times b = |a| \times |b|$$
  ii. and exactly one of a and b is positive while the other is negative, then
$$a \times b = {}^{-}(|a| \times |b|)$$
  iii. and either a or b is zero, then $a \times b = 0$.

Since the absolute value of an integer is always a whole number, the definition reduces the multiplication of integers to the multiplication of whole numbers. For our four problems we have

$$5 \times 4 = |5| \times |4| = 5 \times 4 = 20$$
$$5 \times {}^{-}4 = {}^{-}(|5| \times |{}^{-}4|) = {}^{-}(5 \times 4) = {}^{-}20$$
$${}^{-}5 \times 4 = {}^{-}(|{}^{-}5| \times |4|) = {}^{-}(5 \times 4) = {}^{-}20$$
$${}^{-}5 \times {}^{-}4 = |{}^{-}5| \times |{}^{-}4| = 5 \times 4 = 20$$

On the basis of the definition, each of the following properties can be proved. We shall not be unduly concerned with the proofs of any of these principles, but list them for the sake of completeness.

If Z names the set of integers and $\times$ names the binary operation of multiplication of integers, then
  i. If a and b are in Z, then $a \times b$ is in Z (closure property).
  ii. If a and b are in Z, then $a \times b = b \times a$ (commutative property).
  iii. If a, b, and c are in Z, then $a \times (b \times c) = (a \times b) \times c$ (associative property).
  iv. If a is in Z, then $a \times 1 = 1 \times a = a$. (1 is the multiplicative identity.)
  v. If a, b, and c are in Z, then $a \times (b + c) = (a \times b) + (a \times c)$. (Distributive property of multiplication over addition.)

You will notice that these properties are exactly the same properties that hold for multiplication of whole numbers. The properties of addition of integers are also nearly the same as those for addition of whole numbers. The singular exception was that every integer has an opposite which when added to the integer gives zero.

The definition of division of integers is exactly the same as the definition of division of whole numbers.

> If a, b, and c are integers, then $a \div b = c$ if and only if $a = b \times c$.

As was the case with the set of whole numbers, division is not closed in the set of integers. In other words, given an arbitrary pair of integers, there may not be an integer quotient corresponding to that pair. For example, $^-12 \div 5$ is not an integer.

What operations are closed in the set of integers? Of course, addition and multiplication of integers are closed operations by virtue of the ways in which these operations were defined. How about subtraction? We have agreed that if a and b are integers, then $a - b$ means the same as $a + {}^-b$. Since ^-b always exists as an integer and since the addition of integers is closed, then subtraction of integers is closed. We have just seen that division is not closed, so three of the four fundamental arithmetic operations are closed in the set of integers.

What kinds of equations always have solutions in the set of integers? Analogous to the four fundamental operations of arithmetic are four fundamental types of simple equations suggested by the following examples:

$$\Box + 5 = 17$$
$$\Box - 8 = 12$$
$$5 \times \Box = 17$$
$$\Box \div {}^-4 = 11$$

Can you find integers for each of these equations that form true sentences? For the equation $\Box + 5 = 17$, the integer 12 is a solution. For the equation $\Box - 8 = 12$, the integer 20 is a solution. There is no integer solution for the equation $5 \times \Box = 17$. For the last equation, $\Box \div {}^-4 = 11$, the integer $^-44$ is a solution.

Therefore, all these simple equations, except for the equation $5 \times \Box = 17$, have solutions in the set of integers. If there were a solution to this equation, call it integer c, then we would have $5 \times c = 17$, so that $17 \div 5 = c$. But we know that no such integer exists and we know that no solution exists to this equation, because division of these two integers is not closed. This is a serious deficiency for a system of numbers, and it must be remedied in some way. Of course, you already know what we need to do; we must invent the system of rational numbers so that the number $\frac{17}{5}$ can be used as a solution to this simple equation. All this will be accomplished in Chapter 7.

Here is a summary of these observations about the system of integers.

> The system of integers is closed under the operations of addition, multiplication, and subtraction. It is not closed under division.
>
> If a and b are integers, then there is an integer x that is a solution to the equation
>
> $$a + x = b$$
>
> Likewise, there is an integer y that is a solution to the equation
>
> $$a - y = b$$
>
> There is an integer z that is a solution to
>
> $$z \div a = b$$
>
> Finally, there is no integer solution to the following equation unless a is a divisor of b:
>
> $$a \times \square = b$$

As you will see in Chapter 6, the fact that equations such as $5 \times \square = 17$ have no solutions leads to some interesting developments in the subject matter known as number theory. Just to give you an inkling of this area, consider the equation $2x + 3y = 6$ and see if you can find two or three pairs of integers that, when substituted for the variables x and y, make true statements. One pair that you might discover is to replace x by 0 and y by 2, that is, use the pair (0, 2). This pair makes the sentence true because $2 \bullet 0 + 3 \bullet 2 = 6$. (If you have not seen the raised dot before, it simply is another symbol representing multiplication.) Some of the other pairs are (3, 0), ($^-$3, 4), and (6, $^-$2). One of the intriguing questions you could ask at this point is "How can I find a way to discover *all* pairs of integers (x, y) that make the sentence $2x + 3y = 6$ into a true statement?" You should find the answer to this question in Chapter 6.

Recall that if $a = b$, then $a + c = b + c$ when a, b, and c are integers (the Addition Transformation Principle). Also, recall the converse which stated that if $a + c = b + c$, then $a = b$ (the Cancellation Principle for Addition). Similar principles hold for multiplication of integers.

> If a, b, and c are integers and $a = b$, then $a \times c = b \times c$. (Multiplication Transformation Principle).
>
> If a, b, and c are integers with $c \neq 0$, and if $a \times c = b \times c$, then $a = b$. (Cancellation Principle for Multiplication).
>
> If a and b are integers and $a \times b = 0$, then $a = 0$ or $b = 0$. (The Zero Divisor Property).

EXERCISES (Section 5.4)

1. Here is a brief test of your skills with multiplication and division of integers. You should be able to find the products and quotients in 3 minutes or less with no errors.
   a. 15×7, $^-11 \times 6$, $8 \times ^-14$, $^-9 \times ^-13$
   b. $84 \div 4$, $^-48 \div 6$, $54 \div ^-18$, $^-64 \div ^-4$
   c. 145×9, $^-228 \times 7$, $441 \times ^-9$, $^-271 \times ^-8$
   d. $240 \div 15$, $^-735 \div 21$, $817 \div ^-43$, $^-2,835 \div ^-63$

2. Give an elementary explanation that appeals to you and shows why
   a. $7 \times 3 = 21$ b. $7 \times ^-3 = ^-21$ c. $^-7 \times 3 = ^-21$
   d. $^-7 \times ^-3 = 21$

3. Give two examples that illustrate the following:
   a. If a and b are positive, $a \times b = |a| \times |b|$.
   b. If a and b are negative, $a \times b = |a| \times |b|$.
   c. If a is positive and b is negative, $a \times b = ^-(|a| \times |b|)$.
   d. If a is negative and b is positive, $a \times b = ^-(|a| \times |b|)$.

4. Give two examples that illustrate the distributive property for integers.

5. Number facts for multiplication and division of integers may also be given. For instance,

$$6 \times ^-2 = ^-12, \quad ^-2 \times 6 = ^-12, \quad ^-12 \div 6 = ^-2, \quad ^-12 \div ^-2 = 6$$

   What are the number facts for the following?
   a. 45, $^-9$, $^-405$ b. $^-13$, 16, $^-208$ c. $^-14$, $^-21$, 294

6. As in the set of whole numbers, division is not closed in the set of integers. The division algorithm must be slightly revised to read as follows: If a and b are integers, $b \neq 0$, then there exist unique integers q and r such that $a = bq + r$, where $r = 0$ or $0 < r < |b|$. For instance, if $a = 17$ and $b = ^-3$, then $q = ^-5$ and $r = 2$ (note that $2 < |^-3|$), because $17 = (^-3)(^-5) + 2$.

Find q and r for the following pairs of integers a and b.
a. $a = 91, b = 15$ b. $a = 84, b = {}^-9$
c. $a = {}^-47, b = 12$ d. $a = {}^-71, b = {}^-11$

7. Give at least two examples that confirm the following.
   a. If a and b are integers, then $a \times {}^-b = {}^-(ab)$. For instance, if $a = {}^-3$ and $b = {}^-5$, then ${}^-b = 5$, so that $a \times {}^-b = {}^-3 \times 5 = {}^-15$. Also, $ab = 15$ and ${}^-(ab) = {}^-15$. Therefore, both $a \times {}^-b$ and ${}^-(ab)$ equal ${}^-15$.
   b. If a and b are integers, then ${}^-a \times b = {}^-(ab)$.
   c. If a and b are integers, then ${}^-a \times {}^-b = ab$.

8. Find integer solutions for the following equations.
   a. $14 + x = 8$, $x + 9 = 17$, $45 = 19 + x$
   b. $14 - x = 8$, $x - 9 = 17$, $45 = 19 - x$
   c. $x \div 6 = 5$, $x \div {}^-4 = 11$, ${}^-7 = 6 \div x$

9. Give a convincing argument that $m \times 0 = 0$.

10. Show why the Cancellation Principle for Multiplication excludes "canceling" zero.

11. Using the addition transformation principle, the multiplication transformation principle, and the cancellation principle, solve the following equations for integer solutions if possible. If not possible, state why.
    a. $2x + 5 = 11$ b. $3x - 17 = 4$
    c. $5x - 4 = 2x + 5$ d. $17 - 2x + 5 = 0$
    e. $14 + 5x = 26 + 7x$ f. $13 + x = 31 - 5x$

5.5

ORDERING THE INTEGERS

You probably already have a good, intuitive understanding of the way in which the integers are ordered. No doubt you know that 7 is greater than 2, that 2 is greater than ${}^-5$, and that ${}^-5$ is greater than ${}^-10$. Perhaps you have based your understanding on a mental image of an integer number line and the agreement that of two integers, the one to the right of the other is the greater. This is a very good basis for ordering the integers, but it does depend upon some agreement as to the meaning of "to the right of" as well as an agreement that the positive integers are to the right of zero when represented on an integer number line.

We can give a more satisfactory definition of order for the integers. You may recall that the definition of "greater than" for the set of whole numbers stated that whole number a is greater than whole number b if there exists some nonzero whole number c such that $a = b + c$. Can we use exactly the same definition for integers? Let's try defining "greater than" for integers by saying that integer x is greater than integer y if there exists some nonzero integer z such that $x = y + z$. Then 7 is greater than 2 because $7 = 2 + 5$. However, we could also say that 2 is greater than 7 because $2 = 7 + {}^-5$ and ${}^-5$ is a nonzero integer. So you can see that something must be done about this first try for a definition. One slight change is needed. Instead of requiring that the integer z be nonzero, it must be that z is positive.

> An integer x is greater than integer y if there is a positive integer z such that $x = y + z$. We write "$x > y$" to say that x is greater than y.

Your own elementary school students will probably begin to understand the concept of order for the integers on the basis of pictures of the integer number line and the agreement that "greater than" means "to the right of." You must know that this is an appropriate beginning, but the long-term objective is to reach the given definition. Many of your students will discover the fact that this definition agrees with their intuitive understanding, just as you have done.

Here is another possible definition of "greater than." We know that 12 is greater than 4. $12 - 4$ is a positive integer. We know that 6 is greater than ${}^-3$ and $6 - {}^-3$ is a positive integer. ${}^-4$ is greater than ${}^-10$ and ${}^-4 - {}^-10 = 6$, a positive integer. So, as an alternative definition, one may say that integer x is greater than integer y if $x - y$ is a positive integer. This follows from our earlier definition, because if x is greater than y, then there is some positive integer z such that $x = y + z$. But our definition of subtraction tells us that $x - y = z$ whenever $x = y + z$. Therefore, $x - y$ is a positive integer (z).

> An integer x is greater than integer y if $x - y$ is a positive integer.

The *trichotomy property* for the set of integers stated that if x is an integer then exactly one of the following is true:

$$x \text{ is positive}, \quad {}^-x \text{ is positive}, \quad x \text{ is zero}$$

Given any two integers m and n, then $m - n$ is an integer; so exactly one of the following is true:

$m - n$ is positive, $\quad ^-(m - n)$ is positive, $\quad m - n$ is zero

From what we have seen about "greater than," we can say that exactly one of the following is true:

$$m > n, \quad n > m, \quad m = n$$

Notice that if $^-(m - n)$ is positive, then $^-m + n$ is positive or $n + ^-m$ is positive or $n - m$ is positive. Hence, $n > m$. As a result, we may restate the trichotomy property in terms of "greater than."

> *Trichotomy Property.* If m and n are integers, then exactly one of the following is true:
>
> $$m > n, \quad n > m, \quad m = n$$

You have seen that "greater than" is not a reflexive relation in the set of integers because 5 is not greater than 5, for example. Neither is "greater than" a symmetric relation because, although 5 is greater than 2, 2 is not greater than 5. However, "greater than" is a transitive relation, as you are asked to show in the exercises.

Suppose that a and b are integers and that $a > b$. Then there is some positive integer p such that $a = b + p$. Now for any integer c we know that $a + c = (b + p) + c$ or that $a + c = (b + c) + p$ by virtue of the commutative and associative properties of addition of integers. From the definition of "greater than" it follows that $a + c > b + c$ whenever $a > b$. For example, we know that $21 > ^-4$. If we add 6 to 21 and 6 to $^-4$, we obtain 27 and 2, and we notice that $27 > 2$. If we add $^-8$ to 21 and $^-8$ to $^-4$ we obtain 13 and $^-12$, and notice that $13 > ^-12$.

Again suppose that $a > b$ so that $a = b + p$, where p is some positive integer. Now if c is a positive integer, then $ac = (b + p)c = bc + pc$. Since both p and c are positive integers, then pc is a positive integer. Therefore, $ac > bc$. Thus, if $a > b$ and c *is positive*, then $ac > bc$. For example, $5 > ^-1$, and if we multiply by 7, we obtain 35 and $^-7$, and we can see that $35 > ^-7$. On the other hand, if c is negative, then pc is a negative integer, because the product of a positive integer and a negative integer is a negative integer. Since $ac = bc + pc$, then $ac + ^-(pc) = bc$. But $^-(pc)$ is a positive integer, so it follows from our definition that $bc > ac$. Thus, if $a > b$ and c *is negative*, then $bc > ac$. For example, $5 > ^-1$, and if we multiply by $^-3$, we obtain $^-15$ and 3, and we can see that $3 > ^-15$.

These three properties are summarized as follows. Be careful of the use of the second and third for they depend on whether or not c is positive.

> If a and b are integers and $a > b$, then
> i. $a + c > b + c$, for any integer c.
> ii. $ac > bc$, if c is a positive integer.
> iii. $bc > ac$, if c is a negative integer.

If integer a is greater than integer b, then integer b is less than integer a. We write "$b < a$" to say that b is less than a. Two expressions may therefore be used to say the same thing, either $a > b$ or $b < a$. To say that a is equal to b *or* a is greater than b, we write "$a \geqslant b$." To say that a is equal to or less than b, we write "$a \leqslant b$."

Find all integers that make the following sentence true:

$$23 + x > 14$$

We can add ⁻23 and have

$$^-23 + (23 + x) > {}^-23 + 14$$
or $$(^-23 + 23) + x > {}^-9$$
or $$x > {}^-9$$

So any integer that is greater than ⁻9 is a solution to the original sentence. Sentences like $23 + x > 14$ are called *inequalities*, and a *solution* is a set of integers each of which makes the sentence a true statement. In this case the solution (or solution set) is $\{x; x$ is an integer and $x > {}^-9\}$.

Let's use what we have learned thus far to solve a problem that could arise around income tax time. Suppose that your income for the forthcoming year is fixed at $7,300. You decide to get a part-time job to supplement your income; however, you do not want your income to equal or exceed $10,000 since this will place you in a higher tax bracket. What is the maximum amount of income you can earn (in whole dollars) without equaling or exceeding $10,000? We must solve the following inequality:

$$7,300 + x < 10,000$$

To solve this inequality, we can add ⁻7,300 and have

$$(7,300 + x) + {}^-7,300 < 10,000 + {}^-7,300$$
or $$(x + 7,300) + {}^-7,300 < (2,700 + 7,300) + {}^-7,300$$

or $\qquad x + (7,300 + {}^-7,300) < 2,700 + (7,300 + {}^-7,300)$
or $\qquad\qquad\qquad x + 0 < 2,700 + 0$
or $\qquad\qquad\qquad\qquad x < 2,700$

Therefore, the part-time job must yield less than \$2,700 in order to stay in the same tax bracket.

Find the solution for the following inequality:

$$x \div ({}^-2) > 5$$

Using property iii, multiply by ${}^-2$ and have that

$$x < {}^-10$$

Let us test some of the integers that are less than ${}^-10$. ${}^-12$ is one such integer and ${}^-12$ divided by ${}^-2$ is 6, and 6 is indeed greater than 5. Let's use ${}^-13$ since ${}^-13$ is less than ${}^-10$. ${}^-13$ divided by ${}^-2$ is what integer? There is no such integer! So it is clear that not all integers less than ${}^-10$ are solutions. The difficulty stems from the fact that division of integers is not closed. The solution for this inequality is the set of all integers that are less than ${}^-10$ and have an integer quotient when divided by ${}^-2$.

Here is another inequality involving the concept of absolute value as well. Find all integers that make the sentence true.

$$|x| + {}^-2 < 5$$

Adding 2, we have

$$(|x| + {}^-2) + 2 < 5 + 2$$
or $\qquad\qquad |x| + ({}^-2 + 2) < 7$
or $\qquad\qquad\qquad |x| < 7$

What integers have the property that their absolute values are less than 7? The integers 6, 5, 4, 3, 2, 1, 0, ${}^-1$, ${}^-2$, ${}^-3$, ${}^-4$, ${}^-5$, and ${}^-6$ have this property, and this is the solution. Such integers can be described as those which are greater than ${}^-7$ and at the same time less than 7. We can state the property conveniently as the set of all integers x such that ${}^-7 < x < 7$, that is, such that ${}^-7$ is less than x *and* x is less than 7.

If m and n are integers, we have seen that $|m| \cdot |n| = |m \cdot n|$. Can you show that if m and n are integers, then

$$|m + n| \leqslant |m| + |n|$$

We shall leave this as an exercise for you to do with the suggestion

194

that you consider the possible cases for m and n as either positive or negative integers.

EXERCISES (Section 5.5)

1. What integers belong to each of the following sets?
   a. $\{x; x \text{ is an integer and } 1 \leqslant x \leqslant 7\}$
   b. $\{y; y \text{ is an integer and } {}^-7 < y \leqslant 0\}$
   c. $\{z; z \text{ is an integer and } z < 10\}$
   d. $\{w; w \text{ is an integer and } w < 0 \text{ or } w > 10\}$
   e. $\{x; x \text{ is an integer and } x + 1 = x\}$
   f. $\{x; x \text{ is an integer and } x = 0\}$
   g. $\{x; x \text{ is an integer and } x < 0 \text{ or } x > {}^-2\}$

2. Is it true that there is a least positive integer?
   Is there a least negative integer?
   Is there a greatest positive integer?
   Is there a greatest negative integer?

3. Give two examples each that confirm the following.
   a. If $a > b$, then $a + c > b + c$.
   b. If $a > b$, then $a - c > b - c$.
   c. If $a > b$, and c is positive, then $ac > bc$.
   d. If $a > b$, and c is negative, then $ac < bc$.

4. Analogous to the cancellation principle is the following:
   $$\text{If } ac > bc \text{ and } c \text{ is positive, then } a > b$$
   $$\text{If } ac > bc \text{ and } c \text{ is negative, then } a < b$$
   Give two examples that confirm each of these.

5. Solve the following inequalities:
   a. $x + 5 < 7, x - 5 > 7, 2x + 7 \leqslant 11$
   b. $6x - 11 < 7, 14 - 5x < 9x$
   c. $2x + 3 < 6$ (Note that $2x + 3 = 6$ has no integer solution, but $2x + 3 < 6$ has many integer solutions.)

6. What *integers* are in the solution set for the following?
   $$3x \div 2 < 10$$

7. Find all integers that make the following sentences true.
   a. $|x| < 4$
   b. $|x| + 5 \leqslant 10$
   c. $|x| + 5 < 2$.
   d. $|c| - 9 \leqslant 0$
   e. $|x - 2| < 3$

8. Consider the statement that if m and n are integers then
   $$|m + n| \leqslant |m| + |n|$$
   a. Use the following four pairs of values for m and n and test the statement for these values.

$$m = 5, \qquad n = 2$$
$$m = 5, \qquad n = {}^-2$$
$$m = {}^-5, \qquad n = 2$$
$$m = {}^-5, \qquad n = {}^-2$$

b. Now, without using specific examples, argue that the statement is true when m and n are

both positive
one positive and one negative
both negative

9. Suppose that x is a positive integer and $|a| < x$. Does it follow that $^-x < a < x$? Test this conjecture with some specific examples.

10. Prove that "greater than" is a transitive relation.

5.6

GRAPHING SETS OF INTEGERS

The integer number line has been portrayed as a series of dots as in Figure 5-13. We have agreed that positive integers will be repre-

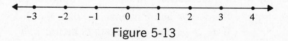

Figure 5-13

sented by dots to the right of the zero dot. There is no reason why we couldn't have represented the integer number line as in Figure 5-14. If we combine the two forms of representations, we produce a means of representing any pair of integers. Suppose that we wish to represent the pair ($^-3$, 2). Then, proceeding almost exactly as in Chapter 1, from the zero point move three spaces left and two spaces up (Figure 5-15).

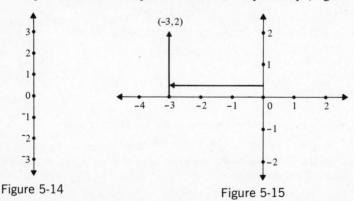

Figure 5-14

Figure 5-15

196

The two lines representing the set of integers are called x and y *axes* and the point they have in common is called the *origin*. The integers in the pair (x, y) are called the *coordinates* of the point, and the four sections created by the two lines are called the *quadrants*. Note that the coordinates of the origin are $(0, 0)$ (Figure 5-16).

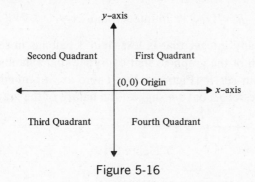

Figure 5-16

A few points with given coordinates have been identified in the Figure 5-17. Notice that the coordinates of any point in the first

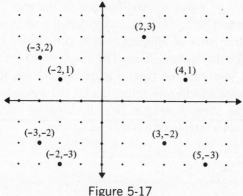

Figure 5-17

quadrant are both positive integers, while those in the third quadrant have negative coordinates. Points in the second and fourth quadrants have one positive and one negative coordinate.

Consider the set of integers

$$S = \{x; \ 2x + 1 = 7\}$$

The only integer that belongs to this set is the integer 3, and it is easy to sketch a graph of this set using just one number line (Figure 5-18). In this case the graph consists of just the one point.

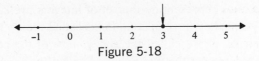

Figure 5-18

Consider the set of integers

$$R = \{x; \; x \text{ is an integer and } 2x + 1 < 7\}$$

In this case, any integer that is less than 3 belongs in set R. We can sketch enough of the graph so that everyone understands what points are included in set R (Figure 5-19). There are an infinite number of integers in the set R, but we suggest the nature of the graph of the set.

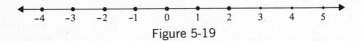

Figure 5-19

Here is a set of pairs of integers:

$$T = \{(x, y); \; x \text{ and } y \text{ are integers and } 2x + 3y = 6\}$$

One pair of integers that makes the sentence true is the pair $(3, 0)$, because $2 \cdot 3 + 3 \cdot 0 = 6$. Another pair is the pair $(0, 2)$, because $2 \cdot 0 + 3 \cdot 2 = 6$. The pair $(^-3, 4)$ also makes the sentence true. There are several other pairs of integers, which you should be able to discover, that make the sentence true. The graph of the set T is especially interesting, as you can see from Figure 5-20. Note that the points representing pairs of integers which make the sentence $2x + 3y = 6$ true seem to lie along a straight line. Because of this, the equation $2x + 3y = 6$ is an example of a *linear equation.*

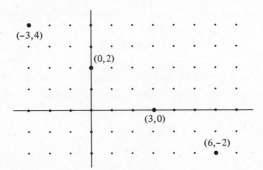

Set $T = \{(x, y); \; x \text{ and } y \text{ are integers and } 2x + 3y = 6\}$

Figure 5-20

198

This set of points is a set of lattice points and represents the *relation* defined in set T. The concepts of relation and function as discussed in Chapter 1 are applicable here. T is a relation on the set of integers. In fact, T is a function from the set of all multiples of 3 to the set of even integers. Test this conjecture by considering several ordered pairs in T.

There is a simple way to determine which pairs of integers make the sentence $2x + 3y = 6$ true, but it falls more appropriately in Chapter 6.

Here is another interesting relation on the set of integers:

$$S = \{(x, y); x \geq 5\}$$

The relation S specifies pairs of integers (x, y) with the only requirement being that each x coordinate is equal to or greater than 5. Some of the pairs included in this relation are $(5, 7)$, $(5, 8)$, $(5, {}^-6)$, $(7, 18)$, and $(112, 0)$. Note that any integral y coordinate is acceptable. The only requirement for inclusion in the relation is that the x coordinate must be equal to or greater than 5. Figure 5-21 is a picture of the graph

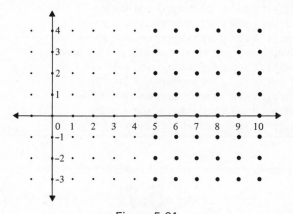

Figure 5-21

of the relation S. You may observe that the relation S is not reflexive [for example, $(3, 3)$ is not an element of S], nor is it a symmetric relation [although $(5, 1)$ is in S, $(1, 5)$ is not, for example]. However, S is a transitive relation. If (a, b) is in S, then $a \geq 5$, and if (b, c) is in S, then $b \geq 5$. But the important thing that you will note is that (a, c) must be in S just because $a \geq 5$. So, if (a, b) and (b, c) are in S, then (a, c) is in S, and S is a transitive relation.

199

EXERCISES (Section 5.6)

1. On a coordinate system, locate the following points and connect them in alphabetic order by straight lines.
   a. $(9, {}^-2)$ b. $(0, 2)$ c. $(6, 2)$ d. $(0, 5)$ e. $(4, 5)$
   f. $(0, 9)$ g. $({}^-5, 5)$ h. $({}^-1, 5)$ i. $({}^-7, 2)$ j. $({}^-1, 2)$
   k. $({}^-10, {}^-2)$

2. Devise some simple, topical figure, such as that from exercise 1, set up coordinates for the essential points of the figure, and draw the figure. Try a jack-o'-lantern, a heart, or a four-leaf clover.

3. Sketch a graph of each of the following sets of integers on a number line.
   a. $\{x : x \text{ is an integer and } x = 7 \text{ or } x = {}^-7\}$
   b. $\{x : x \text{ is an integer and } x^2 = 1\}$ ("x^2" means $x \cdot x$)
   c. $\{x : x \text{ is an integer and } |x| = 1\}$
   d. $\{x : x \text{ is an integer and } 3x - 5 = 4\}$
   e. $\{x : x \text{ is an integer and } 0 < x \leqslant 9\}$
   f. $\{x : x \text{ is an integer and } x > {}^-5 \text{ or } x < 1\}$
   g. $\{x : x \text{ is an integer and } x = 5 \text{ or } x < 2\}$

4. Sketch a graph of the following sets of integer pairs on a coordinate system.
   a. $\{(x, y) : x \text{ and } y \text{ are integers and } x + y = 1\}$
   b. $\{(x, y) : x \text{ and } y \text{ are integers and } x - y = 1\}$
   c. $\{(x, y) : x \text{ and } y \text{ are integers and } x = 3\}$
      [*Note:* Any pair (x, y) such that $x = 3$ is acceptable.]
   d. $\{(x, y) : x \text{ and } y \text{ are integers and } y = {}^-1\}$
   e. $\{(x, y) : x \text{ and } y \text{ are integers and } 2x - 3y = 6\}$
   f. $\{(x, y) : x \text{ and } y \text{ are integers and } x < 5\}$
   g. $\{(x, y) : x \text{ and } y \text{ are integers and } y \geqslant 2\}$
   h. $\{(x, y) : x \text{ and } y \text{ are integers and } x + 1 < y\}$

5.7

ANOTHER CONSTRUCTION OF THE INTEGERS
(Optional)

You have seen how the integers may be invented as an extension of the set of whole numbers through the creation of numbers called opposites of whole numbers. Addition and multiplication of these integers were defined as an extension of what was already known about these operations in the whole numbers. There is at least one other way to create the system of integers, which has been used with prospective elementary school teachers as well as with elementary school youngsters. For the sake of completeness and because the procedure is rather interesting, we shall present one method in this section.

We have spoken of "inventing" or "creating" the set of integers and we should add some clarification. You must realize that all number systems are the invention of man. Any invention must find itself useful for some purpose, and it must be logically consistent with that which has been previously invented. It is in this spirit that we proceed to invent the set of integers in a way quite different than that used earlier.

Beginning with the system of whole number $W = \{0, 1, 2, \ldots,\}$ consider the product set $W \times W$, a portion of which is

:	:	:	:	:	:	.
(0, 5)	(1, 5)	(2, 5)	(3, 5)	(4, 5)	(5, 5)	...
(0, 4)	(1, 4)	(2, 4)	(3, 4)	(4, 4)	(5, 4)	...
(0, 3)	(1, 3)	(2, 3)	(3, 3)	(4, 3)	(5, 3)	...
(0, 2)	(1, 2)	(2, 2)	(3, 2)	(4, 2)	(5, 2)	...
(0, 1)	(1, 1)	(2, 1)	(3, 1)	(4, 1)	(5, 1)	...
(0, 0)	(1, 0)	(2, 0)	(3, 0)	(4, 0)	(5, 0)	...

Do you see that you can find every possible pair of whole numbers somewhere in this scheme? The pair (16, 48) could be found by moving across the bottom until you reach the pair (16, 0) and then moving up that column until you reach the pair (16, 48).

Examine the pairs along the diagonal beginning with the pair (0, 0):

$$(3, 3)$$
$$(2, 2)$$
$$(1, 1)$$
$$(0, 0)$$

Every pair along this diagonal is of the form (a, a), where a is a whole number.

Look at the pairs along the diagonal that begins with the pair (1, 0):

$$(4, 3)$$
$$(3, 2)$$
$$(2, 1)$$
$$(1, 0)$$

Every pair along this diagonal is of the form $(a + 1, a)$, where a is a whole number.

What is the form of the pairs along the diagonal that begins with the pair $(5, 0)$? All pairs along this diagonal have the form $(a + 5, a)$. What is the typical form for pairs along the diagonal that begins with the pair $(0, 3)$? Do you see the pairs $(1, 4)$, $(2, 5)$, $(3, 6)$, and so on, on this diagonal? Then such pairs have the general form $(a, a + 3)$; the second coordinate or component is 3 more than the first coordinate or component.

What would be the first pair along the diagonal that contains the pair $(12, 21)$? Since the second coordinate is 9 more than the first, the pair $(12, 21)$ is found along the diagonal that begins with the pair $(0, 9)$. What pair would be first on the diagonal that contains the pair $(17, 6)$? Do you agree that it would be the pair $(11, 0)$?

For the sake of convenience, let's use some suggestive symbols to represent the set of all pairs along a given diagonal. For the diagonal having the property that all pairs in it have the general form (a, a), let us use the symbol "$[a, a]$" to name the set of all pairs in that diagonal. Of course, "a" is the name of an arbitrary whole number, so $[5, 5]$, $[17, 17]$, and $[0, 0]$ could all be used as names for this set of pairs along this diagonal, which begins with the pair $(0, 0)$. Now for the set of pairs along the diagonal beginning with $(1, 0)$, let's use "$[a + 1, a]$" as a name. Thus,

$$[a + 1, a] = \{(a + 1, a); a \text{ is a whole number}\}$$
$$[a + 2, a] = \{(a + 2, a); a \text{ is a whole number}\}$$
$$[a + 3, a] = \{(a + 3, a); a \text{ is a whole number}\}$$
$$\vdots$$
$$[a + n, a] = \{(a + n, a); a \text{ is a whole number}\}$$

Similarly, for the pairs on the diagonal beginning with $(0, 1)$, the symbol $[a, a + 1]$ is suggestive. Thus,

$$[a, a + 1] = \{(a, a + 1); a \text{ is a whole number}\}$$
$$[a, a + 2] = \{(a, a + 2); a \text{ is a whole number}\}$$
$$\vdots$$

202

Figure 5-22 is the representation of the set $W \times W$ together with the symbols we shall use to name the diagonal sets.

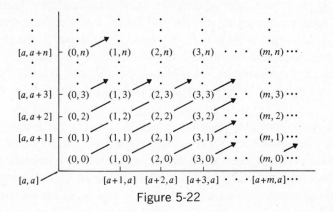

Figure 5-22

Here are names for two diagonal sets. Do they name the same set of pairs?

$$[141, 28], \qquad [178, 65]$$

No doubt you base your answer on whether or not $141 - 28$ is the same as $178 - 65$. Since the difference in each case is 113, you probably agree that the pairs $(141, 28)$ and $(178, 65)$ lie on the same diagonal and therefore that "$[141, 28]$" and "$[178, 65]$" name the same diagonal set. Do you observe any other relationship between the four numbers 141, 28, 178, and 65? Do some scratch work. Try addition relationships.

	141	28	178	65
$141 + 28 = 169$		$178 + 65 = 243$		No help.
$141 + 178 = 319$		$28 + 65 = 93$		So what? Nothing!
$141 + 65 = 206$		$28 + 178 = 206$		Look at that!

It appears that for the pairs $(141, 28)$ and $(178, 65)$, which lie on the same diagonal, $141 + 65 = 28 + 178$. The sum of the first and last components equals the sum of the second and third components.

Let's test a few more pairs that lie on a common diagonal and find whether or not this same relationship holds true. We know that $(16, 7)$ and $(29, 20)$ lie on the same diagonal for they both have the form $(a + 9, a)$ with $a = 7$ in the first pair and $a = 20$ in the second pair. Also note that $16 + 20 = 36$ and $7 + 29 = 36$. Again, the sum of the first and last equals the sum of the second and third components. Test a few more of these to convince yourself that it's not just coincidence.

Here is a way to prove that what we have noticed is not mere coincidence. If two pairs are on the same diagonal, they both must have a common form. Say the first pair is $(a + k, a)$ and the second pair is $(b + k, b)$ so that both do have the same form. Now add the first and last components and obtain $(a + k) + b$ or $a + b + k$. Adding the second and third components, we derive $a + b + k$ also. We have proved that if two pairs (x, y) and (u, v) are on the same diagonal, then $x + v = y + u$.

Suppose that two pairs (x, y) and (u, v) have the property that $x + v = y + u$. Then $x - y = u - v$ (provided $x - y$ and $u - v$ are whole numbers and, if not, then $y - x$ and $v - u$ are whole numbers). So, by our understanding about the common difference of components of pairs along a diagonal, we know that (x, y) and (u, v) are on the same diagonal.

> If (x, y) and (u, v) are ordered pairs of whole numbers, then (x, y) and (u, v) are on the same diagonal in our portrayal of $W \times W$ if and only if $x + v = y + u$.
>
> Two diagonals named by $[x, y]$ and $[u, v]$ are equal if and only if $x + v = y + u$.

The second sentence provides a criterion that may be useful in determining when two diagonals are equal.

To summarize our accomplishments so far, we have built a new object, which has been tentatively called a *diagonal*, that may be named by the symbol $[x, y]$ where the pair (x, y) is any pair along that diagonal. The diagonals consist of ordered pairs of whole numbers, and we have a criterion for equality.

We shall call the set of these diagonals the set of *integers* and use the letter Z to name the set.

$$Z = \{[x, y]; (x, y) \text{ is an ordered pair of whole numbers}\}$$

Upon this new set Z define an operation called addition.

> If $[m, p]$ and $[n, q]$ are integers in set Z, then
> $$[m, p] \oplus [n, q] = [m + n, p + q]$$

This definition of addition has the following properties:

i. $\oplus$ is a *closed* operation on Z, for $[m + n, p + q]$ is certainly the name of an integer (diagonal).

ii. $\oplus$ is a *commutative* operation because

$$[m, p] \oplus [n, q] = [m + n, p + q]$$
$$= [n + m, q + p]$$
(whole number addition is commutative)
$$= [n, q] \oplus [m, p]$$

iii. $\oplus$ is an *associative* operation because

$$[m, p] \oplus ([n, q] \oplus [r, s]) = [m, p] \oplus [n + r, q + s]$$
$$= [m + (n + r), p + (q + s)]$$
$$= [(m + n) + r, (p + q) + s]$$
(whole number addition is associative)
$$= [(m + n), (p + q)] \oplus [r, s]$$
$$= ([m, p] \oplus [n, q]) \oplus [r, s]$$

iv. $[0, 0]$ is an *additive identity* element (called *zero*), for if $[m, p]$ is an integer (diagonal), then

$$[m, p] \oplus [0, 0] = [m + 0, p + 0] = [m, p]$$

v. If $[m, p]$ is an integer (diagonal), then $[p, m]$ is its *additive inverse* or *opposite* because

$$[m, p] \oplus [p, m] = [m + p, p + m] = [m + p, m + p] = [0, 0]$$

We write "$^-[m, p] = [p, m]$."

You may be dismayed at the use of diagonal sets of pairs of whole numbers as a kind of number. However, you can see that the only knowledge required is the knowledge of the set of whole numbers. We are attempting to build from the set of whole numbers a new system of numbers, which we shall call integers. You may already be guessing that the diagonal set named by $[5, 0]$ will be the positive integer 5, that the diagonal set $[0, 0]$ will be the integer 0, and that the diagonal set $[0, 4]$ will be the integer $^-4$. Our motive in proceeding in the way that we have is to create this new system of integers without introducing an undefined term, that is, without using undefined words such as "left" and "right."

The operation of addition as defined for these diagonal sets agrees with integer addition as defined earlier. For example, we know that $7 + {}^-11 = {}^-4$. In terms of diagonal sets, the integer 7 will be the diagonal set $[7, 0]$ (or $[8, 1]$, $[9, 2]$, $[10, 3]$, etc.), the integer $^-11$ will be diagonal set $[0, 11]$ (or $[1, 12]$, $[2, 13]$, $[3, 14]$, etc.), and the integer $^-4$ will be the diagonal set $[0, 4]$ (or $[1, 5]$, $[2, 6]$, $[3, 7]$, etc.). According to the definition of diagonal sets, $[7, 0] \oplus [0, 11] = [7, 11] = [0, 4]$. So the new definition of addition for the new kind of object called integer (as a diagonal) agrees with the definition for addition of integers as given earlier.

As we look next at multiplication, keep in mind the idea that we shall be identifying diagonals with integers in this way.

A suitable definition of multiplication may also be given for this new set of objects.

> If $[m, p]$ and $[n, q]$ are integers, then $[m, p] \odot [n, q] = [mn + pq, mq + pn]$.

The operation of multiplication has the following properties:

i. $\odot$ is a *closed* operation on the set Z because $mn + pq$ and $mq + pn$ are names of whole numbers, so the pair $(mn + pq, mq + pn)$ is a pair of whole numbers.

ii. $\odot$ is a commutative operation on the set Z, for

$$
\begin{aligned}
[m, p] \odot [n, q] &= [mn + pq, mq + pn] \\
&= [nm + qp, np + mq] \text{ (whole number mul-} \\
&\qquad \text{tiplication is commutative)} \\
&= [n, q] \odot [m, p]
\end{aligned}
$$

iii. $\odot$ is an associative operation on the set Z. Here is a start on the proof of this fact. We leave the completion of the argument to you as a good exercise and as a review of the properties of addition and multiplication of whole numbers.

$$
\begin{aligned}
[m, p] \odot ([n, q] &\odot [r, s]) \\
&= [m, p] \odot [nr + qs, ns + qr] \\
&= [m(nr + qs) + p(ns + qr), m(ns + qr) + p(nr + qs)] \\
&= ? \\
&= ? \\
&= [mn + pq, mq + pn] \odot [r, s] \\
&= ([m, p] \odot [n, q]) \odot [r, s]
\end{aligned}
$$

iv. $[1, 0]$ is a multiplicative identity element (called *one*), because if $[m, p]$ is an integer, then

$$[m, p] \odot [1, 0] = [m \cdot 1 + p \cdot 0, m \cdot 0 + p \cdot 1] = [m, p]$$

v. Multiplication of integers is distributive over addition of integers. Again, here is a start on the proof of this fact. Fill in the spaces.

$$[m, p] \odot ([n, q] \oplus [r, s])$$
$$= [m, p] \odot [n + r, q + s]$$
$$= [m(n + r) + p(q + s), m(q + s) + p(n + r)]$$
$$= ?$$
$$= ?$$
$$= ?$$
$$= ?$$
$$= ([m, p] \odot [n, q]) \oplus ([m, p] \odot [r, s])$$

Let us verify for a specific example that the definition of multiplication given here is consistent with that given earlier. Suppose that we use the integers 5 and ⁻2 in our example. You anticipate that the integer 5 is the diagonal set [5, 0] (or [6, 1], [7, 2], [8, 3], etc.) and that the integer ⁻2 is the diagonal set [0, 2] (or [1, 3], [2, 4], [3, 5], etc.). According to the definition of multiplication of integers as diagonal sets,

$$[5, 0] \odot [0, 2] = [5 \cdot 0 + 0 \cdot 2, 5 \cdot 2 + 0 \cdot 0]$$
$$= [0 + 0, 10 + 0]$$
$$= [0, 10]$$

The diagonal [0, 10] is the integer ⁻10, and we confirm the consistency of this definition with the earlier one.

All that remains to be done is to formalize what we have been anticipating.

> The diagonal $[a + n, a]$ will be designated as the integer *positive n*. We write "*n*."
>
> The diagonal $[a, a]$ will be designated as the integer zero.
>
> The diagonal $[a, a + n]$ will be designated as the integer negative *n*. We write "⁻*n*."

Constructing these new objects called diagonals makes an entertaining activity for elementary school youngsters. Over a period of about 2 weeks a chart of these pairs of whole numbers can be constructed, the diagonals can be identified and named in some way, and operations of addition and multiplication (or called anything else that you wish) can be devised.

There are other operations that may be defined on the set of diagonals and may be interesting for you and the youngsters. One operation that children suggest after they have seen the addition operation is the following. Notice that the pattern is the same as that for addition except that whole number multiplication is used instead of whole number addition.

$$[m, p] * [n, q] = [mn, pq]$$

Call this operation "blast." You can show that blasting is closed, commutative, associative, that $[1, 1]$ is an identity element for blasting, and that blasting is distributive over addition of diagonals.

You might ask why blasting isn't used as the operation of multiplication of diagonals. The answer is because it is inconsistent with our earlier definition of integer multiplication. For example $5 \cdot {}^-4 = {}^-20$, yet when we use the diagonals $[5, 0]$ and $[0, 4]$ as names of positive 5 and negative 4 and use blasting as our multiplication, we have

$$[5, 0] * [0, 4] = [5 \cdot 0, 0 \cdot 4] = [0, 0]$$

$[0, 0]$ is a diagonal name for the integer zero, not negative 20.

EXERCISES (Section 5.7)

1. Name the first pair in the diagonal that contains the following:
   a. (16, 4)　　　　b. (11, 26)　　　　c. (143, 195)

2. Name three pairs that are on the same diagonal as
   a. (12, 9)　　　　b. (10, 35)　　　　c. (101, 183)

3. Which of the following pairs of number pairs lie on the same diagonal?
   a. (14, 28), (32, 46)
   b. (171, 97), (231, 157)
   c. (243, 115), (437, 299)

4. What can you say for certain if you know that (m, n) and (p, q) lie on the same diagonal?

5. What can be said for certain if $m + q \neq n + p$?

6. Find the sum of the following by using the definition of the operation called addition. Rename each sum to a simple form.
   a. $[4, 9] \oplus [11, 4]$
   b. $[16, 25] \oplus [27, 11]$
   c. $[14, 14] \oplus [25, 25]$
   d. $[19, 36] \oplus [11, 11]$

7. Rewrite each of the addends in Exercise 6 by naming each, using as its name that pair which occurs first in the diagonal which contains that pair. For instance, part a would be rewritten as

$$[0, 5] \oplus [7, 0] = [\ 2, 0]$$

8. Rewrite each of the addends and sums of Exercise 6 by using the notation that $[a + n, a]$ is named by "n," that $[a, a]$ is named by "0," and that $[a, a + n]$ is named by "^-n."

9. Find the product of the following using the definition of the operation called multiplication. Rename each product by use of the first pair in the diagonal that contains the product pair.
   a. $[4, 9] \odot [11, 4]$ b. $[12, 9] \odot [10, 2]$
   c. $[3, 14] \odot [5, 9]$ d. $[16, 7] \odot [5, 11]$

10. Rewrite each of the factors and products of Exercise 9 using the first pair in the diagonal that contains the given pair. For instance, part a would be written

$$[0, 5] \odot [7, 0] = [0, 35]$$

11. Rewrite each of the factors and products of Exercise 9 using the notation suggested in Exercise 8.

12. Show that the operation "blast" is commutative, associative, and distributive over addition. Here is a start and a finish on the distributivity property. Finish the details.

$$
\begin{aligned}
[a, b] * ([c, d] \oplus [e, f]) &= [a, b] * [c + e, d + f] \qquad \text{Why?} \\
&= [a(c + e), b(d + f)] \qquad \text{Why?} \\
&= ? \\
&= ? \\
&= ([a, b] * [c, d]) \oplus ([a, b] * [e, f]) \qquad \text{Why?}
\end{aligned}
$$

13. An operation called subtraction was not defined for the set of diagonals. Remembering that we always want $a - b = c$ if and only if $a = b + c$, define subtraction for diagonals.

$$[m, n] \ominus [p, q] = ?$$

14. Can you argue that your definition of subtraction provides for closure in the system of diagonals?

15. An operation of division can be defined but will lack closure.
   a. Remembering that we want $a \div b = c$ if and only if $a = b \cdot c$, define division of diagonal elements. Can it be done?
   b. Give an example of the trouble you get into with division of diagonals.

16. What is an appropriate definition of a "positive" diagonal?

    $[a, b]$ is positive if and only if . . . ?   (try some cases)

17. What is an appropriate definition of "less than" for the set of diagonals?

    $[a, b] < [c, d]$ if and only if . . . ?   (try some cases)

René Descartes

(1596–1650)

Today we accept the notion that man has the power to effect changes in nature and that this power is only diminished by our lack of knowledge. We modify the weather, journey to the moon, cure the seemingly incurable, transmit energy, and do thousands of things that are evidence of this power. During the time of Descartes such thoughts were heretical, because it was felt that it was God's will that things were as they were. Descartes felt that *reason* was the means by which man could change the world for the better. It was through logic that man ought to inherit the earth.

Some of Descartes early years were spent as a soldier, and everything we associate with the life of a soldier should be associated with Descartes, for he lived life to its fullest. Holland was an impressive and powerful nation during this time, and Descartes lived there for twenty years, studying mathematics, science, and philosophy. Once a notice was posted and a crowd had gathered to read it. Asking a man to translate the Flemish for him, Descartes learned that it announced a mathematical challenge in the form of a problem to be solved. Descartes remarked that the problem was easy and his translator soon discovered that here was no ordinary fellow. The translator was Isaac Beeckman, who was one of the greatest mathematicians in Holland and who became both a friend and a mentor of Descartes.

The great mathematical discovery attributed to Descartes is that of the formation of analytic geometry. This was to be the first time that algebra and geometry were to be directly related, and it resulted in the development of many other branches of mathematics, especially the calculus.

As a child Descartes was frail and sickly and was allowed to stay in bed late each morning. This habit stayed with him throughout his life, and he often claimed that these late morning hours were among his most productive. In 1649 he was persuaded to go to Sweden to attend Queen Christina at her court, where she had been able to gather a number of scholars. Soon after his arrival the Queen directed him to begin teaching her, which he was willing to do except that she required the instruction to

begin at five in the morning. After more than two months of this early rising and cold weather, which Descartes despised, he became ill of a fever and died soon after. There must be a moral here for all late risers.

Chapter 6

Number Theory

6.1

INTRODUCTION

As many historians have pointed out, the origin of mathematics was probably utilitarian. However, from a very early age the abstract relationships between numbers seem to have interested men. In ancient Greece, mathematics was separated into two main areas: *arithmetic*, which was the theoretical work of the scholar, and *logistic*, which was the practical computation of the businessman. In continental Europe, "arithmetic" is still used today in the classical sense. In America and other English-speaking countries, however, the word "arithmetic" is used in the "logistic" sense.

The study of the properties of numbers, commonly called *number theory*, began with the Greek scholars Thales (600 B.C.) and Pythagoras (540 B.C.), who used symmetric patterns of dots to represent various counting numbers. The use of the geometric shapes to represent numbers gave rise to the term *figurate numbers*.

Triangular numbers are those numbers which can be represented geometrically as symmetric triangles, such as those shown in Figure 6-1. Notice that the addition of consecutive counting numbers beginning with 1 formed the triangular numbers 3, 6, 10, ...

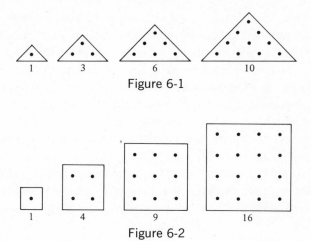

Figure 6-1

Figure 6-2

The sum of consecutive odd counting numbers gave the *square numbers* 1, 4, 9, 16, . . . , which are shown in Figure 6-2.

Undoubtedly, the Greeks were enthralled with the symmetry of the representations of the various figurate numbers. There are, however, other properties of these numbers that are interesting. For example, each of the classifications of numbers given has interesting patterns associated with them. To find the *fifth* triangular, the sum $1 + 2 + 3 + 4 + 5$ would be used. To find the *seventh* square number, the square 7^2 would be used. Other patterns will be identified in the exercises.

In addition to classifying numbers by their geometrical representation, the ancient Greeks distinguished between even and odd numbers. The Greeks thought of numbers as quantities made up of units. Hence, an *even number* was a counting number that could be divided into two equal parts, whereas an odd number was a counting number that could not be divided into equal parts. This classification scheme partitioned the set of counting numbers into two sets: the set of even counting numbers, that is, $\{2, 4, 6, 8, \ldots\}$ and the set of odd counting numbers, that is, $\{1, 3, 5, 7, \ldots\}$.

Number theory, that is, the study of the properties of numbers, is in use in the elementary classroom today. At the earliest levels, the child is asked to recognize the pattern that each whole number is *one more than* the previous whole number. In this way, the child learns that 6 is one more than 5. The distinction between even and odd whole numbers can be used to check the sum of two addends. If an even whole number is added to an odd whole number, the resulting sum must be an odd number; otherwise, the sum is even. Thus, when a child adds two odd whole numbers, his sum should be an even number; otherwise, he has made a mistake in his addition. It is possible that the child will get an even sum and still have an incorrect answer. To use the terminology of Chapter 2, evenness is a necessary but not a sufficient condition for a correct answer.

The rest of the chapter will be concerned with number theory and its use in the elementary classroom. For the most part, only the properties of the nonnegative integers will be considered. The properties of the negative integers may be systematized by renaming each negative integer a as $(-1)(-a)$ and studying the positive integer $(-a)$.

6.2

THE DIVISION ALGORITHM

There are several ways of partitioning the set of whole numbers. One such method was mentioned in Section 6.1, that is, to partition the whole numbers according to evenness and oddness. What we are saying is that every whole number has the form $2 \cdot n$ or $2 \cdot n + 1$, where n is some whole number. The Greeks recognized this property of counting numbers (remember: the Greeks did not use the number 0 in their considerations).

Another method of partitioning the whole numbers is based upon the fact that each whole number has one of the forms $3 \cdot n$, $3 \cdot n + 1$, or $3 \cdot n + 2$, where n is again a whole number. Notice that when $n = 0$, the numbers 0, 1, and 2 are generated. When $n = 1$, the numbers 3, 4, and 5 are generated, and so on.

You should notice at this time that there is a definite pattern resulting from these methods of partitioning the whole numbers. Do you see that another method would entail using the forms $4 \cdot n$, $4 \cdot n + 1$, $4 \cdot n + 2$, and $4 \cdot n + 3$, where n is a whole number? This method could be carried on indefinitely using the pattern that each time we increase the number of forms by 1, with the last form being (constant $\times n$) + (constant $- 1$), where n is a whole number. If we continue our investigation, we observe the following:

1. The constant addend is always greater than or equal to zero and less than the constant factor.
2. As we continue partitioning the whole numbers by expanding the number of forms we use, the constant factor may be changed to any positive whole number. For example, initially the constant factor was 2. It was then changed to 3, and then to 4.
3. Every whole number may be expressed in one of the forms we developed.
4. The variable n is always a whole number.

On the basis of these observations, we state the following conjecture, which is called the *division algorithm:*

If a is a whole number, then a may be expressed in the form $a = b \cdot q + r$, where b is a positive whole number, q is a whole number, and r is greater than or equal to 0 but less than b.

Although we have used the division algorithm to partition the whole numbers and to review the process of inductive reasoning, other uses of the division algorithm will be stressed in forthcoming sections.

EXERCISES (Sections 6.1 – 6.2)

1. Show each of the following figurate numbers as geometric shapes.
   a. 15   c. 21
   b. 25   d. 36
2. Represent each of the following square numbers as a sum of two triangular numbers. Use geometric shapes if necessary.
   a. 4   c. 16   e. 36
   b. 9   d. 25   f. 49
3. What pattern do you observe in Exercise 2?
4. Find each of the following:
   a. The fourth triangular number.
   b. The eighth triangular number.
   c. The sixth square number.
   d. The twelfth square number.
5. A pentagonal number is a number that can be represented as a pentagon (a five-sided polygon). Illustrate geometrically the first four pentagonal numbers.

6. Express the following pentagonal numbers as the sum of a square number and a triangular number.
   a. 5   c. 22   e. 51
   b. 12   d. 35   f. 70

7. In Exercise 5 there is a pattern for determining the nth pentagonal number. What is this pattern?

8. The story is told of a German schoolboy (see p. 260) who was asked to find the sum of the first 100 counting numbers. He found this sum in the following way.

$$\begin{aligned}
\text{sum} &= 1 + 2 + 3 + \cdots + 100 \\
\text{sum} &= 100 + 99 + 98 + \cdots + 1 \\
\text{sum} + \text{sum} &= 101 + 101 + 101 + \cdots + 101 \\
2 \times \text{sum} &= 100 \times 101 \\
\text{sum} &= \frac{100 \times 101}{2} = 5{,}050
\end{aligned}$$

Use this process to find the sum of the first
   a. Ten counting numbers.
   b. Thirty counting numbers.
   c. Six odd numbers.
   d. Ten odd numbers.
   e. Ten even numbers.

9. The division algorithm can be used to generate a set of equivalence classes that partition the set of whole numbers according to the remainder r when a is divided by b. Show the equivalence classes for division by each of the following:
   a. 2   c. 4
   b. 3   d. 5

6.3

PRIME AND COMPOSITE NUMBERS

It is possible to classify the whole numbers according to the number of nonzero divisors each number has. We insist that our divisors be nonzero in the same manner that the teacher insists that the child not try to divide by zero. Division by zero is meaningless in whole number arithmetic.

We state the following definition in terms of integers, reminding the student that our primary consideration is with whole numbers.

An integer a is *divisible* by a nonzero integer b if there exists an integer c such that $a = b \cdot c$. The nonzero

> integer b is called a *divisor* or a *factor* of a. We say "b divides a" and write "$b|a$." We also say that "a is a *multiple* of b."

To illustrate the definition, we say that "5 divides or is a divisor of 20," since $5 \cdot 4 = 20$. We write "$5|20$." Notice that 3 is not a divisor of 20, since we cannot find a whole number c such that $20 = 3 \cdot c$. We write "$3 \!\!\not|\, 20$."

There are some whole numbers with exactly two divisors: 1 and the number itself. We formally define these numbers as follows:

> A whole number p, $p > 1$, is a *prime number* if p has exactly two distinct divisors, itself and 1.

As you might expect, there is also a set of numbers each of which has more than two distinct divisors. We shall require that the set of divisors be finite and have more than one element; hence, we exclude 0 and 1 from this set. We define this set of numbers as follows:

> A whole number n, $n > 1$, that is not prime is a *composite number*.

Before leaving this section we point out that we have partitioned the set of whole numbers into three sets: the set of prime numbers, the set of composite numbers, and the set consisting of the numbers 0 and 1.

Also, it was stated that division by zero is meaningless in whole number arithmetic. This statement warrants further attention. Suppose that 0 does divide 5. Then by our definition there would have to be a whole number c such that $c \cdot 0 = 5$. But this is impossible, since we know that any whole number multiplied by 0 gives 0, not 5. We have reached a contradiction by assuming there is such a whole number c.

Finally, you should notice that every nonzero whole number is a divisor of 0, since $0 = 0 \cdot c$. It was for this reason that we stated that the set of divisors of 0 is infinite, since the set of nonzero whole numbers is infinite.

EXERCISES (Section 6.3)

1. A rectangular number is a number that can be represented as a rectangle. Which of the following numbers can be illustrated as rectangular numbers?

a. 3	d. 6	g. 17
b. 4	e. 8	h. 20
c. 5	f. 11	i. 32

2. Which of the numbers in Exercise 1 are composite numbers?

3. Which of the numbers in Exercise 1 are prime numbers?

4. Use the definition of divisor to show each of the following:
   a. $2|10$ c. $15|90$ e. $4|120$
   b. $3|15$ d. $8|96$ f. $6|0$

5. List the following sets:
   a. {even whole numbers} ∩ {prime numbers}
   b. {odd whole numbers} ∩ {prime numbers}
   c. {prime numbers} ∩ {composite numbers}
   d. {prime numbers} ∪ {composite numbers}
   e. {odd whole numbers} ∪ {even whole numbers}
   f. {0, 1} ∪ {prime numbers} ∪ {composite numbers}
   g. {0, 1} ∩ {prime numbers} ∩ {composite numbers}

6. Draw Venn diagrams to illustrate Exercise 5.

7. Solve each equation. Can you make a conjecture from the pattern?
   a. $5 = (1 \times 6) - n$ d. $19 = (3 \times n) + 1$ g. $73 = (12 \times n) + 1$
   b. $7 = (1 \times 6) + n$ e. $29 = (n \times 6) - 1$ h. $89 = (15 \times n) - 1$
   c. $13 = (2 \times 6) + n$ f. $37 = (n \times 6) + 1$ i. $97 = (n \times 6) + 1$

8. Is the set of prime numbers closed under the operation of addition as defined on W?

9. Is the set of prime numbers closed under the operation of multiplication as defined on W?

10. Is the set of composite numbers closed under the operation of addition as defined on W?

11. Is the set of composite numbers closed under the operation of multiplication as defined on W?

12. Is the set {0, 1} closed under the operation of addition as defined on W?

13. Is the set {0, 1} closed under the operation of multiplication as defined on W?

6.4

PROPERTIES OF PRIMES AND COMPOSITES

The Greek scholars considered the prime numbers to be the building blocks of all counting numbers greater than 1. Their assertion was somewhat justified by the following theorem, which was posed by the Greeks.

The Fundamental Theorem of Arithmetic. Every whole number greater than 1 is either a prime or can be expressed as the product of prime factors in one and only one way except for the order of the prime factors.

As an example of the Fundamental Theorem, consider the *prime factorization* of 42, which may be found by constructing a factor tree that begins with the first prime factor of 42. Each resulting composite factor is, in turn, broken down into a prime factor and a factor that is either prime or composite. The process continues until there are only prime factors on the tree. For example,

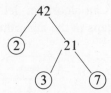

Therefore, $42 = 2 \times 3 \times 7$. The Fundamental Theorem states that 2, 3, and 7 are the only prime factors of 42 and that there is no other way, except for order, to express 42 as a product of primes. We see now why 1 is not considered a prime number. Each nonprime number could be expressed as a product of primes in several different ways, depending upon the number of times the "prime" 1 is used. For example, $42 = 2 \times 3 \times 7 \times 1$ and $42 = 2 \times 3 \times 7 \times 1 \times 1 \times 1$ would be different prime factorizations of 42. It is easier to eliminate 1 from the class of prime numbers, so that the Fundamental Theorem holds for the set of whole numbers greater than 1.

It may seem that the Fundamental Theorem is rather trivial, but we shall point out later that we depend quite heavily upon this theorem in finding the least common multiple and the greatest common divisor of two or more numbers. In fact, the properties of divisibility of whole numbers depend upon this theorem.

Various attempts have been made to give a formula that will yield only primes. For example, the formulas

$$n^2 - n + 41 \qquad \text{and} \qquad n^2 + n + 17$$

will give a prime number for every whole number value of n up to a given number. In the case of $n^2 - n + 41$ each whole number from 0 to 40 will give a prime result. Notice that if $n = 41$, then $41^2 - 41 + 41$

gives a number which is divisible by itself, 1, and 41. Hence it is not a prime number. In the second formula, each whole number from 0 to 16 will yield a prime result. It has been proved that no expression, such as those given (these expressions are called polynomials with integral coefficients), regardless of the degree of the expression, can yield only prime numbers when the domain of the expression is the set of natural numbers.

Is there, then, a procedure for finding prime numbers? In particular, is there a procedure or algorithm for finding all the primes that are less than a given whole number N? The answer is yes, but the procedure is quite cumbersome. The procedure is named after a Greek mathematician who lived around 230 B.C. and is called the Sieve of Eratosthenes. Since this is an algorithm, let us use a flow chart (Figure 6-3) to illustrate the steps in the algorithm.

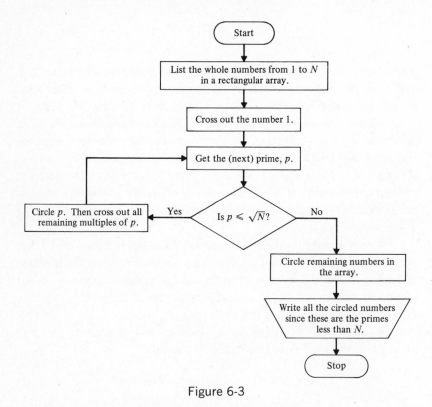

Figure 6-3

As an example of the use of the Sieve of Eratosthenes, let us find all the prime numbers less than 50.

Step 1. List the whole numbers from 1 to 50 in a rectangular array.

Step 2. Cross out the number 1.

Step 3. Get the next prime, which in this case is the first prime 2.

Step 4. Is $2 \leq \sqrt{50}$? Since $\sqrt{50}$ is approximately 7, the answer to this question is yes.

Step 5. Circle 2. Then cross out the remaining multiples of 2 by drawing horizontal lines through the row containing 2 and every second row after the row containing 2.

Step 6. Get the next prime, which is 3.

Step 7. Is $3 \leq \sqrt{50}$? The answer is yes.

Step 8. Circle 3. Then cross out the remaining multiples of 3 by drawing a horizontal line through the third row.

Step 9. Get the next prime, which is 5.

Step 10. Is $5 \leq \sqrt{50}$? The answer is yes.

Step 11. Circle 5. Then cross out the remaining multiples of 5 by drawing diagonal lines from 5 and the multiples of 5 shown in Figure 6-4. Notice each of these diagonal lines begins with a number that is a multiple of 5, five numbers from 5.

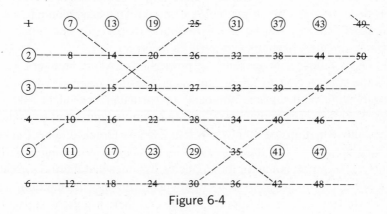

Figure 6-4

Step 12. Get the next prime, which is 7.

Step 13. Is $7 \leq \sqrt{50}$? The answer is yes.

Step 14. Circle 7. Then cross out the remaining multiples of 7 by drawing diagonal lines from 7 and the multiples of 7 shown in Figure 6-4.

Step 15. Get the next prime, which is 11.

Step 16. Is $11 \leq \sqrt{50}$? The answer is no.

223

Step 17. Circle 11 and the remaining numbers that have not been eliminated in the array.

Step 18. All circled numbers are the primes less than 50. We now stop the algorithm.

Figure 6-4 shows the prime numbers less than 50.

It may appear somewhat mysterious why we cross out only multiples of all primes less than or equal to $\sqrt{N}$. In the example only primes less than or equal to 7 were considered. Suppose we felt that possibly 47, one of the numbers left after the sieve process, was indeed composite. Then, by the Fundamental Theorem, 47 can be expressed as the product of two factors, one of which is prime. Also notice that this prime divisor is greater than $\sqrt{47}$, since we have eliminated all prime divisors of 47 that are less than or equal to $\sqrt{47}$. Let us examine the second factor rather closely. It is either prime or it is a composite number less than $\sqrt{47}$, since our first factor is greater than $\sqrt{47}$. If the second factor is a prime, then 47 is a multiple of a prime less than $\sqrt{47}$ and, hence, should have been eliminated in the sieve process. If the second factor is not a prime, then by the Fundamental Theorem it contains a prime factor that is less than $\sqrt{47}$. But this means that the second factor is a multiple of a prime factor which is less than $\sqrt{47}$. This prime multiple should have been eliminated by the sieve process. Hence, our assumption that 47 (or any other remaining number) is composite must be incorrect.

As we further investigate the properties of whole numbers, several questions come to mind. One such question originates from an investigation of the prime numbers. In particular, we might ask: Is there a greatest prime number? This question is equivalent to asking if the number of prime numbers is infinite. The Greek scholar Euclid (300 B.C.) proved the theorem that the number of prime numbers is infinite. His proof, noted for its simplicity, assumes that there is a greatest prime and then shows a contradiction with this assumption. To illustrate Euclid's method, let us assume that there is a greatest prime, such as 79. We now show that we shall arrive at a contradiction by showing that there must be a prime greater than 79. The proof about to be shown is extremely valuable to teachers since it involves an indirect form of reasoning.

Form the number that is the product of all primes 2 through 79. Now add 1 to this product and call the resulting number N. That is,

$$N = (2 \cdot 3 \cdot 5 \cdot 7 \cdot 11 \ldots 79) + 1$$

The number N is larger than 79 and is either prime or composite. If N

is prime, then we have found a prime number greater than 79, the number we assumed to be the greatest prime. Hence, our original assumption that 79 is the greatest prime is false. Therefore, there is no greatest prime. There is, however, the possibility that N is not prime. If this be the case, then N is a composite number greater than 1. We know by the Fundamental Theorem of Arithmetic that N may be expressed as a product of prime numbers in one and only one way. But now consider what the prime factors of this product look like. Certainly 2 cannot divide N since, when we divide by 2, we must get a remainder of 1 (do you see how we would use the division algorithm here?). Likewise, division by 3, 5, 7, . . . , 79 leaves a remainder of 1. Hence, we are assured by the fundamental theorem that N can be expressed as a prime or as a product of primes, and none of the primes 2, 3, 5, . . . , 79 is a factor of N. Our only conclusion is that N is either a prime greater than 79 or is a product of primes greater than 79. In either case, we have contradicted our assumption that there is a greatest prime. This method of proof can be used for any choice of a greatest prime.

If we were to observe a table of prime numbers, we would notice that there are some pairs of prime numbers which differ by 2. Such pairs of numbers are called *twin primes*. Examples of *twin primes* are 3 and 5, 5 and 7, 11 and 13, 17 and 19, and 29 and 31. As we proceed through our table of primes, we find that we can continue finding twin primes; however, they become less numerous as we get sufficiently far out in the table. Is it possible that the twin primes come to an end if we go sufficiently far out in the set of primes or is it the case that there are infinitely many twin primes? There is a conjecture in number theory that the number of pairs of twin primes is infinite. To this day, no proof of this conjecture is known. This statement may surprise you, since one of the more fascinating aspects of number theory is that many of the problems proposed are simple enough for the layman to understand, appreciate, and solve. While many conclusions in number theory seem uncontestable, the proofs of these conclusions are among the most difficult in mathematics to ascertain.

Before leaving this section, let us consider another conclusion of number theory that appears for all intents and purposes to be valid.

Christian Goldbach (1690–1764) proposed the following conjectures in 1742:

1. Every even number greater than 4 is the sum of two odd primes.
2. Every odd number greater than 7 is the sum of three odd primes.

As we look at various values for conjecture 1 alone, we see that

$6 = 3 + 3$	$16 = 3 + 11$ or $5 + 11$
$8 = 3 + 5$	$18 = 7 + 11$ or $5 + 13$
$10 = 5 + 5$ or $7 + 3$	$20 = 7 + 13$ or $3 + 17$

Also, we see that

$9 = 3 + 3 + 3$	$23 = 7 + 5 + 11$
$11 = 3 + 3 + 5$	$25 = 3 + 5 + 17$ or $7 + 7 + 11$
$19 = 3 + 5 + 11$	$57 = 3 + 7 + 47$ or $19 + 19 + 19$

As with the twin prime conjecture, no proof of Goldbach's conjectures has been found. While our intuition may tell us these conjectures are true, the deductive proof necessary for this conjecture to be classified as a theorem still escapes us.

EXERCISES (Section 6.4)

1. Express the following, whenever possible, as prime factorizations.
   a. 12   d. 42   g. 75
   b. 28   e. 54   h. 110
   c. 29   f. 90   i. 113

2. For the following, what is the last prime whose multiples would be eliminated in the sieve of Eratosthenes?
   a. {all primes ≤ 48}   d. {all primes ≤ 100}
   b. {all primes ≤ 64}   e. {all primes ≤ 121}
   c. {all primes ≤ 81}   f. {all primes ≤ 125}

3. Use the sieve of Eratosthenes to find all primes less than or equal to the given number.
   a. 50   d. 80
   b. 60   e. 90
   c. 70   f. 100

4. Illustrate Euclid's proof by assuming that 11 is the greatest prime.

5. Express the following as the sum of two primes.
   a. 8   d. 20   g. 38   j. 62
   b. 12   e. 24   h. 44
   c. 16   f. 28   i. 56

6. Express the following as the sum of three odd primes.
   a. 13   d. 21   g. 35
   b. 15   e. 27   h. 41
   c. 17   f. 29   i. 45

7. The product of two prime numbers is 346. What are the prime numbers? (*Hint:* Can you use evenness to help you?)

$$1 \mid 42 \qquad \text{1 and 42 are divisors}$$
$$2 \mid 42 \qquad \text{2 and 21 are divisors}$$
$$3 \mid 42 \qquad \text{3 and 14 are divisors}$$
$$6 \mid 42 \qquad \text{6 and 7 are divisors}$$

Notice at this point that if we were to continue our process we would be repeating divisors that we had previously determined. In fact, we know that we can stop our divisibility tests after we have considered all whole number divisors less than or equal to $\sqrt{42}$. We are *not* saying that all divisors of 42 are less than 6. What we are stating is that, in using our procedure, all divisors of 42 greater than $\sqrt{42}$ will be determined as we determine divisors less than or equal to $\sqrt{42}$. The argument for this assertion is similar to the argument given in the discussion of the sieve of Eratosthenes. The set of divisors of 42, indicated by D_{42}, then becomes

$$D_{42} = \{1, 2, 3, 6, 7, 14, 21, 42\}$$

Likewise, the set of divisors of 60 is

$$D_{60} = \{1, 2, 3, 4, 5, 6, 10, 12, 15, 20, 30, 60\}$$

The set of common divisors is

$$D_{42} \cap D_{60} = \{1, 2, 3, 6\}$$

The greatest number of this set, 6, is the GCD(42, 60). Notice that 6 is a multiple of every other common divisor of 42 and 60.

Although our procedure guarantees a result, it isn't very practical, particularly if the numbers involved are very large. There is another procedure that involves the prime factorization of the two numbers whose GCD is to be determined. Once again, let us assume that GCD(42, 60) is to be found. We shall use factor trees to express the prime factorizations of 42 and 60.

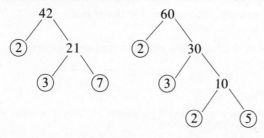

Therefore, $42 = 2 \times 3 \times 7$ and $60 = 2 \times 2 \times 3 \times 5$. The GCD(42, 60)

is the product of the common prime divisors of 42 and 60. Hence, GCD(42, 60) = 2 × 3 or 6.

We said earlier that the Fundamental Theorem of Arithmetic is basic to our work with divisibility. You might ask yourself how the prime factorization method for finding the GCD of two numbers could possibly be used if either of the two numbers had more than one prime factorization. The Fundamental Theorem assures us that this cannot happen.

There is a third method for finding the GCD of two numbers. This method entails the use of the division algorithm and can best be illustrated by an example. Once again, suppose that our task is to find GCD(42, 60). The division algorithm allows us to write

$$60 = 1 \bullet 42 + 18, \quad \text{where } 0 \leqslant 18 < 42$$

Repeating the process, this time using 42 as the dividend and 18 as the divisor, we have

$$42 = 2 \bullet 18 + 6, \quad \text{where } 0 \leqslant 6 < 18$$

Continuing with 18 as the dividend and 6 as the divisor, we obtain the equation

$$18 = 3 \bullet 6 + 0$$

If we collect our equations, we see that

$$60 = 1 \bullet 42 + 18$$
$$42 = 2 \bullet 18 + 6$$
$$18 = 3 \bullet 6 + 0$$

The last nonzero remainder is the GCD(42, 60). That is, GCD(42, 60) = 6. This algorithm is called the *Euclidean algorithm*.

The rationale behind the Euclidean algorithm is based upon the following theorem, which we shall prove because of its simplicity. You are asked to supply the reasons for the proof.

Theorem If a, b and d are whole numbers, where $a > b$, $d \mid a$, and $d \mid b$, then $d \mid (a - b)$.

Statements	Reasons
1. $d \mid a$ means $a = n \bullet d$ and $d \mid b$ means $b = m \bullet d$, where $n, m \in W$	1. Why?
2. $a > b$ and $n > m$	2. Why?
3. $a - b \in W$	3. Why?

4. $a - b = n \cdot d - m \cdot d$ 4. Why?
5. $a - b = (n - m) \cdot d$ 5. Why?
6. $n - m \in W$ 6. Why?
7. $\therefore d \mid (a - b)$ 7. Why?

Now notice that each of the equations that we wrote in the division process can be written in the form

$$\text{remainder} = \text{dividend} - (\text{quotient} \times \text{divisor})$$

In particular,

$$18 = 60 - 1 \cdot 42$$
$$6 = 42 - 2 \cdot 18$$
$$0 = 18 - 3 \cdot 6$$

In applying the theorem just proved to the first equation we see that since 6, GCD(60, 42), divides both 60 and 42, then 6 divides $60 - 42$, which is 18. But notice that 6 is not only a common divisor of 42 and 18, but it must be GCD(42, 18). If there were a common divisor of 18 and 42 greater than 6, GCD(60, 42), this common divisor would also divide 60. But this is not possible, since we said 6 was *the* greatest common divisor of 60 and 42. By continuing this reasoning we see that

$$\text{GCD}(60, 42) = \text{GCD}(42, 18)$$
$$\text{GCD}(42, 18) = \text{GCD}(18, 6)$$
$$\text{GCD}(18, 6) = 6$$

By the transitive property of equality, GCD(60, 42) = 6.

Quite frequently you will encounter situations in which GCD(a, b) = 1. We then say the following:

> If GCD(a, b) = 1, then a and b are said to be *relatively prime*.

A fraction in simplest form has numerator and denominator relatively prime.

A teacher using the prime factorization method of finding the greatest common divisor of two whole numbers must be careful to point out to the children that although 1 is not a member of the prime factorization of two whole numbers it is a divisor of every whole number. Thus, if two whole numbers have no common prime factors, we say GCD(a, b) = 1, since 1 is a common divisor of every pair of whole numbers.

In the addition and subtraction of fractional numbers such as

$\frac{5}{12}$ and $\frac{3}{10}$ a child is taught to find the least common denominator of the two fractions. The least common denominator will be a multiple of each denominator. In fact, we insist that it be the least common multiple of 12 and 10. Our first task then is to specify what we mean by the least common multiple of two numbers, and then to determine a procedure for finding this number.

> *The least common multiple* of two positive whole numbers a and b, written LCM(a, b), is a positive whole number n, such that $a \mid n$ and $b \mid n$, and n divides every other common multiple of a and b (this means that n is the *least common multiple*).

To restate this definition in simpler terms, we insist first that n be a common multiple of a and b and, second, that n be the *least* common multiple of a and b.

There are at least three ways of determining LCM(10, 12). One method again is called a brute-force approach. We begin by finding the set of multiples of 10, designated M_{10}, and the set of multiples of 12, designated M_{12}. These sets are

$$M_{10} = \{0, 10, 12, 20, 30, 40, 50, 60, \ldots\}$$
$$M_{12} = \{0, 12, 24, 36, 48, 60, \ldots\}$$

By finding the intersection of M_{10} and M_{12} we determine the set of common multiples of 10 and 12.

$$M_{10} \cap M_{12} = \{0, 60, 120, \ldots\}$$

Finally, by choosing the least nonzero multiple, we have

$$\text{LCM}(10, 12) = 60$$

If this method were the only method available to find LCM(a, b), many of you would probably consider another choice of profession. Fortunately, there is a simpler algorithm we can use that involves the use of prime factorization. Let us begin by expressing 10 and 12 as prime factorizations; that is,

$$10 = 2 \times 5 \qquad \text{and} \qquad 12 = 2 \times 2 \times 3$$

Now LCM(10, 12) is the product of all the distinct prime factors in the prime factorizations of 10 and 12. However, each prime factor is used the *maximum* number of times it occurs in either of the prime factorizations. In our example, the prime factor 2 occurs once in the factorization of 10 and twice in the factorization of 12. We use the factor 2×2 and write

$$\text{LCM}(10, 12) = 2 \times 2 \times 3 \times 5 = 60$$

We now use our LCM in the least common denominator to find the sum

$$\frac{5}{12} + \frac{3}{10} = \frac{25 + 18}{60} = \frac{43}{60}$$

Again, you are cautioned against using the prime factorization method to find the LCM of two numbers, one of which is the number 1. There is no prime factorization of 1. Does this mean that the LCM cannot be found? The answer is no, since $\text{LCM}(1, a) = a$, where a is any positive whole number. Do you see why?

You may be wondering at this time if there is a simple way to find $\text{LCM}(a, b)$, particularly if a and b are very large. The answer is yes, and we divide the product $a \cdot b$ by $\text{GCD}(a, b)$ to find $\text{LCM}(a, b)$. That is,

$$\text{LCM}(a, b) = \frac{a \cdot b}{\text{GCD}(a, b)}$$

$\text{GCD}(a, b)$ is found most rapidly by using the Euclidean algorithm.

Let us find $\text{LCM}(855, 228)$ to illustrate this procedure. By the Euclidean algorithm, $\text{GCD}(855, 228) = 57$. We found this in three steps. The product, 855×228, is equal to 194,940. $\text{LCM}(855, 228) = 194{,}940/57 = 3420$.

To understand why this algorithm works, we argue as follows. Once again, you should be able to supply the reasons.

Statements	Reasons
1. Suppose $\text{GCD}(a, b) = d$	1. Given
2. Then $a = m \cdot d$ and $b = n \cdot d$	2. Why?
3. $\text{GCD}(m, n) = 1$	3. Why?
4. Therefore, $a \cdot b = m \cdot d \cdot n \cdot d$	4. Why?
5. But $a \cdot n = n \cdot m \cdot d$ and $b \cdot m = m \cdot n \cdot d$	5. Why?
6. Therefore, $n \cdot m \cdot d$ is a multiple of a and a multiple of b	6. Why?
7. But $\text{LCM}(a, b) = n \cdot m \cdot d$	7. Why?
8. $= \dfrac{d \cdot n \cdot m \cdot d}{d}$	8. Why?
9. $= \dfrac{a \cdot b}{\text{GCD}(a, b)}$	9. Why?

If you have difficulty understanding the argument, replace the variables in the argument with numbers, being careful to replace the variables with the *correct* numbers. Now go through the argument. Perhaps this will help you to determine the reasons for each step.

EXERCISES (Section 6.5)

1. List the members of the following:
   a. D_{30} c. D_{144} e. D_1
   b. D_{45} d. D_2 f. D_0

2. List the prime factorizations of the following:
   a. 30 c. 144 e. 65
   b. 45 d. 56 f. 24

3. There is a procedure for finding the number of divisors of a given number. First, list the number N as a prime factorization. That is, $N = a^p \cdot b^q \cdot c^r \cdots$, where $a, b, c, \cdots$ are the prime factors of N raised to the powers $p, q, r, \cdots$, respectively. The number of divisors of N is found by the formula
$$n(D_N) = (p + 1)(q + 1)(r + 1) \cdots$$
until we have exhausted all the exponents.

   Use this formula and Exercise 2 to find the number of divisors of the following.
   a. 30 c. 144 e. 65
   b. 45 d. 56 f. 24

4. Explain how you might use $n(D_N)$ in teaching children.

5. List the members of the following.
   a. M_2 c. M_5 e. M_{10}
   b. M_3 d. M_7 f. M_{12}

6. Which of the following is true? If false, give a counterexample.
   a. D_N is always finite.
   b. M_N is always infinite.
   c. If $D_a \subseteq D_b$, then $b \in M_a$.
   d. If $GCD(a, b) = 1$, then $LCM(a, b) = a \times b$.
   e. $M_2 \cap M_6 = M_6$.
   f. $M_3 \cup M_9 = M_9$.

7. Use prime factorization to find $GCD(a, b)$ and $LCM(a, b)$.
   a. (24, 56) c. (36, 54) e. (31, 7)
   b. (72, 90) d. (12, 40) f. (12, 16, 20)

8. Verify, using Exercise 7, that $a \times b = LCM(a, b) \cdot GCD(a, b)$.

9. Use the Euclidean algorithm to find $GCD(a, b)$ in Exercise 7.

10. Consider the process $*$, defined on the positive whole numbers as follows:
$$a * b = \text{the least common divisor of } (a, b)$$
   a. Is this process an operation?

   b. If so, what properties does this system possess?

11. Give arguments or reasons for the following divisibility tests: divisibility by
   a. 2   e. 6
   b. 3   f. 8
   c. 4   g. 9
   d. 5

12. Tell whether the following are divisible by 2, 3, 4, 5, 6, 8, or 9.
   a. 4,362   b. 123,120   c. 753,801   d. 11,347,101

13. What conclusions regarding N can be drawn from the following?
   a. $n(D_N) = 2$
   b. $n(D_N) = 3$
   c. $n(D_N)$ is an odd number greater than 3

14. What conclusions can be drawn under the following conditions?
   a. If $p, q \in$ {primes}, then GCD(p, q) equals ?
   b. If $p, q \in$ {primes}, then LCM(p, q) equals ?

15. Construct a flow chart to show how you would find the divisors of 40 using the divisibility tests.

16. Construct a flow chart for the Euclidean algorithm.

17. How would you determine the LCM of three numbers?

18. How would you determine the GCD of three numbers?

6.6

CONGRUENCE

As an elementary school teacher you will be placed in the position of choosing classroom helpers to assist you in the management of your classroom. For example, many classrooms have a child who is responsible for taking the attendance, a child who checks the children's desks for orderliness and cleanliness, and a child who is caretaker of the classroom mice, gerbils, and whatever other animals are present in the classroom. Suppose that a selection arises in which six children volunteer for a particular task. The task is of such a nature that you want a particular volunteer to be selected because you know that he will do the best job in carrying out the task. Is there a way that you can make the selection in a manner which appears fair to all the volunteers, yet which will allow you to make the selection of your choice? A variation of a childhood rhyme that is still used by children in choosing teams provides the means. Consider the following rhyme:

> Eenie, meenie, mynie, moe
> Catch a helper by his toe
> If he hollers,
> Let him go.
> Eenie, meenie, mynie, moe.

As the verse is recited, a counting process is begun in which each word of the verse is associated with each volunteer. The word "mynie" is associated with the third child, "catch" with the fifth child, "helper" with the first child, and so forth. Do you see that after we associate a word with the sixth child we return to the first child and begin our word association again? Take a moment and complete Figure 6-5,

Child	1	2	3	4	5	6
	eenie	meenie	mynie	moe	catch	a
	helper	by	?	?	?	?
word	?	?	?	?	?	?
	?	?	?	?	?	?

Figure 6-5

which shows the association of each word with each child. There are 20 words in the rhyme to be assigned to six children. The word list will "end on" the second child. The child you prefer should be placed in the second position in the lineup of volunteers. Notice that there are 3 groups of 6 words with 2 words left over. That is,

$$20 = 3 \cdot 6 + 2 \qquad \text{or} \qquad 2 = 20 - 3 \cdot 6$$

This mathematical statement should suggest the division algorithm to you. Do you see where you would position your selection if 3 children volunteered? If 7 children volunteered?

It is not necessary for you to construct a table like Figure 6-5 each time the number of words in the rhyme or the number of volunteers changes. We shall learn a few mathematical concepts in this section that will greatly simplify our selective procedure. Before we do, consider another situation, which is a result of everyday experience.

Each of us in the course of our lives has had numerous encounters with the calendar. Because of this experience, each of us in looking at the partial calendar of Figure 6-6 can determine the missing days of the month by recognizing that any two Friday dates differ by some multiple of 7. The same is true of any two Monday dates, and so on.

MARCH						
Sun	Mon	Tues	Wed	Thurs	Fri	Sat
				1	2	3
4	5	6	7	8	9	10
11	12	13	14	15		
18	19	20				
25	26					

Figure 6-6

If you were asked if the 3rd and 24th of March were on the same day of the week, you would probably answer yes after a few moments reflection. Either consciously or subconsciously you probably thought as follows:

"Seven days after the 3rd is the 10th."
"Seven days after the 10th is the 17th."
"Seven days after the 17th is the 24th."
"Therefore, the 3rd and the 24th are on the same day of the week."

Notice that your thinking process could have been shortened by thinking that $24 - 3 = 21$, which is a multiple of 7. Hence, the 24th is 3 weeks from the 3rd and must be on the same day of the week as the 3rd.

It is interesting to notice that the seven weekdays not only separate the days of the month into seven groups, but they also do likewise for the days of the year. Many of us have wondered on what day of the week Christmas will fall this year. If we don't have ready access to a calendar, we can still determine the weekday for Christmas. For example, suppose that today is March 3, a Saturday, and the 62nd day of the year (we found this by adding 31 days for January, 28 days for February, and 3 days for March). Christmas, December 25, is the 359th day of the year. Do you see that 365, the number of days in the year, minus 6, the number of days remaining in the year on the 25th, gives 359 days? If Christmas were to fall on the same weekday as today (Saturday), then $359 - 62$, that is, 297, would have to be a multiple of 7. This is not the case since we do not have a zero remainder when we divide by 7. Our remainder is 3. If we think for a moment we see that Christmas must be 3 days from Saturday. That is, Christmas must fall on a Tuesday. For the year 1973, this was true. As a matter of fact, Christmas will always occur 3 days after the weekday upon which March 3 falls.

If we were to number each day of the year with a number from 1 to 365, we see that we have seven distinct classes. Each number of each class is related to every other number of that class by the fact that each number gives the same remainder when divided by 7. For example, the class of days with remainder 3 is given by {3, 10, 17, 24, 31, 38, . . . , 360} and the class of days with remainder 5 is given by {5, 12, 19, 26, . . . , 362}.

We see then that the number 7 partitions the set

$$\{1, 2, 3, \ldots, 365\}$$

into 7 classes. Remember: since this is a partition, each class is disjoint to every other class and the union of the classes gives our original set. This should seem reasonable, since no day of the year can be both a Wednesday and a Friday, and yet the union of all the Sundays through Saturdays of the year gives 365 days.

Is it reasonable to assume that the number 7 partitions the set of integers? If so, what do the classes look like? To answer this question, we need to revisit the Division Algorithm (see p. 217) and extend this algorithm somewhat to include integers.

> *Extended Division Algorithm.* If a is integer, then a may be expressed in the form $a = b \cdot q + r$, where b is a positive integer, q is an integer, and r is an integer greater than or equal to 0 but less than b.

Now, as we consider partitioning the integers in the same manner as previously, we see that each negative integer can be placed in some remainder class and that the remainder classes are limited to those classes which give remainders greater than or equal to 0 but less than 7. The seven classes are

$$\{\ldots -21, -14, -7, \mathbf{0}, 7, 14, 21, \ldots\}$$
$$\{\ldots -20, -13, -6, \mathbf{1}, 8, 15, 22, \ldots\}$$
$$\{\ldots -19, -12, -5, \mathbf{2}, 9, 16, 23, \ldots\}$$
$$\{\ldots -18, -11, -4, \mathbf{3}, 10, 17, 24, \ldots\}$$
$$\{\ldots -17, -10, -3, \mathbf{4}, 11, 18, 25, \ldots\}$$
$$\{\ldots -16, -9, -2, \mathbf{5}, 12, 19, 26, \ldots\}$$
$$\{\ldots -15, -8, -1, \mathbf{6}, 13, 20, 27, \ldots\}$$

Let us agree to call the 0 remainder class [0], the 1 remainder class [1], and so forth. To see that $-15 \in [6]$, notice that $-15 = -3 \cdot 7 + 6$. Remember: in the extended division algorithm the remainder still must be nonnegative.

Up to this point we have been quite wordy in talking about the remainder classes. It is only reasonable to ask if there isn't a concise way of saying what has been said. To do so, we begin by defining a relation on two integers a and b.

> If a and b are integers and n is a positive integer, then *a is congruent to b, modulo n*, if n is a divisor of $a - b$. We write "$a \equiv b$ mod n." The positive integer n is called *the modulus*, which is Latin for "little measure."

This relation is an equivalence relation. You are asked to show in the exercises that the relation "congruence mod n" is reflexive and transitive. Symmetry is shown by observing the following:

1. $a \equiv b$ mod n	1. Given
2. $n \mid a - b$	2. Why?
3. $k \cdot n = a - b$, where $k \in Z$	3. Why?
4. $-k \cdot n = -(a - b)$	4. Why?
5. $-k \cdot n = b - a$	5. Why?
6. $\therefore n \mid b - a$	6. Why?
7. $\therefore b \equiv a$ mod n	7. Why?

You see now that congruence mod n as defined on Z, the set of integers, gives the equivalence classes $[0], [1], \ldots, [n-1]$, where $0, 1, 2, \ldots, (n-1)$ are the possible remainders of division by n.

Let us digress for a moment to relate what has been said thus far to the elementary classroom.

An activity encountered quite early in the mathematics education of a child is that of "skip counting." Instead of counting 1, 2, 3, 4, 5, . . . , a child is asked to skip count by threes in the following manner: 0, 3, 6, 9, 12, ... This activity frequently is done on the number line and is illustrated by jumps of three, as shown in Figure 6-7. Similar examples can be given for steps of 2, 4, 5, and so forth.

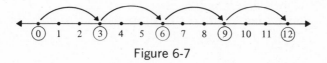

Figure 6-7

If, instead of beginning our skip counting at 0, we begin at 1, our number line becomes that of Figure 6-8. Likewise, by beginning at 2, we

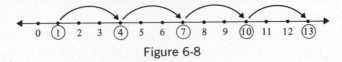

Figure 6-8

obtain the number line of Figure 6-9. The first number line illustrates the multiples of 3, that is, those numbers which, when divided by 3,

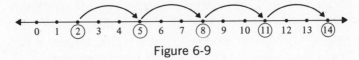

Figure 6-9

give a remainder of 0. The second and third number lines give those numbers which, when divided by 3, give remainders of 1 and 2, respectively. If we were to extend our number lines to include the negative integers, we would have the number lines for those numbers which are congruent to 0, 1, and 2, mod 3, respectively.

We would like now to consider the system consisting of the set of the equivalence classes, mod n, with the two binary operations of addition and multiplication defined upon this set. For notation purposes the set of equivalence classes, mod n, will be denoted by Z_n. As with any mathematical system, we must tell the reader how our operations are to be defined.

Addition. If $[a]$ and $[b]$ are elements of Z_n, then $[a] \oplus_n [b] = [a + b]$. Another way of stating this is to say that a mod $n \oplus_n b$ mod $n = (a + b)$ mod n, where "+" is addition as defined on Z.

As an example of the above definition, suppose that Z_5 is our set of classes. Then $[4] \oplus_5 [4] = (4 + 4)$ mod 5. This is, of course, $[3]$. Let us now build an addition table, modulo 5, and investigate the various properties of Z_5 under addition as defined previously. For convenience sake, let us stop writing brackets to denote our equivalence classes. Hence, we shall write 3 for $[3]$, 2 for $[2]$, and so forth. Our set Z_5 then becomes $\{0, 1, 2, 3, 4\}$.

We notice from Figure 6-10 that we have an additive identity, 0, since $0 + a = a + 0 = a$ for each $a \in Z_5$. Also, each element a of Z_5

Addition Table Mod 5

+	0	1	2	3	4
0	0	1	2	3	4
1	1	2	3	4	0
2	2	3	4	0	1
3	3	4	0	1	2
4	4	0	1	2	3

Figure 6-10

has one and only one additive inverse, which we denote by ^-a. For example, $^-2 = 3$ (read "the additive inverse of 2 is 3"). We know that each additive inverse is unique since the additive identity, 0, appears once and only once in each row or column. We may prove that addition is associative and commutative; however, commutativity may be observed from our figure by observing that there is a symmetry about the diagonal shown in the figure. If we were to cut out the figure and carefully fold it about the diagonal, identical numerals would coincide. A "2" would fold on top of a "2," a "0" on top of a "0," and so forth. Do you see why diagonal symmetry implies commutativity?

A final property which is of interest is that we have a cancellation property for addition. If $a \oplus_5 b = a \oplus_5 c$, then $b = c$ for all $a, b, c \in Z_5$.

Let us summarize what we have said so far regarding Z_5 under the operation of addition.

1. Z_5 is *commutative* under $\oplus_5$.
2. Z_5 is *associative* under $\oplus_5$.
3. There exists an *additive identity* 0 in Z_5.
4. Each element of Z_5 has a unique *additive inverse*.
5. Z_5 has a *cancellation property* under $\oplus_5$.

A mathematical system, such as Z_5, under a binary operation, such as $\oplus_5$, that is associative and possesses an identity and inverse elements is called a *group*.

241

The question may arise in your mind as to what we mean by subtraction mod 5. We treat subtraction mod 5, in the same way we treated
subtraction in the set of integers. Since we have additive inverses for
each element of Z_5, we define subtraction in terms of inverses.

> *Subtraction.* If a and b are elements of Z_n, then $a \ominus_n b =$
> $a \oplus_n {}^-b$, where ${}^-b$ is the additive inverse of b.

To illustrate the definition, let us solve the equation $3 \ominus_5 4 = \square$.
This equation becomes $3 \oplus_5 {}^-4 = \square$. We now add the inverse of 4,
which is 1, to 3 to solve the equation. That is, $3 \oplus_5 1 = 4$.

We now define multiplication. As you might expect, our definition will be constructed in a similar manner as we defined addition.

> *Multiplication.* If $[a]$ and $[b]$ are elements of Z_n, then
> $a \otimes_n b = [a \times b]$. Another way of stating this is to say
> $a \bmod n \otimes_n b \bmod n = (a \times b) \bmod n$, where "$\times$" is mul-
> tiplication as defined on Z.

Once again, suppose that Z_5 is our set of equivalence classes.
Then $4 \otimes_5 3 = (4 \times 3) \bmod 5$. This is 2. Proceeding as we did with the
operation of addition, we now build a multiplication table modulus 5
(Figure 6-11). Investigation of the table reveals that there exists a
multiplicative identity, 1, since $1 \cdot a = a \cdot 1 = a$ for each $a \in Z_5$. Using

Multiplication Table Mod 5

×	0	1	2	3	4
0	0	0	0	0	0
1	0	1	2	3	4
2	0	2	4	1	3
3	0	3	1	4	2
4	0	4	3	2	1

Figure 6-11

the diagonal test put forth earlier, we see we have commutativity. We can also prove associativity.

Two rather interesting questions come to mind. Does each element of Z_5 have an element that acts something like the additive inverse when we considered Z_5 under the operation of addition? Also, does Z_5 have a cancellation property for multiplication? To consider the first question, we need the following definition:

> Let S be a set of elements with a multiplicative identity 1. If, for element n of S, there exists another element n^{-1} of S so that $n \cdot n^{-1} = n^{-1} \cdot n = 1$, then n^{-1} is called the *multiplicative inverse* of n.

In today's elementary classroom, n^{-1} is generally called the reciprocal of n. For example, $\frac{1}{6}$ is called the *reciprocal* of $\frac{6}{1}$, and $\frac{6}{5}$ is called the reciprocal of $\frac{5}{6}$. Using our terminology, $\frac{6}{5}$ is the multiplicative inverse of $\frac{5}{6}$. That is, $\left(\frac{5}{6}\right)^{-1} = \frac{6}{5}$. Notice from the multiplication table that each nonzero element does have a multiplicative inverse. For example, $3^{-1} = 2$ since $3 \underset{5}{\otimes} 2 = 1$. Do you see how to use the table to find the multiplicative inverse of each nonzero element? We find the factor, look along its row until we find the multiplicative identity, and then read upward for the correct factor. Try this procedure to find 2^{-1}. To answer our question, each nonzero element of Z_5 has a multiplicative inverse.

The cancellation property for multiplication of integers was stated in Chapter 5. We restate this property at this time in a more general sense.

> *Cancellation property of multiplication.* If a, b, and c are elements of a set S such that $c \neq 0$ and $a \cdot c = b \cdot c$, then $b = a$.

Is it the case that Z_5 possesses the cancellation property for multiplication? The answer is yes, but the reason for our answer is not apparent. To make our response more reasonable, let us construct a multiplication table for Z_4. This table is given in Figure 6-12. We make the claim that Z_4 does *not* have the cancellation property for multiplication. Let us demonstrate a counterexample (please don't forget the power of a counterexample). Look across the 2 factor row. We see that the products 0 and 2 are repeated. Consider either product; for

Multiplication Table Mod 4

×	0	1	2	3
0	0	0	0	0
1	0	1	2	3
2	0	2	0	2
3	0	3	2	1

Figure 6-12

example, 2. We see that $2 \underset{4}{\otimes} 1 = 2$ and $2 \underset{4}{\otimes} 3 = 2$. Hence, $2 \otimes 1 = 2 \underset{4}{\otimes} 3$. Since $2 \neq 0$, the conditions for investigating the cancellation property are satisfied. Is it the case then that $1 = 3$? If the cancellation property holds, 1 must equal 3. You can see that this is *not* the case. Hence, Z_4 does not have the cancellation property for multiplication. To return to Z_5, we see that there is no repetition of products in any nonzero row or column. What this implies is that, if $c \neq 0$, $a \cdot c = b \cdot c$ means a must equal b. In other words, using the terminology of Chapter 2, $a = b$ is a necessary condition for $a \cdot c = b \cdot c$, or in order for $a \cdot c$ to equal $b \cdot c$, it is necessary for a to equal b.

While we are examining the multiplication table for modulus 4, we should notice that *each* nonzero element of Z_4 does *not* have a multiplicative inverse. The element 2 mod 4 does not have a multiplicative inverse, since there is no element 2^{-1} in Z_4 such that $2 \underset{4}{\otimes} 2^{-1} = 1$.

We state, without proof, that Z_p under multiplication will have a cancellation property and multiplicative inverses if and only if p is prime. Also, if Z_p does not have a cancellation property, then it does not have multiplicative inverses for each nonzero element.

In summary,

1. Z_5 is commutative under $\underset{5}{\otimes}$.
2. Z_5 is associative under $\underset{5}{\otimes}$.
3. There exists a multiplicative identity, 1, in Z_5.
4. Each nonzero element of Z_5 has a unique multiplicative inverse.
5. Z_5 has a cancellation property under $\underset{5}{\otimes}$.

Before considering classroom applications of the material that has been presented thus far in this section, further inspection of the addition and multiplication tables modulus 5 reveals that there is a distributive property of multiplication over addition modulo 5. We shall see how this distributive property is used shortly.

The reader may be asking why division modulo n seems to be having little or no attention paid to it in this section. The answer is simple: the operation of division is not always performable. If we define $a \ominus b$ to be the answer to the question $b \otimes \square = a$, we see that $3 \underset{n}{\ominus} 2$ cannot be performed, since there is no $\underset{n}{\square}$ mod 4 such that $2 \underset{4}{\otimes} \square = 3$. As you may have suspected, if p is prime, nonzero division is always performable in Z_p. Formally,

> *Division.* If $[a]$ and $[b]$ are elements of Z_n, where $[b] \neq [0]$ and n is prime, then $[a] \underset{n}{\ominus} [b] = [a] \underset{n}{\otimes} [b]^{-1}$, where $[b]^{-1}$ is the multiplicative inverse of $[b]$.

Let us now put some of these concepts to work for us. In Section 6.5 we stated that a number is divisible by 9 if the sum of the digits of the number is divisible by 9. To understand why this is true, it is necessary that you first realize that a number a is divisible by a nonzero positive number b if $a \equiv 0 \bmod b$. Notice that $9 \mid 18$ since $18 \equiv 0 \bmod 9$. Now consider the number 252. We maintain that this number is divisible by 9 since $2 + 5 + 2 = 9$, which is divisible by 9. Using the concepts of modular arithmetic,

1. $252 \bmod 9 = (200 + 50 + 2) \bmod 9$ 1. Why?
2. $\quad\quad = (200) \bmod 9 \oplus (50) \bmod 9 \oplus$ 2. Why?
   $(2) \bmod 9$
3. $= (2 \times 100) \bmod 9 \oplus (5 \times 10) \bmod 9 \oplus$ 3. Why?
   $(2) \bmod 9$
4. $= (2 \bmod 9 \otimes 100 \bmod 9) \oplus$ 4. Why?
   $(5 \bmod 9 \otimes 10 \bmod 9) \oplus (2 \bmod 9)$
5. Now $100 \bmod 9 = (99 + 1) \bmod 9$ and   5. Definition of $\oplus$
   $10 \bmod 9 = (9 + 1) \bmod 9$
6. $100 \bmod 9 = 99 \bmod 9 \oplus 1 \bmod 9$ and   6. Why?
   $10 \bmod 9 = 9 \bmod 9 \oplus 1 \bmod 9$
7. Hence, $100 \bmod 9 = 1 \bmod 9$ and   7. Why?
   $10 \bmod 9 = 1 \bmod 9$
8. $252 \bmod 9 = (2 \bmod 9 \otimes 1 \bmod 9) \oplus$ 8. Why?
   $(5 \bmod 9 \otimes 1 \bmod 9) \oplus 2 \bmod 9$
9. $\quad\quad = 2 \bmod 9 \oplus 5 \bmod 9 \oplus 2 \bmod 9$ 9. Why?
10. $\quad\quad = (2 + 5 + 2) \bmod 9$ 10. Why?

11. $= 0 \bmod 9$ 11. Why?
12. But this says that $9 \mid 252$.   12. Why?

What we have shown here is generalizable to any base ten numeral. Do you see why? With certain modifications, this procedure is also generalizable to any base b numeral (see Exercise 13). You will be asked in the exercises to argue the case for divisibility by 3. The preceding argument will be quite useful.

Much of what has been said must appear to be quite "modern" to you, but this is not always the case. The next application of modular arithmetic was used by English and German merchants of the sixteenth century as a check on computational work. This application is best illustrated by examples. In each example, we find the sum, mod 9, of the digits of the numerals with which we are computing. For illustrative purposes we call this sum a *9-sum*. We then check to see if the 9-sum of the sum of the addends equals the 9-sum of the sum; if the 9-sum of the difference of the sum and addend equals the 9-sum of the difference; and if the 9-sum of the factors equals the 9-sum of the product. Hopefully, the examples will make more sense than the description just given. The process is called *"casting out the nines."*

Example	9-sum	Check
326	$3 + 2 + 6 =$ 11 mod 9	11 mod 9 = 2 mod 9
+ 215	$2 + 1 + 5 = +$ 8 mod 9	8 mod 9 = + 8 mod 9
541	$5 + 4 + 1 =$ 10 mod 9	10 mod 9 = 1 mod 9
713	$7 + 1 + 3 =$ 11 mod 9	11 mod 9 = 2 mod 9
− 246	$2 + 4 + 6 =$ 12 mod 9	12 mod 9 = − 3 mod 9
467	$4 + 6 + 7 =$ 17 mod 9	17 mod 9 = 8 mod 9
296	$2 + 9 + 6 =$ 17 mod 9	17 mod 9 = 8 mod 9
× 11	$1 + 1 \quad =$ 2 mod 9	2 mod 9 = × 2 mod 9
3,256	$3 + 2 + 5 + 6 =$ 16 mod 9	16 mod 9 = 7 mod 9

A word of caution is given regarding the use of casting out the nines as a check procedure. In the first example, *if* the sum of 326 and 215 is correct, *then* the 9-sum must check. In other words, "9-sum must check" is a necessary condition (see p. 73) for the answer to be correct. This does not mean that if the 9-sums check then the answer is correct. Notice that if the child arrived at an answer of 631 as his sum, the 9-sum check would still work. The strength of casting out the nines lies in the following assertion: *if* the 9-sums do *not* check, then the sum of 326 and 215 is *not* correct. This you should recognize as the contrapositive of our original implication. If, after a child determines an answer to an addition, subtraction, or multiplication problem, his 9-sum check does *not* work, he has an incorrect answer.

As a final classroom application of modular arithmetic, we ask you to direct your attention to the clock face in Figure 6-13. The numbers represented by the clock face numerals form a finite set: $\{1, 2, 3, 4, 5, \ldots, 12\}$. These numbers may be considered to be equivalence classes, modulo 12, where the number 12 acts like the number 0 (remember, they are in the same equivalence class). Addition and multiplication are defined on our clock in exactly the same manner as we defined these operations modulo 12. If it is 9 o'clock now, the time 11 hours from now can be found by solving the equation

$$9 \underset{12}{\oplus} 11 = \square$$

The time 11 hours from now will be 8 o'clock. If we want to determine the time 33 hours ago, we must solve the equation

$$9 \underset{12}{\oplus} {}^{-}33 = \square$$

The additive inverse of 33 is 3; hence, the time 33 hours ago was 12 o'clock.

A rather interesting classroom activity is to build a circular slide rule such as that shown in Figure 6-15. We begin by constructing a small clock face, which is labeled and then cut out (Figure 6-13). The

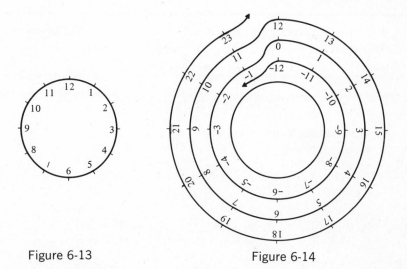

Figure 6-13   Figure 6-14

clock face represents the equivalence classes, modulo 12. On a separate piece of tagboard we devise a circular number line such as that shown in Figure 6-14. These two pieces are joined by a small swivel to give the slide rule (see Figure 6-15).

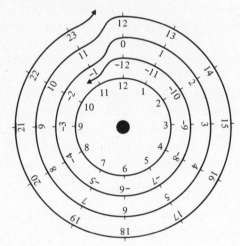

Figure 6-15

To find the sum $5 \underset{12}{\oplus} 11$, these steps are followed:

1. Set the 5 *on the clock face* directly below the 0 on the number line. (Do you see why we do this?)
2. Locate 11 on the *circular number line*.
3. The sum is the number represented *on the clock face* below 11. The sum is 4.

If it is 8 o'clock now, the time 11 hours ago is found by solving the equation $8 \underset{12}{\oplus} {}^-11 = \square$. Our slide rule tells us that our answer is 9. That is, the time 11 hours ago was 9 o'clock.

EXERCISES (Section 6.6)

1. Show that the following are true.
   a. $21 \equiv 0 \bmod 7$
   b. $-4 \equiv 0 \bmod 2$
   c. $-19 \equiv 5 \bmod 6$
   d. $5 \equiv 21 \bmod 8$
   e. $21 \equiv 5 \bmod 8$
   f. $3 \equiv 11 \bmod 2$

2. Which of the following is true, modulus 5?
   a. $0 \in [0]$
   b. $10 \in [0]$
   c. $-5 \in [0]$
   d. $4 \in [1]$
   e. $-4 \in [1]$
   f. $6 \in [1]$
   g. $-6 \in [4]$
   h. $19 \in [4]$
   i. $4 \in [4]$

3. Find the following sums when each number is an equivalence class.

   a. $2 \oplus_5 4$ d. $0 \oplus_{12} 9$ g. $2 \oplus_4 3$

   b. $3 \oplus_7 6$ e. $9 \oplus_{10} 9$ h. $5 \oplus_6 5$

   c. $1 \oplus_2 1$ f. $3 \oplus_9 7$ i. $6 \oplus_8 5$

4. Find the following differences when each number is an equivalence class.

   a. $1 \ominus_4 3$ c. $3 \ominus_4 2$ e. $3 \ominus_8 6$

   b. $2 \ominus_7 6$ d. $1 \ominus_7 5$ f. $4 \ominus_{10} 6$

5. Find the following products when each number is an equivalence class.

   a. $2 \otimes_4 3$ c. $6 \otimes_9 3$ e. $7 \otimes_{12} 3$

   b. $5 \otimes_8 7$ d. $4 \otimes_{12} 6$ f. $7 \otimes_{24} 12$

6. Find the following quotients when each number is an equivalence class.

   a. $2 \oslash_5 4$ c. $8 \oslash_{11} 3$ e. $1 \oslash_3 2$

   b. $2 \oslash_7 4$ d. $7 \oslash_{11} 5$ f. $7 \oslash_{11} 9$

7. Which of the following moduli *will not* have a cancellation property for multiplication?

   a. 2   c. 4   e. 6   g. 41

   b. 3   d. 5   f. 8   h. 51

8. Express each statement in terms of congruences.

   a. 5 divides 25.

   b. 49 is divisible by 7.

   c. 51 is a multiple of 3.

   d. 17 divided by 4 leaves a remainder of 1.

   e. 1 is a divisor of any whole number n.

   f. Every counting number divides itself.

   g. The sum of two even integers is even.

   h. The sum of two odd integers is even.

   i. The sum of an even and an odd integer is odd.

   j. The product of two even integers is even.

   k. The product of two odd integers is odd.

   l. The product of an even and an odd integer is even.

   m. If the sum of the digits of a number is divisible by 3, the number is divisible by 3.

   n. If the sum of the digits of a number is divisible by 9, the number is divisible by 9.

9. Use casting out the nines to tell which of the following is *incorrect*.

   a. $\begin{array}{r} 326 \\ +\,227 \\ \hline 543 \end{array}$ c. $\begin{array}{r} 738 \\ -\,499 \\ \hline 239 \end{array}$ e. $\begin{array}{r} 36 \\ \times\,84 \\ \hline 3{,}024 \end{array}$

   b. $\begin{array}{r} 6{,}834 \\ +\,5{,}217 \\ \hline 12{,}051 \end{array}$ d. $\begin{array}{r} 8{,}132 \\ -\,6{,}376 \\ \hline 1{,}656 \end{array}$ f. $\begin{array}{r} 93 \\ \times\,87 \\ \hline 8{,}081 \end{array}$

10. Build a circular slide rule for a clock. Use this slide rule to find the following.
    a. $5 \underset{12}{\oplus} 64$ c. $3 \underset{12}{\oplus} 16$ e. $11 \underset{12}{\ominus} 28$
    b. $8 \underset{12}{\oplus} 33$ d. $4 \underset{12}{\ominus} 7$ f. $6 \underset{12}{\ominus} 17$

11. Find at least three replacements for x that make the statement true.
    a. $x \equiv 2 \bmod 5$ c. $17 \equiv 2 \bmod x$
    b. $4 \equiv x \bmod 9$ d. $x \equiv 3 \bmod 12$

12. Suppose that January 3 falls on a Monday. On which day of the week will April 3, the 94th day of the year, fall?

13. Casting out the nines works because of a property of a decimal place-value numeration system. It will not work for base five calculations. What analogous check can be used for base five calculations? for base eight calculations? for base b calculations?

6.7

DIOPHANTINE PROBLEMS*

Each of us, at one time or another, has encountered a problem situation in which the problem and the solution to the problem were necessarily in the domain of the integers. Problems that require answers to questions such as how many people, how many cents, and how many units fall into the category of problems requiring integral solutions. Consider the following example.

> Four friends decide to go to a baseball game after work. Upon arrival at the baseball park each of the four friends orders a bottle of beer. Three of the friends also decide to have a hot dog each. Willy, one of the four, pays the bill, telling his friends that they can settle their share of the bill with him after the game. The bill came to $1.90.

> Afterward, Willy tells his three friends that he has forgotten the cost of a hot dog and a bottle of beer. He does remember that the cost of each is a multiple of 5. Can you help Willy and his friends figure the bill?

One way of attacking the problem is to set up an equation that relates the variables and the given information. We are attempting to

* The material in this section has been adapted from a unit developed for prospective elementary school teachers by T. H. Richard of Bemidgi State College, Minnesota.

find the cost of a bottle of beer, call this variable b, and the cost of a hot dog, call this variable h. Four bottles of beer and three hot dogs were purchased at a total cost of 190 cents. The equation that relates this information is

$$4 \cdot b + 3 \cdot h = 190$$

Let us now make a few observations:

1. The values for b and h must be integral, since the cost of a beer and a hot dog cannot be given as fractional parts of cents.
2. It is quite possible that there may be more than one solution for b and, hence, more than one solution for h.
3. If we have a solution to the equation, the replacement(s) for b and h will give a true closed sentence.
4. The equation given can be used to solve an infinite number of problems. If our problem involved the cost of popcorn and iced tea and the purchases remained the same, we would use the same *mathematical model* to solve the problem.
5. The equation is a function of two variables, b and h.

How then do we help Willy and his friends settle the bill? One brute-force technique for solving problems like Willy's lends itself very well to the use of a computer. We begin by expressing one variable, such as h, in terms of the second variable, b. To do so requires a certain amount of algebraic manipulation, which you should be able to do. We then substitute integral values for b and determine values for h. Since b can take on any positive integral value, we call b the *independent variable*. The variable h depends for its value upon the value of b; hence, it is called the *dependent variable*. We know we have a solution to the equation whenever an integral value for b gives an integral value for h. The flow chart of Figure 6-16 depicts the algorithm just described.

Notice that this flow chart does not have a criterion for ending the iterative process. The reason for this is that some equations which require integral solutions have an infinite number of solutions to the equation. Other equations have no solutions, while others have a finite number of solutions. The number of solutions to the type of equation we have been discussing will be examined later in this section.

Let us now use the algorithm to find a solution to Willy's problem. We first decide which of the variables b and h is to be the independent variable. We may choose either, so let us express h in terms of b.

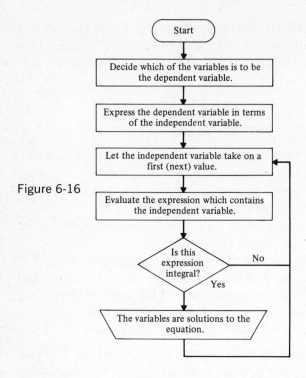

Figure 6-16

That is,

$$h = \frac{190 - 4 \cdot b}{3}$$

We now choose an appropriate value for b and evaluate the expression involving b. Since we know that there was some cost for the beer and that this cost was a multiple of 5, we choose 5 as an initial value for b. Each successive value for b will be the next multiple of 5, until we reach the value 45. We stop inserting values at this point because $b = 50$ produces a negative value for h. Do you see why a negative value for h is unacceptable?

The table of Figure 6-17 is helpful in our search for solutions. We can shorten our search process by remembering that a number is divisible by 3 if the sum of its digits is divisible by 3. If the sum is not divisible by 3, we shall not have an integral evaluation of the expression; hence, we enter a blank in the table.

Upon examination we see that there are three solutions to our equation. These are

b	$4 \cdot b$	$190 - 4 \cdot b$	$(190 - 4 \cdot b)/3 = h$
5	20	170	–
10	40	150	50
15	60	130	–
20	80	110	–
25	100	90	30
30	120	70	–
35	140	50	–
40	160	30	10
45	180	10	–

Figure 6-17

1. $h = 10$, $b = 50$.
2. $h = 25$, $b = 30$.
3. $h = 40$, $b = 10$.

The reasonable solution to Willy's problem is solution 2 unless, of course, it was a 10-cent beer or 10-cent hot dog night.

Problems of the type discussed, in which special restrictions permit *only* integral solutions, are called *Diophantine problems*. Diophantus of Alexandria was a third-century mathematician who brought together the algebraic knowledge of the Greeks in a work called the *Arithmetica*. Diophantine analysis is that branch of number theory which deals with finding integral solutions to problems that may not have a unique solution, that is, those problems which may have more than one solution or which may not have any solutions. In most cases considered in this section we shall be concerned with positive integral solutions to the Diophantine equations.

We may use geometric ideas to better understand and interpret Diophantine equations of the form $a \cdot x + b \cdot y = n$. Recall from Chapter 1 that in a Cartesian coordinate system a point (x, y), where x and y are integers, is called a *lattice point*. The solution set for a Diophantine equation is a set of lattice points. If we construct the graph of the equation $a \cdot x + b \cdot y = n$, where x and y are allowed to take on values other than just integral values, we have the graph of a straight line. If we then determine the lattice points on this line, we have determined the solution set for this Diophantine equation. For example, suppose that we are to find four solutions (if possible) to the Diophantine equation

$$x + y = 5$$

253

In Figure 6-18 we see the straight line that represents the graph of the equation $x + y = 5$. This line passes through the lattice points

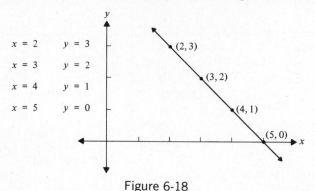

$x = 2$	$y = 3$
$x = 3$	$y = 2$
$x = 4$	$y = 1$
$x = 5$	$y = 0$

Figure 6-18

$(2, 3)$, $(3, 2)$, $(4, 1)$, $(5, 0)$, $(6, -1)$, and so forth. Consequently, four solutions to the Diophantine equation $x + y = 5$ are

$$x = 2, \qquad y = 3$$
$$x = 3, \qquad y = 2$$
$$x = 4, \qquad y = 1$$
$$x = 5, \qquad y = 0$$

If we restrict our solution set to nonnegative integers, we see that the solutions to the Diophantine equation $x + y = 5$ give us the basic facts of 5. By allowing the sum to vary and by placing restrictions on x and y, we may generate the basic facts to 18 as lattice point solutions to Diophantine equations. By considering Diophantine equations of the form

$$y - n \cdot x = 0, \qquad \text{where } n = 0, 1, 2, 3, \ldots, 9$$

we can generate the basic facts for multiplication. For example, if $n = 2$, our equation becomes $y - 2 \cdot x = 0$. If we restrict the replacement set for x to $\{0, 1, 2, 3, 4, 5, 6, 7, 8, 9\}$, then the solution set for our equation becomes

$$\{(0, 0), (1, 2), (2, 4), (3, 6), (4, 8), (5, 10), \ldots, (9, 18)\}$$

which are the basic multiplication facts of 2. Each of these points are lattice points on the graph of the line

$$y - 2x = 0 \qquad \text{or} \qquad y = 2x$$

We mention the preceding to you to point out that the interrelationship of geometry and arithmetic can be used to help children learn skills and to help children see the interrelatedness of mathematics in general.

The question may arise as to how we know if a Diophantine equation has integral solutions. It is foolish to construct a table or to graph the equation of a line in search of integral solutions if indeed integral solutions do not exist. Fortunately, there is a method for checking whether solutions exist. This method makes use of the greatest common divisor of two integers and is given, without proof, as follows.

> Suppose that a, b, and n are integers with a and b both not zero, and suppose that GCD(a, b) = d. Then the equation
>
> $$a \cdot x + b \cdot y = n$$
>
> has at least one integral solution if $d \mid n$, that is, if GCD(a, b) is a divisor of n. Conversely, if $d \nmid n$, then the equation will have no integral solutions.

The following Diophantine equations have integral solutions:

$$x + y = 5, \quad \text{since GCD}(1, 1) = 1 \text{ and } 1 \mid 5$$
$$2x + 4y = 6, \quad \text{since GCD}(2, 4) = 2 \text{ and } 2 \mid 6$$

The following Diophantine equations do *not* have integral solutions:

$$4x + 2y = 5, \quad \text{since GCD}(4, 2) = 2 \text{ and } 2 \nmid 5$$
$$3x + 9y = 4, \quad \text{since GCD}(3, 9) = 3 \text{ and } 3 \nmid 4$$

Earlier we mentioned that a Diophantine problem may have a finite or infinite number of solutions, or no solution at all. If GCD(a, b) $\nmid n$ in the equation $ax + b \cdot y = n$, then there are no integral solutions to the equation. Let us now consider the other possibilities.

If we restrict our solution set to nonnegative integral values for x and y, and require a and b to be positive, we can see that there will be a finite set of solutions, provided solutions exist at all. Examples of restricted Diophantine equations that yield finite solution sets are

$$x + y = 3$$
$$2x + y = 1$$
and
$$2x + 4y = 6$$

Suppose now that we do *not* restrict our solution set to non-

255

negative values of x and y. We claim that if there is a solution to a Diophantine equation then there is an infinite set of solutions to the equation. There is a problem, however, in expressing an infinite set of solutions. We cannot list the solution set; hence, we rely upon the following scheme.

> Suppose that GCD$(a, b) = d$, $d \mid n$, and x_1 (read "x sub one"), y_1 (read "y sub one") is a solution for the Diophantine equation $a \cdot x + b \cdot y = n$. Then the solution set to $a \cdot x + b \cdot y = n$ may be expressed as $\{(x, y);$ $x = x_1 + (b/d)t,\ y = y_1 - (a/d)t$, where $t \in Z$.

It goes without saying that this statement merits further elaboration. There are three important ideas that we call to your attention.

1. If x and y are solutions to the equation $a \cdot x + b \cdot y = n$, then x and y must be integers. The values of x and y are integral, since b/d, a/d, x_1, y_1, and t are all integers. We rely upon the closure of Z under the binary operations of addition, subtraction, and multiplication to ensure this.

2. If x_1 and y_1 are solutions to the equation $ax + by = n$, then upon replacement of these variables with x and y, a true mathematical sentence should result. Suppose that (x_1, y_1) is one solution for $a \cdot x + b \cdot y = n$. If $x = x_1 + (b/d)t$ and $y = y_1 - (a/d)t$ are a solution, then $a \cdot [x_1 + (b/d)t] + b \cdot [y_1 - (a/d)t]$ must equal n. Notice that this is true since

$$a \cdot \left(x_1 + \frac{b}{d}t\right) + b \cdot \left(y_1 - \frac{a}{d}t\right)$$

$$= a \cdot x_1 + \frac{a \cdot b \cdot t}{d} + b \cdot y_1 - \frac{b \cdot a \cdot t}{d}$$

$$= a \cdot x_1 + b \cdot y_1$$

$$= n$$

3. Finally, since $t \in Z$, we have an infinite number of choices for t. Hence, we have an infinite number of solutions for $a \cdot x + b \cdot y = n$.

Consider now the following examples:

Example 1 Suppose that $x_1 = 5$ and $y_1 = 1$ are given as a solution to the Diophantine equation $x + y = 6$. Then we find the solution set in the following manner.

1. $\text{GCD}(a, b) = \text{GCD}(1, 1) = 1$. Therefore, $d = 1$.
2. $b/d = 1/1 = 1$ and $a/d = 1/1 = 1$.
3.

$$x = x_1 + \frac{b}{d} \cdot t \qquad \text{and} \qquad y = y_1 - \frac{a}{d} \cdot t$$
$$= 5 + 1 \cdot t \qquad\qquad\qquad = 1 - 1 \cdot t$$

4. The solution set is

$$\{(x, y) : x = 5 + 1 \cdot t \text{ and } y = 1 - 1 \cdot t, \text{ where } t \in Z\}$$

Example 2 Suppose that $x_1 = 6$ and $y_1 = -1$ are given as a solution to the Diophantine equation $2 \cdot x + 4 \cdot y = 8$. Then we find the solution set in the following manner.

1. $\text{GCD}(a, b) = \text{GCD}(2, 4) = 2$. Therefore, $d = 2$.
2. $b/d = 4/2 = 2$ and $a/d = 2/2 = 1$.
3.

$$x = x_1 + \frac{b}{d} \cdot t \qquad \text{and} \qquad y = y_1 - \frac{a}{d} \cdot t$$
$$= 6 + 2 \cdot t \qquad\qquad\qquad = -1 + 1 \cdot t$$

4. The solution set is

$$\{(x, y) : x = 6 + 2 \cdot t \text{ and } y = -1 + 1 \cdot t, \text{ where } t \in Z\}$$

It may have occurred to you that we have not yet discussed techniques for finding a solution to a Diophantine equation, provided such a solution exists. A simple tabular method will be presented at this time.* The mathematical justification for this algorithm will be omitted because it involves the use of advanced mathematical techniques. We shall call the algorithm the *three-row tabular method* and describe this method by means of the following example.

Example 3 Find an integral solution to the Diophantine equation $60x + 7y = 1$.

1. We begin by finding $\text{GCD}(60, 7)$ by using the Euclidean algorithm. In each equation we shall keep track of the quotient.

---

* For an in-depth treatment of Diophantine analysis see T. H. Richard, "Some Diophantine Problems," unpublished Master's dissertation, Colorado State University, 1968.

257

For example,

$$60 = 8 \cdot 7 + 4, \qquad q_0 = 8$$
$$7 = 1 \cdot 4 + 3, \qquad q_1 = 1$$
$$4 = 1 \cdot 3 + 1, \qquad q_2 = 1 = q_n$$
$$3 = 3 \cdot 1, \qquad \text{we ignore the last quotient}$$

2. Now consider the following three-row table:

q			q_0	q_1	q_2
x	x_{-1}	x_0	x_1	x_2	
y	y_{-1}	y_0	y_1	y_2	

Using the q's from step 1, we have $q_0 = 8$, $q_1 = 1$, and $q_2 = 1$. We *always* define $x_{-1} = 0$, $x_0 = 1$, $y_{-1} = 1$, and $y_0 = q_0$. The partial table then becomes

q			$q_0 = 8$	$q_1 = 1$	$q_2 = 1$
x	$x_{-1} = 0$	$x_0 = 1$	x_1	x_2	
y	$y_{-1} = 1$	$y_0 = 8$	y_1	y_2	

3. Complete the table by using the equations

$$x_1 = x_{-1} + x_0 \cdot q_1 = 0 + 1 \cdot 1 = 1$$
$$x_n = x_2 = x_0 + x_1 \cdot q_2 = 1 + 1 \cdot 1 = 2$$
$$y_1 = y_{-1} + y_0 \cdot q_1 = 1 + 8 \cdot 1 = 9$$
$$y_n = y_2 = y_0 + y_1 \cdot q_2 = 8 + 9 \cdot 1 = 17$$

The table then becomes

q				1	1
x	0	1	1	2	
y	1	8	9	17	

4. One solution to the Diophantine equation $60 \cdot x + 7 \cdot y = 1$ is

$$x = (-1)^2 \cdot x_2 = (-1)^2 \cdot 2 = 2$$
$$y = (-1)^3 \cdot y_2 = (-1)^3 \cdot 17 = -17$$

The exponents are determined by the number of quotients

used in the Euclidean algorithm. The exponent for the x component is the same as the subscript for the last quotient used in the table. The exponent for the y component is one more than this subscript.

5. In checking to see that $(2, -17)$ is a solution to $60 \bullet x + 7 \bullet y = 1$, we see that

$$60(2) + 7(-17) = 120 - 119$$
$$= 1 \quad check$$

Since we have an algorithm that can be used in the solution of a Diophantine equation (provided a solution exists), we can flow chart this algorithm as in Figure 6-19.

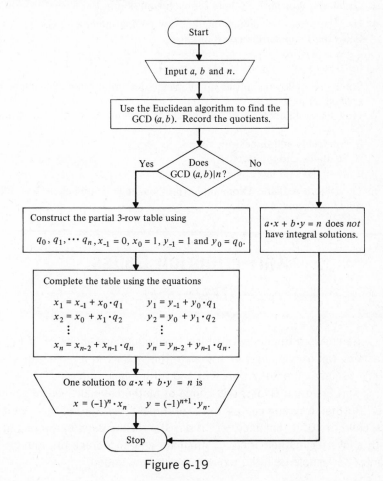

Figure 6-19

EXERCISES (Section 6.7)

1. Which of the following Diophantine equations has a solution?
   a. $2x + 2y = 3$ d. $6x + 3y = 9$
   b. $x + 2y = 3$ e. $4x - 6y = 9$
   c. $2x - 3y = 5$ f. $9y - 3x = 5$

2. In the following a solution to the Diophantine equation is given. Give the general form of the solution set for each and then give three other solutions to the equation.
   a. $x + 4y = 5$ $(1, 1)$ d. $5x - 3y = -11$ $(-1, 2)$
   b. $2x - 3y = 6$ $(0, -2)$ e. $x - y = 4$ $(0, -4)$
   c. $2x + 2y = 8$ $(2, 2)$ f. $x - 3y = 2$ $(-1, -1)$

3. Graph the four lattice points for each equation in Exercise 2.

4. Use the three-row tabular method for finding integral solutions to the following Diophantine equations.
   a. $5x + y = -6$ c. $x + 3y = -6$
   b. $2x + y = 9$ d. $4x - 3y = 17$

5. Solve the following problem by using the brute-force algorithm described on page 252.
   How many different ways can change be made for $2 if the change must be
   a. in nickels and dimes.
   b. in dimes and quarters.
   c. in dimes and half-dollars.

6. Describe a realistic Diophantine problem that is applicable to a fifth-grade mathematics class.

Karl Friedrich Gauss

(1777–1855)

Genius is a quality with which few people are endowed. If we, as teachers, fail to recognize or stimulate this quality in a child, our negligence becomes the loss of present and future generations.

Karl Friedrich Gauss, the Prince of Mathematicians, was a genius. Herr Büttner, a tyrannical teacher of arithmetic, recognized this talent in the child of 10. It remained for his assistant, Herr Bartels, a young man with a love for mathematics, to stimulate and encourage his young student. Eric Temple Bell, the renowned historian, stated:

Archimedes, Newton and Gauss, these three, are in a class by themselves among the great mathematicians, and it is not for ordinary mortals to range them in order of merit.*

Born in 1777 at Brunswick, Germany, Karl Friedrich Gauss was the son of a poor laborer. The precocity of Gauss was evidenced before he was 3 years old when he corrected a payroll sum that his father had erroneously computed. At the age of 10 Gauss astonished his arithmetic teacher, Herr Büttner, by solving, in seconds, a problem of the sort $1 + 2 + 3 + 4 + \cdots + 100$, where the difference between two consecutive terms is constant and a given number of terms (here 100) are to be added. So impressed was Herr Büttner that he purchased with his own funds the best available textbook on arithmetic. Gauss quickly mastered this text. "He is beyond me. I can teach him nothing more" was his teacher's reaction.

Gauss entered college at age 15, vascillating between the study of the classical languages and the study of mathematics. A study of mathematics was decided upon, with the study of the classical languages relegated to that of a lifelong hobby.

Number theory, the study of the properties of integers, became, by his own admission, the first love of Gauss. The statement "Mathematics is queen of the sciences. But arithmetic (number theory) is the queen of mathematics" is attributed to Gauss. In 1801 he published *Disquisitiones Arithmeticae (Arithmetical Researches)*, considered by many to be Gauss'

* E. T. Bell, *Men of Mathematics* (New York: Simon & Schuster, Inc., 1961), p. 218.

greatest masterpiece. The book is in seven sections, each section concerned with some aspect of number theory. Many parts of the text concerned work previously done elsewhere. Gauss unified and generalized these results with his research.

Unfortunately, Gauss was never to return to his first love upon completion of *Disquisitiones*. After its publication in 1801 he broadened his activities to include astronomy, geodesy, and electromagnetism. In the course of his life he provided the first proof of the fundamental theorem of algebra (that is, every algebraic equation of any degree has at least one root), recognized the existence of, and began work on, a non-Euclidean geometry, and did extensive work in analysis. It would take more room than is available here to describe the outstanding contributions of Gauss to mathematics.

On February 23, 1855, Karl Friedrich Gauss died at the age of 78. A mortal died, but the contributions of his genius continue to live in mathematics.

Chapter 7

The Set of
Rational Numbers

7.1

INTRODUCTION

From a mathematical point of view we have seen that the set of whole numbers was deficient in that the set fails to have a solution for the open sentence "$7 + \bigcirc = 3$." It was also apparent that only the whole number zero had an additive inverse. The set of integers contains the set of whole numbers, at least in some sense, and it was seen that a solution to the open sentence given did indeed exist in the set of integers. Furthermore, every integer has an additive inverse in the set of integers. However, there is no solution for the open sentence "$5 \times \bigcirc = 23$" in the set of integers, and only integers 1 and -1 have multiplicative inverses. Therefore, there are some mathematical deficiencies for the set of integers.

From the point of view that mathematics should help us understand the real world, the set of integers is also functionally deficient. In measurement, for example, having established some unit of measure, it rarely happens that an object has a measure that is exactly some positive integer. More often the measure of an object falls between two such consecutive integers. Furthermore, ordinary expression of relationships is not limited to the set of integers, as when we say that there only *half* as many wild-eyed radicals today as there were 20 years ago, or when we say that we are two and one third times as deep in debt now as we were last month. And so we need to build the set of rational numbers.

7.2
A FIELD

Before we go into the matter of creating the set of rational numbers and the operations on that set, let's take a brief detour and examine more carefully a system that we introduced in Chapter 6. You may recall the system of objects called Z_5. Z_5 consists of the set of equivalence classes that we labeled [0], [1], [2], [3], and [4]. Remember that [3], for example, contained all the integers congruent to 3 modulo 5. Therefore,

$$[3] = \{\ldots, -7, -2, 3, 8, 13, 18, \ldots\}$$

If you have forgotten, notice that any two elements of [3] are related in that the difference between them is a multiple of 5; thus, $18 - 3 = 3 \cdot 5$, $13 - (-7) = 13 + 7 = 20 = 4 \cdot 5$, and so on.

As a system of objects we produced two operations on Z_5, which we called "addition" and "multiplication," because they resembled these operations in the set of integers, and used the symbols $\oplus$ and $\odot$ to name addition and multiplication. With the understanding that the brackets used to name these equivalence classes are dropped for the sake of convenient notation, the two tables of addition and multiplication look like this:

$\oplus$	0	1	2	3	4
0	0	1	2	3	4
1	1	2	3	4	0
2	2	3	4	0	1
3	3	4	0	1	2
4	4	0	1	2	3

$\odot$	0	1	2	3	4
0	0	0	0	0	0
1	0	1	2	3	4
2	0	2	4	1	3
3	0	3	1	4	2
4	0	4	3	2	1

What properties do you observe that the set Z_5 and its two operations have? The first thing which is obvious from the tables is that both operations are *closed*, for the sum and product of every pair of elements of Z_5 is another element of Z_5. It may also be seen that both operations are *commutative*, because both tables are symmetric with respect to the main diagonals beginning in the upper left corner of each table. It is not readily visible from the tables that both operations are *associative*, but it can be shown by a simple argument based upon the definitions of addition and multiplication that such is the case.

$$([a] \oplus [b]) \oplus [c] = [a + b] \oplus [c] = [(a + b) + c]$$
$$[a] \oplus ([b] \oplus [c]) = [a] \oplus [b + c] = [a + (b + c)]$$

Since we know that integer addition is associative, we know that addition in Z_5 is associative. You should be able to follow this pattern and show that multiplication in Z_5 is also associative.

From the tables it can be seen that $[0]$ is an *additive identity*, because $[a] \oplus [0] = [a]$ for every $[a]$ in Z_5, and it can be seen that $[1]$ is a *multiplicative identity*, because $[a] \odot [1] = [a]$ for every $[a]$ in Z_5. The inverse for each element, under the operation of addition, may be found from the table if we remind ourselves that we can recognize the inverse of an element a by finding the element which, together with a, produces the additive identity. So the additive inverse of $[0]$ is $[0]$, because $[0] \oplus [0] = [0]$, the inverse of $[1]$ is $[4]$, because $[1] \oplus [4] = [0]$, the inverse of $[2]$ is $[3]$, because $[2] \oplus [3] = [0]$, and so on. Hence, every element has an *additive inverse*. The same is *almost* true for multiplicative inverses; that is, every element except $[0]$ has a multiplicative inverse. How do you recognize a multiplicative inverse when you see it? The product of the element in question and its inverse is the identity $[1]$. Hence, the multiplicative inverse of $[1]$ is $[1]$, because $[1] \odot [1] = [1]$, the multiplicative inverse of $[2]$ is $[3]$, because $[2] \odot [3] = [1]$, the multiplicative inverse of $[3]$ is $[2]$, and the multiplicative inverse of $[4]$ is $[4]$. Hence, every element, except $[0]$, has a *multiplicative inverse*.

Finally, we can give a simple argument which shows that multiplication distributes over addition. If $[a]$, $[b]$, and $[c]$ are elements of Z_5, then by definition of the addition and multiplication operations we have

$$[a] \odot ([b] \oplus [c]) = [a] \odot [b + c] = [a(b + c)] = [ab + ac]$$
$$([a] \odot [b]) \oplus ([a] \odot [c]) = [ab] \oplus [ac] = [ab + ac]$$

Therefore, on the basis of the fact that integer multiplication distributes over addition, we see that in Z_5 *multiplication is distributive over addition.*

Here is a short summary of these observations concerning the operations in Z_5:

Addition	Multiplication
Closed	Closed
Commutative	Commutative
Associative	Associative
Identity ([0])	Identity ([1])
Inverses for all	Inverses for all except [0]
	Distributive over addition

These 11 properties are not unique to the system Z_5, for they are the general properties possessed by any mathematical system that is a *field.*

> A set of at least two elements on which binary operations of addition and multiplication are defined is called a *field* if and only if
>
>   i. Both operations are closed.
>   ii. Both operations are commutative.
> iii. Both operations are associative.
> iv. There are identity elements for each operation.
>   v. Every element has an additive inverse and every nonzero element has a multiplicative inverse.
> vi. Multiplication is distributive over addition.

If you are asked to determine whether or not a system of elements and its operations form a field, you must simply check through this list of properties. If the system has all the properties, it is a field. If the system fails even one property, it is not a field.

Does the set of whole numbers form a field? Several properties of a field are met in the whole numbers, but there are no additive inverses for any whole number except zero and no multiplicative inverses for any whole number except 1, which is its own multiplicative inverse. So the whole numbers do not form a field. What about the set of integers? All the properties of a field are met except the requirement that every element has a multiplicative inverse (except for zero).

267

Therefore, the set of integers is not a field either. The set of rational numbers, yet to be constructed, is our first example of a common number system that is a field.

EXERCISES (Section 7.2)

1. Complete the following table for elements of the field Z_5.

Element	Additive inverse	Multiplicative inverse
[0]		
[1]		
[2]		
[3]		
[4]		

2. What are the elements of the system Z_4?
3. Complete addition and multiplication tables for Z_4.
4. Fill in the blanks in the following table *if possible*. The elements are from the system Z_4.

Element	Additive inverse	Multiplicative inverse
[0]		
[1]		
[2]		
[3]		

5. What are the elements in the system Z_7?
6. Complete addition and multiplication tables for Z_7.
7. Fill in the blanks in the following table *if possible* with the elements coming from Z_7.

Element	Additive inverse	Multiplicative inverse
[0]		
[1]		
[2]		
[3]		
[4]		
[5]		
[6]		

8. Which of the systems Z_4 and Z_7 are examples of a field?

9. Would the system Z_9 be a field? Z_8? Z_6? Z_{10}?
10. Would the system Z_{11} be a field? Z_{13}? Z_{17}? Z_{19}?
11. Can you make a conjecture about when the system Z_n is a field and when it is not?

7.3

WHAT IS A RATIONAL NUMBER?

When we learn a new concept, we rarely learn that concept immediately upon hearing or reading a definition. The correct definition helps us learn the concept, of course, but it is only through thinking about examples, considering allied ideas, and other activities that we come to know the concept. Take a common concept such as "pollution" for example. You have come to know this concept as a result of hearing someone give examples of pollution and examples of things that are not pollution. You have read about pollution and what to do about it. You have described to others what you thought were examples of pollution and may have been corrected on occasion for misunderstandings. Finally, you could probably provide your own definition of pollution based on your set of experiences, your understanding of examples that are and are not pollution, and your realization of the relationship between pollution and other concepts such as "environment," "ecology," and "air quality."

So it is that children in your elementary school classes will come to know certain concepts, such as "rational number," from a basis of earlier experiences as well as the sequence of activities you plan for them. It is unlikely that they will come to know what a rational number is by giving them a stated definition. You will need to use several ways to explain what a rational number is, and we shall need to use more than one way even to provide you with a good, reasonable understanding of the concept and its related ideas.

Let us begin our development of the concept of rational numbers in a way that may appeal to your intuition and that closely resembles the way in which elementary school children begin their study of the concept. Figure 7-1 represents a case of pop bottles. Suppose that 12 of the bottles are full of root beer and 12 are empty. They might look like Figure 7-2. There are now *two* kinds of bottles and an equal num-

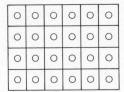

Figure 7-1

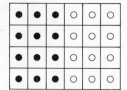

Figure 7-2

ber of each kind, 12 full and 12 empty. *One* kind of bottle is full. What would be a way to say that "Of *two* sets of an equal number each, *one* set is full?" Could you invent some symbol involving the numbers 2 and 1 that would help to express this idea? How about saying that "Of the total set of pop bottles, $\frac{1}{2}$ are full?" Our symbol "$\frac{1}{2}$" means that of *2* equivalent sets (that is, 2 sets each with the same number of objects), 1 set consists of full bottles.

Another way of expressing the idea might be to say that there are 24 bottles altogether and 12 of them are full, so we could say that "There are $\frac{12}{24}$ bottles full of root beer." Someone else may notice that the bottles are arranged in columns and that of 6 columns, 3 are full bottles. "There are $\frac{3}{6}$ bottles full of root beer." One of your clever students may say "If you rearrange the full and empty bottles like this (Figure 7-3), then there are four rows and two of them contain all the full bottles. So I could say that $\frac{2}{4}$ of the bottles are full bottles."

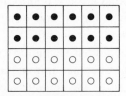

Figure 7-3

Of course, all these ideas are good, and out of them might come at least two major ideas. First, the symbol "$\frac{1}{2}$" means that *one* of *two* equivalent sets is being named. The symbol "$\frac{3}{6}$" means that *three* of *six* equivalent sets are being named. Likewise for the symbols "$\frac{2}{4}$" and "$\frac{12}{24}$." The concept of rational numbers has its beginning in this first idea, that the symbol above the line tells how many of the sets are being considered and the symbol below the line tells how many equivalent sets there are. But — we had better slow up a bit. No one has suggested yet that these symbols name numbers. The notion that these symbols name numbers is hanging in the background. For the moment such symbols simply express a relationship, and it may be some time before the thought arises that these symbols name numbers just as "5" names the number 5.

A second important idea that might come from the look at the pop bottles is that there are several ways to express the relation between the set of full bottles and the entire set of bottles. You have seen that "$\frac{1}{2}$," "$\frac{2}{4}$," "$\frac{3}{6}$," and "$\frac{12}{24}$" all seem reasonable symbols to use to express the relationship. If we agree, then *whatever* it is that is named by "$\frac{1}{2}$" must also be named by "$\frac{2}{4}$," "$\frac{3}{6}$," and "$\frac{12}{24}$."

At this point the typical procedure for further work in the elementary school classroom is to give many different examples of situations in which such symbols can be used to express relationships. Figures 7-4, 7-5, and 7-6 are some samples.

What symbol expresses the relation between the portion of the pie that has been eaten and the whole pie?

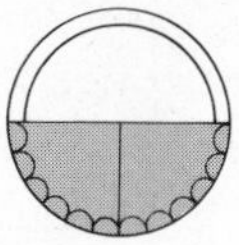

Figure 7-4   Answer _____

Here is a diagram of the playground. The shaded portion is for football. What symbol expresses the relation between the football portion and the whole playground?

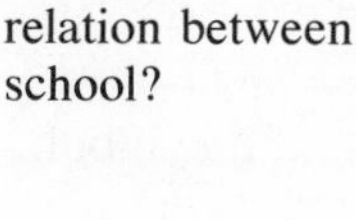

Figure 7-5   Answer _____

Here is a drawing of the street that goes from Manuel's house to school. Manuel has walked as far as the heavy line shows. What symbol shows the relation between how far he has walked and the whole trip from home to school?

Answer _____

Figure 7-6   Home ├──────────────────┤ School

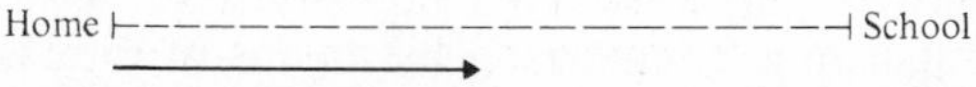

At other times and at other levels in the elementary school curriculum children are introduced to the idea of the *ratio* of two whole numbers (or of two integers). This idea is essentially a *comparison* of two sets or of two numbers, and the symbol used for such comparison is like that introduced previously. For instance, the ratio of 12 apples to 17 apples is named by the symbol "$\frac{12}{17}$."

271

The *quotient* of two whole numbers (or integers) may also be named in this same way. Recall that division may be considered a *partitioning* of a set. For instance, if 4 children come to the party and there are 20 cookies, how many cookies may each child have? The set may be partitioned into 4 equivalent sets of 5 cookies each so each child can have 5 cookies (Figure 7-7). We would write "$20 \div 4 = 5$." Now

Figure 7-7

suppose that there are 4 children and only 3 apples. How much should each child get? The question is "$3 \div 4 = ?$" If we cut the apples as shown in Figure 7-8, line up the pieces, and do the same partitioning

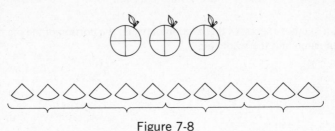

Figure 7-8

as previously, the answer may be found. With regard to a whole apple, each child gets a share that we would name by the symbol "$\frac{3}{4}$," because of 4 equivalent parts of a whole apple, each child gets 3 parts. So an answer to the question is

$$3 \div 4 = \frac{3}{4}$$

provided we are willing to accept "$\frac{3}{4}$" as the name of some kind of number.

So it is that children often come to know that the symbol $\frac{\text{"}a\text{"}}{b}$ has meaning with respect to expressing a relationship between sets, with respect to a comparison by means of ratios, and with respect to division. Out of such meanings comes the idea that these symbols can be used to name numbers. You have seen one indication of this with respect to division, as mentioned previously. Another indication, and a very important one, comes from a closer look at the number line. Figure 7-9 is a magnified picture of the number line showing the point that corresponds to the integer 0 and the point that corresponds to the

Figure 7-9

integer 1. What number do you believe corresponds to the point marked "X"? Do you see that the point at X divides the interval from the point at 0 to the point at 1 into two equivalent sets (equivalent in terms of length)? The interval from the point at 0 to the point at X is one of these two equivalent sets, so a logical symbol to be used for "X" would be "$\frac{1}{2}$." From this point of view it might be seen that there are numbers between 0 and 1 which would be named by our symbols.

To answer the question that began this section, "What is a rational number?", let us use the following definition.

> A *rational number* is the quotient of two integers a and b ($b \neq 0$) and is named by the symbol, "$\frac{a}{b}$."

Let us also agree that two rational numbers are equal if they meet the following criterion.

> If $\frac{a}{b}$ and $\frac{c}{d}$ are rational numbers, then $\frac{a}{b} = \frac{c}{d}$ if and only if $a \times d = b \times c$.

You will recall that in our pop bottle illustration we learned that $\frac{1}{2} = \frac{3}{6}$, and you can see that $1 \times 6 = 2 \times 3$. Similarly, $\frac{4}{8} = \frac{12}{24}$ and $4 \times 24 = 8 \times 12$.

Another version of equality can be derived from the one just given. From our understanding of the commutative and associative properties of multiplication of integers we know that $a \times (b \times m) = b \times (a \times m)$. Therefore, we know that

$$\frac{a}{b} = \frac{a \times m}{b \times m}$$

from the preceding criterion.

> If a, b, and m are integers (b and m not zero) then
> $$\frac{a}{b} = \frac{a \times m}{b \times m}.$$

On the basis of the given definition of rational number and the agreements on equality, we can move directly to the operations of addition and multiplication on the set of rational numbers. In a later section of this chapter we shall provide a formal approach to the system of rational numbers, but for now we rely upon the intuitive development given here.

We must explain something about the words used in discussing rational numbers. First, the symbol $\frac{a}{b}$, which is used to name a rational number, is called a *fraction*. The numeral on the top of the fraction is called the *numerator* and the symbol on the bottom of the fraction is called the *denominator*. The rational number itself has no top or bottom, for it is a concept (specifically, a quotient). Only the symbol that names a rational number has a top and bottom. It is important that we understand the difference between the object (rational number) and its name (fraction), but it is difficult to require our own elementary school students to be precise at all times. As they learn the concept of rational number, they may confuse the object with its name and this is understandable.

There is another problem dealing with symbols. The symbol "$4\frac{5}{6}$" names a rational number because it names the quotient of integers 29 and 6. $29 \div 6 = 4$ with remainder of 5. It may also be said the "$4\frac{5}{6} = 4 + \frac{5}{6}$," so that the rational number may be seen to be the sum of a whole number and a rational number less than 1. You may have used the term "mixed number" when referring to objects like "$4\frac{5}{6}$." Did you mean that the number was mixed or that the symbol was mixed? How can numbers be mixed? If the symbol is mixed, should we call it a mixed numeral? In ordinary classroom use, try to avoid using either "mixed number" or "mixed numeral."

Finally, it is common practice to use the phrase "reduced to lowest terms" or "reduced to lowest form." We have seen that each rational number has many different names. For instance, $\frac{2}{3}$ is named by "$\frac{4}{6}$" and many other symbols. Any application of the principle that $\frac{a}{b} = \frac{am}{bm}$ is essentially a renaming exercise. So the common instruction to youngsters that they should "reduce each fraction to lowest terms" is an admonition to select a certain kind of name from among the many names used to name the rational number. What kind of name is required? That name which has numerator and denominator which name integers that are relatively prime. Since 4 and 6 are not relatively prime, $\frac{4}{6}$ is not "reduced to lowest terms," whereas $\frac{2}{3}$ is so reduced, because

2 and 3 are relatively prime. The rational number $\frac{13}{39}$ is not named in its lowest terms because $\frac{13}{39} = (1 \cdot 13)/(3 \cdot 13)$. Therefore, $\frac{1}{3}$ is the same rational number and uses "lowest terms" in its name.

You may notice that the matter of choosing the name of a rational number which is "in lowest terms" is a matter of finding the greatest common divisor (GCD) of the two integers involved. For instance, $\frac{4}{6}$ is reduced to $\frac{2}{3}$ by recognizing that the GCD of 4 and 6 is 2. Therefore,

$$\frac{4}{6} = \frac{2 \cdot 2}{3 \cdot 2} = \frac{2}{3}.$$

Notice that the factor m which is needed for the "reduction to lowest terms" process is the GCD of 4 and 6. Generally speaking, to reduce any rational number a/b to lowest terms, find the GCD of a and b, write a and b in terms of this GCD (say $a = x \cdot m$ and $b = y \cdot m$), then use the principle for renaming the rational number. In symbols, where m is the GCD of a and b:

$$\frac{a}{b} = \frac{x \cdot m}{y \cdot m} = \frac{x}{y}$$

As an example, reduce $\frac{24}{40}$. The GCD of 24 and 40 is 8 and $24 = 3 \cdot 8$ while $40 = 5 \cdot 8$. Therefore,

$$\frac{24}{40} = \frac{3 \cdot 8}{5 \cdot 8} = \frac{3}{5}$$

The process of renaming rational numbers is also involved in one of the steps of the addition algorithm for rational numbers. More about this in the next section.

EXERCISES (Section 7.3)

1. Find three good examples of concepts that you are coming to know as a result of recent experiences.

2. Develop three activities that will help a youngster learn the concept of 1/3 and the concept of 2/3.

3. Devise some activities (two or more) that will help youngsters visualize the relationship between 2/3, 4/6, and 6/9.

4. Give examples of three activities in which the concept of ratio is relevant to the elementary school child.

5. Describe some simple activities in which sets are partitioned and show the relationship to the operation of division.

6. When children look at your pictures of a number line, they may ask

"What's to the left of zero?" What clever ways can you think of that will inspire a youngster to ask "What's between 1 and 2?"

7. Give four different names for each of the following.
   a. 3/4
   b. 5/6
   c. 12/18
   d. 25/30
   e. 55/75

8. Rename the following by "reducing to lowest terms."
   a. 120/280
   b. 135/225
   c. −27/81
   d. 45/54
   e. 16/−60

9. Here are some rational numbers that you should be able to rename in the form a/b.

   a. $2\frac{5}{6}$ b. $12\frac{7}{11}$ c. $-4\frac{5}{6}$ d. $-10\frac{7}{9}$

   e. $16\frac{5}{9}$ f. $-8\frac{3}{4}$ g. $-1\frac{19}{31}$ h. $75\frac{1}{3}$

10. Here are some rational numbers expressed in the form a/b. Rename them as the sum of an integer and a rational number that is between 0 and 1. (Reduce "to lowest terms.")
    a. 175/50
    b. −137/30
    c. 27/−2
    d. 191/−13
    e. 361/19

11. Do you see a flaw in the language used in the following?

    $\frac{6}{8}$ is a rational number with an even numerator.

    $\frac{6}{8} = \frac{3}{4}.$

    Therefore, $\frac{3}{4}$ has an even numerator.

7.4

ADDITION AND SUBTRACTION OF RATIONAL NUMBERS

Here is a typical addition problem from an elementary textbook. Add $\frac{2}{3} + \frac{1}{4}$. To be able to find the rational number that represents this sum, the child must have several concepts. First, he must have a clear understanding of the meaning of rational numbers and the use of symbols to represent them. Second, he must understand that each rational number has many symbolic names. Third, he must be able to relate this addition to whole number or integer addition. It may be that his thoughts might go something like this: Hmmm, $\frac{2}{3}$ is the same as $\frac{4}{6}$, $\frac{6}{9}$, $\frac{8}{12}$, $\frac{10}{15}$, . . . , and $\frac{1}{4}$ is the same as $\frac{2}{8}$, $\frac{3}{12}$, $\frac{4}{16}$, $\frac{5}{20}$, ... Ah ha! $\frac{2}{3}$ is the same as $\frac{8}{12}$ and $\frac{1}{4}$ is the same as $\frac{3}{12}$ . . . , so $\frac{2}{3} + \frac{1}{4}$ must be $\frac{11}{12}$!!! Back of such knowledge might be experiences with figures as shown in Figures 7-10 and 7-11.

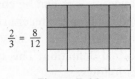

$$\frac{2}{3} = \frac{8}{12} \qquad\qquad \frac{1}{4} = \frac{3}{12}$$

Figure 7-10   Figure 7-11

From these figures, addition of the rational numbers becomes nothing more than counting the number of elements in two disjoint sets (in this case, counting the number of equivalent regions or twelfths), which is the definition of whole number addition. Combining these disjoint sets yields Figure 7-12.

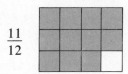

$$\frac{11}{12}$$

Figure 7-12

Similar experiences of many kinds dealing with rational numbers would enable the child to develop the following generalization, although he would hardly say it in the way that we have.

> If a/b and c/d are rational numbers, then
>
> $$\frac{a}{b} + \frac{c}{d} = \frac{ad + bc}{bd}$$

For just a few examples, consider the following:

$$\frac{3}{7} + \frac{5}{11} = \frac{3 \cdot 11 + 7 \cdot 5}{7 \cdot 11} = \frac{33 + 35}{77} = \frac{68}{77}$$

$$\frac{2}{5}+\frac{3}{10}=\frac{2\cdot 10+5\cdot 3}{5\cdot 10}=\frac{20+15}{50}=\frac{35}{50}=\frac{7}{10}$$

$$\frac{4}{9}+\frac{1}{3}=\frac{4\cdot 3+9\cdot 1}{9\cdot 3}=\frac{12+9}{27}=\frac{21}{27}=\frac{7}{9}$$

$$\frac{2}{-7}+\frac{-3}{8}=\frac{2\cdot 8+(-7)(-3)}{(-7)(8)}=\frac{16+21}{-56}=\frac{37}{-56}$$

$$\frac{-3}{4}+\frac{1}{6}=\frac{(-3)(6)+4\cdot 1}{4\cdot 6}=\frac{-18+4}{24}=\frac{-14}{24}=\frac{-7}{12}$$

With these illustrations come some further observations about the addition of rational numbers. For instance, $\frac{2}{5}+\frac{3}{10}$ can be changed to read $\frac{4}{10}+\frac{3}{10}$. The sum can now be found by simple integer arithmetic, and children even do it by counting the "tenths," so $\frac{7}{10}$ may be seen as the sum without appealing to the formal definition. This modification can be satisfactorily generalized as follows.

> If a/k and b/k are rational numbers, then
> $$\frac{a}{k}+\frac{b}{k}=\frac{a+b}{k}$$

Use the first definition and see what happens:

$$\frac{a}{k}+\frac{b}{k}=\frac{ak+kb}{kk}=\frac{ak+bk}{kk}=\frac{(a+b)k}{kk}=\frac{a+b}{k}$$

The third example could be used to illustrate this, because $\frac{4}{9}+\frac{1}{3}=\frac{4}{9}+\frac{3}{9}=\frac{7}{9}$.

The final two examples illustrate that the sum of rational numbers may be determined by negative as well as positive integers.

Check the properties of addition of rational numbers to determine if they agree with the properties of addition in a field.

> i. (*Closure*) Since $b\neq 0$ and $d\neq 0$, then $bd\neq 0$. Hence, $(ad+bc)/bd$ is a rational number.
> ii. (*Commutativity*)
> $$\frac{a}{b}+\frac{c}{d}=\frac{ad+bc}{bd}=\frac{cb+da}{db}=\frac{c}{d}+\frac{a}{b}$$
> iii. (*Associativity*)

$$\frac{a}{b} + \left(\frac{c}{d} + \frac{e}{f}\right) = \frac{a}{b} + \frac{cf + de}{df} = \frac{a(df) + b(cf + de)}{b(df)}$$

$$= \frac{a(df) + [b(cf) + b(de)]}{b(df)}$$

$$\left(\frac{a}{b} + \frac{c}{d}\right) + \frac{e}{f} = ? \quad \text{(Continue the argument!)}$$

iv. (*Identity*)

$$\frac{a}{b} + \frac{0}{1} = \frac{a \cdot 1 + b \cdot 0}{b \cdot 1} = \frac{a}{b}$$

Therefore, $\frac{0}{1}$ is an additive identity (called *zero*). Note that this identity has many names, for $\frac{0}{1} = \frac{0}{6} = \frac{0}{11} \cdots$

v. (*Additive inverse*)

$$\frac{a}{b} + \frac{-a}{b} = \frac{a + (-a)}{b} = \frac{0}{b} = \frac{0}{1} \quad \text{(zero)}$$

Thus, an additive inverse of a/b is $-a/b$.

These are the five properties required of a field addition operation.

Two remarks are in order. Notice again that the additive identity is $\frac{0}{1}$ (or *use any other name* for $\frac{0}{1}$ such as $\frac{0}{2}, \frac{0}{3}, \frac{0}{4}, \ldots$). We shall call this rational number zero, just as the *integer* zero. The other remark has to do with the additive inverse. Recall that we used a special symbol for additive inverses when we introduced the set of integers, that is "$-a$" as the "additive inverse of a" or "the opposite of a." Here we have said that an additive inverse of a/b is $-a/b$. Using the same notion as that used for integers, we could write

$$-\left(\frac{a}{b}\right) = \frac{-a}{b}$$

Confusion can be avoided if this is read "the additive inverse of a over b is the opposite of a over the integer b." It is also true that

$$\frac{a}{b} + \frac{a}{-b} = \frac{a(-b) + ba}{b(-b)} = \frac{a(-b + b)}{b(-b)} = \frac{a \cdot 0}{b(-b)} = \frac{0}{b(-b)} = \frac{0}{1}$$

This shows that $a/-b$ is also an additive inverse of a/b. But it can be shown that such additive inverses are unique (see Exercise 6 of Section 7.4), so we must conclude that $-a/b = a/-b = -(a/b)$. By the way, we can show that $-a/b = a/-b$ because $(-a)(-b) = ab$, as established in Chapter 5 on the set of integers. Here are some specific examples.

$$\frac{2}{5} + \frac{-2}{5} = \frac{2 + (-2)}{5} = \frac{0}{5} = \frac{0}{1}$$

$$\frac{2}{5} + \frac{2}{-5} = \frac{2}{5} + \frac{2(-1)}{-5(-1)} = \frac{2}{5} + \frac{-2}{5} = \frac{2 + (-2)}{5} = \frac{0}{5} = \frac{0}{1}$$

Therefore,

$$-\frac{2}{5} = \frac{-2}{5} = \frac{2}{-5}$$

If a and b are integers, $b \neq 0$, then

$$-\left(\frac{a}{b}\right) = \frac{-a}{b} = \frac{a}{-b}$$

How about the operation of subtraction? Do you recall that for the set of integers $a - b$ means $a + (-b)$? For the set of rational numbers, $a/b - c/d$ means $a/b + (-c/d)$. For instance,

$$\frac{5}{8} - \frac{3}{8} = \frac{5}{8} + \left(-\frac{3}{8}\right) = \frac{5}{8} + \frac{-3}{8} = \frac{2}{8} = \frac{1}{4}$$

So, as for a routine to use in subtracting one rational number from another, we simply can do as we did in the set of integers: add the opposite (or additive inverse).

So far in this section we have developed two definitions: one for addition and one for subtraction.

If a/b and c/d are rational numbers, then

$$\frac{a}{b} + \frac{c}{d} = \frac{ad + bc}{bd}$$

$$\frac{a}{b} - \frac{c}{d} = \frac{a}{b} + \left(-\frac{c}{d}\right)$$

where $-(c/d) = -c/d = c/-d$.

Much remains to be accomplished in terms of suitable *algorithms* for addition and subtraction of rational numbers. Although the definition of addition is adequate, there are routines to make computation simpler. Essentially, the basic algorithm for addition of rational numbers takes advantage of the renaming principle ($a/b = am/bm$) and the concept of the *least common multiple* of integers. In Chapter 6 you learned of the least common multiple (LCM) and used your knowledge of prime numbers to help find the LCM. To illustrate the complete algorithm, consider the typical problem

$$\frac{5}{12} + \frac{1}{18} + \frac{3}{8}$$

We seek a name for each of these three numbers such that the denominators are the same. We examine the prime factorization of each of 12, 18, and 8 and find that $12 = 2 \cdot 2 \cdot 3$, $18 = 2 \cdot 3 \cdot 3$, and $8 = 2 \cdot 2 \cdot 2$. The agreement made in Chapter 6 was that the LCM uses each prime factor the maximum number of times it is used in any number. So the LCM must be $2 \cdot 2 \cdot 2 \cdot 3 \cdot 3 = 72$. This is the name for the denominator of each fraction as we rename them.

$$\frac{5}{12} = \frac{5 \cdot ?}{12 \cdot ?} = \frac{?}{72}$$

$$\frac{1}{18} = \frac{1 \cdot ?}{18 \cdot ?} = \frac{?}{72}$$

$$\frac{3}{8} = \frac{3 \cdot ?}{8 \cdot ?} = \frac{?}{72}$$

Since $12 \cdot 6 = 72$, $18 \cdot 4 = 72$, and $8 \cdot 9 = 72$, then 6, 4, and 9 are needed for the change of names.

$$\frac{5}{12} = \frac{5 \cdot 6}{12 \cdot 6} = \frac{30}{72}$$

$$\frac{1}{18} = \frac{1 \cdot 4}{18 \cdot 4} = \frac{4}{72}$$

$$\frac{3}{8} = \frac{3 \cdot 9}{8 \cdot 9} = \frac{27}{72}$$

Therefore,

$$\frac{5}{12} + \frac{1}{18} + \frac{3}{8} = \frac{61}{72}$$

Once names are found whose denominators name the same number, the algorithm for addition becomes a simple matter of whole number (or integer) addition.

The algorithm for adding rational numbers can be illustrated in flow-chart form as in Figure 7-13.

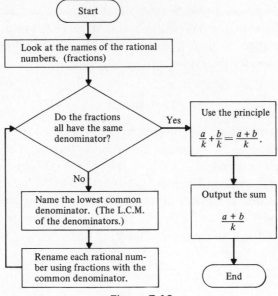

Figure 7-13

Suppose that the sum of two rational numbers is named by the fraction "$\frac{73}{15}$." What principles can be used to rename the rational number in other, perhaps more common, forms?

$$\frac{73}{15} = \frac{60 + 13}{15} \qquad \text{(fact from integer addition, } 73 = 60 + 13\text{)}$$

$$= \frac{60}{15} + \frac{13}{15} \qquad \left(\text{principle that } \frac{a}{k} + \frac{b}{k} = \frac{a + b}{k}\right)$$

$$= 4 + \frac{13}{15} \qquad \left(60 \div 15 = 4 \text{ and } \frac{60}{15} \text{ means } 60 \div 15\right)$$

$$= 4\frac{13}{15} \qquad \text{(notational agreement)}$$

Alternatively, one could say that $\frac{73}{15}$ means $73 \div 15$ and use ordinary division to say that $73 \div 15 = 4$ plus a remainder of 13 or that $73 \div 15 = 4\frac{13}{15}$.

What can you say about the subset of rational numbers

$$I = \left\{\frac{a}{1}; a \text{ is an integer}\right\}$$

Do you agree that $\frac{6}{1}$ *acts like* the integer 6? That $\frac{-12}{1}$ *acts like* the integer -12? If you do agree with this, then you agree with the idea, in general, that the rational number $a/1$ *acts like* the integer a, and the set I is the set of rational numbers that are identified with the set of integers. In this sense, we can say that the set of integers is a subset of the set of rational numbers.

> Under the agreement that the rational number $a/1$ acts like the integer a (or that the integer a can be named by the fraction "$a/1$"), then the set of integers is a subset of the set of rational numbers. We shall agree that
>
> $$\frac{a}{1} = a$$

EXERCISES (Section 7.4)

1. How is your skill with regard to adding and subtracting rational numbers? Test yourself with the following set of problems and see if you can do all of these without error in 5 minutes or less.

   a. $\frac{1}{2} + \frac{2}{3}$, $\frac{3}{4} + \frac{1}{8}$, $\frac{3}{8} + \frac{5}{8}$, $\frac{1}{7} + \frac{5}{6}$

   b. $\frac{7}{8} - \frac{1}{4}$, $\frac{9}{16} - \frac{3}{16}$, $\frac{19}{24} - \frac{23}{24}$, $\frac{9}{16} - \frac{3}{4}$

   c. $2\frac{3}{4} + 5\frac{1}{8} + 9\frac{3}{8}$, $1\frac{1}{3} + 2\frac{1}{4} + 1\frac{5}{6}$

   d. $16\frac{1}{3} - 4\frac{1}{5}$, $3\frac{23}{30} - 1\frac{5}{6}$, $2\frac{9}{10} - 3\frac{1}{4}$

   e. $4\frac{11}{12} - 5\frac{7}{9} + 2\frac{29}{36}$, $17\frac{35}{49} + 8\frac{15}{14} - 15\frac{1}{2}$

2. For the exercises of number 1, did you "reduce to lowest terms"? Would you count it wrong if you did not? Why? Why not?

3. Draw a series of pictures of your own design which will give a clear illustration that

   a. $\frac{3}{4} - \frac{1}{2} = \frac{1}{4}$

   b. $\frac{1}{3} + \frac{2}{9} = \frac{5}{9}$

   c. $\frac{5}{8} + \frac{2}{3} = 1\frac{7}{24}$

4. By simply adding, show that the inverse of

   a. $\frac{3}{4}$ is $\frac{-3}{4}$ as well as $\frac{3}{-4}$.

   b. $\frac{15}{17}$ is $\frac{-15}{17}$ as well as $\frac{15}{-17}$.

5. By appealing to the definition of equality, show why $\frac{137}{-7} = \frac{-137}{7}$.

6. Show that the additive inverse of a rational number x is unique. (Suppose that both y and z were such inverses.)

283

7.5

MULTIPLICATION AND DIVISION OF RATIONAL NUMBERS

The algorithm for multiplication of rational numbers is extremely simple. To make the algorithm appealing to the intuition, however, we should return to fundamentals.

> If a/b and c/d are rational numbers, then
> $$\frac{a}{b} \cdot \frac{c}{d} = \frac{ac}{bd}$$

On the basis of this definition (note that the definition *is* the algorithm), multiplication can be easily shown to be commutative and associative, an identity element can be found, and multiplicative inverses for every rational number *except zero* can be determined. We shall let you show that the commutative and associative principles hold true here, but let us discuss the concept of identity and inverse.

What is a multiplicative identity element? It's some rational number $\bigcirc$ such that for any rational number a/b

$$\frac{a}{b} \cdot \bigcirc = \frac{a}{b}$$

Can you find a rational number that makes this open sentence true? You should discover that the rational number $\frac{1}{1}$ is one rational number which makes the sentence true, because

$$\frac{a}{b} \cdot \left\langle \frac{1}{1} \right\rangle = \frac{a \cdot 1}{b \cdot 1} = \frac{a}{b}$$

If we recall a principle discussed earlier, there are many names for the rational number $\frac{1}{1}$, that is, m/m, where m is any nonzero integer. And it is also true that

$$\frac{a}{b} \cdot \frac{m}{m} = \frac{am}{bm} = \frac{a}{b}$$

which is consistent with another principle we have been using. Therefore, on the basis of the definition of multiplication of rational numbers we have proved that the multiplicative identity for the set of rational numbers is $\frac{1}{1}$ (or, by our identification of integers, it is the integer 1).

Now consider the definition of a multiplicative inverse. The multiplicative inverse of $\frac{2}{3}$ is a rational number $\bigcirc$ such that

$$\frac{2}{3} \cdot \bigcirc = \frac{1}{1} \quad (= 1)$$

Can you find a rational number that makes this sentence true? Your first attempt might be to try the rational number $\frac{3}{2}$ and you find that

$$\frac{2}{3} \cdot \left(\frac{3}{2}\right) = \frac{6}{6} = \frac{1}{1} \quad (= 1)$$

So the multiplicative inverse of $\frac{2}{3}$ is $\frac{3}{2}$. For an arbitrary rational number a/b, the multiplicative inverse must be what?

$$\frac{a}{b} \cdot \frac{b}{a} = \frac{ab}{ba} = \frac{ab}{ab} = \frac{1}{1} \quad (= 1)$$

So you conclude that the multiplicative inverse of a/b must be b/a and you are *almost correct!* What can go wrong? What if $a = 0$? Does "b/a" name a rational number if $a = 0$? No, since the denominator is never zero. We have then established the following general principle.

> If a/b is a rational number with $a \neq 0$, then the *multiplicative inverse* of a/b is b/a. We write, "$(a/b)^{-1} = b/a$" to say that the multiplicative inverse of a/b is b/a.

We shall leave it to you, as an exercise, to show that the multiplication of rational numbers is distributive over addition.

To briefly summarize what has been said about addition and multiplication of rational numbers, we have established (or left as exercises) the following:

> i. (*Closure*) The operations of addition and multiplication of rational numbers are closed. That is, the sum as well as the product of any pair of rational numbers is a rational number.
> ii. (*Commutativity*) The operations of addition and multiplication of rational numbers are commutative.

iii. (*Associativity*) The operations of addition and multiplication of rational numbers are associative.
iv. (*Identities*) The rational number $\frac{0}{1}$ is an additive identity (called *zero*) for the set of rational numbers and the rational number $\frac{1}{1}$ (called *one*) is a multiplicative identity.
v. (*Inverses*) Every rational number a/b has an additive inverse $-a/b$. Every nonzero rational number ab has a multiplicative inverse b/a.
vi. (*Distributivity*) The operation of multiplication of rational numbers is distributive over the operation of addition.

These properties are precisely those which are required of a *field*, as discussed in Section 7.2. Therefore, the set of rational numbers, together with its two operations, is a field. This achievement was one of our principal objectives for this chapter.

As you have seen, much can be done with multiplication of rational numbers from a purely abstract definition of multiplication. However, it should be possible to introduce the operation of multiplication in relation to the set of whole numbers and the set of integers. Do you remember the meaning attached to the expression "3 × 5"? If you recall, it meant that 5 was used as an addend 3 times.

$$3 \times 5 = 5 + 5 + 5$$

What meaning could be given to the expression "$3 \times \frac{2}{11}$"? Logically, it ought to be the case that

$$3 \times \frac{2}{11} = \frac{2}{11} + \frac{2}{11} + \frac{2}{11} = \frac{6}{11}$$

Portrayed on a picture of the number line, it also seems reasonable (Figure 7-14). What is being observed is that a simple algorithm can be used by children to find the product of whole numbers times rational numbers.

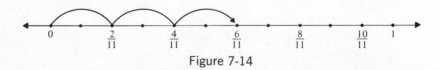

Figure 7-14

$$6 \times \frac{4}{7} = \frac{24}{7} = 3\frac{3}{7}$$

$$4 \times \frac{3}{14} = \frac{12}{14} = \frac{6}{7}$$

$$a \times \frac{b}{c} = \frac{ab}{c}$$

Of course, we can extend this notion to the set of integers rather than just the set of whole numbers; that is,

$$-5 \times \frac{3}{8} = \frac{-15}{8} = -1\frac{7}{8}$$

$$-4 \times \frac{-4}{5} = \frac{16}{5} = 3\frac{1}{5}$$

So, for any integer a and any rational number b/c, we know that $a \times b/c = ab/c$.

What would you say for the case $b/c \times a$? One explanation might be that since multiplication has been seen to be commutative, $b/c \times a = a \times b/c = ab/c = ba/c$. Thus, a neat conclusion is that $b/c \times a = ba/c$. You may argue, however, that kids will be reluctant to accept this until it has been made very clear, from experience, that multiplication is really commutative.

Consider the problem $\frac{3}{4} \times 12 = ?$. Let's go back to the definition of multiplication of whole numbers (Figure 7-15). With this concept, $\frac{3}{4} \times 12$ comes to mean "three fourths *of* twelve," that is, three fourths of a whole where the whole is twelve. Thus, we revert to the *definition* of rational numbers.

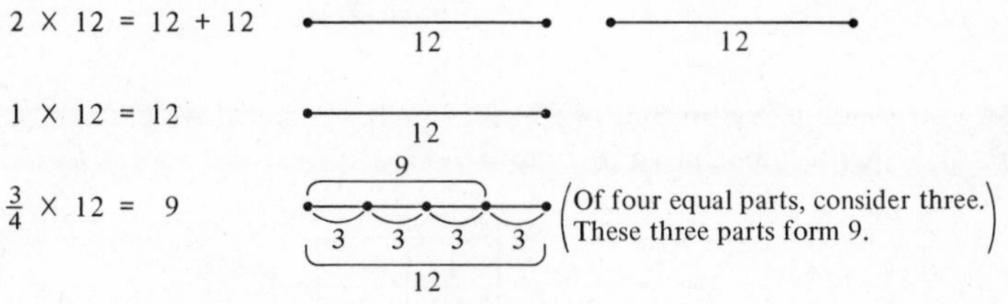

$2 \times 12 = 12 + 12$

$1 \times 12 = 12$

$\frac{3}{4} \times 12 = 9$ (Of four equal parts, consider three. These three parts form 9.)

Figure 7-15

Similarly,

$\frac{2}{3} \times 18 = 12$ Shade in a representation of $\frac{2}{3}$, given Figure 7-16.

287

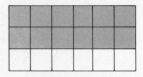

Figure 7-16

If the figure represented 18, what is represented by the shaded region? (12)

$\frac{5}{6} \times 24 = 20$

Here are the 24 pop bottles. Suppose that you fill enough to represent $\frac{5}{6}$ (Figure 7-17).

Figure 7-17

How many pop bottles are filled? (20)

The next illustration leads us back to the formal definition with which we began this section.

$\frac{2}{3} \times 5 = ?$

Figure 7-18 is a picture of 5.

Figure 7-18

Can you shade a region that represents $\frac{2}{3}$? It's easier if we change our picture of 5 slightly, as shown in Figure 7-19.

Figure 7-19

Now shade a region that represents $\frac{2}{3}$, as in Figure 7-20.

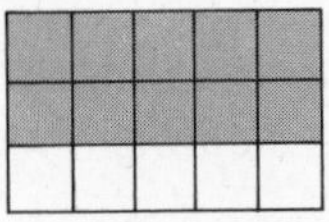

Figure 7-20

What number is represented by the shaded region?
Do you agree that $3\frac{1}{3}$ is a number for the region?
Would you prefer to use the number $\frac{10}{3}$?
Is it true that $3\frac{1}{3} = \frac{10}{3}$?

You have seen that $\frac{2}{3} \times 5 = \frac{10}{3}$. What could be an explanation for some method to find the product $\frac{2}{3} \times \frac{4}{5}$? One method and an explanation might be to use rectangles as in the last few illustrations.

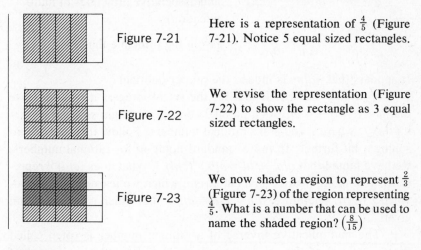

Figure 7-21

Here is a representation of $\frac{4}{5}$ (Figure 7-21). Notice 5 equal sized rectangles.

Figure 7-22

We revise the representation (Figure 7-22) to show the rectangle as 3 equal sized rectangles.

Figure 7-23

We now shade a region to represent $\frac{2}{3}$ (Figure 7-23) of the region representing $\frac{4}{5}$. What is a number that can be used to name the shaded region? $\left(\frac{8}{15}\right)$

Therefore,

$$\frac{2}{3} \times \frac{4}{5} = \frac{8}{15}$$

and the definition of multiplication is confirmed by our intuition. Out of several such activities children come to understand the meaning of the multiplication of rational numbers. It is paradoxical that they gain a skill in computation long before they have a complete understanding of the meaning of the process.

The operation of division of rational numbers is also computationally simple yet difficult to understand in terms of conceptualization. The standard definition is

289

> If a/b and c/d are rational numbers and $c/d \neq 0$, then
> $a/b \div c/d = a/b \times d/c = ad/bc$.

Before we turn to a very few illustrations that may suggest a rationale for the definition, let us again refer to our understanding of division of whole numbers (or of integers). Remember that $24 \div 8 = \langle 3 \rangle$, because $24 = 8 \times \langle 3 \rangle$. Therefore, if division of rational numbers is to be consistent with our earlier thoughts, $a/b \div c/d = \bigcirc$, because $a/b = c/d \times \bigcirc$ (provided $c/d \neq 0$). The definition suggests that the rational number which makes the sentence true is ad/bc. Let us test this.

$$\frac{c}{d} \times \frac{ad}{bc} = \frac{c(ad)}{d(bc)} = \frac{a(cd)}{b(cd)}$$
(by some uses of the commutative and associative principles of multiplication)

$$= \frac{a}{b}$$
$\left(\text{from the principle that } \dfrac{a}{b} = \dfrac{am}{bm}\right)$

It appears that ad/bc is indeed the proper quotient.

You may also recall that for the set of integers it was the case that $a - b = a + (-b)$. As a parallel concept we might say that $r \div s = r \times (s)^{-1}$, where r and s are rational numbers. Follow this line of reasoning a bit further. In more standard notation for rational numbers, we have hinted that $a/b \div c/d = a/b \times (c/d)^{-1}$. What does $(c/d)^{-1}$ represent? The multiplicative inverse of c/d, which we learned is d/c (provided $c \neq 0$). Therefore, $a/b \div c/d = a/b \times d/c$, which is the definition given.

The multiplicative inverse of a rational number is often called the *reciprocal* of the rational number. Therefore, the reciprocal of c/d is d/c. The reciprocal of $\frac{15}{29}$ is $\frac{29}{15}$. Note that the reciprocal of a number times the number itself is one (1).

> If a/b and c/d are rational numbers and $c \neq 0$, then $a/b \div c/d = a/b \times (c/d)^{-1}$. The rational number $(c/d)^{-1}$ is called the multiplicative inverse of c/d or the *reciprocal* of c/d. The product of a rational number and its reciprocal is 1.

In one view of division of whole numbers it was noted that division was repeated subtraction. The question "$24 \div 6$ is what number?" was translated as "How many times may one subtract 6 from 24?" It was also translated as "How many sixes are in twenty-four?" The latter view is perhaps helpful in giving a rationale for the division of rational numbers. For instance, "$\frac{3}{4} \div \frac{1}{3} = $?" could be translated to "How many thirds in $\frac{3}{4}$?"

Consider the representation of $\frac{3}{4}$ in Figure 7-24.

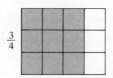

$\frac{3}{4}$

Figure 7-24

On a similar figure consider a representation of $\frac{1}{3}$ (Figure 7-25). Note that a third is represented by four of the small regions.

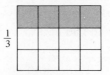

$\frac{1}{3}$

Figure 7-25

Count the number of thirds that can be found in the figure which represents $\frac{3}{4}$ (Figure 7-26).

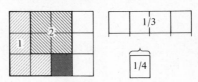

Figure 7-26

In terms of thirds, how much remains to be counted? Do you see that what remains is one fourth of another third?

Therefore, you have seen that

$$\frac{3}{4} \div \frac{1}{3} = 2\frac{1}{4}$$

This is consistent with the definition because

$$\frac{3}{4} \div \frac{1}{3} = \frac{3}{4} \times \frac{3}{1} = \frac{9}{4} = 2\frac{1}{4}$$

Another rationale which might be appealing is suggested by the agreement that "a/b" means "$a \div b$." Therefore, $\frac{3}{4} \div \frac{1}{3}$ could be translated to read

$$\frac{\frac{3}{4}}{\frac{1}{3}}$$

Now using the principle that $a/b = am/bm$ (expanded to allow a, b,

291

and m to be rational numbers rather than integers), the following sequence of equalities seems reasonable:

$$\frac{\frac{3}{4}}{\frac{1}{3}} = \frac{\frac{3}{4} \cdot \frac{3}{1}}{\frac{1}{3} \cdot \frac{3}{1}} = \frac{\frac{3}{4} \cdot \frac{3}{1}}{\frac{3}{3}} = \frac{\frac{3}{4} \cdot \frac{3}{1}}{1} = \frac{3}{4} \cdot \frac{3}{1} = \frac{9}{4} = 2\frac{1}{4}$$

Involved in this set of equalities is the requirement that $\frac{3}{3} = 1$ and $a/1 = a$, where a is any rational number.

You have now studied at least four methods to give some basis for the definition of division of rational numbers. Operationally, the process of multiplying by the reciprocal of the divisor is simple. Intellectually, the concept of division of rational numbers is very difficult for children (and adults) to assimilate.

> If a/b and c/d are rational numbers,
>
> $$\frac{a}{b} + \frac{c}{d} = \frac{ad + bc}{bd}$$
>
> $$\frac{a}{b} - \frac{c}{d} = \frac{a}{b} + \frac{-c}{d}$$
>
> $$\frac{a}{b} \cdot \frac{c}{d} = \frac{a \cdot c}{b \cdot d}$$
>
> $$\frac{a}{b} \div \frac{c}{d} = \frac{a \cdot d}{b \cdot c} \quad \text{(provided } c \neq 0)$$

EXERCISES (Section 7.5)

1. Test your skill with multiplying and dividing rational numbers. See if you can complete the following problems with no errors in 5 minutes or less.

   a. $\frac{2}{3} \cdot \frac{5}{6}, \frac{4}{7} \cdot \frac{3}{5}, \frac{-2}{5} \cdot \frac{3}{7}, \frac{-4}{9} \cdot \frac{3}{16}$

   b. $\frac{6}{7} \div \frac{3}{4}, \frac{3}{5} \div \frac{7}{10}, \frac{4}{-5} \div \frac{-5}{8}, \frac{-12}{15} \div \frac{-7}{-9}$

   c. $\left(\frac{2}{3} \cdot \frac{4}{5}\right) \div \left(\frac{1}{5} \cdot \frac{7}{8}\right)$

   d. $2\frac{3}{4} \cdot 5\frac{7}{8}, 5\frac{4}{5} \cdot 7\frac{1}{10}, 10\frac{12}{13} \cdot (-51)$

   e. $6\frac{1}{3} \div 1\frac{1}{3}, -4\frac{1}{2} \div 2\frac{1}{4}, 16\frac{5}{8} \div 3\frac{1}{4}$

2. If you did not "reduce the results to lowest terms" in Exercise 1, do so.

3. Give a specific example to show that both addition and multiplication of rational numbers are commutative.

4. Give a specific example to show that both subtraction and division of rational numbers are not commutative.

5. Give a specific example to show that addition and multiplication of rational numbers are associative.

6. Give a specific example to show that subtraction and division of rational numbers are not associative.

7. Complete the following table.

Rational number	Additive inverse	Multiplicative inverse
$\frac{3}{4}$		
$\frac{-7}{8}$		
$\frac{8}{-12}$		
$\frac{0}{1}$		
$\frac{0}{5}$		
$2\frac{3}{4}$		
$-3\frac{5}{8}$		
15		

8. Devise at least two activities which could be used to explain that
   a. $\frac{3}{4}$ times 24 equals 18.
   b. $\frac{3}{5}$ times $\frac{2}{3}$ equals $\frac{6}{15}$ or $\frac{2}{5}$.
   c. $\frac{2}{9}$ times $\frac{3}{5}$ equals $\frac{6}{45}$ or $\frac{2}{15}$.

9. Devise some activity which could be used to explain that
   a. 4 divided by $\frac{1}{2}$ equals 8.
   b. 3 divided by 6 equals $\frac{1}{2}$.
   c. $\frac{2}{3}$ divided by $\frac{1}{3}$ equals 2.
   d. $\frac{2}{3}$ divided by $\frac{1}{4}$ equals $\frac{8}{3}$ or $2\frac{2}{3}$.

10. Find the reciprocal of
    a. $\frac{2}{3}$ b. $-\frac{4}{5}$ c. $\frac{1}{3}$ d. 15

11. Rename each of the following rational numbers in the form a/b, where a and b are integers.

    a. $\dfrac{\frac{2}{3}}{\frac{5}{8}}$ b. $\dfrac{\frac{4}{5}}{\frac{5}{8}}$ c. $\dfrac{-\frac{2}{5}}{\frac{4}{10}}$ d. $\dfrac{3\frac{4}{7}}{2\frac{1}{3}}$

    e. $\dfrac{\frac{1}{4}+\frac{2}{3}}{6}$ f. $\dfrac{\frac{5}{6}}{\frac{7}{8}-\frac{4}{9}}$ g. $\dfrac{\frac{12}{15}+\frac{16}{21}}{\frac{14}{25}-\frac{9}{35}}$

7.6
DECIMALS AND PERCENT

Within the foreseeable future the United States will probably adopt a form of the metric system as its official system of measures. As you may know, the base of the metric system is a decimal scheme of relationships between measures. For instance, the meter (approximately 39.37 U.S. inches) is equivalent to 10 decimeters and to 100 centimeters. A liter is 1,000 cubic centimeters. A kilogram is 1,000 grams and a metric ton is 1,000 kilograms. In view of this anticipated change, it is likely that our emphasis, as teachers of mathematics in the elementary school, may shift from the representation of rational numbers by fractional symbols to the representation of rational numbers by decimals. Of course, both forms are in use and will likely continue to be used, yet a change in our system of measures would imply appropriate changes in our study and teaching of the concepts of rational numbers.

You have seen the distinct advantage of the Hindu–Arabic system of numeration as a positional notation. A digit in a numeral has a value determined by its position. The extention to decimals is logically consistent (see Figure 7-27).

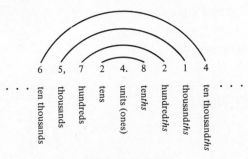

Figure 7-27

There is a convention used as decimal numerals are read aloud, which is that the word "and" is used *only* at the decimal point. Thus, "65,724.8214" is read, "Sixty-five thousand, seven hundred twenty-four *and* eight thousand two hundred fourteen ten thousandths." You may recall other conventions used in reading such numerals aloud; for instance, to the left of the decimal point each group of three digits is read as a block, followed by the name of that block. Therefore, "37,246,433" is read "37 *million*, 246 *thousand*, 433." To the right of the decimal point, we read the numeral as it stands and then affix the name of the last position in the numeral. Therefore, ".236" is read "236 *thousandths*," and ".43291" is read "43 thousand 291 *hundred thousandths*."

The meaning attached to a decimal representation of a rational number is almost given away by the names used. The symbol "14.3" means "fourteen and three tenths" or $14\frac{3}{10}$. The symbol "2.372" means "two and three hundred seventy-two thousandths" or $2\frac{372}{1,000}$. From our knowledge of rational numbers we can write

$$2\frac{372}{1,000} = 2 + \frac{372}{1,000} = 2 + \frac{300}{1,000} + \frac{70}{1,000} + \frac{2}{1,000}$$

$$= 2 + \frac{3}{10} + \frac{7}{100} + \frac{2}{1,000}$$

Now you can see that both notations are consistent and that the positions of the digits continue to determine their value.

You have seen the use of "10^3" as a name for 1,000 with the understanding that $10^3 = 10 \times 10 \times 10$. Let us make a formal definition of such notation (see Chapter 3).

If n is a positive integer, then

$$a^n = \underbrace{a \bullet a \bullet a \bullet \cdots \bullet a}_{n \text{ times}}$$

If n is zero, then

$$a^0 = 1 \quad \text{(provided } a \neq 0\text{)}$$

If n is a negative integer, then

$$a^n = \frac{1}{a^{-n}} \quad \left(= \frac{1}{\underbrace{a \bullet a \bullet a \bullet \cdots \bullet a}_{n \text{ times}}} \right)$$

Here are some illustrations that may help you gain an understanding of the use of these symbols.

$$6^4 = 6 \times 6 \times 6 \times 6 \qquad 12^2 = 12 \times 12 \qquad 5^0 = 1$$

$$3^1 = 3 \qquad\qquad 7^{-2} = \frac{1}{7 \times 7} \qquad\qquad 6^{-4} = \frac{1}{6 \times 6 \times 6 \times 6}$$

$$147^0 = 1 \qquad\qquad 0^0 = \text{not defined} \qquad (-3)^{-3} = \frac{1}{(-3)(-3)(-3)}$$

Again from Chapter 3, you may recall the following:

> In the expression "$a^n = k$" the number a is called the *base*, n is called the *exponent*, and k is called the *n*th *power of a*.

For the expression "$12^2 = 144$," the base is 12, the exponent is 2, and 144 is the second power (or square) of 12. Using exponential notation provides another means for expanded decimal notation as used in Chapter 3. For example,

$$431.67 = 400 + 30 + 1 + \frac{6}{10} + \frac{7}{100}$$

$$= 4 \times 100 + 3 \times 10 + 1 \times 1 + 6 \times \frac{1}{10} + 7 \times \frac{1}{100}$$

$$= 4 \times 10^2 + 3 \times 10^1 + 1 \times 10^0 + 6 \times 10^{-1} + 7 \times 10^{-2}$$

In this expanded notation it can be seen that each digit of the numeral names a power of ten.

The four fundamental operations involving decimals are logical extensions of the operations with rational numbers expressed in fractions. Addition of decimal notated rational numbers is operationally simple. As with whole number algorithms wherein the tens were added to tens, hundreds to hundreds, and so on, in decimal notation one adds tenths to tenths, hundredths to hundredths, and so on. Thus, $26.347 + 145.16 + 1.3562$ can be revised to read

$$
\begin{array}{llll}
26.347 & & 26.3470 & (.347 = .3470; \text{ why?}) \\
145.16 & \text{or to} & 145.1600 & (.16 = .1600; \text{ why?}) \\
+\ \ \ \ 1.3562 & & +\ \ \ \ 1.3562 & (.3562 = .3562) \\
\hline
\end{array}
$$

The purpose of alignment of the decimal point is to ensure that appropriate powers of 10 will be summed.

Subtraction is equally comparable to whole-number subtraction as the example $14.273 - 6.45$ shows.

$$
\begin{array}{ccc}
14.273 & & 14.273 \\
-\ \ 6.45 & \text{or} & -\ \ 6.450 \\
\hline
\end{array}
$$

Do you agree that $.45 = .450$ because of the principle that $a/b = am/bm$? Follow this line of thinking:

$$.45 = \frac{45}{100} = \frac{45 \times 10}{100 \times 10} = \frac{450}{1,000} = .450$$

An algorithm for multiplying rational numbers named by decimals can be derived from a look at an example.

$$2.3 \times 4.16 = 2\frac{3}{10} \times 4\frac{16}{100} = \frac{23}{10} \times \frac{416}{100} = \frac{23 \times 416}{1,000}$$

Before we proceed, notice that the problem has been reduced to one of multiplying 23 times 416 (the digits involved in the two factors) and then dividing by 1,000 or converting to a decimal name by using the definition. Therefore,

$$
\begin{array}{r}
4.16 \\
\times\ 2.3 \\
\hline
1,248 \\
832 \\
\hline
9,568/1,000
\end{array}
$$
Your thinking might resemble this.

$$
\begin{array}{r}
\hline
9.568
\end{array}
$$
Product

The algorithm becomes elementary: find the product of the numbers as if there were no decimal points; locate the decimal point in the product by noting the denominator of the product.

An algorithm for division also derives from knowledge of whole number division and from knowledge of rational numbers named by fractions. For instance, $6.177 \div 2.13$ can be translated as $6.177/2.13$. Again, using the principle that $a/b = am/bm$, we have

$$\frac{6.177}{2.13} = \frac{6.177 \times 1,000}{2.13 \times 1,000} = \frac{6,177}{2,130}$$

Now, from whole number division and an extension to decimals

$$
\begin{array}{r}
2.9 \\
2{,}130\overline{)6{,}177.0} \\
\underline{4{,}260} \\
19{,}170 \\
\underline{19{,}170} \\
0
\end{array}
$$

Ordinarily, the device of multiplying by 1,000 (or 100 or 10 or whatever power of 10 is helpful) is indicated by shifting the decimal point in dividend and divisor. The problem

$$2.13\overline{)6.177}$$

is rewritten as

$$2.13_\wedge\overline{)6.17_\wedge7}\qquad\text{(``$_\wedge$'' is called a \textit{caret})}$$

and carried out as if it were written

$$213\overline{)617.7},\qquad 213\overline{)617.7}$$

$$
\begin{array}{r}
2.9 \\
213\overline{)617.7} \\
426 \\
\hline
1917 \\
1917 \\
\hline
0
\end{array}
$$

The division algorithm outlined very briefly provides a means for deriving both fractional and decimal names for the same rational number.

$$\frac{1}{2} = 1 \div 2 = .5 \qquad \text{because} \qquad
\begin{array}{r}
.5 \\
2\overline{)1.0} \\
1\,0 \\
\hline
0
\end{array}
$$

$$\frac{1}{4} = 1 \div 4 = .25 \qquad \text{because} \qquad
\begin{array}{r}
.25 \\
4\overline{)1.00} \\
8 \\
\hline
20 \\
20 \\
\hline
0
\end{array}
$$

$$\frac{3}{8} = 3 \div 8 = .375 \qquad \text{because} \qquad
\begin{array}{r}
.375 \\
8\overline{)3.000} \\
2\,4 \\
\hline
60 \\
56 \\
\hline
40 \\
40 \\
\hline
\end{array}
$$

What decimal numeral is equivalent to the fractional numeral $\frac{1}{3}$?

$$1 \div 3 = \underline{\quad ? \quad}, \qquad 3\overline{)1.0000\ldots}$$

$$\begin{array}{r} .3333\ldots \\ \hline \underline{9} \\ 10 \\ \underline{9} \\ 10 \\ \underline{9} \\ 10 \\ \underline{9} \\ 10 \end{array}$$

Apparently, the division routine is never "going to come out evenly." What is obvious from this? There is no decimal numeral that is exactly a name for $\frac{1}{3}$. It is approximated by .33 or .333 or .3333, and we can give even better approximations such as .333333, but none of these names exactly the same number that is named by $\frac{1}{3}$. You may see one of the following symbols used to say that "$\frac{1}{3}$ is approximately equal to _____":

$$\frac{1}{3} \doteq .333, \qquad \frac{1}{3} \cong .33, \qquad \frac{1}{3} \sim .3333$$

We shall only devote a few brief paragraphs to the topic of *percent*. We might begin by agreeing that the word "percent" is often translated to mean "hundredths." Thus, 27% means $\frac{27}{100}$; and 10% means $\frac{10}{100}$ or $\frac{1}{10}$. From this understanding a rational number can be seen to have a fractional, decimal, and percent name.

$$\frac{1}{2} = .5 = 50\%$$
$$\frac{1}{4} = .25 = 25\%$$
$$\frac{1}{100} = .01 = 1\%$$
$$\frac{1}{3} \doteq .333 = 33.3\%$$

Sometimes you will see a combination of percent notation with fractional notation. For instance, $7\frac{1}{2}\%$ or $14\frac{1}{4}\%$. The meaning should be clear from the notion that "percent" means "hundredths." So $7\frac{1}{2}\%$ must mean 7 hundredths plus $\frac{1}{2}$ another hundredth. What is $\frac{1}{2}$ hundredth?

$$\frac{1}{2} \times .01 = \frac{1}{2} \times \frac{1}{100} = \frac{1}{200} = \frac{5}{1,000} = .005$$

Therefore, $7\frac{1}{2}\% = .075$. Such an idea makes it possible to name the rational number $\frac{1}{3}$ by $33\frac{1}{3}\%$.

Here are some typical problems involving percents, which will be seen to be reducible to decimal or fractional notation.

> Six percent of the children in this school are in a program of acceleration. If there are 400 children in the school, how many are in this program?

Translated as $\frac{6}{100}$ of the 400 children are in the program, it becomes a problem of multiplying $\frac{6}{100}$ or .06 times 400 to obtain 24. Therefore, 24 children are in this program.

> 25 of the 30 children in this class have drawn good pictures for parent's night. The other 5 have drawn excellent pictures. What percent of the children have drawn excellent pictures?

$\frac{5}{30}$ or $\frac{1}{6}$ of the children have drawn excellent pictures. $\frac{1}{6}$ is the same as $\frac{?}{100}$?

$$\frac{1}{6} = \frac{\bigcirc}{100}$$

We can find a number that makes this sentence true if we recall that $a/b = c/d$ when $a \times d = b \times c$. Therefore,

$$\frac{1}{6} = \frac{\bigcirc}{100}$$

provided $1 \times 100 = 6 \times \bigcirc$. By our knowledge of division, $\bigcirc = 16\frac{2}{3}$. Therefore, $16\frac{2}{3}$ percent of the children drew excellent pictures.

> Twelve percent of all arithmetic texts contain errors. We know that 6 arithmetic texts contain errors. How many arithmetic texts are there all together?

In this case $\frac{12}{100}$ of all such texts equals 6. That is,

$$\frac{12}{100} \times \bigcirc = 6$$

It must be that $12 \times \bigcirc = 600$, so $\bigcirc = 50$.

These three examples illustrate what once were called the "three cases of percent." You can see that your understanding of rational numbers is all that is needed, provided you remember that percent means hundredths.

We close this section with a brief comment on "scientific notation" for decimals. Do you agree that $146 = 1.46 \times 100$? Do you agree that $.0347 = 3.47 \times \frac{1}{100}$? To name a rational number in terms of scientific notation means to name that number as the product of some number between 1 and 10 and another number that is a power of ten. Thus, $146 = 1.46 \times 10^2$ and $.0347 = 3.47 \times 10^{-2}$. Both 1.46 and 3.47 are between 1 and 10 and 10^2 and 10^{-2} are both powers of 10. In the set of exercises you will be led to some conclusions concerning the use of scientific notation as well as some practice in using such notation for fundamental operations.

> A rational number is named by *scientific notation* if it is named as the product of a number a, where $1 \leqslant a < 10$, and a power of 10.
>
> $$a \times 10^n$$

EXERCISES (Section 7.6)

1. Rename each of the following rational numbers, using the definitions of exponents, so that they are named in the form a/b, where a and b are integers.

   a. 2^4 b. $(-2)^4$ c. 2^{-4} d. $(-2)^{-4}$
   e. 5^0 f. $(-5)^0$ g. 5^{-1} h. $(-5)^{-1}$
   i. $\left(\frac{2}{3}\right)^{-1}$ j. $\left(\frac{2}{3}\right)^3$ k. $\left(-\frac{3}{4}\right)^2$
   l. 0^0 m. $\left(\frac{1}{2}\right)^0$ n. $\left(\frac{1}{2}\right)^{-3}$

2. Complete the following table.

N	N^2	N^3	N^4	N^5	N^6
0	0	0	0	0	0
1	1	1	1	1	1
2	4	___	___	___	___
3	___	27	___	___	___
4	___	___	___	___	*
5	___	___	___	*	*
6	___	___	___	*	*

3. Test your skill with the four operations on decimals. Try the following items in 7 minutes and see if you have made any errors.

   a. $1.251 + 21.36 + 17.341 + 101.4$
   b. $15.3 - 9.351 + .014 - 4.005$
   c. $16.23 \times 7.5,\ 156.1 \times 35.01,\ 2{,}145.2 \times 156.1$

d. $47.2 \div 6$, $185.3 \div 9.4$, $15.9 \div .045$

e. $\dfrac{(89.3 + 1.495) \times (18.35 - 4.04)}{275.3}$

4. Complete the following table of equivalent names of rational numbers.

Rational number	Decimal	Percent
$\frac{1}{2}$		
	.375	
		75%
	.70	
$\frac{7}{8}$		
	.833 *	$83\frac{1}{3}\%$
		$12\frac{1}{2}\%$
$\frac{1}{6}$		
		$62\frac{1}{2}\%$
$\frac{4}{5}$		
$\frac{7}{9}$		
	.11$\bar{1}$ *	

5. a. Find 26 percent of 420.
   b. Find 130 percent of 70.
   c. Find .34 percent of 450.
   d. What percent of 36 is 6?
   e. 140 is what percent of 62?
   f. 11 is what percent of 1,543?
   g. 15 is 20 percent of what number?
   h. 250 percent of what number is 40?
   i. 14.2 is .03 percent of what number?

6. Rename each of the following in "scientific notation."
   a. 176.3   b. 14.358   c. .00134
   d. 176,000,000   e. 1.345   f. .0000006791

7. Take advantage of scientific notation and compute the following:
   a. $146,000 \times .0013$
   b. $.000456 \div 36,000$
   c. $\dfrac{13.4 \times .00821}{.000062}$

8. Find typical kinds of problems that illustrate the three kinds of percent problems:
   a. Finding a percent of a number.
   b. Finding what percent one number is of another.
   c. Given that a certain number is a given percent of another number, find the other number.

* See page 326.

7.7

THE RATIONAL NUMBERS AND ORDER

The set of integers is an ordered set in the sense that it is possible to define a relation called "less than" which has properties of transitivity and trichotomy. $-6 < 14$ because $14 = -6 + 20$, where 20 is a positive integer. In many ways the concept of order for the set of rational numbers is much the same as that for the set of integers.

> If r and s are rational numbers, then $r < s$ if and only if there is some *positive* rational number t such that $s = r + t$.
>
> If r and s are rational numbers, then one and only one of the following is true:
>
> $$r < s, \qquad r = s, \qquad s < r$$
>
> This is the law of trichotomy.

Suppose that p, q, and m are rational numbers and suppose that $p < q$ and $q < m$. There must be a positive rational number x such that $q = p + x$ and there must be a positive rational number y such that $m = q + y$. Since $q = p + x$, we can say that

$$
\begin{aligned}
m &= q + y \\
&= (p + x) + y \\
&= p + (x + y)
\end{aligned}
$$

Since both x and y are positive, then $x + y$ is a positive rational number. Therefore, $p < m$, and we have established the transitive property.

> If p, q, and m are rational numbers and $p < q$ and $q < m$, then $p < m$ (*transitive property*).

Here are some properties for the set of rational numbers that you can establish by referring to the model arguments given for the same properties in the set of integers.

> If p, q, r, and s are rational numbers and $p < q$, then $p + r < q + r$ and $p - r < q - r$.
> If, in addition, $r < s$, then $p + r < q + s$.
> If r is a positive rational number, then $pr < qr$.
> If r is a negative rational number, then $pr > qr$.

Figure 7-28 is a picture of the integer number line. Is there an integer between 4 and 5? Between -2 and -3? What do we really

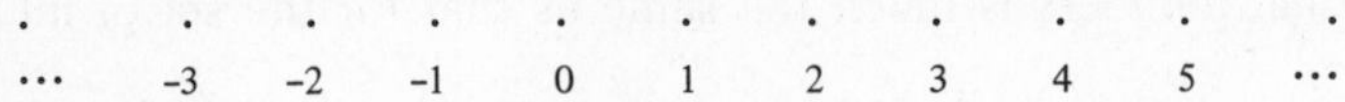

Figure 7-28

mean by the term "between?" An integer would be between 4 and 5 if it were greater than 4 and less than 5. An integer is between -2 and -3 if it is greater than -3 and less than -2. Of course, you can see that there is no integer between 4 and 5 nor is there an integer between -2 and -3. Is there a rational number between 4 and 5? Is there a rational number between -2 and -3? Let's make a formal statement of what is required.

> If p and q are rational numbers and $p < q$, then a rational number r is *between* p and q if $p < r$ and $r < q$.
> If $q < p$, then r is between p and q if $q < r$ and $r < p$.

Can we show that $4\frac{1}{2}$ is a rational number between 4 and 5? We know that $4 < 4\frac{1}{2}$ because $4\frac{1}{2} = 4 + \frac{1}{2}$, and $\frac{1}{2}$ is a positive rational number. Also $4\frac{1}{2} < 5$ because $5 = 4\frac{1}{2} + \frac{1}{2}$, and $\frac{1}{2}$ is still a positive rational number. Therefore, $4\frac{1}{2}$ is between 4 and 5. In a similar way, you can show that $-2\frac{1}{2}$ is between -2 and -3.

Suppose that p and q are rational numbers selected at random and $p < q$. Can we be sure that there is always another rational number between them?

$$p < q \qquad \text{(given)}$$

$p + p < q + p$	and	$p + q < q + q$	(why?)
$2p < q + p$	and	$p + q < 2q$	(why?)
$p < \dfrac{q + p}{2}$	and	$\dfrac{p + q}{2} < q$	(why?)

$$\frac{q + p}{2} = \frac{p + q}{2} \qquad \text{(why?)}$$

So, $(p + q)/2$ is a rational number that is between the rational numbers p and q. Incidentally, $(p+q)/2$ is called the *average* (or *mean*) of p and q.

You have seen that between any two different rational numbers there is another rational number, the average of the two. If we begin with rational numbers 4 and 5, then $4\frac{1}{2}$ is a rational number between them. What rational number is between 4 and $4\frac{1}{2}$ and what rational number is between $4\frac{1}{2}$ and 5? Between 4 and $4\frac{1}{2}$ is the rational number $4\frac{1}{4}$, the average of 4 and $4\frac{1}{2}$. Between $4\frac{1}{2}$ and 5 is the rational number $4\frac{3}{4}$, the average of the two. Is there a rational number between 4 and $4\frac{1}{4}$? Yes, $4\frac{1}{8}$. Is there a rational number between 4 and $4\frac{1}{8}$? Yes, $4\frac{1}{16}$. How long can this go on? Figure 7-29 is a picture of the rational num-

$$\overset{\displaystyle \cdot \quad \cdot \quad \cdot \qquad \cdot \qquad\qquad \cdot \qquad\qquad\qquad\qquad\qquad\qquad \cdot}{\underset{\textstyle 4 \;\; 4\frac{1}{16}\, 4\frac{1}{8} \qquad 4\frac{1}{4} \qquad\qquad\quad 4\frac{1}{2} \qquad\qquad\qquad\qquad\qquad\qquad 5}{}}$$

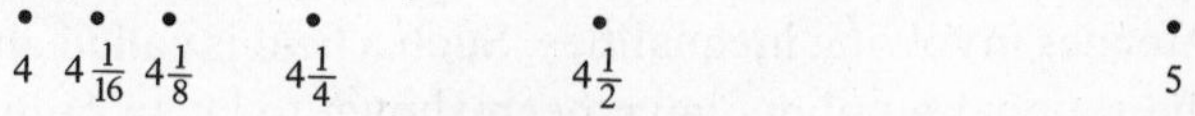

Figure 7-29

bers we are finding between 4 and 5 using the average. Of course, all the steps we are taking could be taken for any pair of rational numbers between 4 and 5 so that a tentative picture of the rational number line between 4 and 5 might look as shown in Figure 7-30. Yet we know that

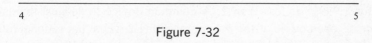

4   5

Figure 7-30

between any pair of such dots representing rational numbers, there must be another dot representing a rational number. So, a revised picture could be that of Figure 7-31. Again, between any two such dots

. . . .

4   5

Figure 7-31

there must be another to represent a rational number. So we are lead to believe that a picture of the number line of rational numbers between 4 and 5 looks like a solid line (Figure 7-32). Remember, however, that it is actually a series of dots that are *very close* together.

4   5

Figure 7-32

In Chapter 8 we shall show why Figure 7-32 is deceptive, because there really are some holes in this apparently solid line.

The fact that between any pair of different rational numbers there is another rational number is referred to as the *density property* of the set of rational numbers.

> The set of rational numbers is *dense*. That is, between any pair of distinct rational numbers there is another rational number.

We have seen that the set of rational numbers is an example of a mathematical system called a field. We have also seen that order can be defined on the set of rational numbers so that both the transitive and trichotomy properties hold true, as well as properties of transformation of sentences involving inequalities. Such a field is called an *ordered field*, so the rational numbers have been shown to be an ordered field. Finally, the rational numbers have been shown to be dense.

> The set of rational numbers with its operations of addition and multiplication forms a *dense, ordered field*.

Graphs of rational number sets are interesting and especially so in contrast to the set of integers.

$$S = \{x; x \text{ is a rational number and } x \leq 2\}$$

Since $2 \leq 2$, then 2 is an element of set S. Every rational number less

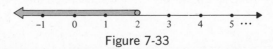

Figure 7-33

than 2 belongs to S, so the heavy line of Figure 7-33 shows this. Here is a set T that is only slightly different from set S just named.

$$T = \{x; x \text{ is a rational number and } x < 2\}$$

The graph of set T must suggest that 2 is not an element of the set, for 2 is not less than 2. Yet it must suggest that 1.99998 is an element of T, for 1.99998 is less than 2. A common device to suggest this is to place an open circle at the dot representing 2 when that rational number is not to be included and a closed circle when it is to be included. Thus, T is as shown in Figure 7-34 and is contrasted with S.

306

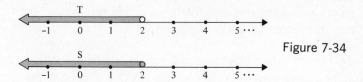

Figure 7-34

In Chapter 5 we sketched the graph of the set of pairs of integers named

$$\{(x, y);\ x \text{ and } y \text{ are } \textit{integers} \text{ and } 2x + 3y = 6\}$$

Let us revise this set slightly and sketch a graph representing such pairs:

$$U = \{(x, y);\ x \text{ and } y \text{ are } \textit{rational numbers} \text{ and } 2x + 3y = 6\}$$

Some pairs that belong to the set U are given here in tabulated form:

x	-3	0	1	2	3	4	$\dfrac{9}{2}$
y	4	2	$\dfrac{4}{3}$	$\dfrac{2}{3}$	0	$\dfrac{-2}{3}$	$-1 \ldots$

Locate these points as we did in Chapter 5 (see Figure 7-35). All these

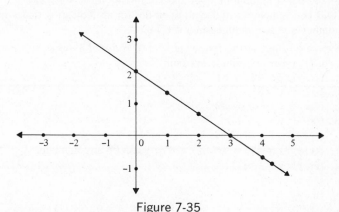

Figure 7-35

points seem to fall on the same straight line, so we connect them with a straight line and make the following conjectures.

Every pair of rational numbers (x, y) having the property that $2x + 3y = 6$ is represented by a dot somewhere along the line.

307

Every dot along the apparently solid line represents some pair of rational numbers (x, y) and $2x + 3y = 6$.

We won't try to prove that these conjectures are true, but they should have some intuitive appeal. They simply say that every pair that makes the sentence true is on the graph and every point that is on the graph makes the sentence true.

EXERCISES (Section 7.7)

1. Show why
   a. $17 < 36$ b. $-5 < 12$ c. $-18 < -4$

2. Give specific rational numbers that exemplify the transitive property.

3. Find four rational numbers that are between $2/3$ and $7/8$.

4. How many rational numbers are between $2/3$ and $7/8$?

5. Graph the following sets of rational numbers on a picture of the rational number line.
   a. $\{x : x \text{ is a rational number and } x \leqslant -2/3\}$
   b. $\{y : y \text{ is a rational number and } y > 5/2\}$
   c. $\{z : z \text{ is a rational number and } -3 < z \leqslant 1\frac{1}{2}\}$
   d. $\{w : w \text{ is a rational number and } w < -5/3 \text{ or } 3/4 < w\}$
   e. $\{v : v \text{ is a rational number and } v < -10/3 \text{ or } v \geqslant -1/2\}$
   (Did you remember to use an open dot for an indication that a rational number was *not* included in a set?)

6. Sketch a graph of the following sets of *rational number pairs* on a rational number coordinate system.
   a. $\{(x, y) : 2x - 3y = 6\}$
   b. $\{(x, y) : y = 3x + 1\}$
   c. $\{(x, y) : y = -2x + 1\}$
   d. $\{(x, y) : y = -x + 1\}$
   e. $\{(x, y) : y = x + 1\}$
   f. $\{(x, y) : x = \frac{1}{2}\}$ (*Note:* $x = \frac{1}{2}$, y can be any number.)
   g. $\{(x, y) : y = -4/3\}$
   h. $\{(x, y) : x = y\}$
   i. $\{(x, y) : |x| = |y|\}$
   j. $\{(x, y) : \text{when } x < 0, y = 1, \text{ and when } x \geqslant 0, y = -1\}$
   k. $\{(x, y) : \text{when } x = 1, y = 2, \text{ otherwise } y = 0\}$

7. If a is a positive rational number, then $a > 0$. Show why $a^2 > 0$.

8. If a is a negative rational number, then $a < 0$. Show why $a^2 > 0$.

9. If $a = 0$, show why $a^2 = 0$.

10. Exercises 7, 8, and 9 show that for every rational number a, _____. (Fill in the blank.)

11. Shade in the regions of the coordinate system for rational numbers named by the following sets of pairs of rational numbers.
   a. $\{(x, y) : x > 2 \text{ and } y \geq \frac{1}{2}\}$

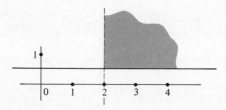

Solution: Note the dashed line for points not in the set.
   b. $\{(x, y) : x \leq -4\frac{1}{4} \text{ and } y < 2\}$
   c. $\{(x, y) : x \leq 2.4 \text{ and } y \geq -3.7\}$
   d. $\{(x, y) : 2x + 3y \leq 6\}$
   e. $\{(x, y) : 2x + 3y > 6\}$
   f. $\{(x, y) : x + y < 1\}$
   g. $\{(x, y) : x < y\}$

12. Of the following pairs of rational numbers, which number is the greater?
   a. $\dfrac{27}{31}, \dfrac{31}{35}$

   b. $\dfrac{-13}{25}, \dfrac{11}{-23}$

   c. $\dfrac{44}{61}, \dfrac{59}{80}$

7.8

A FORMAL CONSTRUCTION OF THE RATIONAL NUMBERS
(Optional)

Given only the set of integers, it is not difficult to create the system of rational numbers in a purely formal way. Let Z represent the set of integers and let Z_0 represent the set of nonzero integers (all the integers except 0). The set $Z \times Z_0$ names a set of ordered pairs of integers, and it is with this set that we begin the construction.

$$Z \times Z_0 = \{(a, b) : a \text{ and } b \text{ are integers}, b \neq 0\}.$$

We need to consider a relation between pairs of elements of $Z \times Z_0$, and if you are thinking "a/b" whenever we write "(a, b)," you may anticipate some of the conclusions.

$(a, b) * (c, d)$ if and only if $ad = bc$.

The relation $*$ on the set of pairs $Z \times Z_0$ has three notable properties.

i. For every pair (a, b), it is true that $(a, b) * (a, b)$. Since $ab = ba$, then, by definition, $(a, b) * (a, b)$.

ii. If $(a, b) * (c, d)$, then $(c, d) * (a, b)$. Since $(a, b) * (c, d)$, then $ad = bc$. But then $bc = ad$ or $cb = da$. From the definition of $*$, it must be that $(c, d) * (a, b)$.

iii. If $(a, b) * (c, d)$ and $(c, d) * (e, f)$, then $(a, b) * (e, f)$. Since $(a, b) * (c, d)$ and $(c, d) * (e, f)$, then from the definition of $*$ we know that $ad = bc$ and $cf = de$. Therefore, $adf = bcf$ and $bcf = bde$. By substitution, $adf = bde$. Since $d \neq 0$, $af = be$, from which it follows that $(a, b) * (e, f)$.

These three properties are called the *reflexive, symmetric,* and *transitive* properties of the relation $*$.

Next, define a special set of pairs from $Z \times Z_0$.

$[a, b] = \{(x, y) : (x, y)$ is in $Z \times Z_0$ and $(x, y) * (a, b)\}$.

For example, $[2, 3]$ contains such pairs as $(2, 3), (4, 6), (6, 9), (-2, -3)$, and so on, because $(2, 3) * (2, 3)$ for $2 \bullet 3 = 3 \bullet 2$

$(2, 3) * (4, 6)$ for $2 \bullet 6 = 3 \bullet 4$, $(2, 3) * (6, 9)$ for $2 \bullet 9 = 3 \bullet 6$

$(2, 3) * (-2, -3)$ for $2 \bullet (-3) = 3 \bullet (-2)$ etc.

Perhaps you can see that $[2, 3]$ names all the pairs of integers which, when used as numerators and denominators, reduce to the rational number $\frac{2}{3}$. We don't need to use any intuition here, however, for we are embarked on a purely formal approach to the development of the rational numbers.

Note that $[a, b] = [c, d]$ if and only if $(a, b) * (c, d)$.

This is not particularly difficult to prove, but we won't be trying to prove much here. Instead we want to show a sequence of steps that can be used to generate the rational numbers.

Let set Q be called the set of rational numbers ("Q" is suggested from the word "quotient") and define Q as

$Q = \{[a, b] : (a, b) \in Z \times Z_0 \text{ and } [a, b] \text{ is as defined earlier}\}.$

Upon set Q define two operations, $\oplus$ and $\odot$.

If $[a, b]$ and $[c, d]$ are rational numbers, then

$$[a, b] \oplus [c, d] = [ad + bc, bd]$$
$$[a, b] \odot [c, d] = [ac, bd]$$

Notice that since $b \neq 0$ and $d \neq 0$, then $bd \neq 0$. Therefore, $[ad + bd, bd]$, called the *sum*, and $[ac, bd]$, called the product of $[a, b]$ and $[c, d]$, are rational numbers in Q.

On the basis of these two definitions, the note about equality, and the properties of the set of integers, it is not difficult to establish the following results.

1. Addition of elements of Q is commutative.
2. Addition of elements of Q is associative.
3. There is an element of Q, that is, $[0, 1]$, which has the property that, for every element $[a, b]$ of Q, $[a, b] \oplus [0, 1] = [a, b]$.
4. For every element $[a, b]$ in Q there is an element, that is, $[-a, b]$, such that $[a, b] \oplus [-a, b] = [0, 1]$.
5. Multiplication of elements of Q is commutative.
6. Multiplication of elements of Q is associative.
7. Multiplication of elements of Q is distributive over addition.
8. There is an element of Q, that is, $[1, 1]$, which has the property that, for every element $[a, b]$ of Q, $[a, b] \odot [1, 1] = [a, b]$.
9. For every element of Q, except $[0, 1]$, there is a multiplicative inverse; that is, if $[a, b]$ is in Q and $[a, b] \neq [0, 1]$, then there is an element, that is, $[b, a]$ such that $[a, b] \odot [b, a] = [1, 1]$.

These nine properties establish the fact that Q is a field.

A *positive* element of Q is defined to be an element $[a, b]$ such that ab is a positive integer. Order for the set Q is defined as in the earlier portions of this chapter. $[a, b] < [c, d]$ if and only if there is some positive element of Q, say $[e, f]$, such that $[a, b] \oplus [e, f] = [c, d]$. Transitive and trichotomy properties follow immediately. So Q is an ordered field. As in Section 7.7, Q is also dense.

Consider the following subset of Q consisting of those elements of Q whose second components are 1:

$$Q_z = \{[a, 1] : a \text{ is an integer}\}$$

If we make an identification of the elements of Q_z such that $[a, 1]$ is identified with the integer a, then you may be able to see that Q_z and the set of integers Z are *essentially* the same. That is, Q_z and Z act in the same way when it comes to addition and multiplication, as well as order. Here are some examples of this idea.

$[4, 1]$ is identified with 4
$[-3, 1]$ is identified with -3
$[4, 1] \oplus [-3, 1] = [4 + (-3), 1] = [1, 1]$
$\qquad 4 + (-3) = 1 \qquad$ (to which $[1, 1]$ is identified)
$[4, 1] \odot [-3, 1] = [4(-3), 1 \bullet 1] = [-12, 1]$
$\qquad 4 \bullet (-3) = -12 \qquad$ (to which $[-12, 1]$ is identified)
$[-3, 1] < [4, 1]$ and $-3 < 4$

From this point of view, the set Q contains a *copy* of the set of integers, this copy being set Q_z.

Finally, if we make an identification of the element $[a, b]$ with the rational number that you know as a/b, you can see that a development of the set of rational numbers can be made from the set of integers alone.

EXERCISES (Section 7.8)

1. Name two other pairs of integers that are $*$-related to the given pair.
   a. $(2, 3)$ b. $(-3, 7)$ c. $(1, 5)$ d. $(-4, -6)$
2. Which of the following are true? Why?
   a. $[3, 4] = [15, 20]$
   b. $[6, 9] = [10, 15]$
   c. $[-12, 20] = [21, -35]$
   d. $[16, -20] = [-8, 12]$
3. Using the definition of addition and multiplication, find the sum and product of the following pairs of elements of Q.

a. [3, 4], [7, 2]
b. [−4, 5], [−8, 3]
c. [2, 3], [5, 6]
d. [−1, 3], [−4, 5]
e. [−11, 2], [7, 11]

4. Fill in the blanks so that the element of Q is positive.
   a. [2, ____]   b. [−3, ____]   c. [____, −5]   d. [____, 7]

5. Find the positive element of Q which will show that
   a. [2, 3] < [7, 8]
   b. [−3, 4] < [1, 2]
   c. [−5, 6] < [−1, 3]

6. The identification of [a, 1] with the integer a can be used to show why
   a. $-5 + 2 = -3$ d. $(-5)(2) = -10$
   b. $7 + (-3) = 4$ e. $(7)(-3) = -21$
   c. $-4 + (-2) = -6$ f. $(-4)(-2) = 8$

   Show how this identification can be used together with the definitions of addition and multiplication in Q.

Richard Dedekind

(*1831–1916*)

Take heart, all dedicated teachers, for your reward for years of inspired teaching may come before heaven, as it did for Richard Dedekind. Although he gave no early sign of the greatness that was later to be his, Dedekind was an excellent student of both science and mathematics. In the middle of the nineteenth century he studied with Karl Gauss and was later to be called the "last pupil of Gauss," not so much because he was one of the last to study with Gauss but more because he seemed to have learned more from Gauss than any of Gauss's later students. At the age of 21 Dedekind obtained his doctor's degree for a rather brief dissertation. Shortly thereafter he was a lecturer at Göttingen and gave the first lectures ever on the subject of Galois theory, which was soon to revolutionize the study of algebra and, in fact, was to become the foundation of a totally new branch of mathematics.

For 50 years Dedekind was a professor at the technical high school in Brunswick, a position that was far below the talents he possessed as a mathematician. No one can seem to explain why he remained in such an obscure post while lesser mathematicians occupied the great chairs of mathematics in Europe's universities. Whatever the reason, Dedekind

was one of the truly great mathematicians of all time and helped to establish the solid foundation on which we now base the calculus. To the theory of irrational numbers he added the concept that is now called a Dedekind "cut," out of which came a clearer view of the set of real numbers. He also added significantly to the subject matter of abstract algebra with his invention of the concept of an "ideal," which helped to resolve the issue of primeness in certain fields.

Dedekind never married and lived with his sister until she died in 1914. He lived to be 85 and had become so well known for so many years that some thought he surely must have died years earlier. In fact, one reputable source listed him as dead on September 4, 1899, to which Dedekind responded that the day might prove to be correct but the year was certainly wrong.

Chapter 8

Real and Complex Numbers

8.1
INTRODUCTION

You have seen that each system of numbers has been created to fill a certain kind of need. The system of natural numbers (and whole numbers) was constructed so that man could count sets of objects and keep accurate records of quantitative data concerning many different kinds of topics. The system of integers was created to provide a means to quantify as well as to designate direction in order that credit and debit, positive and negative, above and below could be given mathematical and hence logical context. The system of rational numbers results from the need to provide for apportionment, subdivision, partitioning, and other needs that demand a sense of fraction. We must show that the set of real numbers also arises from a specific need, and we must also show that this need is not filled by any of the other systems of numbers.

From another point of view, we have emphasized that the set of integers provides a solution to such equations as $x + 7 = 3$ and that no solution for this sentence exists in the whole numbers. Likewise, the rational numbers yield a solution to the equation $2x = 5$ and the integers do not. Finally, consider the equation $x^2 = 2$. We shall show that no rational number exists that makes the sentence true and, therefore, a mathematical need exists for a better number system.

8.2
THE REAL NUMBERS

The ancient Greeks were the first to discover that mathematics could be used to simplify and to organize the world around them. They "mathematized" what they observed in nature and learned much by this method, which we now see as an early scientific method of research. One of the greatest of these thinkers was Pythagoras, who, together with his followers, called Pythagoreans, used numbers not only to organize observations of a scientific nature but also to form a basis for an almost religious philosophy. They believed that all the universe could be reduced to "number" if man only had the knowledge. By "number" the Pythagoreans meant rational number; in fact, they meant positive rational number, because negative numbers were not invented for another 1,500 years or more. So fanatical were they in their belief in the rational numbers that they could not believe that there were any numbers other than the rationals. One of their members finally proved to his own satisfaction that there were numbers which were not rational and went before his brothers to prove this conclusion. He was promptly boiled in oil! However, the seed had been sown and in a few years even the Pythagoreans were convinced that the rational numbers were not the best of number systems.

Here is an argument that is attributed to Euclid, the greatest of all Greek mathematicians, which should convince you that there must be some numbers which are not rational. This argument will show that there is no rational number which makes the sentence $x^2 = 2$ true. Our argument will go like this: we shall assume that there is a rational number which makes the sentence true and follow a correct line of reasoning to reach a conclusion, which we shall see is a contradiction. Since no contradictions are possible, our assumption must be wrong, and so there can be no rational number that makes the sentence true. We begin by assuming that there is a rational number which makes the sentence $x^2 = 2$ true. From among the names of this rational number we can always select the one "in lowest terms," so let us say that

317

a/b is this rational number and that a and b are relatively prime (they have no common divisor except 1). Then $(a/b)^2 = 2$ or $a^2/b^2 = 2$ or $a^2 = 2b^2$. Therefore, a^2 must be an even integer (2 is a factor of a^2). But then a must be an even integer also. (If a were odd then a^2 would be odd.) Say that $a = 2p$ or that $a^2 = 4p^2$. Now from the fact that $a^2 = 2b^2$ we can see that $2b^2 = 4p^2$ or $b^2 = 2p^2$. Therefore, b^2 must be an even integer and so must b also be even. Now we have both a and b even integers, so they have a common factor, 2. But this is a contradiction, since a and b are relatively prime. Therefore, our assumption that there is a rational number which makes the sentence $x^2 = 2$ true must be in error.

We say that since $4 \cdot 4 = 16$, then 4 is a square root of 16. Since $\left(\frac{3}{4}\right)^2 = \frac{9}{16}$, we say that $\frac{3}{4}$ is a square root of $\frac{9}{16}$. We write "$\sqrt{25} = 5$" to say that 5 is a square root of 25. We have just proved that there is no rational number which is the square root of 2, no rational number solution, x, in the equation $x = \sqrt{2}$.

The Pythagoreans were very upset by this development because, first, they had established the famous result that bears their name, the Pythagorean theorem. Given the right triangle of Figure 8-1, the relationship between the length of the sides is that $a^2 + b^2 = c^2$.

$$a^2 + b^2 = c^2 \qquad \text{or} \qquad \sqrt{a^2 + b^2} = c$$

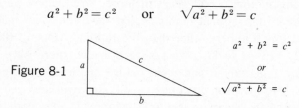

Figure 8-1

$$a^2 + b^2 = c^2$$
$$\text{or}$$
$$\sqrt{a^2 + b^2} = c$$

For a square, with sides each measuring 1 unit, the length of the diagonal squared must be 2 (Figure 8-2).

$$1^2 + 1^2 = 1 + 1 = 2 = c^2$$

Figure 8-2

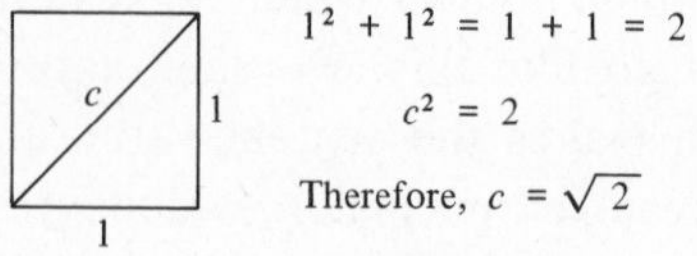

$$1^2 + 1^2 = 1 + 1 = 2$$
$$c^2 = 2$$
$$\text{Therefore, } c = \sqrt{2}$$

Therefore,

$$c = \sqrt{2}$$

Using the lower corner of the square as a center and the length of the diagonal as a radius, form a circle and consider where the circle meets the horizontal line of the square (Figure 8-3). The Pythagoreans had

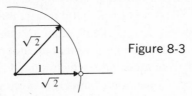

Figure 8-3

expected everything to be measurable with rational numbers, yet we can see that since no rational number when squared gives 2, there can be no rational number to represent that spot along the horizontal line. There *must be a hole* in the rational number line!

Since there must be a hole in the rational number line where $\sqrt{2}$ must go, you should be asking whether or not there are other holes in the rational number line. From an argument similar to that given for proving that $\sqrt{2}$ is not rational, you can show that $\sqrt{3}$, $\sqrt{5}$, $\sqrt{6}$, $\sqrt{7}$, $\sqrt{8}$, and many more square-root expressions name numbers that are not rational. Of course, the square root of 4 is 2 because $2^2 = 4$ and the square root of 9 is 3 because $3^2 = 9$. Therefore, $\sqrt{4}$ and $\sqrt{9}$ are rational numbers. Generally, if x is a rational number and $x = y^2$, where y is some rational number, then $\sqrt{x} = y$, so $\sqrt{x}$ is a rational number. We call such numbers as x *perfect squares*, so 1, 4, 9, 16, 25, $\frac{1}{4}$, $\frac{9}{25}$, and so on, are all perfect squares. We may also consider numbers that are *perfect cubes*. The number 8 is a perfect cube because $8 = 2^3$. $27 = 3^3$, $64 = 4^3$, $125 = 5^3$, and so on. Thus, 27, 64, and 125 are perfect cubes. A cube root of some number x would be a number y such that $y^3 = x$, just as a square root of some number x is a number y such that $y^2 = x$.

> If $a = b^2$, then a is called the square of b and b is called a square root of a. Write "$\sqrt{a} = b$."
>
> If $a = b^3$, then a is called the cube of b and b is called a cube root of a. Write "$\sqrt[3]{a} = b$."
>
> If $a = b^n$, where n is a natural number, then a is called the nth power of b and b is called an nth root of a. Write, "$\sqrt[n]{a} = b$."

Notice that since $5^2 = 25$ and $(-5)^2 = 25$, there are two numbers which are square roots of 25: 5 and -5. Likewise, $(-4)^2 = 16$ and $4^2 = 16$, so -4 is a square root of 16 and 4 is a square root of 16.

There are apparently several holes in the rational number line. We can see that if $\sqrt{2}$ is not a rational number, then $\frac{1}{2} \cdot \sqrt{2}, \frac{1}{4} \cdot \sqrt{2}$, $2 \cdot \sqrt{2}, -\sqrt{2}, (.9) \cdot \sqrt{2}$, and many other rational multiples of the square root of 2 must also be numbers that are not rational. Recall our picture of the rational number line, which looked like a solid line but which we knew was a collection of dots that were very dense (Figure 8-4). We now see that there is a hole at each of the places which repre-

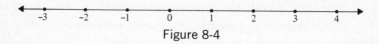

Figure 8-4

sents a number that is not rational. So there are holes at $\sqrt{2}, \sqrt{3}, \sqrt{5}$, $\sqrt{6}, \sqrt{7}, \ldots$, at $-\sqrt{2}, -\sqrt{3}, -\sqrt{5}, \ldots$, at $\frac{1}{2}\sqrt{2}, \frac{1}{2}\sqrt{3}, \frac{1}{2}\sqrt{5}, \ldots$, and many other places (Figure 8-5). Of course, we have just begun to identify the holes, and if we draw a picture of as many holes as we can, the line seems to disappear!!

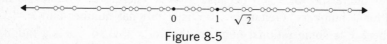

Figure 8-5

The square root of 2 is not a rational number, but it is very close to what rational number? This is an intriguing question because it raises the issue of approximation. Very often we must approximate some real number which is not rational (that is, some *irrational* number) by naming a rational number that is "close" to the irrational number. The word "close" is used to mean that our approximation for the irrational number is in error by some small amount, which we shall not be worried about. Often approximations will be made to the nearest tenth or nearest hundredth, and the routine we shall describe shortly can be used to give results of this sort.

We are faced with the real problem of finding some approximation of the square root of 2 that has an error less than we need worry about. (In measurement our tools usually don't give us a high degree of accuracy anyway.) We can see that $1 < \sqrt{2}$ because $1^2 = 1$, so 1 is not large enough. Also, $2 > \sqrt{2}$ because $2^2 = 4$, so 2 is too large. Therefore, the square root of 2 is between 1 and 2. Suppose we try 1.4 as a first approximation (or first guess). If 1.4 is the square root of 2, what would be the quotient when 2 is divided by 1.4?

320

$$\overset{?}{1.4\overline{)2}}$$

If 1.4 is the square root of 2, then the quotient must be 1.4, for then (1.4) • (1.4) would equal 2. However, we find that

$$
\begin{array}{r}
1.428 \\
1.4\overline{)2.0_\wedge 000} \\
\underline{1.4} \\
6\,0 \\
\underline{5\,6} \\
40 \\
\underline{28} \\
120 \\
\underline{112} \\
8 \text{ (etc.)}
\end{array}
$$

So, the square root of 2 is not 1.4, because the quotient is not 1.4 but rather 1.428 . . . . What can be done? We must try some number that is a little bit larger than 1.4 and a little bit smaller than 1.428. Why not use the average of these two?

$$\frac{1.4 + 1.428}{2} = 1.414$$

Is $1.414 = \sqrt{2}$? Let us divide.

$$
\begin{array}{r}
1.41442 \\
1.414\overline{)2.000_\wedge 00000}
\end{array}
$$

(fill this in as an exercise)

So the square root of 2 is not 1.414 either. It must be a little bit larger than 1.414 and a little smaller than 1.41442. A better guess might be the average of 1.414 and 1.41442, which is 1.41421. This process of dividing and averaging produces better and better approximations for the square root of 2, and you may be ready to accept 1.414 as good enough for your purposes. However, if this is not good enough, simply carry the procedure out as far as you wish. Remember, no amount of effort will yield the exact rational number value for $\sqrt{2}$, because $\sqrt{2}$ is not a rational number.

Here is another irrational number: $\sqrt{41}$. What is an approximation for this real number to the nearest tenth? The divide and average method yields the following results, beginning with 6 as a first approximation.

$$\begin{array}{r} 6.833\ldots \\ 6\overline{)41.000\ldots} \end{array},\qquad \frac{6+6.833}{2}=6.41,\qquad \begin{array}{r} 6.396 \\ 6.41\overline{)41.00{_\wedge}0000\ldots} \\ 38\ 46 \\ \overline{2\ 54\ 0} \\ 1\ 92\ 3 \\ \overline{61\ 70} \\ 57\ 69 \\ \overline{4\ 010} \\ 3\ 846 \\ \ldots \end{array}$$

So $6.41 > \sqrt{41} > 6.396$, and so $\sqrt{41}$ is approximately 6.4 to the nearest tenth.

Since the divide-and-average method is an algorithm for approximating an irrational number by a rational number, we may use the flow chart of Figure 8-6 to describe the algorithm.

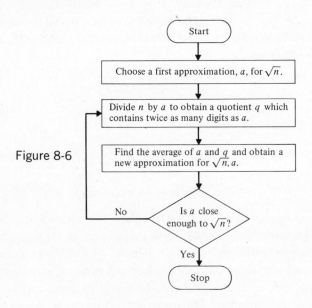

Figure 8-6

EXERCISES (Section 8.2)

1. In a manner similar to that used to show that $\sqrt{2}$ is not a rational number, show that $\sqrt{3}$ is not a rational number. (Note that if a^2 is divisible by 3, then a must be divisible by 3. Why?)

2. The ancient Egyptians must have known about the right-triangle relationship, for they used the concept to form square corners on their pyramids and in surveying land. If the two sides of the right triangle measure
   3 and 4 units, respectively, what must be the measure of the hypotenuse
   (the "slanting" side)? Can you explain how a rope knotted with 12 equal
   intervals could be used to form a right angle? It is contended that this is
   the way the Egyptians formed square corners.

3. What kind of figure could be used to show that there must be a hole in
   the rational number line at $\sqrt{5}$? (Remember that a square, 1 unit on a
   side, was used to form an argument that there must be a hole at $\sqrt{2}$.)

4. The integer 7 is a square root of 49. Can you find another integer which
   is also a square root of 49? Recall that a square root of 16 is an integer x
   such that $x^2 = 16$. What are the square roots of 25? Of 36? Of 0? Of 1?

5. What are the integers that are *fourth* roots of 16? What are the integers
   that are *fourth* roots of 81? What is a cube root of 64? What is a fifth root
   of 32?

6. By use of the divide-and-average method, find an approximation for
   $\sqrt{3}$ to the nearest hundredth.

7. By use of the divide-and-average method, find an approximation for
   $\sqrt{17}$ to the nearest tenth.

8. Using 7 as your first approximation, use the divide-and-average method
   to find the square root of 35.7 to the nearest hundredth.

9. The flow chart illustrated describes an algorithm for finding the square
   root of a number to any desired degree of accuracy. Use this method to
   find a square root of 6,147.

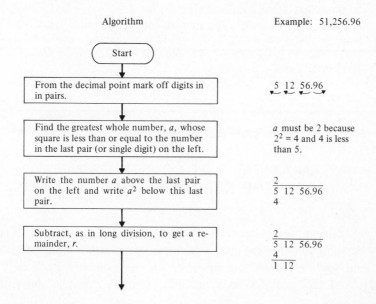

| Algorithm | Example: 51,256.96 |

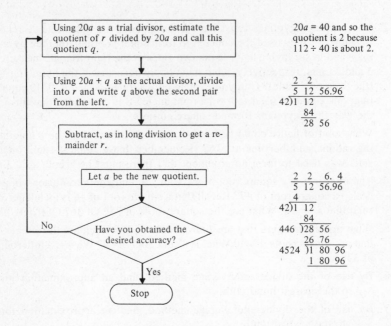

10. We have shown that $\sqrt{2}$ is irrational by use of an indirect argument. There is another argument which shows that $\sqrt{2}$ is irrational by using the prime factorization of integers and the properties of odd and even. We will begin the argument. Determine how a contradiction occurs in the argument and complete the argument.

Suppose that $\sqrt{2}$ is a rational number, say $\sqrt{2} = p/q$, where p and q are integers. Now $p^2 = 2q^2$. The Fundamental Theorem of Arithmetic assures us that p has a certain number of prime factors, and so it must be that p^2 has an even number of prime factors. (How many factors must there be in $2q^2$?)

8.3

AN ATTEMPT AT CONSTRUCTING THE REAL NUMBERS

The relationship between decimal numerals and the set of real numbers is an interesting one. You have seen in Section 8.2 that good rational approximations can be made for real numbers, such as $\sqrt{2}$, $\sqrt{41}$, and the like. Given a decimal numeral, can you determine whether or not it represents a *rational* number? For instance, 6.35 represents what rational number? We know that $6.35 = 6\frac{35}{100} = \frac{635}{100} = \frac{107}{20}$, and so 6.35 is the name of a rational number. What about the decimal 6.24242424 . . . ? This decimal is nonterminating, yet it repeats a cycle of digits. Here is a way to find the rational number named by this decimal. Let N temporarily name the number.

$$
\begin{aligned}
N &= 6.242424 \ldots \\
100N &= 624.242424 \ldots \quad \text{(multiply } N \text{ by 100)} \\
99N &= 618.000000 \ldots \quad \text{(subtract } N \text{ from } 100N) \\
N &= \tfrac{618}{99} = \tfrac{206}{33}
\end{aligned}
$$

Therefore,

$$
6.242424 \ldots = \tfrac{206}{33}
$$

Why multiply N by 100 in this example? Because the length of the repeating cycle of digits was *two* and multiplying by 100 or 10^2 moves the decimal point *two* digits to the right.

Consider the nonterminating repeating decimal numeral 35.1351351351 . . . . Note that the cycle of repeating digits is *three* digits long, so we shall multiply N by $10^3 = 1,000$.

$$
\begin{aligned}
N &= 35.1351351351 \ldots \\
1,000N &= 35135.1351351351 \ldots \\
999N &= 35100
\end{aligned}
$$

So

$$
\begin{aligned}
N &= \frac{35,100}{999} \\
&= \frac{1,300}{37}
\end{aligned}
$$

The decimal numeral .49999 . . . also names a rational number, and you can probably guess what it is. For a proof, let $N = .49999 \ldots$ and $10N = 4.999999$. Then it must be that $9N = 4.5$ or $N = 4.5/9 = \frac{1}{2}$. Thus, .49999 . . . $= \frac{1}{2}$.

From these examples you can see that every nonterminating, repeating decimal names a rational number which can be determined by the routine described in the preceding examples. You have also seen that a terminating decimal names a rational number determined by simply changing the form of the numeral from decimal to fractional. This leaves only the nonterminating, nonrepeating decimal numerals to be considered. For instance, 0.101001100011100001111 . . . is a nonterminating, nonrepeating decimal numeral in which the number of "1's" and "0's" goes from one to two, from two to three, and so on. Such decimal numerals do *not* name rational numbers. They name *irrational numbers*. If we did not already know that $\sqrt{2}$ is an irrational number, we might try to find a decimal numeral for $\sqrt{2}$ which has a cycle of repeating digits, hoping to be able to find the rational number named by $\sqrt{2}$. However, we know that such a search is fruitless, for we have proved that $\sqrt{2}$ cannot be a rational number.

Thus, the set of real numbers is partitioned into the set of rational numbers and the set of irrational numbers. Every terminating decimal names a rational number. Every nonterminating, repeating decimal names a rational number. The nonterminating, nonrepeating decimals name irrational numbers.

Incidentally, notice that you can determine the decimal characteristic of a given rational number by division. For example, $\frac{1}{7} = $ .142847142857 . . . , because

$$\frac{.142857142857 \ldots}{7 \overline{)1.000000000000}}$$

Sometimes it is convenient to name such repeating decimals by drawing a bar over the cycle of repeating digits. Thus $\frac{1}{7} = .\overline{142857}$, with the bar indicating that the cycle of digits which repeats is the six digits covered.

Now we have seen that every rational number can be named by a decimal numeral which either terminates at some convenient point, as with $\frac{3}{4} = .75$, or repeats a cycle of digits as $\frac{1}{6} = .16666 \ldots$. We have assured you that every irrational number is named by a nonterminating, nonrepeating decimal numeral. Therefore, the entire set of real numbers is determined by decimals; that is, every real number can be named by some type of decimal numeral. By constructing concepts of decimal numerals we come close to constructing the set of real numbers.

What properties does the set of real numbers have? We know that addition and multiplication are defined on the set of real numbers. There are some problems with these operations, however, because what is the sum of 3 and $\sqrt{2}$? Intuition tells us that $3 + \sqrt{2}$ is approximately 4.414, because $\sqrt{2}$ is approximately 1.414. But, to be correct, the sum of 3 and $\sqrt{2}$ can best be named by writing "$3 + \sqrt{2}$." What is the product of 3 and $\sqrt{2}$? Again, it is *about* 13.242. The best response, however, is "3 • $\sqrt{2}$."

Much of algebra taught in high school deals with naming real numbers in convenient forms, and you may recall some of this from your study of high school algebra. For example, $\sqrt{2} \cdot \sqrt{3} = \sqrt{6}$, $\sqrt[3]{5} \cdot \sqrt[3]{25} = \sqrt[3]{125} = 5$, $2\sqrt{5} \cdot \sqrt{30} = 10\sqrt{6}$, and so on. We shall not attempt any tasks along these lines, but you should know where the study of real numbers leads.

Ignoring the kinds of details suggested in the preceding paragraph, addition and multiplication of real numbers are closed operations, they are commutative and associative operations, and there are identity elements for each operation, that is, zero and one. Furthermore, for every real number there exists an additive inverse, and for every *nonzero* real number there exists a multiplicative inverse. Finally, multiplication is distributive over addition. All these properties also held true for the set of rational numbers, so you should be asking "What properties does the real number system have that the rational number system does not have?" Remember that the set of rational numbers was *dense;* that is, between any two rational numbers there is another rational number. Between any two real numbers there is also a real number, so the real numbers are also *dense.* In fact, between any pair of distinct real numbers there is a rational *as well as* an irrational number. So both the set of rational numbers and the set of real numbers are dense, ordered fields. What properties has the real number system that the rational number system does not? We have seen that $x^2 = 2$ has no solution in the set of rational numbers but does have the solution $\sqrt{2}$ in the set of real numbers. This is a start on the unique feature of the set of real numbers.

The set of positive real numbers is that set of numbers whose representations on the number line are to the right of zero. Order for the set of real numbers is defined in the same way that it was defined for the set of rational numbers. If a and b are real numbers, $a < b$ if and only if there is a positive real number p such that $a + p = b$. The properties of order described for the set of rational numbers also hold for the set of real numbers. Here is a brief list of these properties:

If a is a real number, one and only one of the following is true: $a < 0$, or $a = 0$, or $0 < a$ (Trichotomy).

> If a, b, and c are real numbers and $a < b$ and $b < c$,
> then $a < c$ (Transitivity).
>
> If a, b, and c are real numbers and $a < b$, then $a + c <$
> $b + c$.
>
> If a, b, and c are real numbers, $a < b$, and c is positive,
> then $ac < bc$, and if c is negative, then $ac > bc$.

The notion of absolute value for real numbers coincides with that given for the set of rational numbers. We may make one further comment, however, in view of the discussion of square roots. We have noted that $\sqrt{(5)^2} = \sqrt{25} = 5$ and you can also see that $\sqrt{(-5)^2} = \sqrt{25} = 5$. Therefore, $5 = \sqrt{(5)^2} = |5|$ and $5 = \sqrt{(-5)^2} = |-5|$. In general, $|a| = \sqrt{(a)^2}$.

> If a is a real number, then
> $$|a| = \sqrt{(a)^2}$$

EXERCISES (Section 8.3)

1. What rational numbers are named by the following decimal numerals?
   a. 4.5555 . . .   d. 1.2413413413 . . .
   b. 27.3000 . . .   e. 1.9̄
   c. .21̄3̄   f. 1,451.45̄14̄5̄

2. Name some real numbers which you are sure are not rational (that is, some irrational numbers) and explain why they are not rational.

3. If the square root of 2 is approximately 1.414, then what would be approximations for the following?
   a. $1 + \sqrt{2}$ d. $2\sqrt{2}$
   b. $1 - \sqrt{2}$ e. $1/\sqrt{2}$
   c. $\sqrt{2}/2$ f. $\sqrt{\sqrt{2}}$

4. What are the decimal numerals that represent the following?
   a. $\frac{1}{2}$ f. $\frac{1}{7}$
   b. $\frac{1}{3}$ g. $\frac{1}{8}$
   c. $\frac{1}{4}$ h. $\frac{1}{9}$
   d. $\frac{1}{5}$ i. $\frac{5}{6}$
   e. $\frac{1}{6}$ j. $\frac{13}{17}$

5. Find real number solutions for the following equations. (Do not approximate.)

a. $x^2 = 2$ c. $-4 + x^2 = 1$

b. $x^2 + 5 = 9$ d. $x^2 - 8 = -5$

6. Find a rational number and an irrational number between each of the following pairs of real numbers.

a. 1, 2   c. $\sqrt{2}$, $1\frac{1}{2}$

b. $\sqrt{2}$, $\sqrt{3}$ d. 1.7, 1.6

7. Solve the following inequalities for the real number solutions.

a. $x + 5 < 7$ d. $\sqrt{2} - 3x \geq 5$

b. $x + \sqrt{5} < 9$ e. $17 \leq \sqrt{3}x - 4$

c. $2x - 5 > \sqrt{3}$ f. $-6 < 3x - \sqrt{7}$

8. Using approximations of the square roots to the nearest tenth, sketch a line graph of the solutions to each of the inequalities given in Exercise 7.

9. Use the square root of $(a)^2$ to give the absolute value of each of the following:

a. -6 d. -4.2

b. 4.3 e. $\sqrt{3}$

c. 5.1 f. $-\sqrt{3}$

10. Here are two arguments that employ a technique used in this section regarding the summation of an infinite number of addends. One argument leads to an absurdity; the other is correct. Determine the incorrect argument and, if possible, tell why this argument is incorrect.

Argument 1   *Argument 2*

$N = 1 + 2 + 4 + 8 + \cdots$ $M = 1 + \frac{1}{2} + \frac{1}{4} + \frac{1}{8} + \frac{1}{16} + \cdots$

$\quad = 1 + 2(1 + 2 + 4 + 8 + \cdots)$ $\quad = 1 + \frac{1}{2}(1 + \frac{1}{2} + \frac{1}{4} + \frac{1}{8} + \cdots)$

$\quad = 1 + 2 \cdot N$ $\quad = 1 + \frac{1}{2} \cdot M$

So $2 \cdot N - N = -1$ So $M - \frac{1}{2}M = 1$

or $N = -1$ or $\frac{1}{2}M = 1$

                         or $M = 2$

8.4

THE COMPLETENESS PROPERTY

We must still answer the query "What property does the set of real numbers have that the rational numbers do not have?" We must take you on a short excursion in order to give you a good answer, although you can already understand a part of the story from your knowledge of $\sqrt{2}$.

Suppose that S is a set of real numbers, say $S = \{1, 3, -5, \sqrt{3},$ 1.345, $2\frac{1}{2}\}$. An *upper bound* of the set S is any real number x such that x is greater than or equal to any element of set S; that is, $x \geq a$ for any a in S. In this view, 5 is an upper bound of set S because

$$5 \geq 1, \quad 5 \geq 3, \quad 5 \geq -5, \quad 5 \geq \sqrt{3}, \quad 5 \geq 1.345, \quad 5 \geq 2\frac{1}{2}$$

Likewise, 4 is an upper bound, $3\frac{1}{2}$ is an upper bound, 3 is an upper bound, 1,000 is an upper bound, and so on. As a matter of fact, 3 is a very special upper bound, for it is the smallest of all the upper bounds. We call 3 the *least upper bound* of the set S. Figure 8-7 is a picture of

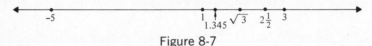

Figure 8-7

set S on a number line. Any real number that is equal to or greater than 3 is an upper bound of set S and 3 is the least upper bound.

What is a lower bound of set S? A *lower bound* is a real number y such that $y \leq a$ for any a in set S. Thus, -10 is a lower bound, -6 is a lower bound, $-1,000$ is a lower bound, and -5 is a lower bound. In fact, -5 is the *greatest lower bound*, because all other lower bounds of S are less than -5.

Here is a summary of the kinds of bounds for a set S of real numbers.

> If S is a set of real numbers, an *upper bound* of set S is a real number x such that $x \geq a$ for every a in set S.
>
> The real number k is the *least upper bound* of set S if k is an upper bound of set S and $k \leq x$ for every upper bound x of set S.
>
> A *lower bound* of set S is a real number y such that $y \leq a$ for every a in set S.
>
> The real number h is the *greatest lower bound* of set S if h is a lower bound of set S and $h \geq y$ for every lower bound y of set S.

For our set $S = \{-5, 1, 1.345, \sqrt{3}, 2\frac{1}{2}, 3\}$ the least upper bound is 3 and the greatest lower bound is -5.

Consider the set T of real numbers:

$$T = \{x : x \text{ is a positive real number and } x^2 < 2\}$$

What are some of the upper bounds of set T? Do you agree that 2 is an upper bound of set T? Since $2 < 2^2$, then every x in set T must be less than 2. Do you agree that $\sqrt{2}$ is an upper bound of set T? If x is an element of T, and $x^2 < 2$, then $x < \sqrt{2}$. The picture of set T shown in Figure 8-8 may portray these ideas more clearly. What is the least

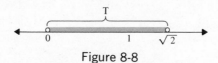

Figure 8-8

upper bound of set T? It must be that $\sqrt{2}$ is the least upper bound of set T, because $\sqrt{2}$ is an upper bound of T and every other upper bound falls to the right of $\sqrt{2}$.

Sketching graphs of sets of numbers provides a good means of contrasting the number systems insofar as these concepts of density are concerned. Consider the set

$$S = \{x : x \text{ is a natural number and } x^2 \leq 5\}$$

The only natural numbers which satisfy the condition that $x^2 \leq 5$ are the numbers 1 and 2. So a graph of this set looks like Figure 8-9, where

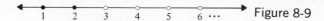 Figure 8-9

we agree that the filled dots represent points of the graph and the empty dots represent natural numbers not in the set S. Consider the same set S but use the whole numbers (Figure 8-10). Now use the set

 Figure 8-10

of integers as replacements for the x (Figure 8-11). With the set of rational numbers as the replacement set for the variable x, we sketch

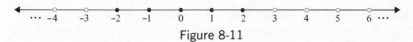

Figure 8-11

a graph that looks like a solid line but which we know has many holes in it. There is no rational number whose square is 5, so we must show a hole at $\sqrt{5}$ and $-\sqrt{5}$ (Figure 8-12). Finally, using the set of real

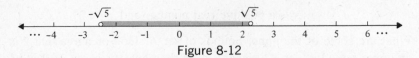

Figure 8-12

numbers as a replacement for the variable x, we sketch a solid line, knowing it has no holes and, since $\sqrt{5}$ is a real number, we show filled dots at $\sqrt{5}$ and $-\sqrt{5}$ (Figure 8-13).

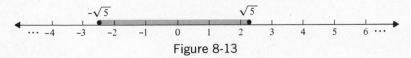

Figure 8-13

Now consider the set of *rational numbers* named in the set U:

$$U = \{x : x \text{ is a positive rational number and } x^2 < 2\}$$

Notice that U and T are almost the same sets, except that U contains only rational numbers, whereas T contains real numbers. What is a rational number upper bound of set U? Do you agree that 2 is such an upper bound? If x is in U, then $x^2 < 2$, so certainly x is less than 2 for $2^2 = 4$, which is greater than 2. Do you agree that 1.5 is an upper bound of U? Since $1.5^2 = 2.25$, then 1.5 is greater than any element of set U. Here is a list of rational numbers each of which is an upper bound of set U, because the square of each of these rational numbers is greater than 2.

N	N^2	
3	9	> 2
2	4	> 2
1.5	2.25	> 2
1.45	2.1025	> 2
1.42	2.0164	> 2
1.415	2.002225	> 2

What is the *rational number* that is the least upper bound of set U? You would like to be able to use $\sqrt{2}$ as this least upper bound, wouldn't you? But we need a rational number! This is the point: there is no rational number that is a least upper bound of set U. We can always find a smaller upper bound than any of those provided in the table, but we shall do so by determining better and better approximations for $\sqrt{2}$.

We have seen that the number line picture of the set of rational numbers, though dense, is full of holes and is therefore an incomplete number line in some sense. The number line picture of the set of real numbers, however, has no holes and is therefore complete. The completeness property is stated not in terms of holes but in terms of the concept of least upper bound.

> *The Completeness Property of the Real Numbers.* Every nonempty set of real numbers having an upper bound has a least upper bound.

You have just seen an example of a set of rational numbers, set U, that has an upper bound, but no least upper bound, in the set of rational numbers. This is the distinguishing characteristic of the system of real numbers. Every nonempty set of real numbers having an upper bound has a least upper bound.

We close this section with an interesting function. Suppose that every real number is paired with either 1 or -1 according to the following rule.

If x is a rational number, x is paired with 1.

If x is an irrational number, x is paired with -1.

Here are some typical pairs in this function: $(2, 1)$, $(3\frac{1}{2}, 1)$, $(-5, 1)$, $(14.253, 1)$, $(\sqrt{2}, -1)$, $(\sqrt{5}, -1)$, $(-\sqrt[3]{26}, -1)$, ... Since every real number is either rational or irrational, every real number is paired with something, either 1 or -1. A graph of this function is particularly interesting, and we construct the graph in stages. First, let us locate a few of the typical pairs of this function, as shown in Figure 8-14. Of

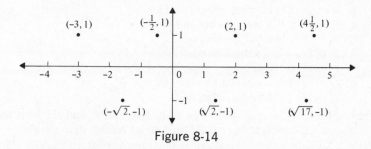

Figure 8-14

course, we know that between any two rational numbers there is another rational number, and between any two irrational numbers there is another irrational number; hence, the points of the graph must be closer than shown in Figure 8-14 (see Figure 8-15). In fact, the points

333

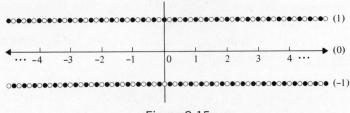

Figure 8-15

of the graph must be much closer than this. They are so dense that we shall not be able to distinguish the points from one another, so the two sets of dots, above and below the number line, must look like straight lines (Figure 8-16). We know that both lines are full of holes!

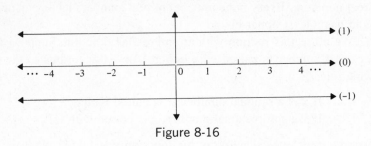

Figure 8-16

EXERCISES (Section 8.4)

1. Consider the following sets of numbers. Find at least two upper and two lower bounds for each set (if such bounds exist).
   a. $A = \{x : x \text{ is a rational number and } x \leq 10\}$
   b. $B = \{x : x \text{ is an integer and } x > 5\}$
   c. $C = \{y : y \text{ is a real number and } y^2 < 4\}$
   d. $D = \{z : z \text{ is a real number and } |z| = 1\}$
   e. $E = \{n : n \text{ is a natural number and } n > 1\}$
   f. $F = \{w : w \text{ is an integer and } -3 \leq w < 7\}$
   g. $G = \{k : k \text{ is a rational number and } k^2 < 3\}$
   h. $H = \{x : x \text{ is a real number and } x^2 < 3\}$

2. For each of the sets A through H in Exercise 1, find the least upper bound if it exists. If there is no least upper bound, state a reason.

3. For each of the sets A through H in Exercise 1, find the greatest lower bound if it exists. If there is no greatest lower bound, state a reason.

4. Sketch graphs of each of the sets A through H in Exercise 1.

5. Here is an interesting function for which you should be able to sketch

the graph and which should show you something interesting. Given that x is a real number:

> If x is an integer, then x is paired with 1.
> If x is not an integer, then x is paired with 0.

Sometimes such a function is named by saying

$$f(x) = \begin{cases} 1, & \text{if } x \text{ is an integer} \\ 0, & \text{if } x \text{ is not an integer} \end{cases}$$

6. Sketch a graph of the following function:

$$H = \{(x, y) : x \text{ and } y \text{ are real numbers and } y = |x|\}$$

7. Sketch a graph of the following function:

$$S = \{(x, y) : x \text{ is a real number, } y \text{ is an integer and } y \leq x < y + 1\}$$

Do you see why this function is called a *step function?*

8.5

THE COMPLEX NUMBERS

The set of real numbers has been shown to be a complete, ordered field with solutions to such an equation as $x^2 = 3$. Can there be any further need for a system of numbers that the set of real numbers cannot fulfill? The answer is yes. The equation $x^2 = -1$ has no solution in the set of real numbers nor any other system invented in this text so far. If you try to use 1 as a solution for the equation $x^2 = -1$, you find that $(1)^2 = 1 \neq -1$. If you try to use -1 as a solution, you find that $(-1)^2 = 1 \neq -1$. So the only likely possibilities are quickly eliminated.

One method to use in creating a new system of numbers, which will have a solution for this equation, is to invent a new number. Let the letter i represent a new number which has the property that $i^2 = -1$. We know that i is not a real number because the square of every real number is never negative. The new number i is a solution for the equation $x^2 = -1$.

To build a totally new system using this new number i, consider the set of numbers given by set C:

$$C = \{a + bi : a \text{ and } b \text{ are real numbers and } i^2 = -1\}$$

Let us agree that two such numbers, for example $a + bi$ and $c + di$, have equality, addition, and multiplication defined as follows:

335

> $a + bi = c + di$ if and only if $a = c$ and $b = d$.
> $(a + bi) + (c + di) = (a + c) + (b + d)i$.
> $(a + bi) \cdot (c + di) = (ac - bd) + (ad + bc)i$.

The set C, together with these three agreements, is called the set of *complex numbers*. Sometimes the a of $a + bi$ is called the real part of the complex number and bi is called the imaginary part of the complex number.

By definition of addition and multiplication, you can see that both operations are closed. You may also see that addition and multiplication are commutative operations for

$$(a + bi) + (c + di) = a + c + (b + d)i$$
$$= c + a + (d + b)i \quad \text{(real number addition is}$$
$$\text{commutative)}$$
$$= (c + di) + (a + bi)$$

and

$$(a + bi) \cdot (c + di) = (ac - bd) + (ad + bc)i$$
$$= (ca - db) + (da + cb)i$$
$$= (c + di) \cdot (a + bi)$$

Likewise, you can show that addition and multiplication are associative operations and that multiplication is distributive over addition.

The additive identity in the set of complex numbers is $0 + 0i = 0$ and the multiplicative identity is $1 + 0i = 1$. The additive inverse of the complex number $a + bi$ must be $-a - bi$, because $(a + bi) + (-a - bi) = [a + (-a)] + [b + (-b)]i = 0 + 0i = 0$.

If $a + bi$ is not the zero or additive identity complex number, then a and b are not both zero. The multiplicative inverse of $a + bi$ can then be named as

$$(a + bi)^{-1} = \frac{a}{a^2 + b^2} + \frac{-b}{a^2 + b^2}i$$

How can we show that the multiplicative inverse of $a + bi$ is the complex number

$$\frac{a}{a^2 + b^2} + \frac{-b}{a^2 + b^2}i?$$

How do we recognize a multiplicative inverse when we see one? The product of the number and its inverse must be the multiplicative identity. Here we must show that $a + bi$ times the number which we think is its inverse gives a product of $1 (= 1 + 0i)$.

$$(a + bi) \cdot \left(\frac{a}{a^2 + b^2} + \frac{-b}{a^2 + b^2} i \right)$$

$$= \left(a \cdot \frac{a}{a^2 + b^2} - b \cdot \frac{-b}{a^2 + b^2} \right) + \left(a \cdot \frac{-b}{a^2 + b^2} + b \cdot \frac{a}{a^2 + b^2} \right) i$$

$$= \left(\frac{a^2}{a^2 + b^2} + \frac{b^2}{a^2 + b^2} \right) + \left(\frac{-ab}{a^2 + b^2} + \frac{ab}{a^2 + b^2} \right) i$$

$$= \frac{a^2 + b^2}{a^2 + b^2} + \frac{0}{a^2 + b^2} i = 1 + 0i = 1$$

So every nonzero complex number has a multiplicative inverse, which is given by the preceding form.

To summarize, the set of complex numbers C, where $C = \{a + bi : a$ and b are real numbers and $i^2 = -1\}$ and where $a + bi = c + di$ if and only if $a = c$ and $b = d$, has the following properties with respect to the operations of addition and multiplication. Addition and multiplication are closed, commutative, and associative operations. Furthermore, multiplication is distributive over addition, $0 = 0 + 0i$ and $1 = 1 + 0i$ are additive and multiplicative identities, and every element has an additive inverse, while every nonzero complex number has a multiplicative inverse. Then it must be that the set of complex numbers is a field.

An interesting portrayal of the set of complex numbers can be achieved by the use of a coordinate system. Let the horizontal axis represent the real number line and let the vertical axis represent the "imaginary number line"; that is, the horizontal axis will represent the a portion of $a + bi$ and the vertical axis will represent the b portion of $a + bi$. To represent the complex number $2 + 3i$, locate a point that is 2 units to the right on the horizontal axis and 3 units up on the vertical axis (Figure 8-17). Similarly, complex numbers $2 - 5i$, $-3 + i$, and $-3 - 2i$ can be represented by means of this coordinate system (Figure 8-18).

This graphical portrayal of the set of complex numbers suggests an alternative approach to the creation of the set of complex numbers. Pretend that you had never heard of complex numbers and begin with the following sequence of ideas.

Let $C = \{(a, b) : a$ and b are real numbers$\}$. Agree that $(a, b) = (c, d)$ if and only if $a = c$ and $b = d$. Define two operations on set C

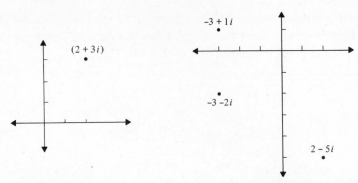

Figure 8-17   Figure 8-18

called addition and multiplication such that $(a, b) + (c, d) = (a + c, b + d)$ and $(a, b) \cdot (c, d) = (ac - bd, ad + bc)$. It is almost obvious that these two operations are closed on the set C because $a + c$, $b + d$, $ac - bd$, and $ad + bc$ are all names of real numbers. Furthermore, $(a, b) + (c, d) = (a + c, b + d) = (c + a, d + b) = (c, d) + (a, b)$, so addition is commutative. Similarly, multiplication is commutative. It can be shown that addition and multiplication are associative operations and also that multiplication is distributive over addition. Notice that $(a, b) + (0, 0) = (a + 0, b + 0) = (a, b)$, so it follows that $(0, 0)$ is an additive identity element. Also, $(a, b) \cdot (1, 0) = (a \cdot 1 - b \cdot 0, a \cdot 0 + b \cdot 1) = (a - 0, 0 + b) = (a, b)$, so it must be that $(1, 0)$ is an identity element for multiplication. Also, $(a, b) + (-a, -b) = (a + -a, b + -b) = (0, 0)$, so the additive inverse of (a, b) is $(-a, -b)$, in other words, $-(a, b) = (-a, -b)$. Finally, if $(a, b) \neq (0, 0)$, then either $a \neq 0$ or $b \neq 0$, so that $a^2 + b^2 \neq 0$. Therefore,

$$\left(\frac{a}{a^2 + b^2}, \frac{-b}{a^2 + b^2} \right) \quad \text{is an element of the set } C$$

More to the point,

$$(a, b) \cdot \left(\frac{a}{a^2 + b^2}, \frac{-b}{a^2 + b^2} \right) = (1, 0)$$

as can be shown through carrying out the operation of multiplication.

In this latter view of the set of complex numbers, note that $(0, 1) \cdot (0, 1) = (0 \cdot 0 - 1 \cdot 1, 0 \cdot 1 + 1 \cdot 0) = (0 - 1, 0 + 0) = (-1, 0)$. If we make the identification of the ordered pair (a, b) with the complex number $a + bi$ as developed earlier in this section, then this latter note shows that $i \cdot i = -1$, because i is represented by the ordered pair $(0, 1)$ and -1 is represented by the ordered pair $(-1, 0)$.

In either view of complex numbers, as numbers of the form $a + bi$, where $i^2 = -1$, or as ordered pairs (a, b), where a and b are real numbers, you can see that the set of complex numbers is a field and that it contains the set of real numbers as a subset. In the view that C is the set of numbers like $a + bi$, the set of real numbers has the form $a + 0i$. In the view of C as a set of ordered pairs, the set of real numbers has the form $(a, 0)$.

Is the set of complex numbers an ordered field? Can you determine which of the complex numbers $2 - 3i$ and $-1 + 4i$ is the greater? In one sense you might be tempted to say that $2 - 3i$ is greater than $-1 + 4i$ because 2 is greater than -1. Someone else may note that 4 is greater than -3 and on this basis contend that $-1 + 4i$ is greater than $2 - 3i$. Neither seems totally correct, does it? Another question that comes up in a discussion of order is whether or not there are positive complex numbers. Recall that greater than (or less than) was defined for integers and rationals by means of positive elements of these systems. Try to give a definition of positiveness for complex numbers and see if you find some difficulties.

Although order and positiveness are not features of the field of complex numbers, there is a concept that resembles the notion of absolute value. For the complex number $a + bi$, the *amplitude* (or magnitude or *absolute value*) of this number is $\sqrt{a^2 + b^2}$. Consider what this means in terms of the graphical portrayal of the complex number $a + bi$ (Figure 8-19). The amplitude of the complex number is the dis-

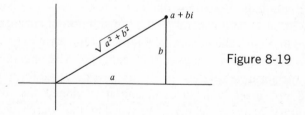

Figure 8-19

tance from the point (a, b) to the point $(0, 0)$, and you can see the role played by the Pythagorean theorem about right triangles.

> If $a + bi$ is a complex number, the *absolute value* (or amplitude or magnitude) of $a + bi$ is given by
> $$|a + bi| = \sqrt{a^2 + b^2}$$

The absolute value of $3 + 4i$ is $\sqrt{9 + 16} = \sqrt{25} = 5$. The absolute value of $3 + 0i = \sqrt{9 + 0} = \sqrt{9} = 3$. The absolute value of $-3 + 0i = \sqrt{(-3)^2 + 0} = \sqrt{9} = 3$. Notice that the absolute value of both $3 + 0i$ and $-3 + 0i$ is 3. Does it follow that the absolute value of complex numbers is consistent with the absolute value of real numbers? Real numbers have the form $a + 0i$ when expressed as complex numbers and $|a + 0i| = \sqrt{a^2 + 0} = |a|$. Therefore, the definition of absolute value for complex numbers is indeed consistent with that given for real numbers.

We have seen that complex numbers provide solutions to equations such as $x^2 = -1$. A solution for $x^2 = -4$ would be $2i$, because $(2i)^2 = 2i \cdot 2i = 4i^2 = 4(-1) = -4$. Solutions for equations like $x^2 + x + 2 = 0$ are not as easily found and fall into the area of study known as algebra. One of the most important questions ever asked was whether or not every equation has a solution. We have emphasized the fact that new systems of numbers have been invented which provide solutions for equations of various kinds. Historically, simple equations of the form $ax + b = 0$ (where x is the variable and a and b are temporary names for numbers) have been easily solved because $x = b/a$ is a solution (provided $a \neq 0$, of course). Equations like $ax^2 + bx + c = 0$ are called quadratic equations, and you may recall from high school algebra that

$$x = \frac{-b + \sqrt{b^2 - 4ac}}{2a} \quad \text{and} \quad x = \frac{-b - \sqrt{b^2 - 4ac}}{2a}$$

are solutions. Equations like $ax^3 + bx^2 + cx + d = 0$ are called cubic equations, and a general method of solution of such equations as well as equations called quartic equations of the form $ax^4 + bx^3 + cx^2 + dx + e = 0$ was discovered over 300 years ago. Attempts to solve equations of the form $ax^5 + bx^4 + cx^3 + dx^2 + ex + f = 0$ for a general solution did not meet with success, and it remained for some nineteenth-century mathematicians to prove that the search was hopeless, for they proved that no general solution to such equations could ever be found.

EXERCISES (Section 8.5)

1. Since $i^2 = -1$ and since $-4 = (-1)4$, then what is $(2i)^2$?
2. If $\sqrt{-1} = i$, find the following:
   a. $\sqrt{-4}$ b. $\sqrt{-36}$ c. $\sqrt{-81}$ d. $\sqrt{-144}$

3. Find the sum and the product of the following pairs of complex numbers. Remember: $(a + bi) + (c + di) = (a + c) + (b + d)i$ and $(a + bi)$ $(c + di) = (ac - bd) + (ad + bc)i$.
   a. $2, 1 + i$
   b. $-3 + 2i, 5$
   c. $1 + i, 1 - i$
   d. $2 + 3i, 2 + 4i$
   e. $6 + i, 5 - 31$

4. Associativity of addition was left as an exercise. Show that addition and multiplication of complex numbers are associative by using the following three complex numbers:

$$2 + 3i, \qquad 4 - i, \qquad 5 + 2i$$

   Note: By using these examples you are not proving that the operations are associative, but you are confirming that these properties hold at least for these three complex numbers. To prove that these properties hold in general, you must use $a + bi$, $c + di$, and $e + fi$.

5. Find the difference between each of the pairs of complex numbers given in Exercise 3. Subtract the second from the first and then subtract the first from the second. Do you notice any interesting feature?

6. Use the three complex numbers of Exercise 4 to confirm that multiplication of complex numbers is distributive over addition (at least for these three numbers).

7. Recall the form for the multiplicative inverse of a nonzero complex number. Find the inverse of each of the following:
   a. 2 b. $3i$ c. $1 + i$ d. $-3 + 2i$

8. Division can be accomplished by using multiplicative inverses because $x \div y = x \cdot y^{-1}$. Divide each pair of complex numbers in Exercise 3. Divide the first into the second.

9. Locate each of the following complex numbers on a coordinate system whose horizontal axis represents the real numbers and whose vertical axis represents the "imaginary" numbers. (Approximate where necessary).
   a. $2 - 3i$ e. $\sqrt{7} + 2i$
   b. $-4 - 2i$ f. $5 - \sqrt{3}i$
   c. $6 + i$ g. $\sqrt{11} + 2\sqrt{5}i$
   d. $-4 + 3i$ h. $5\sqrt{3} - 3\sqrt{7}i$

10. For the complex numbers of Exercises 9a through d find their absolute value (magnitude).

11. For the complex numbers of Exercises 9e through h find their absolute value.

12. Find a solution for each of the following simple equations:
   a. $x^2 = -36$
   b. $x^2 + 144 = 0$

c. $5x^2 + 125 = 0$

d. $2x^2 + 34 = 0$

13. When an equation has the form $ax^2 + bx + c = 0$, $a \neq 0$, we call such an equation a quadratic equation. The solutions have been noted as

$$x = \frac{-b + \sqrt{b^2 - 4ac}}{2a} \quad \text{and} \quad x = \frac{-b - \sqrt{b^2 - 4ac}}{2a}$$

Using these formulas first, identify the values of a, b, and c in the following quadratic equations. Then find the solutions for the equations.

a. $x^2 + 5x + 6 = 0$

b. $3x^2 - 7x + 4 = 0$

c. $2x^2 + 4x + 0 = 0$

d. $2x^2 + 7x + 3 = 0$

e. $3x^2 - 2x - 1 = 0$

f. $3x^2 + 4x + 2 = 0$

8.6

ARE THERE OTHER NUMBER SYSTEMS?

Now that we have developed the set of real and the set of complex numbers, the question naturally arises: "Have we exhausted all the number systems of mathematics?" The answer is an emphatic "no." Mathematicians have invented new number systems whenever there has been good reason to do so. One of the more recent inventions has been the invention of the system of matrices.

> A matrix is a rectangular array of elements appearing in rows and columns.

The elements, or *entries*, of a matrix may be complex numbers, functions, or even matrices themselves. In most cases these elements are real numbers. Here is an example of a matrix, A, in which the entries are integers:

$$A = \begin{bmatrix} 1 & -1 & 3 \\ 2 & 0 & 1 \end{bmatrix}$$

Notice that this is a rectangular array of numbers constructed from two rows and three columns. It is referred to as a 2 by 3 matrix because of the number of rows and columns.

The uses of such "numbers" (for a matrix is just a special kind of number) are many and varied. They can be used to represent inventory items in business, they can be used to represent whole systems of equations, and they are almost indispensible in computer work, for many of the computations of the computer are computations involving matrices.

There is another kind of number that was invented by an Irish mathematician named Hamilton. In effect, Hamilton created a new algebra in which a commutative law for multiplication *did not hold!* You have learned about complex numbers of the form $a + bi$, where $i^2 = -1$. Hamilton's new numbers were of the form $a + bi + cj + dk$, where a, b, c, and d are real numbers (like the a and b of the complex number $a + bi$) and where i^2, j^2, and k^2 all equal -1. Furthermore, the multiplication of the new numbers $i, j,$ and k followed the rules

$$ij = k, \quad jk = i, \quad ki = j,$$
$$ji = -k, \quad kj = -i, \quad ik = -j$$

These new numbers were called *quaternions* by Hamilton, but in later years they have also been referred to as Hamiltonians, in honor of the inventor. Notice that the set of numbers cannot be commutative under multiplication because, for example, $ij = k$ while $ji = -k$.

Many other systems of numbers have been invented and many more will no doubt be invented in the future. The reason for such inventions remains the same as it has always been: when a need exists that is not filled by any existing system of numbers, then we must invent a new system.

EXERCISES (Section 8.6)

1. The addition and multiplication of 2 by 2 matrices is defined in the following way:

$$\begin{bmatrix} a & b \\ c & d \end{bmatrix} + \begin{bmatrix} e & f \\ g & h \end{bmatrix} = \begin{bmatrix} a+e & b+f \\ c+g & d+h \end{bmatrix}$$

$$\begin{bmatrix} a & b \\ c & d \end{bmatrix} \cdot \begin{bmatrix} e & f \\ g & h \end{bmatrix} = \begin{bmatrix} ae+bg & af+bh \\ ce+dg & cf+dh \end{bmatrix}$$

Use these definitions to find the sum and product of the following pairs of matrices.

a. $\begin{bmatrix} 1 & 3 \\ -1 & 2 \end{bmatrix}, \begin{bmatrix} 0 & 1 \\ 1 & -3 \end{bmatrix}$

b. $\begin{bmatrix} 0 & -3 \\ 2 & -1 \end{bmatrix}, \begin{bmatrix} -1 & -2 \\ 0 & 0 \end{bmatrix}$

c. $\begin{bmatrix} 2 & 0 \\ 0 & 2 \end{bmatrix}, \begin{bmatrix} 1 & 2 \\ 3 & 4 \end{bmatrix}$

d. $\begin{bmatrix} 1 & 2 \\ 3 & 4 \end{bmatrix}, \begin{bmatrix} 2 & 0 \\ 0 & 2 \end{bmatrix}$

e. $\begin{bmatrix} 0 & 1 \\ 1 & -3 \end{bmatrix}, \begin{bmatrix} 1 & 3 \\ -1 & 2 \end{bmatrix}$

Consider parts a and e and decide whether or not multiplication of matrices is commutative.

2. Use the definitions of i, j, and k to determine the sum and product of the following pairs of Hamiltonians (or quaternions).

a. $2 + 3i + 2j + 2k, 4i$

b. $2 + 3i, 4 - 5j$

c. $1 + i + j + k, 1 - i - j - k$

3. The congruence systems of Chapter 6 essentially were new number systems created for a special purpose. Remember that $Z_5 = \{0, 1, 2, 3, 4\}$ had interesting addition and multiplication tables.

a. Write out the addition and multiplication tables for Z_5.

b. Write out the addition and multiplication tables for Z_4 and for Z_3.

c. In the system Z_5, what are the multiplicative inverses for the elements 1, 2, 3, and 4?

d. In the system Z_4, what are the multiplicative inverses for the elements 1, 2, and 3?

e. Is the system Z_5 an example of a *field?* Is Z_4?

4. The ratio of the circumference of a circle to its diameter is constant. That is, no matter what circle you use, the quotient of its circumference divided by its diameter is always the same number.

a. Draw a circle (use any weapon handy such as a piece of string tied to a pencil or outline a round powder box).

b. Measure the circumference of the circle. (Stretch a string around the oatmeal box or lay the string around your picture of a circle.)

c. Measure the diameter of the circle (any line segment through the center is a diameter).

d. Divide the measure of the circumference by the measure of the diameter.

e. Did your result of division approximate 3.1416?

5. The number suggested by Exercise 4 is known as pi (π). It is another irrational number, which is just about $\frac{22}{7}$ or nearly 3.1416. The digits never repeat in the decimal numeral that stands for π. The area of a circle of radius r is given by the formula $A = \pi r^2$.

a. What is the area of a circle of radius 5? (Approximate to the nearest hundredth.)

b. What is the circumference of a circle of radius 5?

c. If the circumference of a circle is 12π, what is the measure of the radius?

Karl Weierstrass

(1815–1897)

During the nineteenth century, following a hundred years of exploitation of the new tool of mathematics called the calculus, great mathematicians emerged to give mathematics a firm, logical foundation. One of the greatest of these men was Karl Weierstrass, who, with his students, reduced many of the intuitive concepts of mathematical analysis to such a high degree of rigor that their work became known as the "arithmetization of analysis." Those of us who live and work on the fringes of mathematical development rely on such men as Weierstrass to develop proofs of all the details that are so necessary in the proper development of a theory. Howard Eves, in his *An Introduction to the History of Mathematics,*[*] remarks that "Weierstrassian rigor" came to be synonymous with "extremely careful reasoning." Weierstrass was the "mathematical conscience par excellence."

The period of rigorization of all mathematical development eventually was extended to a period of generalization of mathematical thought. That is, rather than dealing with specific systems, such as the set of integers or the set of rational numbers, study was devoted to abstract systems that had certain generalized properties. The concept of a mathematical *field* is an instance of the generalization notion. The advantage of such generalization is clear, because if we can prove a result to be true in an abstract general system, then we know the result is true in any specific system that is an example of the general system. Thus, any result provable for a field is true in the field of rational numbers, the field of real numbers, the field of complex numbers, and any other system that is a field.

Weierstrass is a counterexample of the popular belief that the productive mathematician does his greatest work before he is 25 years old. He had spent his early youth studying law and finance and was a secondary school teacher until he was 40. He had been working at night on his study of mathematics and included several important papers in the annual high school report prepared for the administration. Such papers were ignored, of course, and it was not until 1854 that he published a

[*] Eves, Howard, *An Introduction to the History of Mathematics*. Boston, Mass.: Allyn and Bacon, Inc., 1969.

paper in *Crelle's Journal* which brought him some recognition. He was given an honorary doctorate, but it was not until 1864, when he was nearly 50, that he became full professor at the University of Berlin.

It is not only as an excellent mathematician that Karl Weierstrass is remembered. Perhaps his experience as a secondary teacher contributed to his lasting reputation as one of the greatest teachers of mathematics of all times. His famous students included Herman Schwarz, Sonya Kovalevski, Georg Cantor, Magnus Mittag-Leffler, and David Hilbert. We owe much to Weierstrass, including the kind of inspiration we all need when we begin to think it is too late for us to accomplish anything significant in our lives.

Chapter 9

Probability and
Statistics

9.1

INTRODUCTION

In Figure 9-1 the young boy is looking at the sign and wondering whether or not it is safe for him to attempt to cross the stream. The boy is 5 feet tall. Should he or should he not attempt to cross the stream?

Consider another situation. Suppose that you have been given

Figure 9-1

the responsibility for planning an outdoor excursion for your third-grade class. Thursday appears to be the best day for such a trip; however, you decide to call the weather bureau to get a forecast for Thursday's weather. The weather forecaster tells you that he sees no current weather conditions which might be conducive to inclement weather. He does add, however, that in the past 50 years it has rained on the particular day you have in mind 32 times. Should you proceed with your plans for a Thursday trip?

The preceding situations are given to emphasize that we live in a world of uncertainty. Decisions must be made on the basis of incomplete or uncertain information. We can improve our chances of making a correct decision in the face of uncertainty by studying *probability*, the study of chance occurrences, and *statistics*, the science of gathering, analyzing, and making inferences from data.

The concepts you will be studying in this chapter are rudimentary concepts of probability and are by no means intended to be complete. We hope to accomplish at least two objectives:

1. To "whet your appetite" for a deeper study of these subjects.
2. To provide you with material that is fun to learn and that can be used for the reinforcement of arithmetic skills.

9.2
SOME FUNDAMENTAL NOTIONS

We introduce some fundamental notions of probability by describing an activity that you might like to use with a group of intermediate-grade students. The activity involves the use of a spinner, which you can easily construct.

We begin by separating the class into three groups of relatively equal number. The groups can be designated as Teams 1, 2, and 3. If the regions of the dial are colored white, red, and gray, appropriate names might be White Team, Red Team, and Gray Team.

Each member of each team (Figure 9-2) is allowed to come forward and spin the spinner once. If the spinner lands in region 1, one point is recorded for Team 1. If the spinner lands in region 2, one point is recorded for Team 2, and so forth for Team 3. If the spinner lands

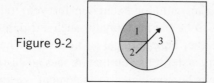

Figure 9-2

on a line, let the child spin again. Scoring can take place after each spin by having the child place a tally mark beside the appropriate team's name. A table similar to that given in Figure 9-3 can be used as a score-board. This table can be drawn on the chalkboard to facilitate scoring.

	Tally	Total
Team 1		
Team 2		
Team 3		

Figure 9-3

The game can be concluded after each member of each team has spun the spinner once and has recorded his tally on the scoreboard. More meaningful results can be obtained if each child has several chances to spin the spinner, thus increasing each team's total. We shall see why this is true in a later section. When the tallies are totaled, the team with the most points is the winner.

You, at this point, may ask the class if they feel that the game was conducted in a manner that was *fair* to each team. In other words, did each team have the same *chance* of winning? Someone will undoubt-edly say (if the complaint had not been registered earlier) that the game is unfair. Children seem to have an uncanny sense of fairness. The size of the regions on the dial influenced the results of the game. The white team had an unfair advantage in playing the game in that the size of region 3 is considerably greater than the size of either region 1 or re-gion 2. The spinner has a better *chance* of landing in region 3 than in landing in either of the two other regions. Indeed, the spinner is *more likely* to land in region 3.

The activity that we just described may be called an *experiment*. The experiment consists of spinning the spinner and observing the region within which the spinner lands. If we disregard the possibility of landing on a line, we may say that there are only three possible *outcomes* for the experiment. The possible outcomes are those of the spinner landing on region 1 or region 2 or region 3. The set of possible outcomes for a particular experiment is called the *sample space* for the experiment. For our activity the sample space is {region 1, region 2, region 3}. It became apparent as the activity progressed that each outcome was *not equally likely;* that is, each outcome did not have the same chance of occurring on a single spin of the spinner. We may make the outcomes equally likely by redrawing the boundaries for the three regions so that the three regions are congruent (of same size and shape).

You may want to redraw the boundaries so that the regions are congruent. The activity may be conducted again with somewhat different results occurring.

EXERCISES (Section 9.1 – 9.2)

1. Which of the following experiments will produce equally likely outcomes?
    a. Flip an unbiased coin and observe whether heads or tails appears.
    b. Roll an unbiased die and observe the numbers that appear on the top of the die.
    c. Place a map of the continental United States on the floor. Then toss a coin on the map and observe which state the coin lands on (assume that you won't land on a boundary).
    d. Throw a ball at two bottles, one a quart bottle, the second a pint bottle. Observe which bottle you knock down.
    e. Reach into a hat and pull out one of three coins, a penny, a quarter, or a half-dollar.
    f. Draw a card from a regular playing deck of cards and observe the suit of the cards.

2. What is the sample space for each of the experiments described in Exercise 1?

3. A coin is tossed. If heads turns up, a whole number is randomly chosen from the set {1, 3, 5}. If tails turns up, a whole number is randomly chosen from the set {2, 4, 6}. Describe a possible sample space for this experiment. Are these outcomes equally likely?

4. Two dice are rolled and the numbers appearing on top of each dice observed. Describe a sample space for this experiment.

5. The activity described in this section can be used to reinforce numeration concepts. Describe how the tallies used in this activity might be used to reinforce nondecimal numeration. Can you devise a game using these tallies and nondecimal numeration?

9.3
THE PROBABILITY OF AN EVENT

We saw in the preceding section that a sample space S, for an experiment A, is the set of all outcomes of the experiment. For example, if we toss a die and observe the number of dots on the top face of the die, our sample space S is $\{1, 2, 3, 4, 5, 6\}$. Each outcome is equally likely, since we assume that each face of the die has the same chance of appearing on top.

We now want to turn our attention to the problem of pairing each outcome of the sample space S with a number that we shall call *the probability of the outcome*. This assignment will not be haphazard. We shall assign probabilities to outcomes in the following manner:

> If an experiment can result in n different, equally likely outcomes, then we assign a probability of $1/n$ to each outcome.

In the experiment of tossing a die and observing the dots on the top face, each outcome is assigned a probability of $\frac{1}{6}$ since there are 6 outcomes. Notice that each probability is a fractional number which is greater than or equal to 0 and less than or equal to 1. Also, the sum of all the probabilities assigned to the outcomes is equal to 1. As you may have suspected, the assignment of a unique number to each outcome defines a function. This is one more instance of the pervasiveness of the function concept in mathematics.

Since we are dealing with a sample space S, which is a set, we may talk about subsets of the set S. In particular,

> *An event E* is a subset of the sample space S. That is, $E \subseteq S$.

Since the event E contains elements of S, each of which has a previously assigned probability $1/n$, we say that an event has a probability and define this probability as follows.

> The *probability of an event E*, written $P(E)$, equals the sum of the probabilities of the elements of the event.

There is a possible source of confusion in what we have said so far. In the development of this section we have assigned probabilities *both* to outcomes, which are elements of the set of outcomes, and to events, which are sets of outcomes. If we agree to consider outcomes to be *elemental events*, that is, singleton sets, we may then say that our probability function will assign probabilities, that is, numbers, to events only. Then if we consider the experiment described earlier of rolling a single die and observing the number of dots on the top face of the die, the outcome 6 will be considered the event $\{6\}$, and we shall consider the probability of the outcome 6 to be the probability of the event $\{6\}$. Hopefully, this simplifies matters somewhat as we now have a function, a *probability* function, whose domain is the set of events of an experiment and whose range is a set of real numbers between 0 and 1 inclusive.

To illustrate the definition of the probability of an event, consider again the experiment of rolling a die and observing the number of dots on the top face of the die. The probability of rolling a 2 or a 4 may be found by determining the probability of the event $E = \{2, 4\}$. In using the preceding definition, $P(E) = \frac{1}{6} + \frac{1}{6} = \frac{1}{3}$. In the same manner, the probability of rolling an odd number is $P(\{1, 3, 5\}) = \frac{1}{6} + \frac{1}{6} + \frac{1}{6} = \frac{1}{2}$.

Two events are of particular interest to us. Suppose that an experiment consists of flipping an unbiased coin and observing whether a head (H) or a tail (T) turns up. The sample space S is equal to $\{H, T\}$. Consider the event of neither a head nor a tail showing up. You may ask if this is an event, since it may at first seem unreasonable to consider such a situation. By definition, an event is a subset of a sample space S. The event of neither a head nor a tail showing up is the empty set, $\emptyset$. The empty set is a subset of every set; hence, $\emptyset \subseteq S$. The question arises as to what probability should be assigned to this event. As you may have guessed, $P(\emptyset) = 0$.

In considering the same experiment, we may ask "What is the probability of a head or a tail showing up?" In this case, $E = \{H, T\}$, which is the sample space S. Hence, $P(E) = P(S) = 1$. We say that we are certain that the event will occur. You now know how to translate the cliché, "The only things that are *certain* are death and taxes," into a probability statement.

EXERCISES (Section 9.3)

1. If an unbiased coin is flipped, what probability should be assigned to the event {heads}? To the event {tails}?

2. If an unbiased die is rolled, what probability should be assigned to each event?
   a. {5}
   b. {6}
   c. {1, 3}
   d. {a prime number is rolled}
   e. {an even number is rolled}
   f. {an odd number is rolled}

3. If 10 pieces of paper with numerals 1, 2, 3, 4, . . . , 10 are placed in a hat and you draw one while blindfolded, what is the probability of each event?
   a. {a 2 is drawn}
   b. {a 9 is drawn}
   c. {a 0 is drawn}
   d. {a 3 or a 4 is drawn}
   e. {a 7, 9, or 10 is drawn}
   f. {a whole number between 0 and 11 is drawn}

4. A card is drawn from a standard deck of 52 cards. What is the probability that this card is
   a. a six
   b. a two
   c. a diamond
   d. a club
   e. black
   f. red
   g. a black ace
   h. a red five
   i. black or red

5. An urn contains 3 blue, 4 black, and 2 white marbles. If a marble is drawn at random from the urn, what is the probability that the marble is
   a. blue
   b. black
   c. white
   d. not blue
   e. neither blue nor black
   f. green

6. Two dice are rolled and the numbers appearing on the top of each die observed, What is the probability that
   a. the sum of the numbers is 7?
   b. the sum of the numbers is 8?
   c. the sum of the numbers is 1?
   d. one, but not both, of the numbers is a 3?
   e. both of the numbers are 4?
   f. the sum of the numbers is not 3?

9.4

ODDS FOR AND AGAINST AN EVENT

As you have seen, the language and concepts of sets can be used as a unifying theme in the study of mathematics. Our development of probability is basically a set approach. Recall from Chapter 1 that the complement of a set E with respect to a set S is the set of elements in S that are not in E. We write E' to designate the complement of E.

Suppose that we have an experiment which consists of drawing a card from a well-shuffled standard deck of 52 cards. The experiment has 52 possible outcomes. The probability of the event of drawing a heart is $\frac{13}{52}$, since there are 13 hearts in the deck, each having an elemental probability of $\frac{1}{52}$. If we now consider the probability of *not* drawing a heart, that is, $P(E')$, we see that $P(E') = (52 - 13)/52$ or $\frac{39}{52}$. By definition $E \cup E' = S$; hence,

$$P(E) + P(E') = P(S) \quad \text{and} \quad P(E') = 1 - P(E)$$

We may now use the concept of $P(E')$ to interpret a word that is used quite frequently in the world of gambling, the word "odds." Precisely what does it mean when we hear that the odds of team A winning the football game are 3 to 2, written "$\frac{3}{2}$"? What we are stating is that the ratio of $P(E)$ to $P(E')$ is 3 to 2. The *probability* that team A will win is $\frac{3}{5}$; the *probability* that team A will *not* win is $\frac{2}{5}$. The odds that team A will win are $\left(\frac{3}{5}\right)/\left(\frac{2}{5}\right)$, that is, 3 to 2.

In general, we state

In an experiment where $P(E) \neq 1$ or 0, the *odds in favor* of the event E are $P(E)/P(E')$. The *odds against* the event E are $P(E')/P(E)$.

The probability of an event happening and the odds in favor of such an event should not be confused. The probability of rolling a 3 in a single roll of the die is $\frac{1}{6}$. The odds in favor of rolling a 3 are $\frac{1}{5}$. As you can see, there is a difference between the two concepts.

EXERCISES (Section 9.4)

1. If the probability of a team winning is $\frac{1}{3}$, what is the probability that the team will *not* win?

2. If the probability of rain on a given day is .65, what are the odds in favor of rain? What are the odds against rain?

3. The probability of answering a question is $\frac{1}{2}$. What are the odds in favor of answering the question? What are the odds against answering the question?

4. The odds in favor of a horse winning a race are 3 to 2. What is the probability that the horse will win the race?

5. If a card is drawn at random from a standard deck of 52 cards, what are the odds that the card is
   a. a 2?   d. a red king?
   b. a 5?   e. not a diamond?
   c. a black 6?   f. not a king?

6. Suppose that a horse has run 100 races and has won 10 of these races. What odds might you give *against* this horse winning the next race?

7. Suppose that a "fair" coin has been flipped 33 times and a head has turned up each time. What are the odds that a head will turn up on the next flip?

9.5

COMPOUND EVENTS

In Section 1.6 an experiment was described in which a brilliant blue die and a sensational red die are rolled and the numbers represented on the top face of each die are recorded as an ordered pair (a, b), where a represents the number on the blue die and b represents the number on the red die. The sample space S for this experiment is simply the cross product $B \times R$, where $B = \{$numbers appearing on the blue die$\}$ and $R = \{$numbers appearing on the red die$\}$. We now ask the question "How does one determine the probability of the union of two events of S?" It is reasonable to assume that if A and B are events of S, then $A \cup B$ will be an event of S. We call $A \cup B$ a *compound event*. In particular, can we use our knowledge of $P(A)$ and $P(B)$ to determine $P(A \cup B)$? Consider the following possibilities for events A and B of S, the sample space of the experiment described.

Suppose that A is the event that the sum of the two dice is 5 and B is the event that a 6 will occur on the blue die. In listing these events we see that $A = \{(1, 4), (2, 3), (3, 2), (4, 1)\}$ and that $B = \{(6, 1), (6, 2), (6, 3), (6, 4), (6, 5), (6, 6)\}$. What is the probability of obtaining, on a single toss of the dice, a sum of 5 *or* a blue 6? Using set notation, we ask: What is $P(A \cup B)$; that is, what is $P(\{(1, 4), (2, 3), (3, 2), (4, 1), (6, 1), (6, 2), (6, 3), (6, 4), (6, 5), (6, 6)\})$? Since each outcome of $A \cup B$ is an elemental outcome, $P(A \cup B) = \frac{4}{36} + \frac{6}{36} = \frac{10}{36}$. In this case

$$P(A \cup B) = P(A) + P(B)$$

Now consider A to be the event that the sum of the two dice is 5 and B is the event that a 2 will occur on the blue die. In listing these events we see that

$$A = \{(1, 4), (2, 3), (3, 2), (4, 1)\}$$
$$B = \{(2, 1), (2, 2), (2, 3), (2, 4), (2, 5), (2, 6)\}$$

Again, we ask what $P(A \cup B)$ is. In forming the compound event $A \cup B$ we have

$$A \cup B = \{(1, 4), (2, 3), (3, 2), (4, 1), (2, 1), (2, 2), (2, 4), (2, 5), (2, 6)\}$$

Notice that we did *not* list (2, 3) twice in our set. Hence, $P(A \cup B) = \frac{4}{36} + \frac{5}{36} = \frac{9}{36}$. In this case,

$$P(A \cup B) \neq P(A) + P(B)$$

There is a basic difference between the two examples. In the first example the events are *disjoint;* in the second example, the events are *not* disjoint.

If A and B are *disjoint* events, that is, $A \cap B = \emptyset$, the events are said to be *mutually exclusive.*

We saw in the first example that the probability of the union of two mutually exclusive events is the sum of the probabilities of each event. That is,

If A and B are mutually exclusive events of a set S, then the probability that either A or B will occur in a single trial of an experiment is

$$P(A \cup B) = P(A) + P(B)$$

What then are we to do with events that are not mutually exclusive? We saw earlier that for these events

$$P(A \cup B) \neq P(A) + P(B)$$

The difficulty arises in the fact that we cannot count common outcomes twice in forming the union of A and B. However, in finding $P(A)$ and $P(B)$ we count each common outcome twice, once in A and once in B. We can reconcile $P(A \cup B)$ and $P(A)$ and $P(B)$ by agreeing to count common outcomes once instead of twice. Using set terminology, we see that

> If A and B are any events of S, then $P(A \cup B) = P(A) + P(B) - P(A \cap B)$.

If the events A and B are mutually exclusive, then $A \cap B = \emptyset$. Hence, $P(A \cap B) = 0$, giving the case we described earlier.

Let us now consider some examples of the use of the concepts we have developed in this section.

Example 1 Let A be the experiment of drawing a single card from a standard deck of 52 cards. What is the probability that this card will be a 3 or a 5?

SOLUTION: If we let E be the event that a 3 is drawn and F be the event that a 5 is drawn, then $E = \{3$ of hearts, 3 of diamonds, 3 of clubs, 3 of spades$\}$ and $F = \{5$ of hearts, 5 of diamonds, 5 of clubs, 5 of spades$\}$. Since $E \cap F = \emptyset$, then $P(E \cup F) = P(E) + P(F)$. That is, $P(E \cup F) = \frac{4}{52} + \frac{4}{52} = \frac{8}{52}$.

Example 2 Let C be the same experiment described in Example 1. What is the probability of drawing a heart or a 10?

SOLUTION: If we let A be the event that a heart is drawn and B be the event that a 10 is drawn, then $A = \{$all hearts in the deck$\}$ and $B = \{10$ of diamonds, 10 of hearts, 10 of clubs, 10 of spades$\}$. In this instance $A \cap B \neq \emptyset$; hence, $P(A \cup B) = P(A) + P(B) - P(A \cap B)$. That is, $P(A \cup B) = \frac{12}{52} + \frac{4}{52} - \frac{1}{52} = \frac{15}{52}$.

EXERCISES (Section 9.5)

1. Suppose that a single die is rolled. Which of the following pairs of events are mutually exclusive?
   a. An odd number is shown; an even number is shown.
   b. A prime number is shown; an even number is shown.
   c. A prime number is shown; an odd number is shown.
   d. One is shown; a number less than 3 is shown.
   e. A number greater than 2 is shown; a number less than 2 is shown.
   f. A 5 is not shown; a 2 is not shown.

2. What is the probability of each of the compound events described in Exercise 1?

3. Enrollment in all the Mathematics 192 classes shows the following:

	Males	*Females*
Freshmen	27	73
Sophomores	63	142
Juniors	10	60
Seniors	5	35
Totals	105	310

   What is the probability that a student, chosen at random, will be
   a. a sophomore?
   b. a male sophomore?
   c. a female or a junior?
   d. a male junior or a male senior?
   e. not a female junior?

4. In a survey conducted at the University of Northern Colorado it was found that 76 percent of the female students preferred male athletes, 58 percent of the female students preferred male mathematics majors, and 63 percent of the female students preferred male mathematics majors who are athletes.
   a. What is the probability that a female student, chosen at random, prefers either male athletes or male mathematics majors?
   b. What is the probability that a female student, chosen at random, prefers neither?

5. There are 560 sophomores at Aims College. Of these sophomores 270 are enrolled in science, 130 are enrolled in mathematics, and 100 are enrolled in both mathematics and science.
   a. What is the probability that a sophomore, randomly chosen, will be in either mathematics or science?
   b. What is the probability that a sophomore, randomly chosen, will not be in a mathematics course?

c. What is the probability that a sophomore, randomly chosen will not be in a science course?

d. What is the probability that a sophomore, randomly chosen, will not be in a science and a mathematics course?

6. There is a law of probability which states that if A, B, and C are events of an experiment, then

$$P(A \cup B \cup C) = P(A) + P(B) + P(C) - P(A \cap B) - P(A \cap C) - \\ P(B \cap C) + P(A \cap B \cap C)$$

Use this law to solve the following problem. If a person takes a ride in the country near Greeley, Colorado, the probability that he will see a steer is .87, a horse .62, a sheep .31, a horse and steer .55, a horse and sheep .45, a steer and sheep .30, and all three .03. What is the probability that he will see at least one of the three animals?

9.6

STATISTICS

In previous sections we started our discussions with probabilities which were assigned to events that arose from an experiment. Each outcome was equally likely; hence, the task of assigning a probability to the outcome was relatively simple.

Suppose, however, that we consider the dilemma of the third-grade teacher who has the responsibility for planning the outdoor excursion which we talked about in Section 9.1. From the information at hand, she can *infer* or *estimate* that the probability of inclement weather on the day of the excursion is $\frac{32}{50}$, since in the past 50 years it has rained 32 times on the day of the picnic. The teacher must now decide whether the risk of rain is "too high" to plan a trip for that particular day.

Consider also the dilemma of the baseball manager who has a right-handed pitcher pitching to a left-handed batter in a baseball game. It is the bottom of the ninth, the manager's team is winning 2 to 1, and there are base runners at first and second base. Data collected up to this game show that this particular batter has a batting average of .450 against right-handed pitchers and a batting average of .219 against left-handed pitchers. Should the manager put in a left-handed pitcher to pitch to this batter? Again, the probability that the left-handed batter will get a hit is unknown; however, based on the previous data we *infer* that the probability of a hit against a right-handed pitcher is .450. The manager, like the third-grade teacher, must now make a decision based upon the statistics at hand.

We may use *descriptive statistics*, which is concerned with organizing and presenting data in such a manner that the data can be easily understood and analyzed, to help us arrive at a reasonable probability of an event.

Suppose that a small machine manufacturer produces 10 machines a day. During the first 15 days of production the number of defective machines is determined and recorded. On the basis of these data, what would be a reasonable estimate for the number of defective machines per day?

We begin by constructing a simple table that shows the number of days, the *number* of defective machines, the *cumulative* number of defective machines, and the *cumulative percent* of defective machines. The cumulative percent is the ratio of cumulative number defective to the cumulative number of machines times 100. This table is shown in Figure 9-4.

Day number	1	2	3	4	5	6	7	8	9	10	11	12	13	14	15
Defective no.	3	5	2	2	3	2	2	1	3	2	1	1	2	3	2
Cumulative defective no.	3	8	10	12	15	17	19	20	23	25	26	27	29	32	34
Cumulative % defective no.	.3	.4	.33	.3	.3	.28	.27	.25	.26	.25	.24	.225	.223	.229	.227

Figure 9-4

We now construct the graph of the *cumulative frequency distribution* (Figure 9-5). By connecting the 15 points we obtain a curve. We use the cumulative percent of defective machines occurring on the fifteenth day as the *probability* that a machine will be defective on a given day.

In most experiments, such as the one described, if we increase the number of trials, the cumulative frequency percentage will approach the theoretical probability. For example, as we increase the number of tosses of a coin, the ratio of the number of heads occurring to the total number of trials will approach the theoretical probability of $\frac{1}{2}$.

It is wise for you as a teacher to remember the preceding state-

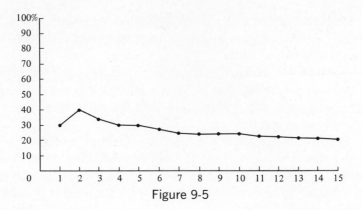

Figure 9-5

ment when conducting an experiment in your classroom to determine the empirical probability of an event. It is also wise to remember that each time the experiment is performed, it must be performed under identical, or very similar, conditions. Many teachers have found themselves in embarrassing situations either because the experiment was not conducted a sufficient number of times to allow the empirical probability to reasonably approach the theoretical probability, such as in a coin-flipping experiment, or because the experiment was not repeated under identical, or at least, similar conditions, such as in a spinner activity when the spinner became defective after considerable usage.

There are situations in everyday life when decisions are made on the basis of *sampling*. For example, Gallup polls and Nielson ratings are based upon the idea that a random sample of a population can be used to make inferences regarding the whole population under consideration. An ideal method of conducting a political survey would be to contact every person in the voting population and ask their political preference. In most cases this is unrealistic because of cost or because of inability to contact every member of the population. What we do instead is draw a *sample* from the population and make *inferences* to the population from this sample. Statisticians insist that the sample be unbiased. To avoid biased samples, we select the sample by a *random process*, such as selecting names from a hat or by any of several other random sampling methods. On the basis of this sample, for example, we might infer that 43 percent of the voting population favors candidate X.

EXERCISES (Section 9.6)

1. A store has two brands of low-phosphate detergents: Brand A and Brand B. Each month the store sells 30 cases of Brand A and 20 cases of Brand B. A customer enters the store to buy a low-phosphate detergent. What is the probability that she will purchase Brand A? Brand B?

2. You have been assigned the task of determining which cereal is most preferred by freshmen, sophomores, juniors, and seniors eating breakfast at your university. It has been determined that .15 of the people who eat breakfast at the university are seniors, .25 are juniors, .30 are sophomores, and .30 are freshmen. You have decided on a sample of 1,000 students. Which of the following sampling procedures would you follow:

   a. Randomly sample 1,000 students taken from the freshman, sophomore, junior, and senior classes.
   b. Take a random sample of 250 students from each class.
   c. Take random samples of 150 seniors, 250 juniors, 300 sophomores, and 300 freshmen.

3. A teacher decides to run an analysis of the questions asked on a test. Each time the test is administered to 20 students, and the number of students that miss each question is recorded.

   a. Complete the following table.

Test	1	2	3	4	5	6	7	8	9	10
No. missing question 7	15	13	11	12	10	6	15	7	14	15
Cumulative no.										
Cumulative %										

   b. Construct the graph of the cumulative frequency distribution.
   c. What is the probability of a student missing question 7 the next time the test is administered?

4. The data for question 8 are as illustrated.

Test	1	2	3	4	5	6	7	8	9	10
No. missing question 8	3	7	5	8	1	3	3	6	5	15
Cumulative no.										
Cumulative %										

   a. Complete the table.
   b. Construct the graph of the cumulative frequency distribution.

363

c. What is the probability of a student missing question 8 the next time the test is administered?

Blaise Pascal

(*1623–1662*)

Blaise Pascal, co-founder of the mathematical theory of probability, was born in Clermont, France, on June 19, 1623. His father was a man of culture and became the teacher of his son. It was decided that young Blaise should not study mathematics early in his education because of his frailty. The theory was used that the use of the mind might overstrain an already poor physical health. Persistence was not to go unrewarded. At the age of 12, Pascal coaxed a description of geometry from his father. The enthusiasm with which this description was received and the subsequent pursuit of geometry by the young prodigy are a legend in the history of mathematics. At the age of 14, he attended weekly scientific discussions with a group of famous mathematicians and scientists. From this group developed the French Academy of Sciences. At the age of 16, he proved a highly original theorem in descriptive geometry, which bears his name. At the age of 18, he invented the first mechanical calculating machine in history. In 1654, he became a co-founder of the mathematical theory of probability, the main concern of this chapter.

As one might expect, the theory of probability grew out of a gambling problem. In 1654, the Chevalier de Méré, an amateur mathematician and professional gambler, proposed the following problem to Pascal. On each play of a game, one of two players scores a point, and the two players have an equal chance to make the point. Three points are required to win. If the players must end the game when one player has two points and the other player one point, how should the stakes be divided? Pascal's solution to the problem was that the stakes should be divided 3 to 1 in favor of the man who was ahead. How would you have divided the stakes if each player had one point?

The renowned Pascal triangle, shown here was so named because of Pascal's use of the triangle in probability. This triangle is also well known because of the patterns one can find associated with it. For example, sum the numbers in each row to find one such pattern.

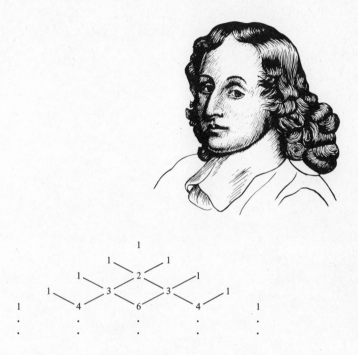

Blaise Pascal died in 1662 while suffering convulsions. He did most of his great work while in severe physical pain. Acute indigestion and chronic insomnia plagued him to the end of his life at age 39.

Chapter 10

Geometry

10.1

INTRODUCTION

In this chapter we shall consider geometric concepts that arise quite naturally in the child's experience. A tack or a sharp pencil gives rise to the geometric notion of point, which the child associates with the concept of sharpness. The edge of a book or the edge of a table, a pair of railroad tracks, and other such items give forth the idea of straightness, which is later associated with the geometric concept of line. The child's world is geometric. He observes, categorizes, and describes this world according to roundness, straightness, squareness, and many other geometric properties that he will later formalize.

It is not the objective of this chapter to construct a formal deductive system of geometry. Hopefully, many of you have studied a course in formal deductive geometry, which began with undefined terms, defined terms, and axioms. With these elements you proceeded to reason deductively to arrive at conclusions called theorems.

Our approach to geometry will be informal in that geometry will be approached intuitively, as it is with the young children whom you will teach. We shall continually remind you that geometry is part of the elementary school curriculum and we shall occasionally suggest procedures for teaching geometric concepts. It is our sincere hope that you will leave this chapter with the belief that geometry is fun and that geometry is a necessary part of the child's mathematical experience.

10.2
POINTS, LINES, PLANES, AND SPACE

The building block for geometry is the concept of point. A *point* has no dimension, but rather is thought of as a location in space. The concept of point may be visualized in the physical world as the head of a needle, the tip of a tack, or the tiny hole in a piece of paper that has been pricked with a pin. Each of these physical forms is geometrically inadequate for representing the concept "point." Many teachers have had children point out to them that the teacher had not drawn a point on the blackboard with her chalk. The mark that was made is a picture of a point. This mark necessarily has some width associated with it; hence, "the point" is given dimension. Our geometric description of point does not allow for dimension.

We usually choose to label points (really the picture of a point — we assume you know what we mean) by capital letters such as A, B, and so on. With young children fun can be had by considering each of the children in the room to be a point and calling the "points" by the children's first names.

A *line* is a set of points, which can be visualized as the edge of a ruler, a taut string, or any other object that illustrates straightness. For our purposes we shall speak only about straight lines. A fundamental assumption that we shall make is the following:

> Two points determine one and only one line.

If we allowed "curved" lines, Figure 10-1 illustrates that an infinite number of "lines" could pass through two points. This would contradict our stated assumption.

Simple manipulative devices can be built to convince the children that our assumption regarding straight lines is, at least, reasonable. Consider the spinner shown in Figure 10-2. The dial on the spinner spins freely through the point C and can take on ideally an infinite

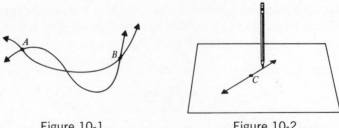

Figure 10-1   Figure 10-2

number of positions on the face of the dial. Each different position may be thought of as a representation of a different line. If we were to stop the spinner with a pencil, as is shown in the figure, a single line is determined. The pencil point may be considered as the second determining point.

There are two properties of a line that are not obvious to young children. The first is that a line is of infinite length. The second is that a line is an infinite set of points. We try to remind children of these properties by drawing continuous straight lines and by representing these lines with arrowheads on each side of the picture of the line, such as is shown in Figure 10-3.

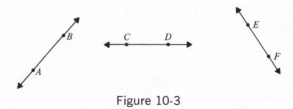

Figure 10-3

Since two points determine one and only line, we generally use the names of any two distinct points on the line to name the line. To remind the reader that we are indeed talking about a line, a two-headed arrow is written above the names of the points. For example, the names for each of the lines in Figure 10-3 are $\overleftrightarrow{AB}$, $\overleftrightarrow{CD}$, and $\overleftrightarrow{EF}$.

We may consider *a plane* to be a two-dimensional extension of a line, just as a line may be considered a one-dimensional extension of a point. In the physical world a plane can be visualized as the top of a desk, the wall or floor of a room, or as a piece of flat paper. Once again, difficulty arises in conceiving that a plane is infinite in both dimension and number of points. One of the more fascinating theorems in set theory states that there are as many points on a line as there are in a plane. This statement defies intuition.

If one point determines one and only point and two points determine one and only one line, we may ask how many points are needed to fix or determine one and only one plane? Our first inclination is to answer that three points must determine one and only one plane. This statement is only partially true in that we cannot choose any three points. Our points must not be collinear, that is, not all the points are on the same line. We make the following statement.

Any three noncollinear points determine one and only one plane.

Each of us is familiar with a three-legged stool. Regardless of the length of each leg of the stool, the stool will not wobble since the three noncollinear legs determine a unique plane. It is interesting to observe the result of adding another leg to the stool. Will the stool wobble?

We generally name planes by using lowercase letters, such as p for the plane depicted in Figure 10-4.

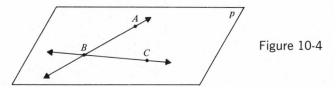

Figure 10-4

Finally, we state that since we are discussing sets of points, our universal set shall be what we call space.

Space is the set of all points.

One final word is in order. The terms "point," "line," "plane," and "space" deliberately were not defined in this section. Suppose that we state that the definition for a line is that a line is a set of points that are infinite in length. To understand the word "line," we must know what a point is. A point might be described as a part or element of the set of points that constitutes a line. We have a circularity of definition that always occurs when we attempt to define basic terms. For this reason we say that point, line, plane, and space are undefined terms from which other geometric terms can easily be defined.

EXERCISES (Section 10.2)

1. Name the geometric concept suggested by each of the following.
   a. a speck of dust
   b. the floor of your classroom
   c. outer space
   d. a firefly

2. Name a physical model for each of the following.
   a. a point
   b. a line
   c. a plane
   d. space

3. Complete the following table. Then conjecture the number of lines determined by n points if no more than two points are collinear. Draw a picture if necessary. [*Hint:* Use the idea of triangular numbers (Chapter 6).]

Number of points	Number of lines
1	0
2	1
3	?
4	?
5	?
.	.
.	.
.	.
n	?

10.3

A COORDINATE SYSTEM FOR A LINE

Each of you has had extensive experience in using the number line to learn and to teach mathematics. Each of us rather take the number line for granted in that we usually don't bother to ask such questions as:

How in heaven's name did we get something like numbers associated with a geometric entity called "line"?

Does it make any difference with which point on the line I choose to associate the number 0?

To answer these questions we make some rather fundamental assumptions, called the Ruler Assumptions. These assumptions furnish us with an infinite ruler that can be placed on any line and used to measure distances along the line.

Ruler Assumptions. The set of points on a line can be put into one-to-one correspondence with the set of real numbers in such a way that
1. Any particular point on the line can be paired with the number 0.
2. To each pair of points there exists a unique real number called the *distance* between the points.

We can see that we use the Ruler Assumptions each time we build and use a number line. We generally begin by drawing a straight line on the chalkboard. We then choose some point with which we associate the number 0. Which point we choose is irrelevant since the line is infinite. We choose some unit length and then assign the coordinate 1 to the end point of the part of line that is one unit from the 0 coordinate. The distance between these points is 1. The rest of the number line is then laid off using unit distances. Notice that the length of the unit is optional. Also, the assignment of the number 0 to point O and the number 1 to point D (see Figure 10-5) uniquely determines

Figure 10-5

a linear function (there is that concept again) from the set of all points on the line to the set of all real numbers.

What we need now is some method for determining the distance between two points such as those appearing in Figure 10-5. Our intuition tells us that the distance between A and O, written AO, is 4 (notice that distance can never be negative). The distance between A and C is 9. Is there an easy way to determine the distance between two points without counting? Our dilemma is resolved by the following definition.

On a coordinatized line the *distance* between two points having coordinates a and b is $|a - b|$.

We see that $AO = |-4 - 0| = 4$ and $AC = |-4 - 5| = 9$. If we extend our thinking somewhat, we see that our unifying concept of function is again present. Given the two points A and B we have a distance function d, which associates a real number with the points A and B. That is, $d(A, O) = 4$, $d(A, C) = 9$, and so forth.

EXERCISES (Section 10.3)

1. When we use the Ruler Assumptions, we make an assumption about the number of points on a line. What is this assumption?

2. How would you explain to a child that distance is never negative?

3. How would you explain to a child that the order in which the points A and B are chosen does not make a difference in determining the distance between A and B?

4. Which of the following are false?
   a. The distance between two points may be zero.
   b. There are as many points on a line as there are real numbers.
   c. There may be more than one distance assigned to two points on a coordinatized line.
   d. Coordinatized lines must be horizontal.
   e. A coordinatized line may have either direction of the line negative.

5. Find each distance:
   a. OH d. FI
   b. GD e. HE
   c. GC f. OF

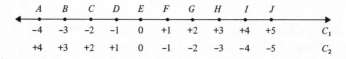

6. In the accompanying diagram two coordinate systems, C_1 and C_2, of a line l are indicated. Use this diagram to help you answer the following questions.

	A	B	C	D	E	F	G	H	I	J	
	-4	-3	-2	-1	0	$+1$	$+2$	$+3$	$+4$	$+5$	C_1
	$+4$	$+3$	$+2$	$+1$	0	-1	-2	-3	-4	-5	C_2

   a. What number is associated with point A under the coordinate system C_1?
   b. What number is associated with point G under the coordinate system C_1?
   c. What number is associated with point A under the coordinate system C_2?
   d. What number is associated with point G under the coordinate system C_2?
   e. What rule converts C_1 coordinates to C_2 coordinates?
   f. Is $d(B, F)$ under C_1 equal to $d(B, F)$ under C_2?
   g. Given two different coordinate systems C_i and C_j, do you feel it is always possible to convert C_i coordinates to C_j coordinates by means of a rule?

10.4

SUBSETS OF A LINE

We shall now use the Ruler Assumptions to help us define select subsets of a line. Remember that the Ruler Assumptions guaranteed us that there is a one-to-one correspondence between the set of real numbers and the set of points on a line. In particular, these assumptions enabled us to build a number line such as the one shown in Figure 10-6.

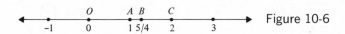

Figure 10-6

Consider now what we mean when we say algebraically that the number $\frac{5}{4}$ is *between* the number 1 and 2. What we are stating is that $1 < \frac{5}{4}$ *and* $\frac{5}{4} < 2$. We can now define what we mean geometrically when we say that point B is between points A and C.

> Suppose that A, B, and C are three points on a number line. Point B is *between* points A and C if and only if the coordinates a, b, c of A, B, C are such that $a < b < c$ or $a > b > c$.

If we now take the points O and C and all points between O and C, we have a subset of the line $\overleftrightarrow{OC}$. This particular subset of $\overleftrightarrow{OC}$ is a line segment and is formally defined as follows:

> The *line segment AB*, written $\overline{AB}$, is the set of points whose elements are the distinct points A and B and all the points between A and B on a given line through A and B.

A consequence of these definitions is that a point B is between two points A and C whenever $AB + BC = AC$. Remember that AB, BC, and AC are distances; hence, we are adding numbers, not line segments. To illustrate this assertion, we see from Figure 10-6 that point B is between points A and C, since $|1 - \frac{5}{4}| + |\frac{5}{4} - 2| = |1 - 2|$.

There is a point that is of particular interest to us, since it is not

375

only *between* A and C but it is also the same distance from A and C. We call this point the midpoint of AC and give the following definition.

> The *midpoint of the segment* $\overline{AC}$ is the point M on $\overline{AC}$ such that $AM = MC$.

Since the point M is one half the distance from A to C, we have $AM = \frac{1}{2} \cdot AC$. The coordinate m of M is $(a + c)/2$, where a and c are the coordinates of points A and C, respectively.

If we consider point C and all those points whose coordinates are less than or equal to that of C, we have another subset of a line, which is called a ray.

> Consider a line $\overleftrightarrow{CO}$. A *ray* with endpoint C and containing O is the union of segment $\overline{CO}$ and the set of all points X on $\overleftrightarrow{CO}$ such that O lies between X and C.

If we delete the endpoint C of the ray $\overrightarrow{CO}$, we have what is called a *half-line*, designated by $\overrightarrow{CO}$.

What we have said to this point may be summarized by the following table.

$\overleftrightarrow{AB}$ the line through A and B	← $\quad A \quad B \quad$ →
AB the distance from A to B	$\lvert a - b \rvert$
$\overline{AB}$ the segment with endpoints A and B	$A \longrightarrow B$
$\overrightarrow{AB}$ the ray with endpoint A	$A \quad B$ →
$\overrightarrow{AB}$ the half-line without endpoint A	$A \quad B$ →

It should be noted that whenever any line is coordinatized, then any line segment, ray, or half-line of that line is also coordinatized. Also, lines, half-lines, and rays do not have midpoints. Only segments have midpoints. Figure 10-7 shows line l intersecting the segment $\overline{CD}$ in its midpoint M. Line l is an example of a bisector of the segment CD. In general, we say

> A line, ray, or segment whose intersection with a given segment $\overline{CD}$ is the midpoint M of $\overline{CD}$ is called a *bisector of the segment* $\overline{CD}$.

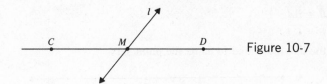

Figure 10-7

EXERCISES (Section 10.4)

1. Use the definition of betweenness to show the following.

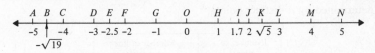

a. *D* is between *A* and *G*.   d. *G* is between *E* and *I*.

b. *B* is between *A* and *K*.   e. *H* is between *C* and *M*.

c. *F* is between *D* and *N*.   f. *O* is between *A* and *N*.

2. Use the statement that *B* is between *A* and *C* if $AB + BC = AC$ to show parts a through f of Exercise 1.

3. Find the midpoint of the following segments:

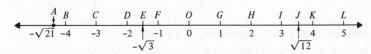

a. *AB*   c. *GD*   e. *GJ*   g. *KB*

b. *BF*   d. *EJ*   f. *OL*   h. *LE*

4. Explain why each line segment cannot have more than one midpoint.

5. Explain why each line segment has an infinite number of bisectors.

6. Explain why lines, rays, and half-lines do not have midpoints.

7. Which of the following is true?

a. A half-line has one endpoint.

b. A line segment has two endpoints.

c. A ray has no endpoints.

d. A line segment is a subset of a line.

e. A ray may be a subset of a line segment.

f. A ray may be a subset of a line.

g. The union of two rays is always a line.

h. The union of two rays may be a line.

i. The union of two half-lines may be a line.

j. The midpoint of $\overline{AB}$ is the same as the midpoint of $\overline{BA}$.

k. If $\overline{AB}$ is a subset of $\overline{CD}$ and *X* is between *A* and *B*, then *X* is between *C* and *D*.

l. $\overrightarrow{EF} = \overrightarrow{FE}$.

m. $\overleftrightarrow{AB} = \overleftrightarrow{BA}$.

n. $\overline{AB} = \overline{BA}$.

8. Use the line illustrated to name the point sets.

a. $\overline{AB} \cup \overline{AC}$ d. $\overrightarrow{CA} \cup \overrightarrow{BE}$ g. $\overleftarrow{BA} \cup \overrightarrow{AD}$

b. $\overline{AB} \cap \overline{AC}$ e. $\overrightarrow{BD} \cup \{B\}$ h. $\overline{AB} \cap \overrightarrow{BC}$

c. $\overrightarrow{AC} \cup \overline{BE}$ f. $\overrightarrow{BA} \cap \overrightarrow{DE}$ i. $\overline{AB} \cap \overrightarrow{BC}$

9. Complete the following table. Conjecture how many line segments are determined by n distinct points.

Number of points	Number of line segments
1	0
2	1
3	?
4	?
.	.
.	.
.	.
n	?

10. How many rays are determined by n points on a line?

11. Reread Sections 10.3 and 10.4. In what ways are the properties of the real numbers used to define or discuss geometric concepts.

12. In Chapter 8 you learned that the real numbers are dense. How may this property be used to show that between any two points on a line there are an infinite number of points?

10.5
ANGLES

As we look around us we find everyday examples of angles. The hands of the clock, the corner of a building, a shadow, and numerous other examples connote the idea of angle. In many instances, most people find themselves thinking about the measure of the angle and not the angle itself when asked what is meant by the concept angle.

Figure 10-8 shows two angles. Investigation of the figures shows

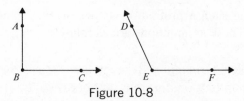

Figure 10-8

that there are two rays in each figure. Each pair of rays has a common endpoint. From these observations we state that

> *An angle* is the union of two noncollinear rays that have a common endpoint.

The common endpoint is called the *vertex* of the angle and the rays are called the *sides* of the angle. It is customary to name an angle by its vertex, such as $\angle B$, or, if confusion can arise, to name the given angles $\angle ABC$ or $\angle CBA$.

If we look rather closely at the shadow cast by a pencil, we would see that the shadow, which closely resembles an angle, separates the desk top into three distinct sets of points: the interior of the shadow, the boundary of the shadow, and the exterior of the shadow. In a similar sense, an angle separates the plane into three sets of points: the interior of the angle, the angle, and the exterior of the angle. If someone were to ask what you meant by the interior of the angle, you might simply draw a picture of an angle and point to the interior. If pressed for a little more rigor, you might say that a point K is in the interior of angle B if it lies in the intersection of the set of points above $\overrightarrow{BC}$ and the set of points below $\overrightarrow{BA}$ (see Figure 10-9). There is a more formal way of stating what we mean by the interior of an angle, but this might belabor the point.

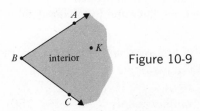

Figure 10-9

If someone were to ask you to measure an angle, most of you would use some sort of a protractor, such as that shown in Figure

379

10-10. In using such a protractor we are making some rather basic assumptions. These assumptions are as follows.

> *Protractor Assumption*: To each angle, say ABC, there corresponds a unique real number r, called the *measure* of the angle, such that $0 < r < 180$. We write $m \angle ABC = r$.

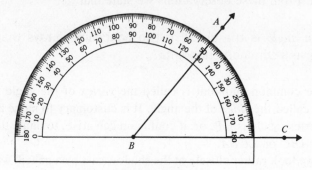

Figure 10-10

Once again we see the ubiquitous notion of function. Given a geometric entity called "angle," we are assigning to this angle a number called the measure of the angle. The Protractor Assumption assures us that we can indeed do this. In this text we shall express angle measures in terms of *degrees*, probably the most common unit of measure for angles. Other units of measure can be used, such as a *radian*, but we would necessarily have to change our Protractor Assumption so that the measure of the angle would take on somewhat different values than those given.

There are several methods of classifying angles. If we use a metric approach, that is, an approach in which the *measure* of the angle is emphasized, we have the following definition.

> Let A be an angle with measure r. Then A is
> 1. An *acute angle* if $0 < r < 90$.
> 2. A *right angle* if $r = 90$.
> 3. An *obtuse angle* if $90 < r < 180$.

Examples of these angles are shown in Figure 10-11.

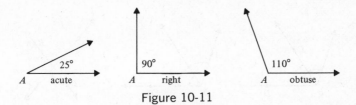

Figure 10-11

Pairs of angles may be classified by either metric or nonmetric means. The first definition given is a metric definition.

> Let A and B be two angles. Then A and B are
> 1. *Complementary* angles if m $\angle A$ + m $\angle B$ = 90.
> 2. *Supplementary* angles if m $\angle A$ + m $\angle B$ = 180.

In Figure 10-12 $\angle C$ and $\angle D$ are complementary angles, while $\angle C$ and $\angle F$ are supplementary angles.

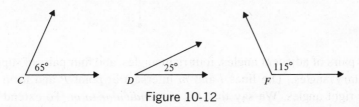

Figure 10-12

A nonmetric classification of angles in the same plane is as follows:

> Two angles are *adjacent* angles if they have
> 1. A common vertex and a common side.
> 2. No common interior points.

Also,

> Two angles are *vertical angles* if the sides of one angle are rays opposite the sides of the other.

Notice in Figure 10-13 that part a illustrates adjacent angles while part b does not. Do you see why? Part c illustrates two sets of vertical angles. Can you name them?

381

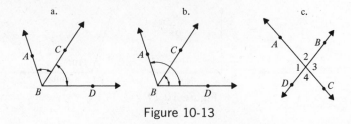

Figure 10-13

If we now look at Figure 10-14, we can tie together many of the ideas contained in this section. There are two pairs of vertical angles,

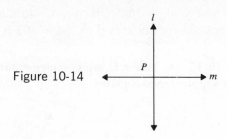

Figure 10-14

four pairs of adjacent angles, four right angles, and four pairs of supplementary angles. The lines *l* and *m* intersect at point *P* and form the four right angles. We say that *l is perpendicular to m*. To extend our definition of perpendicularity to rays and line segments, we state the following:

> Two lines, rays, or line segments are said to be *perpendicular* if the lines containing them form a right angle.

Notice that when two lines are perpendicular, four right angles are always found. There are several possibilities when a line and a ray, a line and a segment, a ray and a segment, or a segment and a segment are perpendicular. You are asked to discuss these possibilities in the exercises.

If a line, ray, or line segment is perpendicular to a line segment at the midpoint *M* of a segment, then the line, ray, or line segment is called a *perpendicular bisector of the line segment.*

Just as line segments can be bisected, so may angles. Our definition of an angle bisector will allow only for a ray to bisect an angle.

> A ray $\overrightarrow{BE}$ is the *bisector of* $\angle ABC$ if
> 1. E lies in the interior of ABC.
> 2. m $\angle ABE =$ m $\angle CBE$.

A major part of your teaching responsibility in geometry is to take the concepts presented in this section and present them to the children in a meaningful manner. Several of the exercises ask you to translate from the abstract to the physical world of geometry.

EXERCISES (Section 10.5)

1. What is wrong with the definition that an angle is
   a. The union of two noncollinear rays.
   b. The union of two collinear rays that have a common endpoint.

2. Find the measure of A if A and B are complementary angles and B is
   a. 33°   c. 18°   e. 49°
   b. 45°   d. 37°   f. 82°

3. Find the measure of C if C and D are supplementary angles and D is
   a. 37°   c. 21°   e. 136°
   b. 65°   d. 112°   f. 95°

4. Use the accompanying figure to name the measure of each of the following angles. Assume that rays AF and AG are collinear and bisect angles BAC and DAE, respectively.
   a. *DAG*   d. *BAE*
   b. *CAF*   e. *CAD*
   c. *GAE*

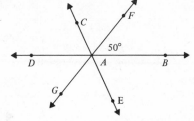

5. Use the accompanying figure to show that for each angle all complements of the angle have the same measure ($x = y$).

6. Argue that for each angle all supplements of the angle have the same measure.

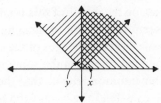

383

7. Use the accompanying figure to show that vertical angles have the same measure. (*Hint:* Use Exercise 6.)

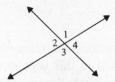

8. Two intersecting lines form two pair of vertical angles. What is the measure of each angle if all four vertical angles have the same measure? What are the lines called?

9. If two lines intersect, two pair of vertical angles are found. What is true of the adjacent angles?

10. Suppose that $\overrightarrow{AB}$ is a coordinatized line and that $\overleftrightarrow{CD}$ is the perpendicular bisector of $\overline{AB}$. What is the coordinate of *M*? (See the accompanying figure.)

11. When two lines are perpendicular, four right angles are always formed. How many right angles may be formed when each of the following are perpendicular?

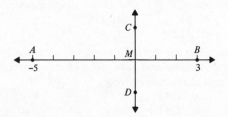

    a. a line and a ray   c. a ray and a segment
    b. a line and a segment   d. a segment and a segment

10.6

PARALLEL LINES

If we were to imagine the cover of this book as part of an infinite plane, then it would seem reasonable to imagine that the pair of horizontal edges and the pair of vertical edges of the cover would not meet, no matter how far extended. We form the same impression with a pair of telephone wires. Our intuition tells us that the wires would remain equidistant if we were to extend the wires infinitely far in space. Here we are relying upon the physical world to define the geometric concept of parallelism.

> If m and l are coplanar lines with no points in common, m and l are said to be *parallel lines*.
>
> If m and l are noncoplanar lines whose intersection is empty, m and l are called *skew lines*.

Either horizontal edge of the back cover of your book will not intersect either vertical edge of the front cover. A horizontal edge of the back cover and a vertical edge of the front cover depict skew lines.

The Greeks, who first formalized geometry into a deductive system, believed that geometry should describe the physical world. Euclid (300 B.C.), an Alexandrian scholar, who first collected in *The Elements* the existing geometric knowledge in a formal deductive manner, put forth a fundamental assumption regarding parallel lines. His postulate became known as the famous fifth postulate and was the subject of much controversy in the years following Euclid's death. Many outstanding scholars tried, in vain, to prove Euclid's assumption.

> *Euclid's Parallel Postulate.* If a straight line meets two straight lines so as to make the two interior angles on the same side of it taken together less than two right angles, these straight lines being continually produced shall at length meet on that side on which are the angles which are less than two right angles.

There are numerous substitutes for Euclid's postulate that are somewhat easier to understand. The postulate we see most frequently is attributed to John Playfair (1748–1819), a Scotsman.

> *Playfair's Postulate.* Through a given point P, not on a line l, only one line parallel to the given line l may be drawn.

We are assuming, of course, that P and l are coplanar, that is, in the same plane.

Again, this assumption seems reasonable if we look to the physical world for an interpretation of this postulate. It appears so reason-

385

able, in fact, that this postulate was looked upon as "truth" rather than as an assumption for almost 2,200 years. It was not until the Hungarian Bolyai and the Russian Lobachevski challenged Euclid's assumption that the world realized that a consistent geometry could be created by substituting a postulate regarding parallel lines which was quite different than that put forth by Euclid. The work of Bolyai and Lobachevski established mathematics as a work of the intellect, not of the senses, and rejected the notion of self-evident truths in favor of acceptable assumptions. We mention this to emphasize that geometry has a rich cultural heritage with profound ramifications on Western culture. We turn now to concepts associated with parallelism.

We begin by stating that a *transversal* is a line which intersects two given lines in two distinct points. $\overleftrightarrow{AB}$ is a transversal in Figure 10-15. Line $\overleftrightarrow{AB}$ determines a number of angles, some of which are

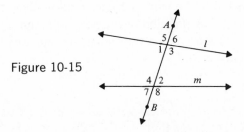

Figure 10-15

already known to us. For example, angles 2 and 7, 4 and 8, 1 and 6, and 3 and 5 are vertical angles, while angles 2 and 8, 7 and 8, 4 and 7, and 4 and 2 are adjacent angles. Of particular interest are angles 4 and 3, and angles 1 and 2. Both pair of angles occur on the interior of lines *l* and *m* and both pair of angles occur on alternate sides of the transversal *AB*. Angles 4 and 3 and angles 1 and 2 are called *alternate interior angles*. Angles 8 and 3, 2 and 6, 7 and 1, and 4 and 5 are called *corresponding angles*.

Now consider the parallel lines *l* and *m* cut by the transversal $\overleftrightarrow{AB}$, as shown in Figure 10-16. If we were to measure angles 1 and 2 and angles 3 and 4, we would find m ∡1 = m ∡2 and m ∡3 = m ∡4. We state without proof the following theorems.

If two parallel lines are cut by a transversal, then any pair of alternate interior angles has the same measure. The converse of this theorem is also true.

Further examination of Figure 10-16 would reveal that corresponding angles have equal measures. Hence,

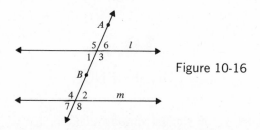

Figure 10-16

If two parallel lines are cut by a transversal, any pair of corresponding angles has the same measure. The converse of this theorem is also true.

There are other relationships between the angles found by the transversal of two parallel lines. You will be asked to conjecture some of these relationships in the exercises.

EXERCISES (Section 10.6)

1. Use the accompanying figure to name each of the following:
   a. All alternate interior angles.
   b. All corresponding angles.
   c. All supplementary angles.
   d. All vertical angles.

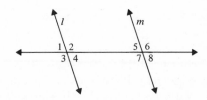

2. Use the figure from Exercise 1 to name the measure of the following if the measure of angle 2 is 50. Assume $l \parallel m$.

   a. 1   c. 6   e. 5

   b. 3   d. 8   f. 7

3. Argue that if two parallel lines are cut by a transversal, alternate exterior angles have equal measure.

4. Draw a picture to depict Euclid's postulate.

5. Use a reference book to write a short biographical sketch of each of these men.

   a. János Bolyai   d. Girolami Saccheri

   b. Johann Bolyai   e. Karl F. Gauss

   c. John Playfair   f. Georg Riemann

6. Cite examples from the physical world that may be used to demonstrate Playfair's postulate. Describe how these examples may be used in the instruction of children.

10.7

CONGRUENCE

In Chapter 1 you studied various relations that were defined on given sets of numbers. For example, you learned that two numbers *a* and *b* were equal if and only if "*a*" and "*b*" were two names for the same number. You learned that the equals relation is an equivalence relation.

There is a rather important relation that is defined on the set of all geometric figures. This relation is best illustrated by examining Figure 10-17. Notice that parts a and b "look alike." Upon closer ex-

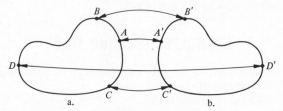

Figure 10-17

amination we would probably say that part a is a duplicate of b, and vice versa. If we trace part a and match this figure with b in such a way that a coincides with b, we shall have established a rather important relation between parts a and b.

> Two figures *a* and *b* are *congruent*, written *a* ≅ *b*, if and only if there is a one-to-one correspondence between *a* and *b* such that *a* and *b* coincide.

There are several ways of viewing congruence. Motion, or transformation, geometry involves the intuitive notion of moving one figure so that the image of this figure coincides with another figure. Under such a movement collinearity, betweeness of points, angle measure, and distance are preserved.

EXERCISES (Section 10.7)

1. If two angles are congruent, what can we say about their measures.
2. If two line segments are congruent, what can we say about their lengths?
3. Are all lines congruent?
4. Are all rays congruent?
5. Is each geometric figure congruent to itself? How do you know?
6. If figure A is congruent to figure B, is B congruent to A? How do you know?
7. Suppose that A is congruent to B and B is congruent to C. Is $A \cong C$? How do you know?
8. Suppose that you wanted to show the children that a given angle A is congruent to a given angle B *without* involving the concept of measurement. Describe, in detail, how you would organize the presentation of this concept.

10.8
CONSTRUCTIONS

Geometers make a distinction between a *drawing* and a *construction*. We continually find ourselves making pictures or drawings of geometric relationships in order to easily visualize these relationships. For example, we might make the drawing shown in Figure 10-18 to

Figure 10-18

help us visualize one possible intersection of a plane and a cone. We are allowed to use freehand methods and any instrument we please to obtain a reasonable visualization of our geometric figures. Our procedures may involve measuring either with a ruler or a protractor.

Constructions, however, are restricted to the use of the unmarked straightedge and/or a compass (the use of a pencil or pen is reasonable). These restrictions have their roots in the history of mathematics, since the Greeks (in particular, Plato, 375 B.C.) first imposed the ruler and straightedge limitation. Euclid, in his *Elements*, made a distinction between a *problem* in which something, usually a construction, was required to be performed, and a *theorem*, in which a new principle was asserted to be true. Both problems and theorems fell under the general heading of *proposition*. The first three propositions of Book 1 of the *Elements* require the proofs of geometric constructions.

We now introduce the technique for several basic constructions of geometry. We shall not give reasons as to why these constructions "work," since our primary concern is in the realm of informal geometry, which is the area of geometry with which you shall have most frequent contact when you enter the profession.

CONSTRUCTION 1. Construct a line segment congruent to a given line segment.

Given segment $\overline{AB}$, we begin by constructing a line segment $\overline{CD}$ with our straightedge. With A as center, construct an arc that passes through point B. Construct an arc, using the same compass setting and C as the center, that intersects the line segment $\overline{CD}$ in point E (if the arc does not intersect $\overline{CD}$, extend $\overline{CD}$ so that the intersection is nonempty. $\overline{CE} \cong \overline{AB}$ (Figure 10-19).

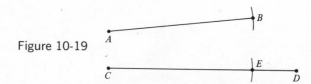

Figure 10-19

CONSTRUCTION 2. Construct an angle congruent to a given angle.

Given angle ABC, we begin by constructing a segment $\overline{PQ}$. With B as center draw an arc of a circle with radius less than $\overline{PQ}$ so that the arc intersects $\overline{BA}$ and $\overline{BC}$ at points E and F, respectively. With P as center and using the same compass setting, construct an arc that intersects PQ at R. With F as center, construct an arc passing through E. With R as center and using the same compass setting, construct another arc that intersects the arc through point R. Call this point S. The points P and S determine a line segment. Angle $SPR \cong$ angle ABC (Figure 10-20).

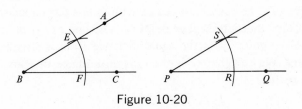

Figure 10-20

CONSTRUCTION 3. Construct the perpendicular bisector of a line segment.

Given segment $\overline{AB}$. Use the endpoints A and B as centers of circles with radii of equal measure to construct arcs that intersect at points E and F. The segment $\overline{EF}$ bisects $\overline{AB}$ (Figure 10-21).

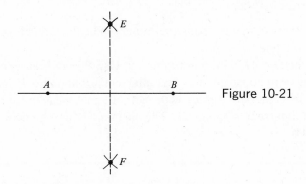

Figure 10-21

CONSTRUCTION 4. Construct the bisector of an angle.

Given angle A. Use A as the center of a circle to construct arcs that intersect the sides of A at points B and C. Use B and C as centers of circles with radii of equal measure to construct arcs that intersect at point T. Ray $\overrightarrow{AT}$ is the bisector of angle A (Figure 10-22).

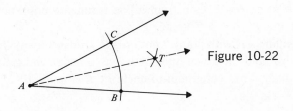

Figure 10-22

CONSTRUCTION 5. Construct a perpendicular to a given line from a point not on the line.

Given line $\overleftrightarrow{AB}$ with point P not on $\overleftrightarrow{AB}$. Use P as the center of a circle with radius r to construct arcs that intersect $\overleftrightarrow{AB}$ at points E and F. Use E and F as centers of circles with radius the same as before to construct arcs that intersect at point G. The line $\overleftrightarrow{PG}$ is perpendicular to $\overleftrightarrow{AB}$. Also, point G is the same distance from $\overleftrightarrow{AB}$ as P. That is, $PM = MG$. We say that G is the *reflection* image of P over the line $\overleftrightarrow{AB}$ (Figure 10-23).

Figure 10-23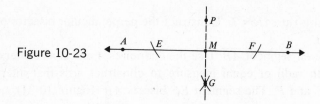

CONSTRUCTION 6. Construct a perpendicular to a given line at a point on the line.

Given line $\overleftrightarrow{AB}$ with point P on $\overleftrightarrow{AB}$. Use P as the center of a circle with radius r to construct arcs that intersect AB at points E and F. Use E and F as centers of circles with radii of equal measure to construct arcs that intersect at point G. The line $\overleftrightarrow{PG}$ is perpendicular to $\overleftrightarrow{AB}$ (Figure 10-24).

Figure 10-24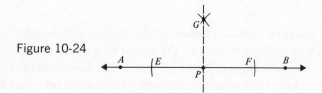

CONSTRUCTION 7. Construct a line through a point and parallel to a given line.

Given line $\overleftrightarrow{AB}$ with point P not on $\overleftrightarrow{AB}$. Construct any transversal $\overleftrightarrow{CP}$ through P and the given line. With P as a vertex and $\overrightarrow{CP}$ as a side, construct angle CPD congruent to angle PCB (Figure 10-25).

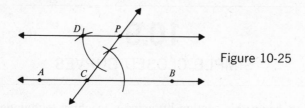

Figure 10-25

CONSTRUCTION 8. Construct the reflection image of segment $\overline{AB}$ over line r.

Given segment $\overline{AB}$ and the reflecting line r. Use construction 5 to find the reflection image C of point A. Again use construction 5 to find the reflection image D of point B. $\overline{CD}$ is the reflection image of $\overline{AB}$ (Figure 10-26).

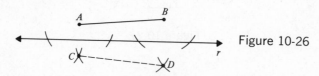

Figure 10-26

We shall use these constructions throughout the rest of this chapter.

EXERCISES (Section 10.8)

1. Explain the rationale behind construction 7.
2. In construction 8, how would you show that $\overline{AB} \cong \overline{CD}$?
3. Use construction 8 to construct a line segment congruent to a given line segment (construction 1).
4. Use construction 8 to construct an angle congruent to a given angle.
5. How can you use the idea of a reflection to bisect a given angle?
6. Construct a triangle that is congruent to a given triangle using reflections. How many image points are necessary for the construction?

10.9
SIMPLE CLOSED CURVES

Let us begin this section by using a teaching technique that we have used to introduce new concepts to young children. Our method is a "compare and contrast" method. It goes something like this:

The symbols in Figure 10-27 are garos. The symbols in Figure

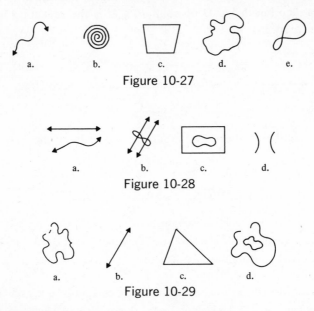

Figure 10-27

Figure 10-28

Figure 10-29

10-28 are *not* garos. Which of the symbols in Figure 10-29 are garos? As we examine our garos we see the following:

1. They may or may not be infinite in length.
2. They may or may not be closed.
3. They may or may not intersect themselves.
4. They may or may not be made up of lines or line segments.
5. They are drawn by a single continuous motion of the pencil wherein the pencil never leaves the paper.

A comparison of Figure 10-27 with 10-28 reveals that the apparent difference between those figures which are garos and those figures

394

which are not garos is that garos are drawn by a single continuous motion of the pencil with the pencil never leaving the paper and no portion of the curve other than a finite number of points is retraced. The term "garo" is, of course, used to represent a curve. We assume that all the curves used in this text will be plane curves, that is, curves lying in a plane.

As we begin refining our notion of a curve, we see that some of the curves in Figure 10-27 begin and end at the same point. Parts c, d, and e are examples of *closed curves*. Furthermore, we see a distinct difference between curves c and d, and curve e. Curve e "crosses itself," whereas curves c and d do not. This leads us to the definition:

> A *simple closed curve* is a curve that begins and ends at the same point without ever "crossing itself."

Every simple closed curve partitions a plane into three distinct sets of points: the exterior of the curve, the interior of the curve, and the curve itself. When we consider the union of the curve and its interior, we have a *region* whose boundary is the curve. In Figure 10-30 the region of a familiar curve is shown.

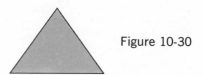

Figure 10-30

We may use the notion of boundary and region to distinguish between two rather important kinds of simple closed curves. We shall use Figure 10-31 to make this distinction. In parts a and d it is possible

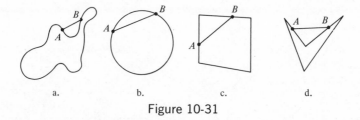

a.   b.   c.   d.

Figure 10-31

to find at least one pair of points, *A* and *B*, on the boundary of the curve such that the line segment joining *A* and *B* lies at least partially *outside* the region determined by the curve and its interior. Such regions are called *concave regions*. A mnemonic device for remembering the definition of concave regions is that some portion of the region appears to be "caved in." If all pairs of boundary points determine line segments that are subsets of the region, the region is called a *convex region*.

Before leaving this section we should observe that some simple closed curves can be the union of line segments. We make the following definition:

> A *polygon* is a simple closed curve which is the union of line segments. No two segments with a common endpoint are collinear.

Polygons may form regions that are concave or convex and may be further classified by the number of line segments, commonly called the *sides* of the polygon, which make up the union of line segments.

The following table gives the names of the polygons with the given number of sides.

Number of sides	Name	Number of sides	Name
3	Triangle	7	Septagon
4	Quadrilateral	8	Octagon
5	Pentagon	:	
6	Hexagon	:	
		n	n-gon

EXERCISES (Section 10.9)

1. Which of the following are simple, closed curves?

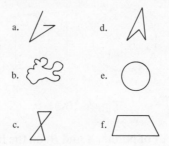

a.   d.

b.   e.

c.   f.

2. Which of the following are convex figures?

a.　　　　　　　b.　　　　　　　c.　　　　　　　d.

3. Can a triangle be concave?

4. Is the intersection of two convex simple closed curves always convex?

5. What is wrong with each of the following definitions: A polygon is
   a. the union of three or more line segments.
   b. a closed curve that is the union of line segments.
   c. a simple curve that is the union of line segments.

6. Which of the following are false?
   a. A straight line is a curve.
   b. All polygons are convex.
   c. A curve may be simple and not closed.
   d. A curve may be closed and not simple.
   e. In every closed curve the line segment that connects an interior point to an exterior point must intersect the curve.
   f. Every closed curve has exactly one interior.

7. Suppose that a child asks you where the boundary for a simple closed curve "ends" and the interior of the curve "begins." What response would you give the child?

8. Suppose that a child asks you how a straight line can be considered a curve. What response would you give to the child?

9. Cite at least five examples of simple closed curves from the physical world.

10.10
TRIANGLES

As we saw in the previous section, a triangle is a polygon with three sides. The points of intersection of the three sides are called the *vertices* of the triangle. The vertices are used to name the triangle. The triangle in Figure 10-32 is named *ABC* and is written △*ABC*.

We may consider the triangle to be the most basic polygon to discuss; hence, we shall use this figure to unify and expand many of

Figure 10-32

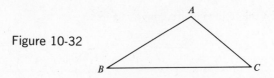

the concepts presented earlier in this chapter. For example, we saw that one of the methods for classifying angles is to use a *metric approach* in which the angles were classified as acute, right, and obtuse. Similarly, triangles may be classified as acute, right, or obtuse depending upon whether the triangle has three acute angles (acute), one right angle (right), or one obtuse angle (obtuse). Also, if the measures of the three angles of a triangle are equal, the triangle is called *equiangular*.

In a right triangle, the side opposite the right angle is called the *hypotenuse* and the remaining sides are called the *legs* of the triangle.

Triangles may also be classified according to the measures of the sides of the triangle. If no two measures of the sides of a triangle are equal, the triangle is called *scalene*. If *at least* two measures are equal, the triangle is called *isosceles*. If all three measures are equal, the triangle is called *equilateral*.

Figure 10-33 shows these classifications:

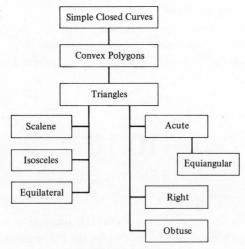

Figure 10-33

We turn now to a rather important result, which is dependent upon Euclid's fifth postulate. We may state the result as a *theorem*, that is, as a statement which can be proved deductively by making basic assumptions and reasoning from these assumptions. The theorem is as follows:

> The sum of the measures of the angles of a triangle is 180.

To show the dependence of this theorem upon the Fifth Postulate, we may look at Figure 10-34 and reason as follows:

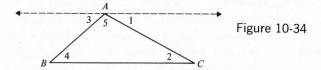

Figure 10-34

We may construct a single line through point A, parallel to the line containing $\overline{BC}$. This is Euclid's Fifth Postulate. Sides $\overline{AC}$ and $\overline{AB}$ are now subsets of the transversals $\overleftrightarrow{AC}$ and $\overleftrightarrow{AB}$. We now state that m $\angle 1 =$ m $\angle 2$ and m $\angle 3 =$ m $\angle 4$. Why? But m $\angle 3 +$ m $\angle 5 +$ m $\angle 1 =$ 180. Why? Therefore, m $\angle 4 +$ m $\angle 5 +$ m $\angle 2 = 180$. Why? Hence, the sum of the measures of the angles of a triangle is 180.

The crux of the proof is based upon the fact that there is exactly one line through A parallel to $\overline{BC}$. If we change this basic assumption, we change the results of our theorem.

There is a very important theorem associated with right triangles. This theorem was discovered by Pythagoras (584–495 B.C.) and his sect.

> *Pythagorean Theorem.* In any right triangle, the square of the measure of the length of the hypotenuse is equal to the sum of the squares of the measures of the lengths of the legs. That is, if a is the measure of the hypotenuse and b and c are the measures of the legs, then $a^2 = b^2 + c^2$.

This theorem may be used to find the measure of the third side of a right triangle if we are given the measure of the other two sides of the triangle. For example, in Figure 10-35, since $c = ?$, $a = 5$, and $b = 3$, then to find c we use the Pythagorean relationship: $a^2 = b^2 + c^2$. That is, $5^2 = 3^2 + c^2$ or $c^2 = 25 - 9$. Since length cannot be negative, $c = \sqrt{16}$ or 4.

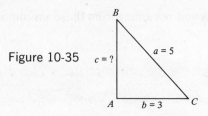

Figure 10-35 $c = ?$

In Section 10.7 the general notion of congruence was discussed. We said that two figures a and b are congruent, written $a \cong b$, if and only if there is a one-to-one correspondence between a and b such that a and b coincide. A question arises as to how is such a definition used if we are to show that two triangles are congruent? Must we show that corresponding angles and corresponding sides are respectively congruent to show congruence of the figures? If we look at Figure 10-36, this would mean that we would have to show that

$$
\begin{array}{ccccc}
A \leftrightarrow Y & & \angle A \cong \angle Y & & a \cong y \\
B \leftrightarrow Z & \text{and} & \angle B \cong \angle Z & \text{and} & b \cong z \\
C \leftrightarrow X & & \angle C \cong \angle X & & c \cong x
\end{array}
$$

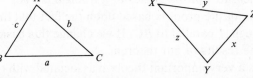

Figure 10-36

This is quite cumbersome because six facts are not needed to show the congruence of the two triangles. If we make the following assertion, we can prove several ways of showing triangles congruent. The theorems will be stated without proof.

> *SAS Postulate.* If two sides and the included angle of one triangle are congruent to the corresponding two sides and included angle of another triangle, the triangles are congruent (SAS $\cong$ SAS).

Using this postulate and other basic assumptions, we may show that two triangles are congruent if

1. Three sides of one triangle are congruent to the corresponding three sides of another triangle (SSS $\cong$ SSS).

2. Two angles and the included side of one triangle are congruent to the corresponding two angles and the included side of another triangle (ASA ≅ ASA).
3. Two angles and the nonincluded side of one triangle are congruent to the corresponding two angles and nonincluded side of another triangle (AAS ≅ AAS).

EXERCISES (Section 10.10)

1. What is the measure of each angle of an equilateral triangle?
2. In Exercise 6 of Section 10.5 you were asked to argue that supplements of the same or equal angles have the same measure. Use this assumption and the accompanying figure to show that the measure of an exterior angle ($\angle$1) is equal to the sum of the measures of the two opposite interior angles ($\angle$3 and $\angle$4).

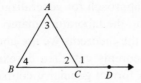

3. Construct a triangle congruent to a given triangle by using
   a. the SAS postulate and constructions 1 and 2.
   b. construction 8.
4. Develop a laboratory exercise to be used with fifth graders which is designed to show that in an isosceles triangle the measures of the angles opposite the sides of equal measure are equal.
5. Give an example of two triangles whose corresponding angles have equal measure, yet the triangles are *not* congruent.
6. Natural numbers that satisfy the relationship $c^2 = a^2 + b^2$ are called *Pythagorean triples* and are written (a, b, c). $(3, 4, 5)$ is one such triple. Determine two other Pythagorean triples.
7. Multiples of Pythagorean triples are also Pythagorean triples. For example, $(3, 4, 5)$ and $(6, 8, 10)$ are Pythagorean triples. Present an argument showing that multiples of Pythagorean triples are also Pythagorean triples.
8. What are the measures of the angles of an isosceles right triangle?
9. Argue each of the following: two right triangles are congruent if
   a. the hypotenuse and leg of one triangle are congruent respectively to the corresponding hypotenuse and leg of the second.
   b. the legs of the one triangle are congruent respectively to the corresponding legs of the second.

401

c. a side and an acute angle of the first triangle are congruent respectively to the corresponding side and acute angle of the second.

10. Develop a laboratory exercise to show that the sum of the measures of the angles of a triangle is 180.

10.11

OTHER THEOREMS RELATED TO TRIANGLES

As an elementary school teacher you will be very concerned with helping the child to make generalizations based upon empirical observations. In Chapter 2 we called these generalizations conjectures. In this section we shall state several theorems of geometry that lend themselves to a laboratory approach for generalizations. We hope that you take the time to develop the laboratory materials which will guide the children to conjecture the theorems we are about to present. The formal proof of these theorems can then be exposited when the child becomes involved in a formal geometry course at a later stage in his mathematical development.

We begin by stating a definition of a term whose name is derived from the Italian mathematician Giovanni Ceva (1647–1736) (pronounced Chāva).

> A line drawn from a vertex of a triangle that is neither parallel to, nor contains a side of, a triangle is called a *cevian* of the given triangle.

In Figure 10-37 $\overleftrightarrow{BQ}$ and $\overleftrightarrow{BT}$ are cevians. The vertex and the point of intersection with the opposite side are generally used in naming cevians.

Figure 10-37

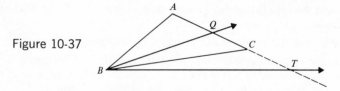

In 1678, Ceva published a treatise on geometry in which he proved the following theorem:

Ceva's Theorem. If three cevians $\overleftrightarrow{AD}$, $\overleftrightarrow{BE}$, and $\overleftrightarrow{CF}$ are concurrent (meet in a common point), then $(AF/FB) \cdot (BD/DC) \cdot (CE/EA) = 1$. Notice that AF, FC, BD, DC, CE, and EA are distances.

This theorem can be demonstrated by choosing three cevians in a triangle, one cevian from each vertex of the triangle, that are concurrent. Regardless of the choice of cevians, the product of the ratios in the theorem will be 1.

There is also a converse to Ceva's theorem, which is widely used for showing that three cevians are concurrent.

Converse to Ceva's Theorem. If three points D, E, and F are taken one on each side of the triangle ABC such that $(AF/FB) \cdot (BD/DC) \cdot (CE/EA) = 1$, then the cevians $\overleftrightarrow{AD}$, $\overleftrightarrow{BE}$, and $\overleftrightarrow{CF}$ are concurrent.

We can now use the constructions that we learned in Section 10.8 to introduce some rather special cevians.

A median is a cevian that passes through the midpoint of the side of a triangle.

By using the converse of Ceva's theorem we can show that the medians of a triangle intersect in a point called *the centroid* of the triangle. We can also show that if we construct a line segment connecting the midpoints of two sides of a triangle (the feet of two medians) then two things are true. First, this segment is parallel to the third side of the triangle and, second, the measure of the length of this segment is equal to one half the measure of the length of the third side. Both of these generalizations can be discovered by elementary school children by using laboratory methods.

An *altitude* is a cevian that is perpendicular to a side of a triangle.

Again, we can show that the altitudes of a triangle intersect at a given point called the *orthocenter* of the triangle.

The angle bisectors of a given triangle are also cevians which are concurrent at a point that is called the *incenter* of the triangle. This point is appropriately named, since the incenter is the center of a circle such as that shown in Figure 10-38. Notice that the circle touches each

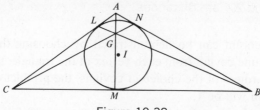

Figure 10-38

side of the triangle in exactly one point, *L*, *M*, and *N*, respectively. The cevians $\overleftrightarrow{AM}$, $\overleftrightarrow{BL}$, and $\overleftrightarrow{CN}$ are called Gergonne lines and are concurrent at a point *G* called the *Gergonne point*.

One final cevian warrants our attention. If in △*ABC* we construct the angle bisector $\overrightarrow{AE}$ and the median $\overleftrightarrow{AF}$, then the cevian $\overleftrightarrow{AG}$ that is on the opposite side of $\overleftrightarrow{AF}$ such that m ∡*GAE* = m ∡*FAE* is called a *symmedian*. As you might expect, the symmedians of a triangle are concurrent at a point called the *Lemoine point*.

A summary of our work with concurrent cevians is given in the table:

Cevians	*Point of concurrency*
Medians	Centroid
Altitudes	Orthocenter
Angle bisectors	Incenter
Gergonne lines	Gergonne point
Symmedians	Lemoine point

In conclusion, it is interesting to note that much of the geometry that was introduced in this section is post-Euclidean geometry, developed by men who lived in the seventeenth, eighteenth, and nineteenth centuries. We mention this because many people believe that synthetic geometry ended with Euclid. Quite the contrary is true. Interestingly enough, much of the recent synthetic work is appropriate in the elementary school geometry curriculum.

EXERCISES (Section 10.11)

1. Construct a triangle and then construct the following:
   a. An altitude of the triangle.
   b. A median of the triangle.

c. An angle bisector of the triangle.

d. A symmedian of the triangle.

2. Construct a triangle and then determine the following by construction:

a. The orthocenter of the triangle.

b. The centroid of the triangle.

c. The incenter.

d. The Lemoine point.

3. Develop, in detail, a laboratory exercise for intermediate-grade children to show the following:

a. Ceva's theorem.

b. The converse of Ceva's theorem.

c. In $\triangle ABC$ if $\overleftrightarrow{AD}$ and $\overleftrightarrow{BE}$ are angle bisectors such that $\overline{AD} \cong \overline{BE}$, then $\triangle ABC$ is isosceles.

d. In $\triangle ABC$ the line segment $\overline{EF}$, which connects the midpoints of two sides of a triangle, is parallel to and has measure equal to one half the measure of the third side.

e. The medians of a triangle meet at a point two thirds of the distance from each vertex.

f. In any triangle the measure of the angle between two bisectors of two angles of the triangle equals one half the measure of the third angle plus 90.

g. The sum of the distances from any point within an equilateral triangle is a constant equal to the measure of the altitude.

4. Which of the following may *not* be in the interior of a triangle?

a. Centroid   c. Incenter

b. Orthocenter   d. Lemoine point

5. Under what circumstances will the centroid, orthocenter, incenter, and Lemoine point coincide?

10.12

QUADRILATERALS

A quadrilateral is a polygon with four sides. Figure 10-39 shows examples of several quadrilaterals, some of which are concave. As we begin to classify quadrilaterals, we must ask ourselves a rather basic question: What criterion should we use for classification? In Section 10.10 we saw that triangles can be classified according to angles or

Figure 10-39

sides. We find that both of these classifications can again be used after we use a new classification, that of parallelism of sides. The simplest category of quadrilaterals meeting a criterion of parallelism is that class of quadrilaterals with exactly one pair of opposite sides parallel. We use the word "opposite" in the sense that if two sides of a quadrilateral are not adjacent then these sides are considered opposite. We then state

If $ABCD$ is a quadrilateral such that $\overline{AB} \parallel \overline{CD}$ and $\overline{BC}$ is not parallel to $\overline{AD}$, then $ABCD$ is a *trapezoid*.

It is not at all unusual to see trapezoidal classrooms with overhead projectors positioned in the front of the room for instructional purposes. The trapezoidal shape of the room provides for ideal viewing (see Figure 10-40).

Figure 10-40

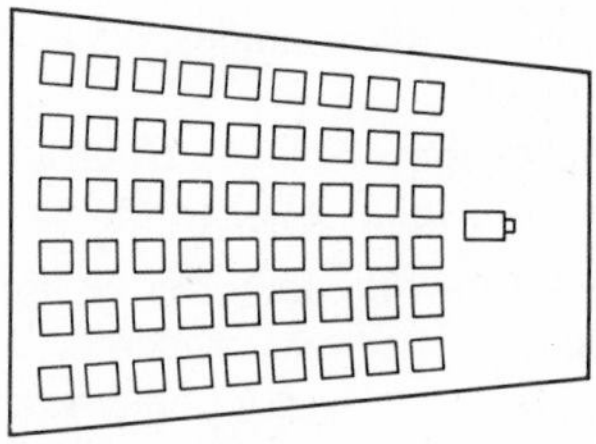

Quadrilaterals with two pairs of opposite sides parallel are called parallelograms. Formally,

If $ABCD$ is a quadrilateral such that $\overline{AB} \parallel \overline{CD}$ and $\overline{AD} \parallel \overline{BC}$, then $ABCD$ is a *parallelogram*.

We now use the congruence of angles and the congruence of sides to further classify parallelograms:

If $ABCD$ is a parallelogram such that $\overline{AB} \cong \overline{BC} \cong \overline{CD} \cong \overline{DA}$, then $ABCD$ is a *rhombus*.

If $ABCD$ is a parallelogram such that $\angle A \cong \angle B \cong \angle C \cong \angle D$, then $ABCD$ is a *rectangle*.

Finally, we use the definition of a rhombus and of a rectangle to define a square.

> If *ABCD* is a rhombus and a rectangle, then *ABCD* is a *square*.

There are two quadrilaterals that have no sides parallel, but yet have pairs of adjacent sides congruent. If the quadrilateral is convex, it is called a *kite*. If the quadrilateral is concave, it is called a *chevron* (see Figure 10-41). Some texts consider a chevron to be a special case of a kite. We have not done so in this text.

Figure 10-41

kite   chevron

You, as a teacher, can use the preceding definitions to introduce or review the concepts of all, some, and none. For example, all squares are rectangles but not all (some) rectangles are squares. Also, some rhombi (plural for rhombus) are rectangles. Notice that no trapezoids are parallelograms. These concepts are illustrated in the Venn diagrams of Figures 10-42, 10-43, and 10-44.

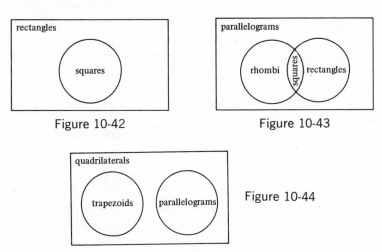

Figure 10-42   Figure 10-43

Figure 10-44

The investigation of special properties of quadrilaterals can be a source of interest and fun for both the child and teacher alike. Laboratory activities using compass and ruler can be devised to aid the child to discover the following theorems (which will have to be accepted as conjectures):

1. If the midpoints of consecutive sides of *any* quadrilateral are connected, the resulting figure is a parallelogram.
2. In a parallelogram, opposite sides and angles are congruent.

If we define a *diagonal* of a quadrilateral as a segment determined by two nonadjacent vertices, we can show that

3. The diagonals of a parallelogram bisect each other.
4. Each diagonal and the sides of a parallelogram form two congruent triangles.
5. The sum of the measures of the interior angles of a quadrilateral equals 360.

Finally, while polygons with more than four sides will not be discussed in this section, Exercise 8 gives a very nice inductive technique for determining the sum of the measures of the interior angles of an *n*-sided polygon.

Classification of Quadrilaterals

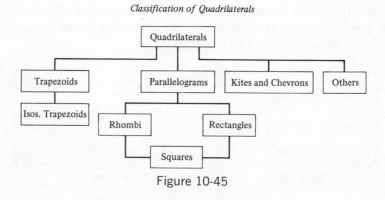

Figure 10-45

EXERCISES (Section 10.12)

1. Construct a convex quadrilateral. Bisect the sides of the quadrilateral and connect the consecutive midpoints. What figure results?
2. Repeat Exercise 1 with a concave quadrilateral. What figure results?
3. Develop in detail a laboratory exercise for intermediate-grade children to show the following:
   a. In a parallelogram, opposite sides and angles are equal.

b. In any quadrilateral the sum of the measures of the angles equals 360.

c. The diagonals of a parallelogram bisect each other.

d. Each diagonal and the sides of a parallelogram form two congruent triangles.

4. Do the diagonals of a kite bisect each other?

5. Are there any pairs of congruent angles in a kite? in a chevron?

6. Which quadrilateral is determined if two consecutive angles are supplementary?

7. Which of the following are false?
   a. All rectangles are quadrilaterals.
   b. If the diagonals of a quadrilateral are congruent, the quadrilateral is a square.
   c. Each diagonal and the sides of an isosceles trapezoid form two congruent triangles.
   d. The segment joining the midpoints of the parallel sides of an isosceles trapezoid divides the trapezoid into two congruent quadrilaterals.

8. Complete the following table. Then conjecture the sum of the measures of the interior angles of a convex polygon with n sides.

Number of sides	Number of triangles formed	Sum of measures
3	1	180
4	2	360
5	?	?
.	.	.
.	.	.
.	.	.
n	?	?

10.13
CIRCLES

If you were to ask a child "What is a circle?," he would probably respond in any one of a number of ways. Each description would probably involve the concept of roundness. One 6-year-old described a circle as "something that looks like this," with the finger tracing in the air the outline of a circle. Another child described a circle as "something that is perfectly round." A last child said that a circle "was the top of a can." Mathematically, we define a circle in the following manner.

> A *circle* is the set of all points in a plane at a fixed distance from a given point in the plane called the *center* of the circle. The segment from the center to any point on the circle is called the *radius* of the circle.

There are other terms associated with a circle. A line segment with endpoints on the circle is called a *chord* of the circle. If a chord contains the center of the circle, the chord is called a *diameter* of the circle. A *central angle* of a circle is an angle whose vertex is the center of the circle. The measure of a central angle is assigned in the usual manner (see Figure 10-46).

A rather interesting phenomenon occurs when we try to define what we mean by the arc of a circle. An arc can be modeled in the physical world by a rainbow or a part of a bicycle tire, but the mathematical definition is a bit more illusive. Consider Figure 10-47. If we

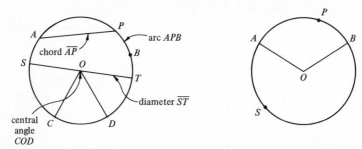

Figure 10-46   Figure 10-47

were asked to describe arc AB, written $\overarc{AB}$, we would probably want to say that arc $\overarc{AB}$ is the set of all points on a circle consisting of two points on the circle, A and B, and all the points on the circle *between* A and B. A problem arises with the use of the word "between." We have used this word when talking about linear relationships, but our relationship now is not linear but rather curvilinear. The points A and B determine two arcs, not one. One arc appears larger than the second arc; hence, we call this arc a *major arc* of the circle. The smaller arc is called a *minor arc* of the circle. To avoid confusion as to which arc we are considering, a third letter is used. We can now refer to arc $\overarc{APB}$ or to arc $\overarc{ASB}$.

Arcs may be assigned measures in the same manner that we assigned measures to angles and to line segments. If we separate a circle into 360 congruent arcs, each arc may be considered as one unit of *arc degree*. The number of arc degrees in an arc determines the arc degree measure for that arc. We can show that each arc of measure 1 in arc degrees determines a central angle of measure 1 in degrees. The opposite is true also. We say that a central angle of measure 1, in degrees, *intercepts* an arc of measure 1 in arc degrees. An arc of measure 90 in arc degrees determines a central angle that is a right angle. There is a distinction between degrees and arc degrees. The first is used to measure angles; the second is used to measure arcs. Notice also that the degree measure of an angle may not exceed 180, while the arc measure of an arc may not exceed 360. Technically, we need an arc assignment postulate, such as the Ruler and Protractor postulates given earlier, to assign arc degrees to arcs.

As with triangles and quadrilaterals, there are numerous theorems that can be conjectured as a result of well-planned laboratory work. A few of these results are as follows:

1. *All radii and all diameters of the same circle are congruent.*
2. *In the same circle, chords that are equally distant from the center are congruent.*
3. *A diameter that is perpendicular to a chord bisects the chord and its two arcs.*

Before leaving this section, we shall try to unify several of the concepts presented in this chapter. It was mentioned in Section 10.10 that the angle bisectors of a triangle intersect in a point called the in-center (*I*). This point is the center of a circle that can be *inscribed* in the given triangle (see Figure 10-48). If we construct the perpendicular bisector of the sides $\overline{AB}$, $\overline{BC}$, and $\overline{CA}$, we determine a single point *O* called the *circumcenter* of the triangle *ABC*. This point is the center of a circle that can be *circumscribed* about the triangle *ABC* (see Figure 10-49).

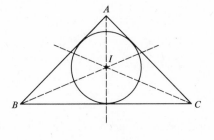

Figure 10-48

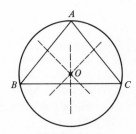

Figure 10-49

The following results relate the centroid (C), the orthocenter (H), and the circumcenter O of a given triangle:

4. C, H, and O are collinear such that $2 \cdot OH = CH$.
5. The midpoints of the sides of a triangle, the feet of the altitudes, and the midpoints of the lines joining the orthocenter (H) to the vertices of the triangle are on a circle with center T, where T is the midpoint of the segment $\overline{OH}$. This circle is called the *nine-point circle*.

Result 4 was first proved by L. Euler, a Swiss mathematician (1707–1783). Result 5 was due to K. W. Feuerbach, a German mathematician (1800–1834). Again, both of these results were produced considerably after the Euclidean era.

EXERCISES (Section 10.13)

1. Which of the following are true?
   a. The center of a circle is not part of the circle.
   b. The radius of a circle is not part of the circle.
   c. Two circles are congruent if and only if their radii have equal measures.
   d. A diameter is the longest chord in a circle.
   e. A central angle of 90 degrees intercepts an arc of 180 arc degrees.
   f. A minor arc has greater arc degree measure than a major arc.
   g. A circle is a polygon.
2. What are the possible number of points of intersection for two circles?
3. Name at least three physical models in your classroom that are circular.
4. In the accompanying figure, minor arcs $\overarc{AB}$, $\overarc{BC}$, and $\overarc{CD}$ are congruent, and $\overline{AD}$ is a diameter of the circle.

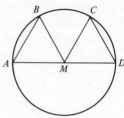

   a. Are chords $\overline{AB}$ and $\overline{CD}$ congruent? Why?
   b. Is $\overline{AM} \cong \overline{MD}$? Why?
   c. Is $\triangle ABM \cong \triangle MCD$? Why?
   d. What is m $\angle AMB$?
5. Describe in detail a laboratory exercise designed to show each of the following:

   a. All radii and all diameters of the same circle are congruent.

   b. In the same circle, chords that are equally distant from the center are congruent.

   c. A diameter that is perpendicular to a chord bisects the chord and its two arcs.

   d. The nine-point circle theorem.

6. Is the measure of the radius of the incircle always greater than the measure of the radius of the circumcircle?

7. Must the incenter of a triangle always lie inside the triangle?

8. Must the circumcenter of a triangle always lie inside the triangle?

9. Will the circumcenter and the orthocenter of a triangle ever coincide?

10. Construct a circle and choose any four points on the circle. Connect these points to form a quadrilateral. This quadrilateral is called a *cyclic quadrilateral.* Use a protractor to measure the opposite angles of the quadrilateral. Record the results and repeat the procedure with a different cyclic quadrilateral. What conjecture can you make?

11. An angle is said to be *inscribed* in an arc if its sides contain the endpoints of the arc and its vertex is a point of the arc other than an endpoint. The measure of an inscribed angle is equal to one half the measure of its *intercepted* arc. Use this theorem to argue your conjecture from Exercise 10.

10.14
THREE-DIMENSIONAL FIGURES

Thus far we have discussed planar or two-dimensional figures such as angles, triangles, quadrilaterals, and circles. Our everyday experiences, however, take place in a three-dimensional world. The classroom in which you sit is three-dimensional. The books that you read and the pencil you hold are models for three-dimensional figures. We therefore turn our attention to three space, which we may consider to be an extension of two space. You remember that we agreed that space is an undefined term and is used to signify the set of all points.

As we extend our thinking to a third dimension, we soon realize that we must broaden our geometric perspectives. In a plane, two lines are either parallel or meet in a point; in space, we must allow for another possibility. Consider the intersection of the front wall of your classroom with the floor of the room. This intersection can be interpreted as representing a straight line. Now consider the intersection of the ceiling of your room with a side wall. Again we have the representation of a straight line. If we assume that your room is rectangular (see Figure 10-50), the two lines just described will never meet; yet

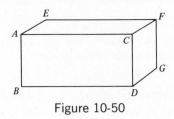

Figure 10-50

they are not parallel, since they do not lie in the same plane. Such lines are called skew lines.

> *Skew lines* are lines that are not in the same plane and do not meet.

$\overleftrightarrow{DG}$ and $\overleftrightarrow{AC}$ are skew lines. Can you name other pairs of skew lines in the figure?

A line such as $\overrightarrow{PA}$ is perpendicular to a plane at a given point A if the line is perpendicular to at least two lines passing through A. To see why two lines are necessary for perpendicularity, consider Figure 10-51, which shows a pencil touching a piece of paper. It is possible

Figure 10-51

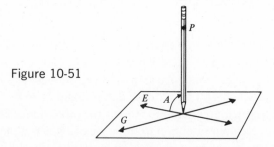

for angle EAP to be a right angle while angle GAP is not. Fence builders use the double-line principle to assure themselves that a fence pole is indeed perpendicular to the ground.

Two planes are perpendicular if one of the planes contains a line perpendicular to the other plane. Again, carpenters and bricklayers use the criteria for a plane perpendicular to a plane in the construction of the walls of a building.

414

Simple closed surfaces are the three-dimensional extension of simple closed curves. They partition space into three sets of points: the *interior*, the *exterior*, and the *surface*. We shall consider two subsets of simple closed surfaces: polyhedrons and nonpolyhedrons.

> *A polyhedron* is a simple closed surface whose *faces* are polygonal regions (polygon and the interior). The vertices of the polygon are called the *vertices* of the polyhedron and the sides of the polygon are the *edges*.

The simplest polyhedron that is part of the everyday experience of a child is a *rectangular prism*, commonly called a box. If we use an ordinary shoe box as our model of a rectangular prism, we see that the *bases* of the box are congruent polygons and their interiors. All prisms, rectangular and otherwise, have this characteristic. In the case of a box, the bases are congruent rectangular regions. The remaining faces of the box are polygonal regions. If the prism is a *right prism*, as is a box, the sides of the prism are perpendicular to the bases. Figure 10-52 illustrates various prisms, both right prisms and other prisms.

Figure 10-52

Each of us has either seen pictures of, or heard of, a polyhedron that, unlike the prism, has only one base. The models of these polyhedra are preserved in Egypt and are, of course, *pyramids*. The bases of the pyramids in Egypt are rectangular; however, any polygon may be used as the base of a pyramid. Pictures of several pyramids are shown in Figure 10-53.

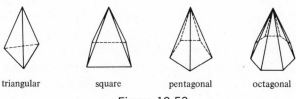

triangular   square   pentagonal   octagonal

Figure 10-53

415

A rather interesting occurrence of polyhedrons in nature is in the form of mineral crystals. Rock salt crystals are models of right prisms; quartz crystals may take on several forms, one of which is pyramidal. Crystal forms are interesting and can be put to good use in a combined mathematics–science class. Crystals give the elementary school teacher an excellent opportunity to point out the omnipresence of geometry in nature.

The nonpolyhedron class of simple closed surfaces includes cylinders, cones, and spheres. Again, we begin with the most familiar of these figures, the sphere. Most small children have had the opportunity to see, feel, and play with a ball of some kind. Later, in geography, the children will learn that the planet upon which they live is "almost" spherical. Mathematically, a sphere is merely an extension of a circle to three space.

> A *sphere* is the set of all points in space at a fixed distance from a point *C* called the *center* of the sphere.

A very nice way to illustrate that a sphere is an extension of a circle is to tie a small piece of thread or string to a circular bracelet. Ask the children to describe the figure that results as they spin the bracelet, as is shown in Figure 10-54. If you are clever, the children can actually see a ball as the bracelet spins about the string.

Figure 10-54

Ice cream cones, conical paper cups, and the funnel created by water flushing down a sink are each suggestive of the geometric surface that we call *a cone*. We may generate a cone by first constructing a circle on our paper. We now let the end of the eraser on our pencil represent a point *P* not in the plane of the circle and the pencil point represent a point *A* on the circle. By holding the eraser (point *P*) fixed, we now move the pencil so that it passes through each point on the circle. The result is a cone, as shown in Figure 10-55.

The point *P* is the vertex of the cone and the circular region is

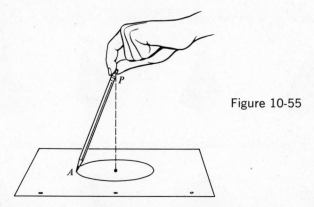

Figure 10-55

the base of the cone. If the line from *P* to the center of the circle is perpendicular to the plane of the circle, we have a *right cone*.

The last nonpolyhedron that we shall study in this section is again
quite familiar to the young child. Few children in this day and age have
failed to see and feel a soup can or some other cylindrical can that has
been used for food storage. Telephone poles, water pipes, and most
water glasses are each suggestive of a cylinder. Each of these models
has two congruent circular regions as bases, and the line segment connecting the centers of the circles is perpendicular to the plane of each
circle. In this case we say we have a *right circular cylinder*. Actually,
the bases of both a cone and a cylinder do not have to be circular. Any
simple closed curve will do for the base; however, the models for cones
and cylinders that we generally see in everyday life are circular. Figure 10-56 shows several examples of cones and cylinders.

Figure 10-56

EXERCISES (Section 10.14)

1. Name each of the polyhedra. Be as specific as possible.

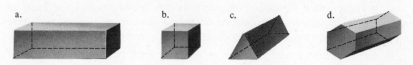

a. b. c. d.

2. Name each of the polyhedra. Be as specific as possible.

a.
b.
c.
d.

3. Name each of the simple closed surfaces. Be as specific as possible.

a.
b.
c.
d.

4. In the accompanying figure, name the following:
   a. Three sets of parallel planes.
   b. Three sets of parallel segments.
   c. Three sets of skew segments.
   d. Four segments that are perpendicular to the same or different planes.

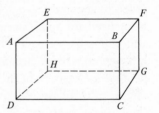

5. Give at least two models occurring in our world for a
   a. Right triangular prism.
   b. Right rectangular prism.
   c. Right triangular pyramid.
   d. Right rectangular pyramid.
   e. Sphere.
   f. Right circular cylinder.
   g. Right circular cone.

6. On page 416 a procedure was described for generating a sphere from a bracelet and a piece of string. Describe a procedure for generating a
   a. Right circular cone from a right triangle.
   b. Right circular cylinder from two circles and a line.
   c. Right circular cone from a right pyramid.
   d. Right circular cylinder from a right prism.

7. A *regular polyhedron* is a polyhedron in which all faces are congruent polygons with all sides congruent. It can be shown that the faces of regular polyhedra can only be triangles, squares, or pentagons. There are only five regular polyhedra. Can you describe these polyhedra?

8. Go to your school library and examine at least two elementary mathe-

matics series (K–6) to determine the extent of study of three-dimensional surfaces.

9. Describe the possible figures that can result from the intersection of a plane and a
   a. Sphere.
   b. Right triangular prism.
   c. Right rectangular prism.
   d. Right triangular pyramid.
   e. Right rectangular pyramid.
   f. Right circular cone.
   g. Right circular cylinder.

10.15
MEASUREMENT

The world in which we live and work is a world of measurement. Housewives buy commodities using a cost-per-unit or a cost-per-weight basis. Carpets are purchased on a cost-per-square-yard factor and fertilizer is guaranteed to cover so many square feet. Our highways abound with signs telling the distance between various cities. In each of these instances the concept of measurement is used.

Let us consider the concept of measurement and see how a child is generally introduced to this rather important concept. For instructional purposes we shall work, whenever possible, in the metric system, which may or may not be familiar to you. A brief table of equivalences of linear units in the metric system follows ($\approx$ is read "is equivalent to").

$$10 \text{ millimeters (mm)} \approx 1 \text{ centimeter}$$
$$10 \text{ centimeters (cm)} \approx 1 \text{ decimeter}$$
$$10 \text{ decimeters (dm)} \approx 1 \text{ meter}$$
$$1,000 \text{ meters (m)} \approx 1 \text{ kilometer (km)}$$

An examination of this table indicates an obvious advantage of the metric system over the English system. The metric system uses a decimal base for conversion from one linear unit to another unit. The English system has no such common base for conversion purposes.

In order that you might appreciate what a child goes through when he first is introduced to measurement, suppose that we ask you to measure the width of your desk. This, at first, may seem trivial to you. Some of you will place a ruler (if you are fortunate enough to have one) on your desk top and simply state that your desk top is *n* (depending, of course, upon what this number is) centimeters wide. You may experience some difficulty in that your desk top is not *exactly n* centimeters wide, so you say that the desk top is "approximately" *n* centimeters wide. But suppose we tell you that you cannot use a rule to measure the desk top. Now the difficulty of the activity increases somewhat. You are probably asking "What in heaven's name are we supposed to use if a ruler is disallowed?" You now must think about the *act of measuring*. The first realization is that you have been asked to make a *linear* measurement. You must now choose some convenient unit to perform this measurement. You can't use a ruler, which eliminates centimeters or inches; hence, you look for some other convenient unit of measurement; but this unit must be linear. The length of a pencil may come to mind as one such unit. Someone may decide to use the width of this book as the choice of unit. Regardless of what linear unit is chosen, you must now decide *how many* units wide your desk top is. This is generally decided by matching the linear unit with the width of the desk top, as is shown in Figure 10-57. You generally real-

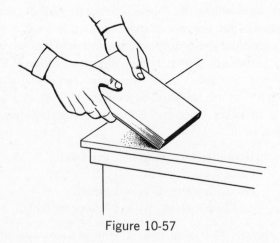

Figure 10-57

ize the first time you perform this measurement that you have *approximated* the width of the desk top. The width of the desk top is approximately *n* (whatever this number is) pencils or bookwidths wide.

On the basis of the preceding activities, the following points become evident:

1. To measure is a process whereby we compare the object being measured with a given unit.
2. On the basis of the comparison given, we assign a number, called the *measure*, to the object being measured.
3. We name the *measurement* of an object as a number of units.
4. To measure an object, we generally make a physical comparison between the object being measured and some unit of measurement. It is assumed that the unit being used is a linear unit if the measurement requires length, a unit of weight if the measurement requires weight, and so on.
5. All physical measurements are approximate, since the device used in the measurement is necessarily inaccurate and our observation techniques are limited.
6. Standard units are generally used in measurement for ease in communication. If, for example, you used a pencil to measure your desk top, your measurement of n pencils will undoubtedly differ from the measurement of other colleagues who also used a pencil to measure the desk top. The unit, which in this case is the length of a pencil, can (and usually does) vary from student to student. For this reason, we use the unit centimeter or inch to convey measurements. The length of a centimeter or an inch has been standardized.

We list separately one more point for emphasis. The process of assigning a number to an object is another example of a function. We may call this function a measurement function if you like. The domain of the function is the set of objects being measured, the functional rule is "match an object with a number of units," and the range is the measures of the measurements.

EXERCISES (Section 10.15)

1. Name at least three standard *English* units that are used in the measurement of each of the following:
   a. time
   b. weight
   c. liquid capacity
   d. dry capacity
   e. area
   f. volume

2. Name at least three standard metric units that are used in the measurement of the following:
   a. weight   c. area
   b. length   d. volume

3. Name the equivalent relationships between each of the units in Exercises 1 and 2. For example, 2 pints ≈ 1 quart.

4. Solve the following (≈ means "is equivalent to"):
   a. 1 km ≈ n m   d. 7 cm ≈ n m   g. 2.1 m ≈ n mm
   b. 3 km ≈ n m   e. 50 dm ≈ n cm   h. .3 km ≈ n cm
   c. 45 km ≈ n m   f. 6.3 cm ≈ n mm   i. .6 m ≈ n dm

5. Describe a laboratory exercise which could be used to show that
   a. 300 cm ≈ 3 m   c. 2,000 grams ≈ 2 kilograms
   b. 8 pints ≈ 1 gallon   d. 2 hours ≈ 120 minutes

10.16

LENGTH, AREA, AND VOLUME OF GEOMETRIC FIGURES

We conclude this chapter with a brief consideration of the measurement of simple closed curves and simple closed surfaces. To fully describe the development of each of the relationships given in this section would exceed the page limitations of this text. Hence, our exposition will be brief.

The simplest notion with which we begin is that of *perimeter*. The perimeter of a simple closed curve is the length of the path from the initial point of a curve to the terminal point of the curve. The perimeter of a polygon is the measure of the union of the line segments that form the polygon. In order that we may speak more freely, we shall focus our attention throughout the remainder of this section on equations that relate the measures of the various point sets which compose the figures we shall discuss. We shall not emphasize the unit of measurement. For example, the perimeter of a square will be expressed as

$$P = 4 \cdot s$$

where P is the measure of the perimeter and s is the measure of the length of a side of the square.

The perimeter of a circle is called the *circumference* of the circle and is given by the equation

$$C = 2 \cdot \pi \cdot r$$

where C is the measure of the circumference, π is a constant defined to be the ratio of the circumference of the circle to the diameter of the same circle, and r is the radius of the circle.

Figure 10-58

The measurement of the length of a curve such as that shown in Figure 10-58 will not be discussed in this text. The methods for finding such lengths fall in the realm of the calculus.

As we learned earlier, a simple closed curve partitions the plane into the curve, the interior of the curve, and the exterior of the curve. The perimeter of a curve is concerned with the length of the curve itself. We now consider the measure of the interior of a simple closed curve. We shall call this measure the *area* of the curve, and again we shall only concern ourselves with the areas of polygons and circles.

The area of a rectangle is simply the product of the height of the rectangle times the base of the rectangle. That is,

$$A = b \times h$$

This relationship may be easily proved in a formal geometry course, but we may use graph paper to show that this relationship is indeed true (see Figure 10-59). If we have a rectangle with a base of

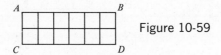

Figure 10-59

6 units and height of 2 units, we see that there are 12 square units in the rectangular region. In our measurement process we match the rectangular region with 12 square units. Again, we have our measurement function in operation.

The question arises as to what is the area of any parallelogram. Once again we may use a laboratory activity to show that the relation-

423

ship $A = b \times h$ holds for any parallelogram. If we begin with graph paper and construct a parallelogram such as that shown in Figure 10-60, we may cut the polygonal region so that a rectangular region is found (Figure 10-61).

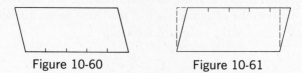

Figure 10-60   Figure 10-61

Since the diagonal of a parallelogram separates the parallelogram into two congruent triangles, each triangle must be one half the area of the parallelogram. That is,

$$A = \tfrac{1}{2} \bullet b \bullet h$$

where A is the area of a triangle and h is an altitude to a side b of the triangle.

We state without proof that the area of a circle (circular region) is given by the formula

$$A = \pi \bullet r^2$$

There are several approaches to this formula. One approach involves constructing a circle on a piece of paper. If we now partition the circular region into 16 congruent regions and arrange these regions as shown in Figure 10-62, we obtain a figure that approximates a rec-

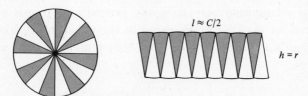

Figure 10-62

tangular region. The base of the rectangle is approximately half the circumference of the circle, and the height of the rectangle is the radius of the circle. By approximating the area of this rectangular region we can approximate the area of the circle. That is,

$$\begin{aligned} A &\approx (\tfrac{1}{2} \times C) \times r \\ &\approx \tfrac{1}{2} \times (2 \times \pi \times r) \times r \\ &\approx \pi \bullet r^2 \end{aligned}$$

A simple closed surface separates space into three disjoint sets of points: the surface, the interior of the surface, and the exterior of the surface. If we form the union of the surface with its interior, we have a *solid*.

We begin our investigation of the volume of cylinders and prisms by making a few intuitive observations. We may think of a cylinder or a prism such as those pictured in Figure 10-63 as the union of an infinite number of slices. Each slice is a circular or polygonal region whose area we can compute. We may think of the volume of a cylinder or prism as the sum of the measures of the area of each of these thin slices. Since the sum of the measures of thickness of these slices is the height (h) of the solid, the volume of a cylinder or a prism may be given by

$$V = B \cdot h$$

where V is the volume of any cylinder or any prism, B is the area of the base, and h is the height of the solid.

Figure 10-63

If T is a cone or a pyramid with base area B and height h, then the volume of T is given by

$$T = \tfrac{1}{3}B \cdot h$$

This relationship is not immediately obvious. Young children may be led to this conjecture by using plastic models of cones and cylinders of equal base and height. The plastic cones are filled with water and emptied into the corresponding plastic cylinders, which have been premarked to show thirds of volume. Each time the experiment is performed the ratio of the volume of cone to cylinder is one to three. We are assuming that the height and base of the figures being compared are equal. We conclude this section by considering the problem of determining the surface area of a right circular cylinder. The area will include the area of both bases and the area of the surface included between the bases. We know the area of a circular base to be $\pi \cdot r^2$. If we "unroll" the surface between the bases (see Figure 10-64), we

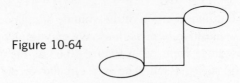

Figure 10-64

have a rectangle whose area is $b \times h$. But the base is the circumference of a circle and the height is the height of the cylinder. Hence,

$$SA = 2 \cdot \pi \cdot r^2 + 2 \cdot \pi \cdot r \cdot h$$

The following table summarizes the equations that have been discussed in this section.

Figure	Measure	Equation
Square	Perimeter	$P = 4 \cdot s$
Circle	Circumference	$C = 2 \cdot \pi \cdot r$
Parallelogram	Area	$A = b \cdot h$
Triangle	Area	$A = \frac{1}{2} \cdot b \cdot h$
Circle	Area	$A = \pi \cdot r^2$
Cylinders	Volume	$V = B \cdot h$
Prisms	Volume	$V = B \cdot h$
Cone	Volume	$V = \frac{1}{3} \cdot B \cdot h$
Pyramid	Volume	$V = \frac{1}{3} \cdot B \cdot h$
Cylinder	Surface area	$SA = 2 \cdot \pi \cdot r^2 + 2 \cdot \pi \cdot r \cdot h$

EXERCISES (Section 10.16)

1. Find the circumference and area for each circle of given radius r.
   a. $r = 2$ c. $r = 3$ e. $r = \sqrt{3}$
   b. $r = \frac{1}{2}$ d. $r = \frac{3}{8}$ f. $r = 2\sqrt{5}$

2. Approximate the area of the simple closed curve in the accompanying figure.

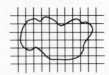

3. Describe a procedure for getting a better approximation to the preceding figure.

4. Suppose that a young child asks you how he can find the area of any quadrilateral. What would be your response?

5. Suppose that a child asks you if the boundary of a region "adds" any area to the region. What would be your response?

6. The area of triangle APB is equal to the area of triangle ATB. Why?

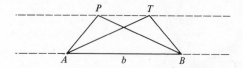

7. What generalization can be made using the figure given in Exercise 6?

8. Find the volume of each cylinder or prism of given base B and height h.
   a. $B = 6$
   $\quad h = 3$
   b. $B = 2$
   $\quad h = 5$
   c. $B = 5 \cdot \pi$
   $\quad h = 3$
   d. $B = \sqrt{8} \cdot \pi$
   $\quad h = \sqrt{2}$

9. Find the volume of each pyramid or cone of given base B and height h.
   a. $B = 3\pi$
   $\quad h = 5$
   b. $B = \frac{1}{3}\pi$
   $\quad h = 6$
   c. $B = 6$
   $\quad h = \sqrt{6}$
   d. $B = 2\sqrt{5}$
   $\quad h = \sqrt{7}$

10. Find the surface area of each right circular cylinder of given radius r and height h.
    a. $r = 3$
    $\quad h = 4$
    b. $r = 2$
    $\quad h = 6$
    c. $r = \sqrt{5}$
    $\quad h = \frac{5}{2}$
    d. $r = 2\sqrt{3}$
    $\quad h = 6.2$

Nikolai Lobachevski

(1793–1856)

Nikolai Ivanovich Lobachevski was born in Makarief, Russia, in 1793, the second son of a minor government official. He entered the University of Kazan at the age of 14, received his master's degree at the age of 18, and was appointed a professor at the unusually early age of 23. He taught mathematics, physics, and astronomy at the University of Kazan.

Because of the efficient manner in which he carried out his academic responsibilities, Lobachevski was made university librarian, museum curator, and rector. He believed strongly that in order to get a job done to your liking you had either do it yourself or know enough about its execution to make intelligent and constructive criticism. Consequently,

he was quite eager to forsake coat and collar to engage in the ever-present manual labor tasks of his university. On one occasion, he was mistaken for a janitor or workman by a distinguished foreign visitor and was asked to serve as a guide through the university libraries and museum collections. The visitor, being very impressed by the charm and intelligence of the obliging workman, tendered a handsome tip upon parting. Lobachevski was insulted by the foreigner's impudence. The foreigner left bewildered, only to encounter the Rector that evening at a social function. Apologies were offered and accepted on both sides.

One wonders how any substantive work in mathematics could have been accomplished in addition to the many responsibilities and distractions associated with administrative work. Yet in 1826 Lobachevski publicly outlined his work on non-Euclidean geometry before The Physical-Mathematical Society of Kazan. In his work he publicly challenged Euclid's fifth postulate, which had been looked upon for 2,000 years as an absolute truth. This challenge was extremely important in the future development of mathematics, since the postulates of mathematics must be regarded as acceptable assumptions rather than self-evident truths. Lobachevski produced a geometry as logically consistent as that of Euclid by assuming the postulate that there is not *one* parallel through a fixed point to a given straight line but *two*. Neither of these parallel lines meets the line to which they are parallel.

By 1842 the notoriety of Lobachevski had spread to Western Europe and, in particular, to Karl F. Gauss. He was elected a foreign correspondent of the Royal Society of Göttingen (Gauss's university) for his creation of non-Euclidean geometry. Unfortunately, the mathematical work that won him much esteem among his mathematical peers may have been instrumental in his downfall. In 1846 Lobachevski was relieved of his university responsibilities by the Russian government. No explanation for this action was given. One can only conjecture that the work which challenged an "accepted truth" of 2,000 years may have appeared heretical and threatening to the government.

The death of his son contributed to failing health and, on February 24, 1856, Nikolai Lobachevski, the Copernicus of geometry, died, a blind and broken man at the age of 62.

Answers to
Selected Exercises

CHAPTER 1

Section 1.2

1. a. Statement. b. Statement. c. Open sentence, variable "she."
   d. Open sentence, variable "*x*." e. Statement. f. Statement.
   g. Meaningless sentence. h. Open sentence, variable "she."

3. a. 71. b. 8. c. 27. d. 3.
   e. Several pairs may be used. For example the pair 11, 10 because
      $12 > 11 > 10$ is a true statement.

5. $-(P \wedge Q)$ is equivalent to $-P \vee -Q$.   (DeMorgan's
   $-(P \vee Q)$ is equivalent to $-P \wedge -Q$.   Laws)
   $P \vee Q$ is equivalent to $Q \vee P$.   (Commutative
   $P \wedge Q$ is equivalent to $Q \wedge P$.   Laws)
   $(P \vee Q) \vee R$ is equivalent to $P \vee (Q \vee R)$.   (Associative
   $(P \wedge Q) \wedge R$ is equivalent to $P \wedge (Q \wedge R)$.   Laws)
   $P \wedge (Q \vee R)$ is equivalent to $(P \wedge Q) \vee (P \wedge R)$. (Distributive
   $P \vee (Q \wedge R)$ is equivalent to $(P \vee Q) \wedge (P \vee R)$. Laws)

7. Just remember that two contradictory statements have opposite truth
   values and that two contrary statements cannot both be true at the same
   time but they may both be false at the same time.

9. a. Roses are not red or violets are not blue.
   b. Juanita is not seven nor is she eight years old.
   c. You shouldn't get out or else you shouldn't stay out.
   d. $-(-P) \vee -(-Q)$ which is equivalent to $P \vee Q$.
   e. $-P \wedge -(-Q)$ which is equivalent to $-P \wedge Q$.
   f. $-(-P) \wedge -Q$ which is equivalent to $P \wedge -Q$.

Section 1.3

1. a. $A = \{4\}$.　　b. $B = \{1, 3, 5, 7, 9\}$.　　c. $C = \{\frac{3}{5}, -\frac{3}{5}\}$.
   d. $D = \{8\frac{1}{2}\}$.　　e. $E = \{-6, -5, -4, -3, -2, -1\}$.
   f. $F = \{4, -4\}$.　　g. $G = \emptyset$.

3. a. True.　　b. False.　　c. True.　　d. False.　　e. False.
   f. False.　　g. True.　　h. True.　　i. True.　　j. True.
   k. False.

5. a. The open sentence $2x^2 + x - 1 = 0$.
   b. The empty set.
   c. $A = \{-1\}$ because $2(-1)^2 + (-1) - 1 = 0$.
   d. $A = \{-1, \frac{1}{2}\}$.

7. "17" is the symbol that represents the number seventeen. "{17}" is the symbol that represents a set containing the single element 17.

9. a. There are no elements in the empty set.
   b. There is one element in set A.
   c. There is one element in set B.
   d. There are two elements in set C.
   e. There are 101 elements in set D. (Don't forget zero.)
   f. Set E contains more elements than we can count. Say that it has an infinite number of elements.
   g. Again, there are more elements than we can count.

Section 1.4

1. a. False. Change "reflexive" to "symmetric."
   b. False. Change "symmetric" to "transitive."
   c. True.　　d. True.
   e. False. By the definition of division, $13 = 52 \div 4$.

3. a. $\{a\}, \{b\}, \{c\}, \{a, b\}, \{a, c\}, \{b, c\}, \emptyset$.
   b. $\{a, b, c\}$.
   c. 8.

5. The only subset of $\emptyset$ is $\emptyset$.

7.

Number of elements	Number of one-to-one correspondences	
1	$1 (= 1$	$= 1!^*)$
2	$2 (= 2 \bullet 1$	$= 2!)$
3	$6 (= 3 \bullet 2 \bullet 1$	$= 3!)$
4	$24 (= 4 \bullet 3 \bullet 2 \bullet 1$	$= 4!)$
5	$120 (= 5 \bullet 4 \bullet 3 \bullet 2 \bullet 1 = 5!)$	
$\vdots$		
n	$n(n-1)(n-2) \cdots 3 \bullet 2 \bullet 1 = n!$	

* The symbol "!" is used as a shorthand notation to name the product of the factors from the number given down to 1. Thus $4! = 4 \bullet 3 \bullet 2 \bullet 1$.

9. The set of even whole numbers is equivalent to the set O of odd whole numbers as shown by the following matching.

$$
\begin{array}{ccccccc}
E & 0 & 2 & 4 & 6 & 8 \ldots 2n & \ldots \\
  & | & | & | & | & | & \\
O & 1 & 3 & 5 & 7 & 9 \ldots 2n+1 \ldots
\end{array}
$$

11. Use the multiples of four (call this set F).

$$
\begin{array}{cccccc}
E & 0 & 2 & 4 & 6 & 8 \ldots 2n \ldots \\
  & | & | & | & | & | \\
F & 0 & 4 & 8 & 12 & 16 \ldots 4n \ldots
\end{array}
$$

Section 1.5

1. a. 2, 7.   b. 1, 2, 4, 5, 6, 7.   c. 3, 4.   d. 3, 4, 5, 8.
   e. 3, 4, 5, 8.   f. 2, 3.   g. 5, 6.   h. 4, 6, 7.   i. 6.
   j. 2, 6, 7.   k. 1, 3, 4, 6.   l. 4, 5.   m. 5, 8.
   n. 2, 6, 7.   o. 7.   p. 4, 6, 7.   q. 1, 2, 3, 4, 6, 7.
   r. Ø.   s. 1, 2, 3, 4, 6, 7.   t. Ø.   u. 1, 3, 4, 6.

3. Relations: equality, subset, not a subset, proper subset, improper subset, equivalent sets, disjoint sets.
   Operations: intersection, union, complement (difference or separation),
   product (see the next section).

Section 1.6

1. {(H, H), (H, T), (T, H), (T, T)}.

3. He must remove three sox because he must have either 3 black sox, 2
   brown and 1 black, 2 black and 1 brown, or 3 brown sox. In any case he
   has a pair of matching sox.

5. If $A = B$, then $A \times B = B \times A$. If either A or B is the empty set, then both
   $A \times B$ and $B \times A$ are empty sets and hence equal.

7. Let $A = \{1, 2\}$, $B = \{a, b\}$, and $C = \{m, n, p\}$. Then
   $A \times (B \cup C) = \{(1, a), (1, b), (1, m), (1, n), (1, p), (2, a), (2, b)$
   $(2, m), (2, n), (2, p)\}$ and
   $(A \times B) \cup (A \times C) = \{1, a), (1, b), (1, m), (1, n), (1, p), (2, a)$
   $(2, b), (2, m), (2, n), (2, p)\}.$

9. No, it doesn't make sense. If we let $A = \{a\}$, $B = \{b\}$ and $C = \{c\}$ then
   $A \cup (B \times C) = \{a, (b, c)\}$ while $(A \times B) \cup (A \times C) = \{(a, c), (b, c)\}.$

11. $A = \{9, 6, 0, 3\}$ and $B = \{7, 4, 1, 2\}$. What has been called $A \times B$ must be
    in error because there should be 16 pairs included and formed from the
    sets A and B just named. The set given must be a subset of the real
    $A \times B$.

Section 1.7

1. (1, 6), (2, 5), (3, 4), (4, 3), (5, 2), (6, 1), (6, 5), (5, 6).

3. (1, 1), (2, 2), (3, 3), (4, 4), (5, 5), (6, 6).

5. ". . . is in the same class as . . . ." ". . . is as tall as . . .," ". . . is older
   than . . . ."

7. $\{(1, a), (2, a)\}, \{(1, a)\}, \{(1, b)\}$. 3 . 2.

9. 2 n $2n$ 2^{2n-1}
   m n mn 2^{mn-1}.

11.
Relation	Domain	Range
R	$\{1, 4\}$	$\{1, 2, 4\}$
S	$\{1, 2, 3, 4\}$	$\{1, 2, 3, 4\}$
T	$\{1, 2\}$	$\{2, 3\}$
U	$\{1, 3, 4\}$	$\{1, 3, 4\}$

13. a. $\{(a, b), (b, a), (b, e), (e, b), (a, a), (d, d)\}$.
    b. $\{(a, a), (b, b), (c, c), (d, d), (e, e), (a, e), (b, c)\}$.
    c. $\{(a, b), (b, c), (a, c), (b, d), (a, d)\}$.
    d. $\{(a, a), (b, b), (c, c), (d, d), (e, e), (a, b), (b, a)\}$.
    e. $\{(a, b), (b, a)\}$.
    f. $\{(a, a), (b, b), (c, c), (d, d), (e, e), (a, e)\}$.
    g. $\{(a, b), (b, a), (a, a), (b, b)\}$.

Section 1.8

1. $\{(7, s)\}, \{(7, s), (7, t), (8, p)\}, \{(7, p), (8, t), (9, s), (9, t)\}$.

3. a. $\{(1, a), (2, a), (3, b), (4, d)\}$.   b. $\{(a, 1), (a, 2), (b, 3), (d, 4)\}$.
   c. No. Yes.
   d. $\{(1, d), (2, c), (3, b), (4, a)\}$ is the function. Its inverse is a function from B to A: $\{(d, 1), (c, 2), (b, 3), (a, 4)\}$.

5. $((2, 3), 5), ((16, 12), 28)$, and $((8, 0), 8)$ belong to the sum function. $((6, 1), 8), ((7, 5), 35)$ and $(3, 5)$ do not belong to the sum function.

CHAPTER 2

Section 2.2

1. a. 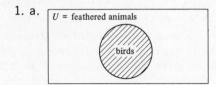   b.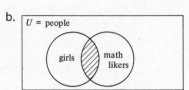

   c. 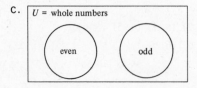   d.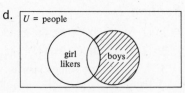

e.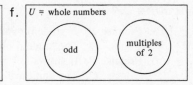

U = whole numbers

even

f. U = whole numbers

odd

multiples of 2

3. a. Valid.   b. Invalid.   c. Invalid.   d. Valid.   e. Invalid.
   f. Invalid.   g. Invalid.   h. Valid.   i. Valid.   j. Invalid.

5. Answers will vary. Some likely responses are:
   "School is not fun."
   "Mathematics is hard."
   "I never get the right answer."

Section 2.3

1. a. 11, 13, 15, 17, 19.   b. 36, 49, 64, 81, 100.   c. 1, 16, 1, 32, 1.
   d. 13, 21, 34, 55, 89.   e. 8, 7, 10, 9, 12.   f. 6, 7, 8, 9, 10.
   g. d, 8, 9, 10, e.   h. N, T, E, T, T.

3. a. $1 \cdot 2 \cdot 3 = 6 \cdot 1$ Each product of three consecutive inte-
      $2 \cdot 3 \cdot 4 = 6 \cdot 4$ gers can be expressed as a multiple of
      $3 \cdot 4 \cdot 5 = 6 \cdot 10$ six.
      $4 \cdot 5 \cdot 6 = 6 \cdot 20$.

   b. $4 = 2 + 2$ Every even number greater than two can
      $6 = 3 + 3$ be expressed as the sum of two primes.
      $8 = 5 + 3$
      $10 = 7 + 3$.

   c. $1 \cdot 2 \cdot 3 \cdot 4 = 5^2 - 1$ Each product of four consecutive inte-
      $2 \cdot 3 \cdot 4 \cdot 5 = 11^2 - 1$ gers can be expressed as the difference
      $3 \cdot 4 \cdot 5 \cdot 6 = 19^2 - 1$ of a perfect square and 1.
      $4 \cdot 5 \cdot 6 \cdot 7 = 29^2 - 1$.

   d. $1 = 1^2$ The sum of the first n consecutive odd
      $1 + 3 = 2^2$ numbers is n^2.
      $1 + 3 + 5 = 3^2$
      $1 + 3 + 5 + 7 = 4^2$.

   e. $3^2 - 1 = 8 \cdot 1$ Each odd number squared, minus 1, is a
      $5^2 - 1 = 8 \cdot 3$ multiple of eight.
      $7^2 - 1 = 8 \cdot 6$
      $9^2 - 1 = 8 \cdot 10$.

   f. $2 = 1 + 1$ Every prime number of the form $4n + 1$
      $5 = 1 + 4$ can be expressed as the sum of 2 squares.
      $13 = 4 + 9$
      $17 = 1 + 16$.

5. 10, 14, 15, 51.

7. Incorrect conjecture: $a \times b = a + b$.
   Correct conjecture: The above statements are true when $a = x/(x - 1)$
   and $b = x$, $x \neq 1$.

Section 2.4

1. a. Premise *P:* A student evades the draft.
      Concl. *Q:* The student breaks the law.
   b. Premise *P:* It snows.
      Concl. *Q:* The game will be cancelled.
   c. Premise *P:* x is a whole number greater than one.
      Concl. *Q:* x^2 is greater than x.
   d. Premise *P:* 1m $=$ 100 cm.
      Concl. *Q:* 10m $=$ 1000 cm.
   e. Premise *P:* 1 km $=$ 1000 m.
      Concl. *Q:* 5 km $=$ 5000 m.
   f. Premise *P:* a, b, c are whole numbers greater than zero.
      Premise *Q:* b is greater than c.
      Concl. *R:* $a \cdot b$ is greater than $a \cdot c$.

3. a. If a student studies hard, then the student will pass the course.
   b. If I know him, then I love him.
   c. If you are meek, then you shall inherit the land.
   d. If Heiny doesn't foul out, then the game shall be won.
   e. If you err, then you are human.
   f. If we are to have world preservation, then we must have peace.
   g. If you are happy, then you will smile.
   h. If you have faith, then you will be saved.
   i. If you are a responsible citizen, then you will vote.
   j. If you fly to Hawaii, then you must go to California.
   k. If a number is even, then it is divisible by two.
   l. If $b = 2$, then $4 \times b = 8$.
   m. If two lines intersect, then they are not parallel.
   n. If I date someone else, then she cries.

5. Answers will vary.

7. Transitive property.

Section 2.5

1. a. Some men are not married.
   b. No girls are pretty.
   c. All days are beautiful.
   d. Some work is fun.
   e. No equation has a solution.
   f. All numbers are prime.
   g. You go to school and you must not study.
   h. You measure water in liters and you are not using the metric system.
   i. All numbers are perfect squares.
   j. If a number is a negative number, then it is less than zero.
   k. There is at least one x such that x is less than zero.
   l. For no x, $x^2 = 9$.
   m. For no x, $x/x \neq 1$.
   n. x is not greater than zero and $x/x = 1$.

3.

P	Q	P → Q	−Q	P ∧ −Q	−(P ∧ −Q)
T	T	T	F	F	T
T	F	F	T	T	F
F	T	T	F	F	T
F	F	T	T	F	T

5. $(P \rightarrow Q)$ is equivalent to $-P \lor Q$.

Section 2.6

1. a.

P	Q	R	−P	−Q	−R	P ∨ Q	(P ∨ Q) → R	(−P ∧ −Q)	−R → (−P ∧ −Q)
T	T	T	F	F	F	T	T	F	T
T	T	F	F	F	T	T	F	F	F
T	F	F	F	T	T	T	F	F	F
F	F	F	T	T	T	F	T	T	T
T	F	T	F	T	F	T	T	F	T
F	T	T	T	F	F	T	T	F	T
F	F	T	T	T	F	F	T	T	T
F	T	F	T	F	T	T	F	F	F

b.

P	Q	R	−P	−Q	−R	Q ∧ R	P → (Q ∧ R)	(−Q ∨ −R)	(−Q ∨ −R) → −P
T	T	T	F	F	F	T	T	F	T
T	T	F	F	F	T	F	F	T	F
T	F	F	F	T	T	F	F	T	F
F	F	F	T	T	T	F	T	T	F
T	F	T	F	T	F	F	F	T	F
F	T	T	T	F	F	T	T	F	T
F	F	T	T	T	F	F	T	T	T
F	T	F	T	F	T	F	T	T	T

c.

P	Q	R	−P	−Q	−R	Q ∨ R	P → (Q ∨ R)	(−Q ∧ −R)	(−Q ∧ −R) → −P
T	T	T	F	F	F	T	T	F	T
T	T	F	F	F	T	T	T	F	T
T	F	F	F	T	T	F	F	T	F
F	F	F	T	T	T	F	T	T	T
T	F	T	F	T	F	T	T	F	T
F	T	T	T	F	F	T	T	F	T
F	F	T	T	T	F	T	T	F	T
F	T	F	T	F	T	T	T	F	T

d.

P	Q	R	−P	−Q	−R	P ∧ Q	(P ∧ Q) → R	(−P ∨ −Q)	−R → (−P ∨ −Q)
T	T	T	F	F	F	T	T	F	T
T	T	F	F	F	T	T	F	F	F
T	F	F	F	T	T	F	T	T	T
F	F	F	T	T	T	F	T	T	T
T	F	T	F	T	F	F	T	T	T
F	T	T	T	F	F	F	T	T	T
F	F	T	T	T	F	F	T	T	T
F	T	F	T	F	T	F	T	T	T

3. a. Invalid.   b. Valid – contrapositive.   c. Invalid.
   d. Valid – law of detachment.   e. Valid – law of detachment.
   f. Invalid.   g. Valid – contrapositive.   h. Invalid.   i. Invalid.
   j. Invalid.   k. Valid – contrapositive.
   l. Valid – law of detachment.   m. Valid – law of detachment.
   n. Invalid.   o. Invalid.   p. Invalid.

Section 2.7

1. a.

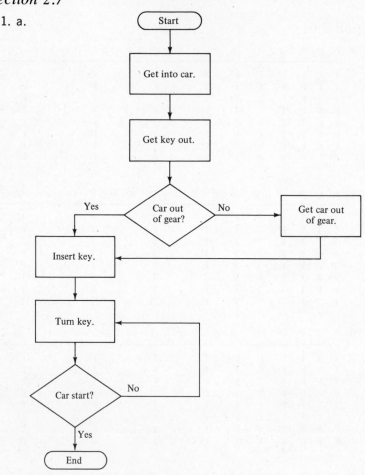

b.

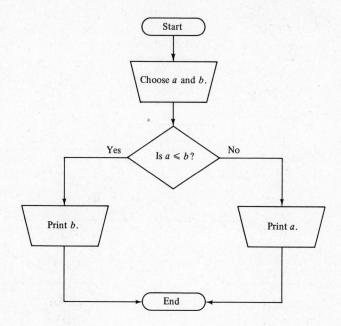

c.

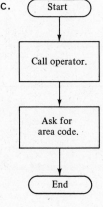

d.

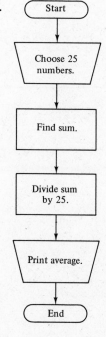

e.

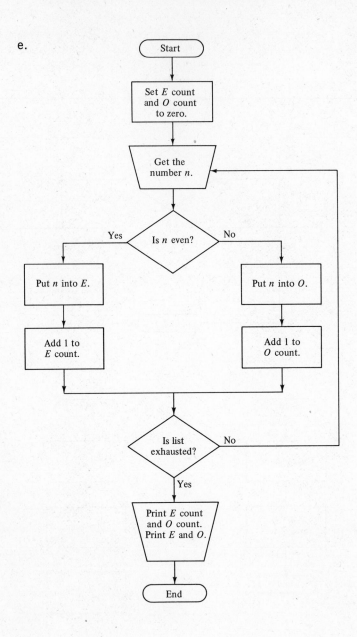

3.

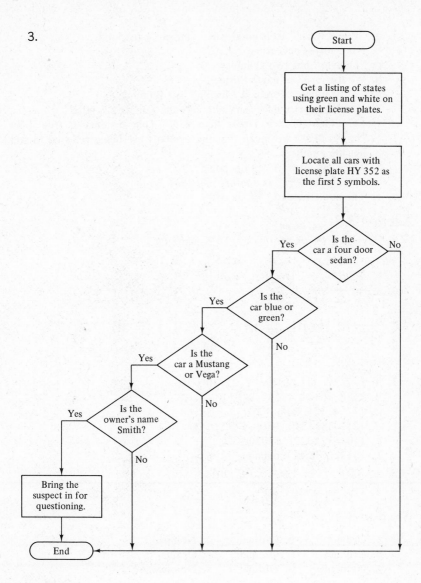

CHAPTER 3

Section 3.2

3. a. $\{(a, a), (b, b), (c, c), (d, d), (a, b)\}$.
   b. $\{(a, c), (c, d), (a, d), (d, a), (a, a), (d, c), (c, c), (d, d)\}$.
   c. $\{(a, a), (b, b), (c, c), (d, d), (a, c), (c, d), (c, a), (d, c)\}$.
   d. $\{(a, a), (b, b), (c, c), (d, d), (a, c), (c, d), (a, d)\}$.
   e. $\{(a, a)\}$.

7. a. "Walla Walla" feels good when you say it out loud.
   b. No changes necessary.
   c. "Denver" has two syllables.
   d. We use "13" to name thirteen.
   e. Can you use "Abraham Lincoln" in a sentence?
   f. No changes are necessary although the sentence is false. "17.145690314" is larger than "36." This sentence is true if by "larger than" we mean that the symbols are being referred to and not the numbers.
   g. The numerator of "$\frac{17}{18}$" is odd.
   h. The symbol "$\frac{34}{36}$" is another name for $\frac{17}{18}$.
   i. The numerator of "$\frac{34}{36}$" is odd.

Section 3.3 ααα

3. Egyptian: ααα   Roman: $\overline{\text{DC}}$.

5. a. 2^4 or 16.   b. 6.   c. 5^{10}.   d. 1.
   e. 5^4 or 625.   f. 3^8.   g. 1.   h. 7^{-1} or $\frac{1}{7}$.

9. a. T ≡ π   b. I = IIII I I

   c. − III ⊥ TTT ≡ III   d. I I ≡ III

Section 3.4

1. a. 1, 2, 10, 11, 12, 20, 21, 22, 100, 101, . . . , 1212.
   b. 2122, 10122, 12202, 210110.
   c. 17, 64, 185, 244.
   d. 1211, 1111210, 1011, 1202.
   e. 1101, 1110221, 120200221.
   f. 1012, 20 with remainder 121.

3. a. 2401.   b. 1343.   c. 2011.

5. a. 129.   b. 105.   c. 1573.   d. 2530.   e. 226,389.

Section 3.5

1. a. Ordinal.   b. Ordinal.   c. Nominal.
   d. Ordinal.   e. Ordinal.   f. Ordinal.
   g. Nominal.   h. Ordinal.   i. Nominal.

CHAPTER 4

Section 4.2

1. a. No—a may not have a sister or a may have more than one sister.
   b. No—$(8 + 6)/2 = 7$ which is not an even number.
   c. No—parent not unique.
   d. Yes.

e. Yes.
f. Yes.
g. No—$(3 + 5)/2 = 4$ which is not an odd number.
h. Yes.

3. $a * b = 2 \cdot (a + b) -$ yes.

Section 4.3

1. a. Commutative.   b. Closure.   c. Commutative.   d. Identity.
   e. Commutative.   f. Commutative.
   Note: closure was used in each of the above.

3. $9 + 6 = 9 + (1 + 5) = (9 + 1) + 5 = 10 + 5 = 15.$

5. $n(A) = 8$, $n(B) = 6$. Therefore, $8 + 6 = 12 + 2.$

7. a. Yes.   b. No.   c. Yes.

9. $a * b = (a + b) + 7$ where $a, b \in W.$

Section 4.4

1. a. Distributive.   b. Commutative.   c. Commutative.   d. Identity.
   e. Associative.   f. Closure.

3.
$$\cdot(1,6)\cdot(2,6)\cdot(3,6)\cdot(4,6)\cdot(5,6)\cdot(6,6)$$
$$\cdot(1,5)\cdot(2,5)\cdot(3,5)\cdot(4,5)\cdot(5,5)\cdot(6,5)$$
$$\cdot(1,4)\cdot(2,4)\cdot(3,4)\cdot(4,4)\cdot(5,4)\cdot(6,4)$$
$$\cdot(1,3)\cdot(2,3)\cdot(3,3)\cdot(4,3)\cdot(5,3)\cdot(6,3)$$
$$\cdot(1,2)\cdot(2,2)\cdot(3,2)\cdot(4,2)\cdot(5,2)\cdot(6,2)$$
$$\cdot(1,1)\cdot(2,1)\cdot(3,1)\cdot(4,1)\cdot(5,1)\cdot(6,1)$$

5. a. $2 \cdot 10 + 3 \cdot 10 = (2 + 3) \cdot 10 = 50.$
   b. $2^2 \cdot 5 + 2^2 \cdot 3 = 2^2 \cdot (5 + 3) = 32.$
   c. $3^3 \cdot 1 + 3 \cdot 2 = 3(3^2 \cdot 1 + 1 \cdot 2) = 33.$
   d. $(a + b)3 = 3a + 3b.$
   e. $x(x + 1).$
   f. $(1 + c)(a + b + 3).$

7. Answers will vary—a paperfolding exercise where children construct a cube is one such activity.

9. a. Yes.   b. Yes—1.   c. Yes.   d. Yes.

Section 4.5

1. Answers may vary—one method is to remove the proper subset A, leaving the elements in B that are not in A.

3. a. $\{0, 1, 2, 3, 4, 5\}$.   c. $\{0, 1, 2, 3\}$.   e. $\{4, 5\}$.   g. $\emptyset$.
   b. $\{0, 1, 2\}$.   d. $\{0, 1, 2, 3, 4\}$.   f. $\{6\}$.   h. $\emptyset$.

5. Trichotomy.

Section 4.6

1. a. $\{a, b, c\}, \{f\}.$ b. $\{1\}, \{3, 4, 5\}.$ c. $\emptyset, \emptyset.$ d. $\{1, 4\}, \emptyset.$
3. a.

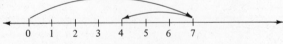

   b. $A = \{1, 2, 3, 4, 5, 6, 7\}, B = \{1, 2, 3\}.$
      $A - B = \{4, 5, 6, 7\}.$
   c. $7 - 3 = ?, ? + 3 = 7,$ therefore, $? = 4.$

5. Not always $-$ if $a \div c \in W$ and $b \div d \in W$ then $a \div c < b \div d.$
7. $a > b \Rightarrow a + n = b \Rightarrow (a - b) + n = 0 \Rightarrow a - b > 0.$
9. $a = b, a \neq 0.$
11. Yes $-$ if $a = b = c = 1.$

Section 4.7

1. a. $\begin{aligned} 33 &= 30 + 3 \\ + 16 &= 10 + 6 \\ \hline 40 &+ 9 = 49 \end{aligned}$ b. $\begin{aligned} 41 &= 40 + 1 \\ + 32 &= 30 + 2 \\ \hline 70 &+ 3 = 73 \end{aligned}$

   c. $\begin{aligned} 63 &= 60 + 3 \\ + 87 &= 80 + 7 \\ \hline 140 &+ 10 = 150 \end{aligned}$ d. $\begin{aligned} 115 &= 100 + 10 + 5 \\ + 496 &= 400 + 90 + 6 \\ \hline 500 &+ 100 + 11 = 611 \end{aligned}$

3. a.

   b.

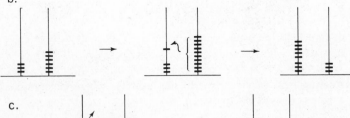

   c.

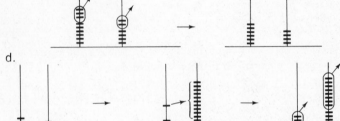

   d.

446

5. a.
$$\begin{array}{r} 16 \\ \times\ 8 \\ \hline 48 \\ +\ 80 \\ \hline 128 \end{array}$$
b.
$$\begin{array}{r} 25 \\ \times\ 12 \\ \hline 10 \\ 40 \\ 50 \\ +\ 200 \\ \hline 300 \end{array}$$
c.
$$\begin{array}{r} 153 \\ \times\ 6 \\ \hline 18 \\ 300 \\ +\ 600 \\ \hline 918 \end{array}$$
d.
$$\begin{array}{r} 113 \\ \times\ 27 \\ \hline 21 \\ 70 \\ 700 \\ 60 \\ 200 \\ +\ 2000 \\ \hline 3051 \end{array}$$

7. a.
$$\begin{array}{r} 8 = q \\ 7\overline{)58} \\ 56 \\ \hline 2 = r \end{array}$$
b.
$$\begin{array}{r} 7 = q \\ 12\overline{)84} \\ 84 \\ \hline 0 = r \end{array}$$
c. $a = 162 + 6 = 168.$

d.
$$\begin{array}{r} 2 = q \\ 40 \\ 15\overline{)639} \\ 600 \\ \hline 39 \\ 30 \\ \hline 9 = r \end{array}$$
e.
$$\begin{array}{r} 6 = q \\ 300 \\ 16\overline{)4903} \\ 4800 \\ \hline 103 \\ 96 \\ \hline 7 = r \end{array}$$
f.
$$\begin{array}{r} 4 = q \\ 20 \\ 306\overline{)8611} \\ 6120 \\ \hline 1491 \\ 1224 \\ \hline 267 = r \end{array}$$

9. a. 0, 1, 2.   b. 0, 1, 2, 3, 4.   c. 0 through 10.
   d. 0 through 19.   e. 0 through 24.   f. 0 through 39.

11. a. $7\overline{)86}$

70	10
16	
14	2
2	12

b. $8\overline{)93}$

80	10
13	
13	
5	11

c. $17\overline{)236}$

170	10
66	
51	3
15	13

d. $21\overline{)493}$

420	20
73	
63	3
10	23

e. $426\overline{)6834}$

4260	10
1574	
1278	3
296	13

f. $637\overline{)9301}$

6370	10
2931	
2548	4
383	14

CHAPTER 5

Section 5.2

1. a. 40, 33, 113.
   b. 59, 255, 23.
   c. 1252, 811, 1011.
   d. 697, 972, 1928.
   e. 2432, 3612, 60,754.
   f. 36 R5, 46, 44 R 14.
   g. 270 R 7, 14 R 4, 83 R 15.

3. Zero is neither to the left of nor to the right of zero.

5. a. 6.   b. ⁻6.   c. 3.   d. ⁻5.
   e. ⁻7.   f. ⁻4.   g. 2.   h. 0.

7. The absolute value of any integer is not less than zero.

9. Subtraction is a binary operation so we subtract in terms of pairs of integers.

Section 5.3

1. a. 9, ⁻12, 101, 82.
   b. 136, −103, 2, 114.
   c. ⁻72, 23, 34.
   d. ⁻53, ⁻683.
   e. 1673.

3. a. $17 + 9 = 26, 9 + 17 = 26, 26 − 9 = 17, 26 − 17 = 9$.
   b. $25 + {}^-11 = 14, {}^-11 + 25 = 14, 14 − 25 = {}^-11, 14 − (⁻11) = 25$.

5. a. $16 + x$.   b. $m + 3$.   c. $t + 247$.   d. $500 − x$.

7. Since $16 − 9 = 7$ and $9 − 16 = {}^-7$, then subtraction is not commutative. Since $(15 − 11) − 12 = {}^-8$ while $15 − (11 − 12) = 16$, then subtraction is not associative.

Section 5.4

1. a. 105, ⁻66, ⁻112, 117.
   b. 21, ⁻8, ⁻3, 16.
   c. 1305, ⁻1596, ⁻3969, 2168.
   d. 16, ⁻35, ⁻19, 45.

5. a. $45 × {}^-9 = {}^-415, {}^-9 × 45 = {}^-415, {}^-415 ÷ {}^-9 = 45, {}^-415 ÷ 45 = {}^-9$.

11. a. $x = 3$.   b. $x = 7$.   c. $x = 3$.   d. $x = 11$.
    e. $x = {}^-6$.   f. $x = 3$.

Section 5.5

1. a. 1, 2, 3, 4, 5, 6, 7.
   b. ⁻6, ⁻5, ⁻4, ⁻3, ⁻2, ⁻1, 0.
   c. 9, 8, 7, 6, 5, ...
   d. All integers *except* 0, 1, 2, 3, 4, 5, 6, 7, 8, 9, 10.
   e. No integers belong to this set.
   f. 0.
   g. All integers belong to this set.

5. a. $x < 2, x > 12, x \leqslant 2$.
   b. $x < 3, 1 < x$.
   c. $x < 1$ (or $x < 1\frac{1}{2}$).

7. a. ⁻3, ⁻2, ⁻1, 0, 1, 2, 3.
   b. ⁻5, ⁻4, ⁻3, ⁻2, ⁻1, 0, 1, 2, 3, 4, 5.
   c. No integer solution.
   d. ⁻9, ⁻8, . . . , 0, . . . , 8, 9.
   e. 0, 1, 2, 3, 4.

Section 5.6

1.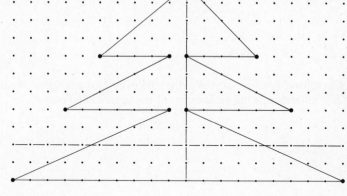

3. a.

    b. $\overset{\bullet\;\;\bullet\;\;\bullet}{\underset{-1\;\;0\;\;1}{\cdot}}$ c. Same as b.

    d. $\underset{0\qquad\;\;3}{\cdots\;\;\cdot\;\cdot\;\;\bullet}$

    e. $\underset{0\;1\;2\;3\;4\;5\;6\;7\;8\;9}{\cdot\;\cdot\;\bullet\;\bullet\;\bullet\;\bullet\;\bullet\;\bullet\;\bullet\;\bullet\;\bullet}\cdot$

    f. Sketch the entire set of integers.

    g. $\overset{\bullet\;\bullet\;\bullet\;\bullet}{\underset{\longleftarrow\;\;0\;1\;2\;3\;4\;5}{}}$

Section 5.7

1. a. $(12, 0)$.   b. $(0, 15)$.   c. $(0, 52)$.

3. a. Same.   b. Same.   c. Different.

5. (m, n) and (p, q) do not lie on the same diagonal.

9. a. $[0, 35]$.   b. $[24, 0]$.   c. $[44, 0]$.   d. $[0, 54]$.

11. a. $^-35$.   b. 24.   c. 44.   d. $^-54$.

13. $[m + q, n + p]$.

15. a. No.

17. $[a, b] < [c, d]$ if and only if there exists some $[x, y]$ where $x > y$ such that $[a, b] \oplus [x, y] = [c, d]$.

CHAPTER 6

Section 6.2

1. a.   b.   c.   d.

3. Each square number can be represented by two triangular numbers whose difference is the square root of the square number.

5.

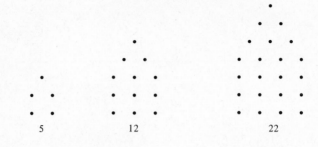

     1   5   12   22

7. The nth pentagonal number is equal to the sum of the nth square number and the $(n-1)$th triangular number.

9. a. [0], [1].   b. [0], [1], [2].   c. [0], [1], [2], [3].
    d. [0], [1], [2], [3], [4].

Section 6.3

1. *b, d, e, h, i.*

3. 3, 5, 11, 17.

5. a. {2}.   b. {3, 7, 11, · · ·}.   c. Ø.   d. {2, 3, 4, 5, · · ·}.
    e. *W*.   f. *W*.   g. Ø.

7. a. 1.   b. 1.   c. 1.   d. 6.   e. 5.   f. 6.   g. 6.
    h. 6.   i. 16.
    Each prime number greater than three can be expressed either as one more or one less than a multiple of six.

9. No$-3 \times 3 = 9$.

11. Yes.

13. Yes.

Section 6.4

1. a. $3 \times 2 \times 2$.   b. $7 \times 2 \times 2$.   c. Not possible.   d. $7 \times 2 \times 3$.
    e. $2 \times 3 \times 3 \times 3$.   f. $2 \times 3 \times 3 \times 5$.   g. $3 \times 5 \times 5$.
    h. $11 \times 2 \times 5$.   i. Not possible.

3. a. 2, 3, 5, 7, 11, 13, 17, 19, 23, 29, 31, 37, 41, 43, 47.
   b. Same as a. with 53, 59.
   c. Same as b. with 61, 67.
   d. Same as c. with 71, 73, 79.
   e. Same as d. with 83, 89.
   f. Same as e. with 97.

5. a. $5 + 3$.   b. $7 + 5$.   c. $11 + 5$.   d. $17 + 3$.   e. $17 + 7$.
   f. $23 + 5$.   g. $31 + 7$.   h. $41 + 3$.   i. $53 + 3$.   j. $59 + 3$.

7. 2×173.

Section 6.5

1. a. $\{1, 30, 2, 15, 3, 10, 5, 6\}$.   b. $\{1, 45, 3, 15, 5, 9\}$.
   c. $\{1, 144, 2, 72, 3, 48, 4, 36, 6, 24, 8, 18, 9, 16, 12\}$.   d. $\{1, 2\}$.
   e. $\{1\}$.   f. N

3. a. 8.   b. 6.   c. 15.   d. 8.   e. 4.   f. 8.

5. a. $\{0, 2, 4, 6, \cdots\}$.   b. $\{0, 3, 6, 9, \cdots\}$.   c. $\{0, 5, 10, 15, \cdots\}$.
   d. $\{0, 7, 14, 21, \cdots\}$.   e. $\{0, 10, 20, 30, \cdots\}$.
   f. $\{0, 12, 24, 36, \cdots\}$.

7. a. GCD is 8   b. GCD is 18   c. GCD is 18
      LCM is 168.   LCM is 360.   LCM is 108.
   d. GCD is 4   e. GCD is 1   f. GCD is 4
      LCM is 120.   LCM is 217.   LCM is 240.

11. a. A number divisible by two must be even.
    b. Consider the number 252.
$$252 = (2 \times 10^2) + (5 \times 10) + 2$$
$$= 2 \times (99 + 1) + 5 \times (9 + 1) + 2$$
$$= (2 \times 99) + (2 \times 1) + (5 \times 9) + (5 \times 1) + 2$$
$$= (2 \times 99) + (5 \times 9) + (2 + 5 + 2)$$
$$= (2 \times 33 + 5 \times 3) \times 3 + (2 + 5 + 2).$$
    Now, since three divides the term with three as a factor, it will divide
    252 if it divides the sum, $(2 + 5 + 2)$.
    c. Any number of hundreds is divisible by four, therefore, one need only
    consider the tens' and ones' digits.
    d. All multiples of 5 end in a 0 or a 5.
    e. Since $6 = 3 \times 2$, any number which is divisible by 2 and by 3 is divis-
    ible by 6.
    f. Any number of thousands is divisible by 8, therefore, one need only
    consider the hundreds', tens', and ones' digits.
    g. Same argument as for b, applied here.

13. a. N is prime.
    b. N is the square of a prime.
    c. N is the square of a composite.

451

15.

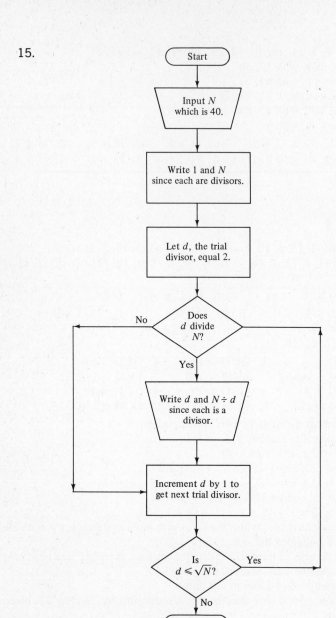

17. LCM(a, b, c) = LCM(LCM(a, b), c).

Section 6.6

1. a. $7 \mid (21 - 0)$.   b. $2 \mid (-4 - 0)$.   c. $6 \mid (-19 - 5)$.
   d. $8 \mid (5 - 21)$.   e. $8 \mid (21 - 5)$.   f. $2 \mid (3 - 11)$.

3. a. 1.   b. 2.   c. 0.   d. 9.   e. 8.   f. 1.   g. 1.
   h. 4.   i. 3.

5. a. 2.   b. 3.   c. 0.   d. 0.   e. 9.   f. 12.

7. a. Yes.   b. Yes.   c. No.   d. Yes.   e. No.   f. No.
   g. Yes.   h. No.

9. a. $\underline{\begin{array}{l} 3 + 2 + 6 = 11 \bmod 9 \\ 2 + 2 + 7 = 11 \bmod 9 \end{array}}$ $\underline{\begin{array}{l} 11 \bmod 9 = 2 \\ 11 \bmod 9 = +2 \end{array}}$
   $5 + 4 + 3 = 12 \bmod 9$ $12 \bmod 9 \neq 4$ therefore incorrect.

   b. $\underline{\begin{array}{l} 6 + 8 + 3 + 4 = 21 \bmod 9 \\ 5 + 2 + 1 + 7 = 15 \bmod 9 \end{array}}$ $\underline{\begin{array}{l} 21 \bmod 9 = 3 \\ 15 \bmod 9 = +6 \end{array}}$
   $1 + 2 + 0 + 5 + 1 = 9 \bmod 9$ $9 \bmod 9 = 9$ check – possibly
   correct answer.

   c. $\underline{\begin{array}{l} 7 + 3 + 8 = 18 \bmod 9 \\ 4 + 9 + 9 = 22 \bmod 9 \end{array}}$ $\underline{\begin{array}{l} 18 \bmod 9 = 9 \\ 22 \bmod 9 = -4 \end{array}}$
   $2 + 3 + 9 = 14 \bmod 9$ $14 \bmod 9 = 5$ check – possibly
   correct answer.

   d. $\underline{\begin{array}{l} 8 + 1 + 3 + 2 = 14 \bmod 9 \\ 6 + 3 + 7 + 6 = 22 \bmod 9 \end{array}}$ $\underline{\begin{array}{l} 14 \bmod 9 = 5 \\ 22 \bmod 9 = -4 \end{array}}$
   $1 + 6 + 5 + 6 = 18 \bmod 9$ $18 \bmod 9 \neq 1$ therefore incorrect.

   e. $\underline{\begin{array}{l} 3 + 6 = 9 \bmod 9 \\ 8 + 4 = 12 \bmod 9 \end{array}}$ $\underline{\begin{array}{l} 9 \bmod 9 = 0 \\ 12 \bmod 9 = \times 3 \end{array}}$
   $3 + 0 + 2 + 4 = 9 \bmod 9$ $9 \bmod 9 = 0$ check – possibly
   correct answer.

   f. $\underline{\begin{array}{l} 9 + 3 = 12 \bmod 9 \\ 8 + 7 = \bmod 9 \end{array}}$ $\underline{\begin{array}{l} 12 \bmod 9 = 3 \\ 15 \bmod 9 = \times 6 \end{array}}$
   $8 + 0 + 8 + 1 = 17 \bmod 9$ $17 \bmod 9 \neq 0$ therefore incorrect.

11. a. $-8, -3, 2, 7, 12$.   b. $-5, 4, 13, 21$.   c. $3, 5, 15$.
   d. $-9, 3, 15, 27$.

13. a. Cast out fours.
   b. Cast out sevens.
   c. Cast out $(b - 1)$s.

Section 6.7

1. *b, c, d.*

3. a. 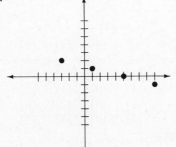   b.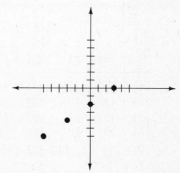

c.

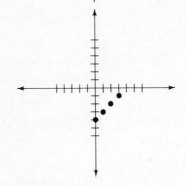

d.

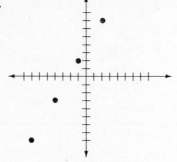

e.

f.

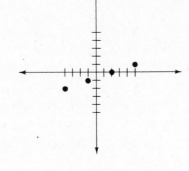

5. a. 19 (or 21 if 0 dimes or 0 nickels).
   b. 3 (or 5 if 0 dimes or 0 quarters).
   c. 3 (or 5 if 0 dimes or 0 half dollars).

CHAPTER 7

Section 7.2

1.

Element	Additive inverse	Multiplicative inverse
[0]	[0]	None exists
[1]	[4]	[1]
[2]	[3]	[3]
[3]	[2]	[2]
[4]	[1]	[4]

3.

+	[0]	[1]	[2]	[3]
[0]	[0]	[1]	[2]	[3]
[1]	[1]	[2]	[3]	[0]
[2]	[2]	[3]	[0]	[1]
[3]	[3]	[0]	[1]	[2]

×	[0]	[1]	[2]	[3]
[ ]	[0]	[0]	[0]	[0]
[1]	[0]	[1]	[2]	[3]
[2]	[0]	[2]	[0]	[2]
[3]	[0]	[3]	[2]	[1]

5. {[0], [1], [2], [3], [4], [5], [6]}.

7.

Element	Additive inverse	Multiplicative inverse
[0]	[0]	None exists
[1]	[6]	[1]
[2]	[5]	[4]
[3]	[4]	[5]
[4]	[3]	[2]
[5]	[2]	[3]
[6]	[1]	[6]

9. No. No. No. No.

11. Z_n is a field provided n is a *prime* number.

Section 7.3

7. a. $\frac{6}{8}, \frac{9}{12}, \frac{12}{16}, \frac{15}{20}$.

   b. $\frac{10}{12}, \frac{15}{18}, \frac{20}{24}, \frac{50}{60}$.

   c. $\frac{2}{3}, \frac{4}{6}, \frac{6}{9}, \frac{24}{36}$.

   d. $\frac{5}{6}, \frac{10}{12}, \frac{15}{18}, \frac{75}{90}$.

   e. $\frac{11}{15}, \frac{22}{30}, \frac{33}{45}, \frac{44}{60}$.

9. a. $\frac{17}{6}$.   b. $\frac{139}{11}$.   c. $-\frac{29}{6}$.   d. $-\frac{97}{9}$.

   e. $\frac{149}{9}$.   f. $-\frac{35}{4}$.   g. $-\frac{50}{31}$.   h. $\frac{226}{3}$.

11. The error lies in the fact that both the symbol and the number are being referred to.

Section 7.4

1. a. $\frac{7}{6}, \frac{7}{8}, 1, \frac{41}{42}$.

   b. $\frac{5}{8}, \frac{3}{8}, -\frac{1}{6}, \frac{-3}{16}$.

   c. $17\frac{1}{4}, 5\frac{5}{12}$.

   d. $12\frac{2}{15}, 1\frac{14}{15}, -\frac{7}{20}$.

   e. $1\frac{17}{18}, 11\frac{2}{7}$.

5. $7 \times 137 = 959$ and $(-7) \times (-137) = 959$ so $7 \times 137 = (-7) \times (-137)$ and, by definition, $\frac{137}{-7} = \frac{-137}{7}$.

Section 7.5

1. a. $\frac{5}{9}, \frac{12}{35}, -\frac{6}{35}, -\frac{1}{12}$.

   b. $\frac{8}{7}, \frac{6}{7}, \frac{32}{25}, -\frac{36}{35}$.

   c. $\frac{64}{21}$.

   d. $\frac{517}{32}, \frac{2059}{50}, -\frac{7242}{13}$.

   e. $\frac{19}{4}, -2, \frac{133}{26}$.

3. $\frac{3}{4} + \frac{2}{3} = \frac{17}{12} = \frac{2}{3} + \frac{3}{4}$.

   $\frac{3}{4} \times \frac{2}{3} = \frac{1}{2} = \frac{2}{3} \times \frac{3}{4}$.

5. $\frac{1}{2} + \left(\frac{3}{4} + \frac{2}{3}\right) = \frac{1}{2} + \frac{17}{12} = \frac{23}{12} = \frac{5}{4} + \frac{2}{3}$
$\quad = \left(\frac{1}{2} + \frac{3}{4}\right) + \frac{2}{3}.$
$\frac{1}{2} \times \left(\frac{3}{4} \times \frac{2}{3}\right) = \frac{1}{2} \times \frac{1}{2} = \frac{1}{4} = \frac{3}{8} \times \frac{2}{3}$
$\quad = \left(\frac{1}{2} \times \frac{3}{4}\right) \times \frac{2}{3}.$

7.

Rational number	Additive inverse	Multiplicative inverse
$\frac{3}{4}$	$-\frac{3}{4}$	$\frac{4}{3}$
$-\frac{7}{8}$	$\frac{7}{8}$	$-\frac{8}{7}$
$\frac{8}{-12}$	$\frac{8}{12}$	$-\frac{12}{8}$
$\frac{0}{1}$	0	None exists
$\frac{0}{5}$	0	None exists
$2\frac{3}{4}\left(\frac{11}{4}\right)$	$-2\frac{3}{4}$	$\frac{4}{11}$
$-3\frac{5}{8}\left(-\frac{29}{8}\right)$	$\frac{29}{8}$	$-\frac{8}{29}$
15	-15	$\frac{1}{15}$

11. a. $\frac{16}{15}$. b. $\frac{32}{25}$. c. $-\frac{1}{1}$. d. $\frac{75}{49}$.
e. $\frac{11}{72}$. f. $\frac{60}{31}$. g. $\frac{5740}{1113}$.

Section 7.6

1. a. $\frac{16}{1}$. b. $\frac{16}{1}$. c. $\frac{1}{16}$. d. $\frac{1}{16}$.
e. $\frac{1}{1}$. f. $\frac{1}{1}$. g. $\frac{1}{5}$. h. $\frac{1}{-5}$.
i. $\frac{3}{2}$. j. $\frac{8}{27}$. k. $\frac{9}{16}$. l. Not defined.
m. $\frac{1}{1}$. n. $\frac{8}{1}$.
3. a. 141.352. b. 1.958.
c. 121 725, 5465.061, 334,865.72.
d. $7.86\overline{6}$, 19.712^+, $353.3\overline{3}$.
e. 4.7194^+.
5. a. 109.20. b. 91. c. 1.53. d. $16\frac{2}{3}\%$.
e. 229.03^+. f. $.7^+\%$. g. 75. h. 16. i. $473\frac{1}{3}$.
7. a. 18.98. b. .00000001266. c. 1935^+.

Section 7.7

1. a. $17 < 36$ because 19 is a positive number and $17 + 19 = 36$.
b. $-5 < 12$ because 17 is a positive number and $-5 + 17 = 12$.
c. $-18 < -4$ because 14 is a positive number and $-18 + 14 = -4$.
3. Since $\frac{2}{3} = \frac{16}{24}$ and $\frac{7}{8} = \frac{21}{24}$, then $\frac{17}{24}, \frac{18}{24}, \frac{19}{24}$, and $\frac{20}{24}$ are between $\frac{2}{3}$ and $\frac{7}{8}$.

5.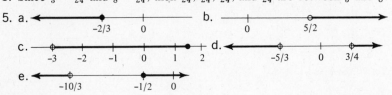

Section 7.8

1. a. (4, 6), (6, 9).   b. (−6, 14), (−9, 21).
   c. (2, 10), (5, 25).   d. (4, 6), (−2, −3).

3. a. [34, 8], [21, 8].   b. [−52, 15], [32, 15].
   c. [27, 18], [10, 18].   d. [−17, 15], [4, 15].
   e. [−107, 22], [−77, 22].

5. a. [5, 24] because [2, 3] ⊕ [5, 24] = [7, 8].
   b. [5, 4] because [−3, 4] ⊕ [5, 4] = [1, 2].
   c. [1, 2] because [−5, 6] ⊕ [1, 2] = [−1, 3].

7. Since $a > 0$ then $a \bullet a > a \bullet 0$ for multiplying both terms of an inequality by a positive rational number maintains the direction of inequality. Therefore, since $a \bullet a = a^2$ and $a \bullet 0 = 0$, it must be that $a^2 > 0$.

9. By substitution $a^2 = a \bullet a = 0 \bullet 0 = 0$.

11. b. 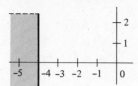   c.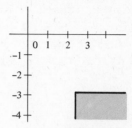

    d. 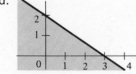   e.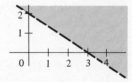

    f.   g.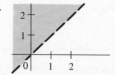

CHAPTER 8

Section 8.2

1. Suppose that $\sqrt{3} = a/b$ where a and b are relatively prime integers. Then $3 = a^2/b^2$ or $3b^2 = a^2$. Therefore, 3 is a factor of a^2 and hence is a factor of a. Let's say $a = 3x$ so that $3b^2 = a^2 = (3x)^2 = 9x^2$. Then $b^2 = 3x^2$ and 3 is a factor of b^2 and hence is a factor of b. But now 3 is a factor (divisor) of both a and b so a and b are not relatively prime. This is a contradiction of our assumption so it must be that $\sqrt{3}$ is not a rational number.

3. Use a rectangle with one leg 2 units long and the other 1 unit long. Then the diagonal of the rectangle must be $\sqrt{2^2 + 1^2} = \sqrt{5}$ units long.

5. $\pm 2, \pm 3, 4, 2.$

7. 4.1 $(4.123 \ldots)$.

9. Between 78.402 and 78.403.

Section 8.3

1. a. $\frac{41}{9}$. b. $\frac{273}{10}$. c. $\frac{213}{999}$ $\left(\frac{71}{333}\right)$.
   d. $\frac{12401}{9990}$. e. 2. f. $\frac{1450000}{999}$.

3. a. $2.4.4$. b. $-.414$. c. $.707$.
   d. 2.828. e. $.707$ (Compare with c.). f. 1.146.

5. a. $\pm\sqrt{2}$. b. ± 2. c. $\pm\sqrt{5}$. d. $\pm\sqrt{3}$.

7. a. $x < 2$. b. $x < 9 - \sqrt{5}$. c. $x > (5 + \sqrt{3})/2$.
   d. $x \le (5 - \sqrt{2})/-3$. e. $21/\sqrt{3} \le x$. f. $(\sqrt{7} - 6)/3 < x$.

9. a. 6. b. 4.3. c. 5.1. d. 4.2. e. $\sqrt{3}$. f. $\sqrt{3}$.

Section 8.4

1. a. 10, 11; no lower bounds.
   b. No upper bounds; 5, 0.
   c. 2, 3; −2, −3.
   d. 1, 2; −1, −2.
   e. No upper bounds; 1 is the only lower bound.
   f. 7, 8; −3, −4.
   g. 1.8, 1.9; −1.8, −1.9.

3. a. No lower bounds.
   b. 5.
   c. −2.
   d. −1.
   e. 1.
   f. −3.
   g. There is no greatest lower bound because there is no negative rational number whose square is 3 yet there is always another rational number between any lower bound and $-\sqrt{3}$.

5.

458

7.

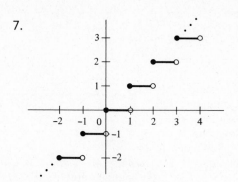

Section 8.5

1. $(2i)^2 = 2i \cdot 2i = 4i^2 = 4(-1) = -4.$

3. a. $3 + i, 2 + 2i.$
   b. $2 + 2i, -15 + 10i.$
   c. $2, 2.$
   d. $4 + 7i, -8 + 14i.$
   e. $11 - 2i, 33 - 13i.$

5. a. $1 - i, -1 + i.$
   b. $-8 + 2i, 8 - 2i.$
   c. $2i, -2i.$
   d. $-i, i.$
   e. $1 + 4i, -1 - 4i.$
   Notice that the two results are opposites.

7. a. $\frac{1}{2}$ because $2 \cdot \frac{1}{2} = 1.$ (or $\frac{1}{2} + 0i$).
   b. $-i/3$ (or $0 + \frac{-1}{3}i$).
   c. $\frac{1}{2} - \frac{1}{2}i.$ (Try it: $(1 + i)(\frac{1}{2} - \frac{1}{2}i) = \frac{1}{2} + \frac{1}{2} + \frac{1}{2}i - \frac{1}{2}i = 1.$)
   d. $\frac{-3}{13} - \frac{2}{13}i.$

9.

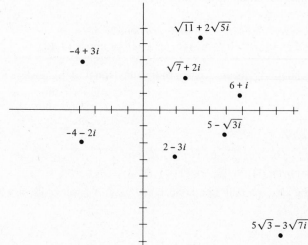

11. e. $\sqrt{7+4} = \sqrt{11}$.
    f. $\sqrt{25+3} = \sqrt{28} = \sqrt{4} \cdot \sqrt{7} = 2\sqrt{7}$.
    g. $\sqrt{11+20} = \sqrt{31}$.
    h. $\sqrt{75+63} = \sqrt{138}$.

13. a. $a = 1$, $b = 5$, $c = 6$. Solutions: $-2, -3$.
    b. $a = 3$, $b = -7$, $c = 4$. Solutions: $1, \frac{4}{3}$.
    c. $a = 2$, $b = 4$, $c = 0$. Solutions: $0, -2$.
    d. $a = 2$, $b = 7$, $c = 3$. Solutions: $-\frac{1}{2}, -3$.
    e. $a = 3$, $b = -2$, $c = -1$. Solutions: $1, -\frac{1}{3}$.
    f. $a = 3$, $b = 4$, $c = 2$. Solutions: $(-4 + \sqrt{8}i)/6$, $(-4 - \sqrt{8}i)/6$. Or, using the fact that $\sqrt{8} = \sqrt{4} \cdot \sqrt{2} = 2\sqrt{2}$, the solutions are: $(-2 + \sqrt{2}i)/3$, $(-2 - \sqrt{2}i)/3$.

Section 8.6

1. a. $\begin{bmatrix} 1 & 4 \\ 0 & -1 \end{bmatrix}$, $\begin{bmatrix} 3 & -8 \\ 2 & -7 \end{bmatrix}$.
   b. $\begin{bmatrix} -1 & -5 \\ 2 & -1 \end{bmatrix}$, $\begin{bmatrix} 0 & 0 \\ -2 & -4 \end{bmatrix}$.
   c. $\begin{bmatrix} 3 & 2 \\ 3 & 6 \end{bmatrix}$, $\begin{bmatrix} 2 & 4 \\ 6 & 8 \end{bmatrix}$.
   d. $\begin{bmatrix} 3 & 2 \\ 3 & 6 \end{bmatrix}$, $\begin{bmatrix} 2 & 4 \\ 6 & 8 \end{bmatrix}$.
   e. $\begin{bmatrix} 1 & 4 \\ 0 & 1 \end{bmatrix}$, $\begin{bmatrix} -1 & 2 \\ 4 & -3 \end{bmatrix}$.

3. a.

+	0	1	2	3	4
0	0	1	2	3	4
1	1	2	3	4	0
2	2	3	4	0	1
3	3	4	0	1	2
4	4	0	1	2	3

b.

×	0	1	2	3	4
0	0	0	0	0	0
1	0	1	2	3	4
2	0	2	4	1	3
3	0	3	1	4	2
4	0	4	3	2	1

   c. 1, 3, 2, 4.
   d. 1, 2 has no multiplicative inverse, 3.
   e. Yes, no.

5. a. $25\pi \doteq 25 \times 3.1416 = 78.5400$ or about 78.54.
   b. $2\pi \cdot 5 = 10\pi \doteq 10 \times 3.1416 = 31.416$ or about 31.42.
   c. 6.
   (The symbol "$\doteq$" means "is approximately equal to.")

CHAPTER 9

Section 9.2

1. a. Yes. b. Yes. c. No. d. No.

3. (H, 1), (H, 3), (H, 5), (T, 2), (T, 4), (T, 6)—yes.

5. Have the children tally in a nondecimal base. Answers will vary for the game.

Section 9.3

1. $\frac{1}{2}, \frac{1}{2}$.
3. a. $\frac{1}{10}$.   b. $\frac{1}{10}$.   c. 0.   d. $\frac{2}{10}$.   e. No.   f. Yes.
5. a. $\frac{3}{9}$.   b. $\frac{4}{9}$.   c. $\frac{2}{9}$.   d. $\frac{6}{9}$.   e. $\frac{2}{9}$.   f. 0.

Section 9.4

1. $\frac{2}{3}$.
3. a. $\frac{1}{1}$.   b. $\frac{1}{1}$.
5. a. $\frac{4}{48}$.   b. $\frac{4}{48}$.   c. $\frac{2}{50}$.   e. $\frac{39}{13}$.   f. $\frac{48}{4}$.
7. $\frac{1}{1}$.

Section 9.5

1. a, e.
3. a. $\frac{205}{415}$.   b. $\frac{63}{415}$.   c. $\frac{320}{415}$.   d. $\frac{15}{415}$.   e. $\frac{355}{415}$.
5. a. $\frac{300}{560}$.   b. $\frac{430}{560}$.   c. $\frac{290}{560}$.   d. $\frac{460}{560}$.

Section 9.6

1. .60, .40.
3. a.

15	28	39	51	61	67	82	89	103	118
.75	.7	.65	.6375	.61	.5583	.5857	.5562	.5722	.59 .

b.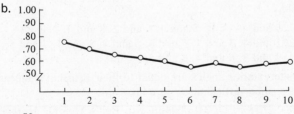

c. .59.

CHAPTER 10

Section 10.2

1. a. A point.   b. Plane.   c. Space.   d. Point.
3. 3, 6, 10, 15, 21, $\cdots n(n-1)/2$.

Section 10.3

1. The number of points on the line is infinite.
3. $|A - B| = |B - A|$.
5. a. 2.   b. $2 + \sqrt{5}$.   c. $\sqrt{2} + \sqrt{5}$.   d. 1.6.   e. 5.   f. 3.

Section 10.4

1. a. $-5 < -3 < -1$.   b. $-5 < -\sqrt{19} < \sqrt{5}$.   c. $-3 < -2 < 5$.
   d. $-2.5 < -1 < 1.7$.   e. $-4 < 1 < 4$.   f. $-5 < 0 < 5$.
3. a. $(-\sqrt{21} + {}^-4)/2$.   b. -2.5.   c. $-.5$.   d. $(-\sqrt{3} + \sqrt{12})/2$.
   e. $(1 + \sqrt{12})/2$.   f. 2.5.   g. 0.   h. $(5 - \sqrt{3})/2$.
5. An infinite number of lines can be passed through a single point.
7. a. F.   b. T.   c. F.   d. T.   e. F.   f. T.   g. F.
   h. T.   i. T.   j. T.   k. T.   l. F.   m. T.   n. T.
9. $n(n - 1)/2$.
11. Answers will vary.

Section 10.5

1. a. Need a common endpoint.   b. Cannot be collinear.
3. a. $143°$.   b. $115°$.   c. $159°$.   d. $68°$.   e. $44°$.   f. $85°$.
5. $y = 90 - t$, $x = 90 - t$, therefore, $x = y$.
7. 3 is a supplement of 2; 1 is a supplement of 2; therefore, $m(1) = m(3)$.
   The same argument applies for angles 2 and 4.
9. They are supplementary.
11. a. 0, 2, or 4.   b. 0, 2, 4.   c. 0, 2, 4.   d. 0, 2, 4.

Section 10.6

1. a. 2 and 7, 5 and 4.   b. 5 and 1, 6 and 2, 8 and 4, 7 and 3.
   c. 1 and 2, 2 and 4, 3 and 1, 5 and 6, 6 and 8, 8 and 7, 7 and 5.
   d. 1 and 4, 2 and 3, 6 and 7, 8 and 5.
3. The alternate exterior angles are equal to their respective alternate interior angles since vertical angles are involved.
5. Either Eves' *History Of Mathematics* or Bell's *Men Of Mathematics* are excellent references.

Section 10.7

1. They are equal.
3. Yes.
5. Yes — by definition of congruence.
7. Yes — by definition of congruence.

Section 10.8

1. Congruent alternate interior angles have been constructed; hence, the lines are parallel.
3. The reflection image of a line segment is congruent to the pre-image.
5. The angle bisection will be the reflecting line which reflects one side of the angle into the second side.

Section 10.9

1. $b, d, e, f.$
3. No.
5. a. Not necessarily closed.   b. Not necessarily simple.
   c. Not necessarily closed.
7. This is synonymous to asking what the next rational number after 0 is — you can always find another.
9. Answers will vary.

Section 10.10

1. 60.
3. Construction necessary.
5. Similar triangles.
7. Let (a, b, c) be a Pythagorean triple and (na, nb, nc) be a multiple of the first triple. Then $a^2 + b^2 = c^2$. Multiplying both sides of the equation by n^2, we have $n^2a^2 + n^2b^2 = n^2c^2$. Therefore, (na, nb, nc) is a Pythagorean triple.
9. a. The third sides must be congruent by the Pythagorean relation. Hence, SSS $\cong$ SSS.
   b. Same as a.
   c. The second acute angle of each triangle must be congruent. Therefore, all the angles of the triangles are congruent. Hence, ASA $\cong$ ASA.

Section 10.11

1. Construction.
3. The answers will vary.
5. If the triangle is equilateral, these points will coincide.

Section 10.12

1. A parallelogram.
3. Answers will vary.
5. Opposite angles in a kite — the pair of angles which have a side in common with the obtuse angle.
7. $b, c.$

Section 10.13

1. $a, b, c, d.$
3. Answers will vary — a clock, circular table, the top of a paint can, etc.
5. Answers will vary.
7. Yes.
9. Yes — in an equilateral triangle.

11. The union of the two arcs intercepted by the opposite angles is the whole circle. Hence, $\frac{1}{2} \cdot 360 = 180$.

Section 10.14

1. a. Rectangular prism.　　b. Cube.　　c. Right triangular prism.
   d. hexagonal prism.

3. a. Circular cone.　　b. Cylinder.　　c. Right circular cylinder.
   d. Right cone.

5. a. A tent, an A frame house, certain rulers.
   b. A cigar box, a refrigerator.
   c. Certain crystals, architecture.
   d. Pyramids of Egypt, architecture.
   e. A ball, the sun.
   f. A tin can, a flag pole.
   g. The sharpened portion of a pencil, a water cup, ice cream cone, a funnel.

7. Tetrahedron – four faces, each a triangle.
   Cube – 6 faces, each a square.
   Octahedron – 8 faces, each a triangle.
   Duodecahedron – 12 faces, each a pentagon.
   Icosahedron – 20 faces, each a triangle.

9. a. A point, a circle.
   b. A point, a right triangle, a triangle, a line segment.
   c. A point, a segment, a rectangle.
   d. A point, a triangle, a segment.
   e. A point, a segment, a rectangle, a triangle.
   f. A point, a segment, a circle, an ellipse, a parabola.
   g. A point, a segment, an ellipse, a circle.

Section 10.15

1. a. Seconds, minutes, hours.　　b. Ounces, pounds, tons.
   c. Cups, pints, quarts.　　d. Pints, pecks, bushels.
   e. Sq. inches, sq. feet, sq. yards.　　f. Cu. inches, cu. feet, cu. yards.

3. a. 60 seconds ≈ 1 minute　b. 16 ounces ≈ 1 lb　c. 2 cups ≈ 1 pint
   　 60 minutes ≈ 1 hour.　　　 2000 lbs ≈ 1 ton.　　 2 pints ≈ 1 quart.

   d. 16 pints ≈ 1 peck　　e. 144 sq. in. ≈ 1 sq. ft
   　 4 pecks ≈ 1 bushel.　　 9 sq. ft ≈ 1 sq. yd.

   f. 12^3 cu. in. ≈ 1 cu. ft
   　 27 cu. ft ≈ 1 cu. yd.

5. Answers will vary.

Section 10.16

1. a. $C = 4\pi, A = 4\pi$.　　b. $C = \pi, A = \frac{1}{4}\pi$.　　c. $C = 6\pi, A = 9\pi$.
   d. $C = \frac{6}{8}\pi, A = \frac{9}{64}\pi$.　　e. $C = 2\sqrt{3}\pi, A = 3\pi$.
   f. $C = 4\sqrt{5}\pi, A = 20\pi$.

3. Use a smaller grid.

5. It does not add any area to the region.

7. Any triangle with base b and the remaining vertex on line $\overleftrightarrow{PT}$ will have the same area as triangle APB.

9. a. $V = 5\pi$. b. $V = \frac{6}{9}\pi$. c. $V = 2\sqrt{6}\pi$. d. $V = \frac{2}{3}(\sqrt{35}\pi)$.

Index